PRAISE FOR
Jump-Starting America

"Jonathan Gruber and Simon Johnson's important *Jump-Starting America* argues that public investment in knowledge and research can help put American economic growth back on track.... Gruber and Johnson have produced a superbly argued case.... Their analyses are always insightful.... One way or another, our economy could use a jump-start, and the authors' vision of a research- and education-led American comeback is compelling."

—Ed Glaeser, writing in the *Wall Street Journal*

"Something has gone profoundly wrong with the US economy over the last two decades. Economic growth has been disappointing, and the little of it we have witnessed has benefited the already rich and left everybody else behind. This wonderfully readable book by two leading scholars explains why and what to do about it. It is a powerful call for action for the government to get involved, encourage innovation in local clusters, and help the economy get back to creating good jobs for ordinary Americans. A must read."

—Daron Acemoglu, coauthor of *Why Nations Fail*, and Elizabeth and James Killian Professor of Economics, MIT

"In this meticulously researched, highly readable, and exquisitely timed book, Jonathan Gruber and Simon Johnson of MIT propose a new, national plan, rooted in expanded scientific research, for accelerating US growth, reducing inequality, and jump-starting regions of America which have been falling behind. And, they show the funding mechanisms, federal and local decision-making processes, and actual areas of new research which would undergird it. It is brilliant at historical, economic, and political levels."

—Roger Altman, former deputy secretary of the Treasury, founder and senior chairman of Evercore

"This brilliant book brings together economic history, urban economics, and the design of incentives to build an ambitious proposal to jump-start growth across geographies and mitigate inequality."

—Susan Athey, Economics of Technology Professor and director, Initiative for Shared Prosperity and Innovation, Stanford University

"Opportunities for technological breakthroughs have never been greater, but America is fumbling its historic leadership. Gruber and Johnson explain with clarity, authority and insight how America can regain its innovation mojo."

—ERIK BRYNJOLFSSON, director of the MIT Initiative on the Digital Economy, and coauthor of *The Second Machine Age*

"What has been missing from our ongoing debate about inequality and bringing the fruits of prosperity to a much wider segment of people is an approach to make it happen in a way that is familiar to American society, tradition, and historical political success. Jon Gruber and Simon Johnson provide that missing link by demonstrating how smart public investment in science will build the capabilities and infrastructure that is the *sine qua non* for the investment that will generate returns in the form of new products, services, and other benefits that employ millions and are widespread geographically."

—ELLEN DULBERGER, member of the Board on Science, Technology, and Economic Policy, the National Academies of Science, Engineering, and Medicine

"This is the book America needs now. The blueprint for a dazzling future, filled with invention and growth, can be found in our recent past. Johnson and Gruber have resurrected the lost history of American science, and the era of big government that funded it. They have written a manifesto brimming with novel proscriptions that are themselves evidence that this country hasn't lost its capacity to innovate."

—FRANKLIN FOER, author of *World Without Mind*

"In *Jump-Starting America*, Jonathan Gruber and Simon Johnson present an innovative and compelling case to invest more in innovation, and they propose a bold plan to ensure that the benefits are shared throughout the US and the money is spent wisely. Nothing less than the preeminence of the US economy hangs in the balance."

—ALAN B. KRUEGER, former chairman of The Council of Economic Advisors, and Bendheim Professor of Economics and Public Affairs, Princeton University

"*Jump-Starting America* is a brilliant, fascinating, timely, and important book. It makes a compelling case that thoughtful government investment in science is the key to achieving a second golden age for the American economy. A joy to read."

—STEVE LEVITT, coauthor of *Freakonomics*, and William B. Ogden Distinguished Service Professor of Economics, University of Chicago

"America's future prosperity depends on investing in our entire country, most especially those areas 'left behind.' Gruber and Johnson show us the way through ingenious ideas based on how it was done in the past and that cut through today's political gridlock, providing the inspiration and optimism we need for enabling many more Americans to secure an economically bright future."

—ERIC SCHMIDT, former CEO and executive chairman of Google

"Long derided, at best for the hubris of officials trying vainly to do science and pick winners and at worst for its cronyism, industrial policy is making a comeback in many countries. Jonathan Gruber and Simon Johnson show how the government can promote innovation while avoiding the classic pitfalls of such policies. The United States of DARPA, NASA, the NIH or the NSF offers a perhaps-unexpected role model. This very important book by two world leading academics is a must-read not only for scholars, but also for all policymakers, from those who still doubt the power of industrial policy to those who might be tempted to apply it carelessly."

—JEAN TIROLE, Toulouse School of Economics,
2014 Nobel laureate in economics

JUMP-STARTING
AMERICA

*How Breakthrough Science
Can Revive Economic Growth
and the American Dream*

Jonathan Gruber
and
Simon Johnson

PUBLICAFFAIRS
NEW YORK

PublicAffairs
Hachette Book Group
1290 Avenue of the Americas, New York, NY 10104
www.publicaffairsbooks.com
@Public_Affairs

Printed in the United States of America
Originally published in hardcover and ebook by PublicAffairs in April 2019
First Trade Paperback Edition: May 2023

Published by PublicAffairs, an imprint of Perseus Books, LLC, a subsidiary
of Hachette Book Group, Inc. The PublicAffairs name and logo is a trademark
of the Hachette Book Group.

The Hachette Speakers Bureau provides a wide range of authors for speaking
events. To find out more, go to hachettespeakersbureau.com or email
HachetteSpeakers@hbgusa.com.

The publisher is not responsible for websites (or their content) that are not owned
by the publisher.

Print book interior design by Linda Mark.

Library of Congress Cataloging-in-Publication Data
Names: Gruber, Jonathan, author. | Johnson, Simon, 1963– author.
Title: Jump-starting America : how breakthrough science can revive economic
  growth and the American dream / Jonathan Gruber and Simon Johnson.
Description: New York, NY : PublicAffairs, 2019. | Includes bibliographical
  references and index.
Identifiers: LCCN 2018059898 (print) | LCCN 2019002380 (ebook) |
  ISBN 9781541762503 (ebook) | ISBN 9781541762480 (hardcover)
Subjects: LCSH: Technological innovations--Economic aspects--United States. |
  Economic development--United States.
Classification: LCC HC110.T4 (ebook) | LCC HC110.T4 G78 2019 (print) |
  DDC 338/.0640973--dc23
LC record available at https://lccn.loc.gov/2018059898

ISBNs: 9781541762480 (hardcover); 9781541762503 (ebook);
      9781541762497 (paperback)

LSC-C

Printing 1, 2023

JONATHAN:

To my wife, Andrea, who was devoted to this project from the start and whose "wife test" was an invaluable guide to the creation of the book

SIMON:

To Mary, Celia, and Lucie, for everything

Contents

Prologue:

Everyone Else

In 2017, Amazon—one of the most prominent tech companies in the world—announced it intended to build a second headquarters-type operation somewhere in North America. Amazon stated that HQ2 would hire, over ten to fifteen years, as many as fifty thousand employees, with "average annual total compensation" over $100,000. The company launched a public competition and gave localities just six weeks to submit bids, a very short deadline. The response was impressive: 238 cities and regions threw their hats into the ring, representing forty-three states, Puerto Rico, and the District of Columbia.

These bids reportedly included generous inducements to Amazon, including billions of dollars in tax benefits, infrastructure improvements, real estate deals, and other inducements.[1] There are obvious major risks involved in making expensive commitments to any firm in a fast-changing industry, as it is hard to know who will be a large successful employer in a decade. A major investment by a company like Amazon is also not an unmixed blessing; if it drives up real estate prices and rents while undermining local public finances, it can actually worsen outcomes for some residents.

Why are so many local political and business leaders desperate to attract this number of jobs when, supposedly, the American economy is doing so well? After all, according to the White House and the Federal Reserve, the economy is close to full employment, which is officially defined as meaning that everyone who wants a job now has a job, and wages are increasing. The president of the United States in 2018 described recent economic growth as "amazing," argued that recent performance is "very sustainable," and emphasized, "Everywhere we look, we are seeing the effects of the American economic miracle."[2]

Unfortunately, these headline numbers are deeply misleading. People in many parts of the country feel they have been—or soon will be—left behind by the growing importance of technology in our economy. Millions of good jobs have been lost to automation in recent decades, particularly in manufacturing. Yes, the service sector has expanded, but too many of the new jobs pay low wages that make it difficult for families to survive, let alone prosper. The low official unemployment rate also hides the fact that many discouraged workers have given up entirely on looking for work and are therefore not included in the statistics.

As our economy recovered from the financial crisis of 2008, some places and some people forged ahead. But many more places—meaning a large number of people—feel increasingly frustrated. This frustration felt by millions of Americans is legitimate and reflects the decades-long failure of policy, from both Democratic and Republican administrations, to create the conditions that foster sufficiently rapid and shared economic growth.

Disappointment with national-level policies naturally leads to local initiatives—sometimes with support across the political spectrum—that include trying to win Amazon's HQ2. While these local efforts have positive dimensions, they can also lead to a race to the bottom that reduces local revenue and makes it harder to maintain public infrastructure, including schools. America's communities are increasingly trapped between fear of missing out on the next generation of good jobs and undermining the essential public services that make them safe and attractive places to live.

It does not have to be this way. Our book is intended for everyone who is tired of the old rhetoric and willing to try something different. We aim to tap into today's local energy for sharing economic prosperity, by proposing an update and (we hope) an improvement on the national-level policies that promoted economic growth just a few decades ago.

The United States of America has always been defined by the notion of forward progress. For a long time, the engine that drove this technological and economic progress was simple: innovation, through which new ideas become commercial products.

American innovation led the way in the nineteenth century for railroads, steel, automobiles, electricity, and radio. In the twentieth century, as science advanced, the United States strengthened its technical leadership: atomic power, digital computers, jet planes, microelectronics, and satellites. From 1940 through to the 1970s, it is hard to think of any significant area of rapid technological change in which the United States did not play a formative role.

During the post–World War II boom years, a broad cross section of Americans shared in the rewards that come with being first to market with new ideas. Across almost all groups and almost all locales, people experienced higher incomes, improved standards of living, better health, and more opportunities for their children. The United States became one of the most dynamic nations on earth, and to a substantial and unprecedented degree, much of the newly created wealth was shared around the country.

This American engine of progress and prosperity is now in serious trouble. Job-creating innovation has slowed, resulting in a stalled standard of living for the middle class. Rewards from the remaining advances have become increasingly concentrated in the hands of a small number of people living in a few big cities. What went wrong?

The private sector has always been, and will remain, key to American prosperity. However, the major—and now mostly forgotten—lesson of the post-1945 period is that modern private enterprise proves much more effective when government provides strong underlying support for basic and applied science and for the commercialization of the resulting innovations.

Why is government financing of research and development so important? Because firms are interested in innovation only to the extent that it improves their own bottom line—and not if it benefits others. "Spillovers" from innovation are incredibly important, creating the basic scientific knowledge and also many of the more applied ideas that power further innovation and create jobs in all corners of the economy. But they are limited by private companies' unwillingness to invest when they do not receive the full or sufficient benefits from that investment. Meanwhile, financiers who support start-ups are, understandably, reluctant to take risks on large, expensive investments with potentially distant payoffs—despite the fact that such investments help create the high-value-added jobs of the future.

The innovation that led to rapid growth after World War II was the direct result of a fruitful partnership between the private sector, the federal government, and universities that allowed us to generate and capture these spillovers as a country. Almost every major innovation in this era relied in an important way on federal government support along the chain of its development. This support was provided by both Democratic and Republican administrations.

Unfortunately, since the late 1960s, the federal government has retreated from this leadership role because of a combination of concerns—from both the Right and the Left—including about short-term budget math and the proper role of science in society. Predictably, this retreat has coincided with a slowdown in the productivity growth that powered the postwar United States economy and boosted living standards across all income groups.

On its current course, America seems unlikely to continue its dominance of invention. Intensely innovative competitors are gaining strength around the world, in large part because other nations are doing a better job of reading American history. Government-financed research initiatives in other nations, including China, are helping to create the technologies of tomorrow, along with the associated well-paid jobs.

America can regain the path to good jobs through innovation. In fact, we are uniquely positioned to update and apply our previous winning formula. We have the best universities in the world, along with entrepreneurs and investors who are eager to partner—as well as thousands of creative students, US born and immigrant, who want to build good companies. The American economic environment for technology entrepreneurs is good. What is missing?

All we need, in our view, is a more strategic view regarding how government can expand on its role as a catalyst for private enterprise. The post-1945 years, with tweaks to reflect modern realities, show us how this can be done.

But the politics of recent decades teach us another lesson—the benefits must be shared more widely across society. There are many geographic areas with the potential for innovative success, with resources ranging from strong educational institutions to entrepreneurial residents. A serious plan to jump-start the American growth engine must focus on all these places of opportunity.

In early November 2018, Amazon announced its much-awaited HQ2 decision. The projected jobs will be split between two locations: Crystal City (now rebranded as National Landing), part of Arlington, in Northern Virginia, across the Potomac River from Washington, DC; and Long Island City, in the borough of Queens, across the East River from Manhattan, New York City. In other words, the "winners" are two of the most economically successful regions of recent decades and places that both already have plenty of good jobs. The potential for Amazon to transform lagging communities remains unfulfilled.[3]

The lesson from the HQ2 bidding experience is clear. Established big tech companies, left to their own devices, will bring a significant number of good jobs—along with congestion, high house prices, and perhaps even more inequality—to a small set of already successful cities, most of which are located on the East or West Coast.

This book is for everyone else.

Introduction to the Paperback Edition:
America, Jump-Started

In early 2020, the world was again at war—this time fighting a deadly virus. Just as in the early days of World War II, the United States found itself insufficiently prepared for a global struggle. But, exactly as Vannevar Bush correctly perceived in May 1940, we once again held one ace card: science.

To be specific, what the United States had was relevant knowledge among scientists, strong capabilities of biotech firms, and sufficient understanding on the part of public health officials. But just as in early 1940, the task was to pivot this potential quickly into top priority applications—particularly effective vaccines, produced and distributed at massive scale.

If you are reading these words in public anywhere in the world, look around. If you see people interacting normally and with few masks visible, this is because new vaccines dragged us back from the edge of what could otherwise have become a global virus-induced depression.

Why was a government intervention needed? Why didn't the private sector react quickly by itself to develop a vaccine for COVID-19, given the enormous potential profits? The answer is also an explanation for decades of underinvestment in vaccines by pharmaceutical companies. Vaccine development is costly—and risky. By the time a vaccine is developed, the infectious disease in question may have abated on its own or evolved in a way that renders any recently developed vaccine ineffective, leaving companies holding the bag for billions of dollars in research and development (R&D) costs. Company executives thinking about this kind of opportunity would rather invest their dollars in potential therapeutic drugs that are certain to be in demand once developed, such as treatments for cancer or heart conditions or Alzheimer's disease.

Given that, left to its own devices, the private sector chronically underinvests in vaccines, what worked in 2020? Two types of government intervention can promote vaccine development. The first is "push" incentives, of the type we highlight in this book: public funding for the underlying scientific research and for speedy development of new vaccines. The other is "pull" incentives: a public guarantee to purchase large quantities of the new vaccine, removing the risk that there will not be a market. The United States made a major commitment of public resources along both dimensions.

The new vaccines, developed by Moderna and BioNTech (partnered with Pfizer), relied on a recently developed technology. For their entire history, vaccines have functioned by exposing the body to a small amount of virus, training the immune system to fight off that virus should it arrive. This approach traditionally requires years of trial and error to assess the right amount of exposure, including lengthy trial periods.

Both Moderna and BioNTech had for several years been working on a radically different approach to treating disease, using messenger RNA (mRNA)—described as "a wisp of genetic code from a virus"—to prompt development of appropriate antibodies. Much of the research on which this approach was based had been funded in large part by the National Institutes of Health, but at the beginning of 2020 there was no authorized mRNA vaccine—and therefore no such vaccine had ever been manufactured at large scale.

Executives and researchers at the relevant companies immediately realized that the technology they had been developing could be readily applied to COVID-19 vaccines. With push and pull incentives provided by the federal government, the companies pivoted quickly and their employees worked hard. The results saved millions of lives and reopened economies.

Does this mean that we—as American taxpayers or global citizens—should be relaxed about future pandemics and our ability to cope in terms of public health capabilities, drawing on our stock of scientific knowledge? On the contrary, COVID-19 confirmed exactly what we argued in *Jump-Starting America*, which was published in hardcover in the spring of 2019. There is a lot more that we can and should do in terms of investing in publicly funded R&D in the United States and more effectively using our greatest resource, which is millions of smart people across the country who want better jobs and who can boost how much new scientific knowledge we produce and use productively.

The ultimate test of any model is its "out of sample prediction"—the ability of a theory to explain data observed after the model was created. The COVID-19 vaccine experience is a compelling out-of-sample test for the central hypothesis in *Jump-Starting America*: government funding of research and development can have outsized returns by catalyzing, rather than displacing, private investment.

The pandemic offers broader lessons that further support what we suggested in *Jump-Starting America*.

For example, consider the pressure on—and near collapse of—supply chains around the world in 2020 and 2021, with difficulties still evident in 2022. No one was prepared for the extent of disruption to global commerce, affecting the production of goods and services. The pandemic, along with the brutal 2022 Russian invasion of Ukraine and ongoing trade tensions with China (as well as that country's Zero-COVID policy), have significantly elevated interest in "onshoring" production—i.e., producing more in the United States and reducing the length of supply chains.

Despite the rise of remote work, there is no evidence of a pandemic-induced decline in the preeminence of existing technology hubs. As we emphasized in *Jump-Starting America*, a few coastal cities still dominate the innovation economy in the modern United States. A recent study carried out by a team at the Brookings Institution highlights a striking fact that illustrates this point—in recent years, 75 percent of all jobs created in high-tech sectors are in just six cities. The economic bonanza associated with the development of the new vaccines was concentrated disproportionately in Boston, home of Moderna and already one of the leading tech cities in the nation.

Much of the debate about technology hubs revolves around the "economies of agglomeration" discussed in our book, which arise from person-to-person interaction. Do such economies persist when individuals work from home more—and can do so flexibly from all over the world? A rash of news stories suggested that the existing tech hubs lost some of their predominance during the pandemic, for example, as people moved from Silicon Valley and New York City to places with lower population density. But more than two years later, there is no widespread evidence for declining attractiveness of superstar cities. Working from home several days per week does not seem to discourage highly skilled individuals from wanting to live in the same metropolitan areas as people with similar skill levels.

A fundamental problem arising from our excessive reliance on superstar cities was highlighted even further in the wake of the pandemic— there is a limited supply of housing, leading to sky-high real estate prices. One policy response would be to build more housing in places like San Francisco and Boston, but such ideas consistently run into local opposition and seem unlikely ever to gain sufficient traction.

At the same time, the pandemic may have created a new balance of power between the quality of jobs and the quality of life. While some companies would prefer that everyone show up every day, the tighter labor market means that management needs to pay attention to how talented people want to arrange their lives. At least in part, this means thinking about moving tasks away from those crowded and expensive coastal areas to places with more affordable real estate and shorter commutes. In *Jump-Starting America*, we identified more than 100 places with the potential to become next-generation tech hubs—as laid out on our website, Jump-StartingAmerica. com. This list quickly attracted attention on how best to think about building new hubs and what exactly the federal government could do to better match where people already live and where good jobs are created.

Perhaps most encouraging for us is that our vision helped inspire a major piece of legislation: the CHIPS and Science Act, signed into law by President Biden on August 9, 2022. This law was the merger of two separate pieces of legislation. The first is the Creating Helpful Incentives to Produce Semiconductors (CHIPS) bill, a $52.7 billion investment over five years in onshoring production of semiconductors. This attempts to address a major supply chain bottleneck exposed by COVID-19—the enormous dependence of the U.S. economy on semiconductors, which are largely manufactured overseas.

As with other examples emphasized in our book, from flat-screen displays to synthetic biology, semiconductors are yet another technology that was invented in the United States but for which most of the employment has moved overseas. This issue is particularly timely given ongoing tension between the United States and China over Taiwan, where 65 percent of semiconductor fabrication takes place, as well as all of the fabrication of the most advanced chips. The CHIPS and Science Act provides $52 billion in subsidies along with a 25 percent investment tax credit to support production in the United States. This legislation also prohibits funded companies from expanding their manufacturing of semiconductors in China.

The second piece of legislation was the Endless Frontiers Act (EFA), an effort led by Senator Chuck Schumer of New York. This legislation reflected in many important ways the arguments of our book, including focusing attention on the significant decline in public R&D funding as a share of GDP and on the ongoing concentration of technology jobs in a small set of superstar cities.

The EFA went through several permutations before it was finally attached to the CHIPS bill as part of a combined package that passed Congress with bipartisan support—a rarity in today's supercharged partisan environment. The final bill aims to inject more than $75 billion in new federal spending (above the previously set baseline) over five years on public R&D. While smaller than what we had proposed initially, this represents a 10 percent increase in publicly funded R&D and would reverse a decades-long trend of decline. (Full disclosure: we were delighted to participate in some of these discussions, but we were not in charge of final details or the legislative language.)

The bill also includes a $10 billion investment in a new technology hubs program that would set up new regional technology hubs outside existing superstar cities. The law proposes to do so through exactly the type of apolitical competitive mechanism emphasized in *Jump-Starting America*. The Commerce Department will evaluate proposals on a set of defined criteria, granting up to $150 million to at least twenty new hubs around the country in a first round, with the goal of much larger follow-up funding if the initial round is deemed successful.

One reason to believe that such a model can succeed is that a smaller-scale version was piloted as part of the American Rescue Plan, which passed Congress in spring 2021. That program provided $1 billion to finance the "Build Back Better Challenge," charged with awarding $25 million to $75 million to areas to transition to tech hubs. The winners of this competition were announced on September 2, 2022, and they are a broad coalition of places from around the country and across the technology space. The winners include locations in twenty-four states, with clusters in biotechnology and health, advanced mobility (such as autonomous and electric vehicles), natural resource and agricultural in-dustries, next-generation manufacturing, and clean energy (including one hub focused on the type of hydrogen-powered energy we discuss in the last chapter of this book). Perhaps most important for illustrating the feasibility of such place-based policy, there has been (so far) no crit-icism of this process as being influenced by politics—this is the type of apolitical competition that can work at larger scale.

In line with this approach, the National Science Foundation recently announced its Regional Innovation Engines program, which aims to promote economic development in a way that is new for this agency. NSF funding continues to prioritize potentially important research, but the agency explains the program is particularly designed for areas "without well-established innovation ecosystems." An essential element is the development of a workforce that can contribute in high-tech areas like biotechnology. Over ten years, the program will make $160 million available for these potential regional engines.

While these legislative and executive actions represent a major step forward, the ambitious agenda of *Jump-Starting America* is far from real-ization. Most immediately, the new R&D and tech hub spending is now authorized, but Congress needs to support this through appropriations. Good intentions are not enough to change the trajectory of economic progress in the United States, and continued funding is far from certain in a highly partisan political environment. Appropriations to build and support enhanced public funding for R&D are essential, and we remain engaged on the advocacy front to this end.[1]

In the longer run, U.S. public R&D financing as a share of our economy remains well below the level of our competitors. Even with this proposed increase, the United States will not regain its position among the top ten countries in public R&D financing relative to GDP. By some calculations, our public R&D spending as a share of GDP remains less than half that of China, where investing in science is seen as a major economic and security priority. The CHIPS and Science Act supports significant R&D investments in semiconductors and clean energy but provides no new funding for investments in other critical areas such as biomedicine. And perhaps most worrisome, the United States may not be learning the lessons of COVID-19 in terms of push and pull investments that support critical public health technologies. It is essential that the investments in the CHIPS and Science Act become the beginning, and not the end, of our nation's renewed commitment to boosting science.

This major investment in technology hubs has the potential to create a virtuous cycle of support for more investment in federally funded science. If voters around the country experience first-hand the economic benefits that scientific research can bring to their communities, this should broaden the base of support for larger federal spending on R&D. Even the relatively modest $10 billion investment in technology hubs in the CHIPS and Science Act, along with existing programs at the Commerce Department and the NSF, could generate enormous social dividends down the road by catalyzing support for science and for robust, sustained federal funding in pursuit of breakthrough innovations.

There is a saying in Washington, DC: your policy proposals are gaining traction when you sit down to lunch with someone, and that person carefully explains the importance of your own idea and why it should be adopted immediately—all without realizing that you came up with this suggestion originally.

This has been our experience with *Jump-Starting America*. We have lost track of how many people have taken these ideas on board and then explained them with commendable clarity. It is immensely gratifying to see so many people claim to be among the parents of these ideas.

When we first proposed and began to develop these ideas in late 2016 and early 2017, our emphasis on place-based economic development was deeply unfashionable. Some distinguished colleagues advised us to head in other directions, and experienced people close to the political process opined that such suggestions had no chance of gaining traction.

But the point of writing books that develop policy proposals is not, in our view, to restate the obvious or pander to whatever notions are currently fashionable. Instead, we recommend the approach in *Jump-Starting America*: define the problem to be solved, assess the various options available, and then offer a way forward.

The goal of books like *Jump-Starting America* is not to write legislation—elected politicians and their expert advisers will do that. Our goal was simply to get some new or rejuvenated ideas into the mix, and then to help develop messages that will persuade people everywhere to lend their support. Specifically, this is what we currently suggest, to anyone who will listen: Create more good jobs now, build the technologies that we obviously need, and prepare for whatever crisis, disaster, or conflict next comes our way.

To achieve this, a strong positive vision of science, with economic gains for everyone, must rise again.

Introduction:

Endless Invention

A nation which depends upon others for its new basic scientific knowledge will be slow in its industrial progress and weak in its competitive position in world trade, regardless of its mechanical skill.

—Vannevar Bush, head of the US World War II scientific effort[1]

IN JUNE 1940, THE FUTURE OF THE WORLD HUNG IN THE BALANCE. GERMANY HAD ATTACKED THE Netherlands, Belgium, and France just over a month earlier, and the Nazi victories were nothing short of stunning. Using military technology in new and inventive ways, the Germans demonstrated a form of warfare that combined quick movement, powerful weaponry, and dominance of the air. On paper, and according to conventional thinking, the combined British and French forces should have been able to stop the German advance, but within six weeks, the British were scrambling to evacuate their beleaguered forces from Dunkirk, and Paris fell.

America waited indecisively on the fringes of this fast-spreading conflict, with a competent but small navy, an air force that had fallen behind its potential adversaries, and an army that was so short of rifles that soldiers had to practice with brooms instead. In all of 1939, the United States built only six medium tanks.[2]

US military technology at the start of World War II was also seriously flawed. There were "grave defects with the depth-control mechanism and the exploder" in US torpedoes; many did not detonate when they hit targets.[3] There was no consistently reliable way to track the presence of German U-boats in the Atlantic—thousands of sailors died as a result, and Britain came close to starvation.[4] American armor was initially no match for what the Germans had in the field and under development.

A mere four years later, led by newly developed American technology, the Allies scored a decisive victory against both Germany and Japan. The United States had transformed warfare through the development and rapid deployment of advanced radar, proximity fuses, more effective armor, automated fire control mechanisms, amphibious vehicles, and high-performance aircraft—as well as by more effective ways to limit bacterial infections and control malaria.[5] The German submarine fleet, once so close to victory in the Atlantic, was broken by the use of techniques, including radar detection, that seemed fantastical just a few years before. Japan's surrender was forced by the detonation of two atomic bombs, based on essentially brand-new science.

How did this technological transformation happen—and so quickly? Start with June 12, 1940, and a visit to the White House by Vannevar Bush.

Vannevar Bush was an accomplished man. Previously vice president and dean of engineering at MIT, on the eve of World War II, he was running the Carnegie Institution for Science, a leading research organization in Washington, DC. Tough and experienced as an administrator, Bush was also a technology visionary and an entrepreneur with two successful start-ups under his belt, including as cofounder of Raytheon—an early technology company that grew up to become a substantial military contractor.

Bush represented American private enterprise, both academic and profit-making, at its best. Like many private-sector leaders of his generation, he also had a deeply rooted dislike of government involvement both in the economy and in science.

Bush had good reason to feel on edge waiting for his first White House meeting with President Franklin Delano Roosevelt. Despite the urgency of the moment, Bush did not have a new weapon or potential technology to unveil. Instead, his idea was prosaic and literally written on a single sheet of paper. In short, Vannevar Bush wanted to create a new government committee.

Washington, DC, has never been short of committees, and the summer of 1940 was no exception. But what Bush had in mind was no ordinary additional level of bureaucracy. The powerful people, with a clear mandate to develop weapons, would no longer just be admirals and generals or established industrial companies or even the private sector's top research labs but rather Bush and a few university colleagues, none of whom had experienced combat. By any political standards, this was a breathtaking move—and by outsiders with very little political experience. Thirty years later, this was Bush's assessment:

> There were those who protested that the action of setting up N.D.R.C. [the National Defense Research Committee] was an end run, a grab by which a small company of scientists and engineers, acting outside established channels, got hold of the authority and the money for the program of developing new weapons. That, in fact, is exactly what it was.[6]

It worked. FDR was well aware that war was approaching—and was looking for good ideas that would not trigger congressional opposition. The president's prior experience as assistant secretary of the navy encouraged him both to think about military technology and to be skeptical of admirals. Bush had prepared the ground well through key advisors, and FDR approved the idea inside of fifteen minutes. The National Defense Research Committee (NDRC) sprang into being.

Bush proved an inspired choice, abrasive enough to get the job done but also always focused on improving coordination and cooperation, even among people who did not like him. His friends were good at recruiting and managing talented scientists—other founding members of the NDRC included Karl Compton (president of MIT), James B. Conant (president of Harvard), Frank B. Jewett (president of Bell Labs and the National Academy of Sciences), and Richard C. Tolman (dean of the graduate school at Caltech).

Bush had long rubbed shoulders with all the smartest scientific people, who worked on everything from theories about the atom to far-fetched notions about how electricity passes through various materials. His new government committee idea was, in effect, simply about harnessing these individuals and their protégés in a productive manner to the coming effort of national defense.

This team, and the people they worked with, built—for its day—an enormous operation. At the peak of the activity, Bush directed the work of around thirty thousand people, of whom six thousand were scientists. Perhaps two-thirds of all physicists in the United States were employed in this operation.[7] There had never been a greater concentration of scientific effort in the world.

In 1938, on the eve of world war, federal and state governments spent a combined 0.076 percent of national income on scientific research, a trivial amount. By 1944, the US government was spending nearly 0.5 percent of national income on science—a sevenfold increase, most of which was channeled through Bush's organization from 1940.[8] The effects of this unprecedented surge were simply incredible and, for America's enemies, ultimately devastating.

Then, in 1945, Vannevar Bush had what may be considered his most profound insight. The war had been won, in part, because scientists under his general direction had figured out how to apply the existing stock of knowledge for military purposes and because American industry proved very good at turning those ideas quickly into a large number of physical goods—weapons of war.

What was needed next, Bush argued, was a redirection to focus on winning the peace. In a simple yet forceful way, Bush asked: What are the scientists to do next? His answer: a lot more science—funded by the federal government. In a 1945 report titled *Science: The Endless Frontier*, prepared for President Roosevelt, Bush argued dramatically that more than narrowly defined national security was at stake. Invention, including in ways that could not be forecast, would save lives, increase the standard of living, and create jobs.

Government itself should not do science. Bush was scathing about bureaucracy in general and had the metaphorical scars to prove that military bureaucracy in particular was not conducive to scientific inquiry.

At the same time, based on Bush's deep personal experience, the private sector—firms, rich individuals, and the best universities—by itself could not fund and carry out the innovative science that was required. Private business was very good at incremental change based on existing knowledge. But by the mid-twentieth century, the age of individual inventors providing breakthroughs by themselves was substantially over, and private sector science was being carried out in large-scale corporate labs. The executives running these labs were not generally inclined to fund the invention of new technologies that could undermine or even ruin their company's existing business model.

The controversial yet deep insight of Bush's wartime model was combining the traditionally quite separate world of corporate management with the quirky faculty of universities to find solutions for what the military needed—sometimes even before the military knew precisely what that was. In his report, Bush proposed that the United States combine that university–private sector partnership with ongoing large-scale government funding to produce a postwar innovation machine.

This is—eventually—exactly what the United States did. The idea of large-scale government funding for university-based science took a while to gain traction, and the precise structures created were not exactly what Bush had in mind.[9] Nevertheless, in the decades that followed World War II, his broad vision was implemented to a substantial degree.

An essential part of this approach was a transformation of higher education, including a great expansion in the number of university-trained engineers and scientists—made possible through federal government support, beginning with the GI Bill of 1944. New sectors developed, millions of jobs were created, and these vacancies, including occupations that had not previously existed, were filled by people with recently acquired high levels of skill. For example, the government backed investments in the technology needed to develop jet aircraft, creating the basis for a large commercial sector, which in turn needed—and was able to hire—thousands of skilled mechanics and engineers.

This combination of new technology and a larger number of skilled people increased productivity and created the scientific and practical basis for almost everything that characterizes our modern economy. For the next two decades, wages rose for university-educated people and—a key point—also for those with only a high school diploma.

The catalyst for this effort was federal government funding at a scale never previously experienced, which generated some of the highest-return investments the world has ever seen.

From 1940 to 1964, federal funding for research and development increased twentyfold. At its peak in the mid-1960s, this spending amount was around 2 percent of annual gross domestic product—roughly one in every fifty dollars in the United States was devoted to government funding of research and development (equivalent, relative to GDP, to almost $400 billion today). The impact on our economy, on Americans, and on the world was simply transformational.

There is a good chance you are alive today because of this work. Penicillin was a pre–World War II British invention—a brilliant albeit accidental discovery. But it was the Americans, under Bush's leadership, who figured out how to scale up production and distribute millions of high-quality doses around the world.[10] This effort sparked interest in other potentially important soil microorganisms, leading indirectly to the development of streptomycin (effective against tuberculosis) and other antibiotics.[11] Cortisone and other steroids were created.[12] An ambitious worldwide anti-malaria campaign was launched.[13] Childhood vaccination, the decline in maternal mortality, and the control of infectious disease more broadly all sprang directly from this work. The leading American pharmaceutical companies of today owe their expansion and subsequent fortune to this public push, which began under Bush's auspices, to improve medical science.[14]

Digital computers are another area where the federal government had great impact.[15] By 1945, the US military saw that it faced important problems—from the automated control of naval guns to the management of complex early-warning radar systems—that called out for faster computation than was humanly possible. Their funding for both basic research and more applied development eventually made possible both the development of new machines (hardware)—including transistors, which became the essential silicon-based component—and the instructions that run on those machines (software). From this national defense–oriented investment flowed everything that has changed how we handle, analyze, and use information—up to and including Apple's iPhone.

The examples go on, including jet aircraft, satellites, improved telecommunications, and the internet. It is hard to find any aspect of modern life that has not been profoundly affected by innovation that can be traced back either to the Bush-era efforts or to inventions that were supported by various government programs in the years that followed.

Prior to 1940, university education was primarily a luxury, available to only a few people. Subsequent to the expansion in the potential for technological progress—and the availability of government support for research and teaching—the number and quality of places for studying science, engineering, and all their applications greatly increased. For the first time, the United States became the best country in the world to study, develop, and commercialize new technology.

The backbone of the US economy in the postwar years was built on a visionary model that created not just great companies and amazing products but also a large number of good jobs—the basis for the largest and most successful expansion of a middle class that the world has ever seen. The fruits of government investment were indirectly shared with all citizens through a US corporate sector that provided stable employment at high wages with relative equality, at least by today's standards.

Median family income in the United States doubled from 1947 through 1970. The increase in wealth was shared throughout the country, with growth not only on the coasts but in the industrial Midwest and the newly dynamic South.

The broader benefits of this new technology were felt around the world. There was a general American desire to support a more stable world—primarily to avoid a repetition of the Great Depression and two world wars. However, what drove the spread of useful and productivity-enhancing technology was not primarily any form of altruism or even a deliberate desire to help. Ideas, once manifest in the form of a usable technology, are hard to control and spread to wherever people find them appealing.

Naturally, other countries responded—by investing in their own scientific endeavors, in effect trying to create their own version of what was working well in the United States. This became the age of deliberate government-supported but private sector–led technological innovation.

WHAT WENT WRONG?

Despite a remarkable run of technological and economic success, the United States now faces serious problems. In World War II and during the Cold War, the country built a powerful and stable engine of growth through the application of scientific research to practical problems. The associated technologies proved transformative, resulting in new products, new companies, and an almost insatiable demand for American goods and services around the world.

Unfortunately, we failed to maintain the engine. From the mid-1960s onward, based on concerns about the environmental, military, and ethical implications of unfettered science, compounded by shortsighted budget math, the government curtailed its investments in scientific research. Economic difficulties during the 1970s, followed by the Reagan Revolution and the anti-tax movement, resulted in an even broader retreat from federally funded activities. Most recently, the impact of a global financial crisis in 2008 and consequent economic pressures—known as the Great Recession—have further squeezed investments in the scientific future.

Federal spending on research and development peaked at nearly 2 percent of economic output in 1964 and over the next fifty years fell to only around 0.7 percent of the economy.[16] Converted to the same fraction of GDP today, that decline represents roughly $240 billion per year that we no longer spend on creating the next generation of good jobs.

Should we care? If there is socially beneficial research and product development to be done, surely the innovative companies of today will take this on?

In fact, they won't. Invention is a public good, in the sense that every dollar of spending on science by a private company is paid for by that company (a private cost), while some of the benefits from discoveries invariably become public—ideas, methods, and even new products (once patents expire) are shared with the world.

The private sector, by definition, focuses solely on assessing if the private returns—to this firm, its managers and investors—of any investment are high enough to justify the risks. Executives running these companies do not account for the spillover benefits that accrue from producing general knowledge, and they do not share proprietary research that might benefit others.

Moreover, new invention in the private sector is constrained by financing. The venture capital sector that has created so many high-tech success stories has, at the same time, avoided the type of very-long-run and capital-intensive investments that lead to technological breakthroughs—and create new industries and jobs.

As a result, the government retreat from research and development has not been fully offset by the private sector. Consequently, our stock of knowledge increased more slowly than it would have otherwise—over time, this means lower growth and less job creation.

Missed opportunities for invention directly contribute to the stagnation of incomes. From World War II through the early 1970s, our economy—total gross domestic product—grew close to 4 percent per year on average.[17] Over the last forty years, our growth performance has slipped, averaging under 3 percent per annum since the early 1970s and decelerating further to under 2 percent per annum since 2000.[18] By the mid-2020s, the Congressional Budget Office expects annual growth in total GDP will average only 1.7 percent per year.[19]

At its core, economic growth is all about what happens to productivity—how much we collectively produce per person.[20] The information technology revolution is much hyped—smartphones for everyone!—but has proven profoundly disappointing in terms of its impact on productivity, and there is no sign this will soon change. The boom-bust decade that started the 2000s only further undermined our ability to grow.

Good jobs—at decent wages with reasonable benefits—are disappearing and being replaced by low-paying jobs that do not support a sufficient standard of living. A process of job destruction is a normal part of any market economy and also existed during the boom years of the 1950s and 1960s. But the new information technology that failed to boost overall productivity growth served to accelerate the elimination of high-paying jobs that were previously held by people with just a high school education. As a result, after doubling in only twenty-three years after World War II, the median US household income grew by only 20 percent over the next forty-five years.

While we have retreated from Vannevar Bush's innovation engine, the rest of the world is picking up the slack. Total research funding is growing at a much faster rate, relative to the economy, in the rest of the world than it is in the United States, led in many countries by active government policies. This is particularly true in our largest economic rival, China, whose rising investments have paid off, including in areas such as computing and, increasingly, medical research, where the United States once dominated.

The middle class is already under enormous pressure, with stagnant wages and a rising cost of higher education that makes it harder and harder to move up the economic ladder. At the same time, there is a discernible and hard-to-reverse geographic impact: good jobs are created disproportionately in a small number of cities, largely on the East and West Coasts. Restrictive zoning policies and high land prices in these cities make it difficult for many people to migrate to where the good jobs are, leaving them behind in slower-growing areas and contributing to a sense of economic unease.

We need a transformative and politically sustainable new way to boost growth and create jobs—by jump-starting our growth engine.

JUMP-STARTING THE ENGINE

The economic slowdown of the past few decades is not inevitable. Our economy can become dazzling again—both in terms of inventions and, more importantly, in terms of the prospects for most Americans. To do this, America needs to become much more of a technology-driven economy. That sounds surprising because most of us think we are a country driven by leading technologies and technological players. After all, isn't Silicon Valley already the engine of world growth?

Actually, no—Silicon Valley impacts only a small part of the US economy.[21] The American private sector invests in new products but not in basic science. To really improve the performance of the American economy—and to raise incomes across the board—we need to invest heavily in the underlying science of computing, human health, clean energy, and more.

The necessary conditions are largely in place. We have the world's leading universities, favorable conditions for starting new business, and plenty of capital willing to take risks. We have learned a great deal about what works and what does not in terms of the public-private partnership around science and innovation.

What we need is a sustained public- and private-sector push that scales up the innovation system, focusing on the creation of ideas that can be converted into technology—just like the early work on digital computers ended up creating an entirely different structure for the organization and dissemination of information. This will require the type of commitment to the federal funding of science that helped support our post–World War II boom.

We should support this with a major expansion in science education across all ages, with the goal of producing—and employing—many more university graduates with technical skills. This combined increase in demand and supply can, over time, create millions of new, high-paying jobs.

But to make this push both economically sensible and politically sustainable, we need to distribute the benefits of growth more broadly, in two senses.

First, we must ensure that the new high-tech jobs do not follow the pattern of the past forty years and fall into just a narrow set of "superstar" cities on the East and West Coasts. There are dozens of other cities throughout the United States that meet the conditions for creating a new technology hub. These are cities that have the preconditions for success—a large pool of skilled workers, high-quality universities, and a low cost of living—and where people desperately want more jobs at good wages. But they are places that are losing out today because they do not have enough scientific infrastructure to become new centers of innovation, nor do they have the base of venture capital that can turn new ideas into profitable companies.

The federal government can select the best places using the type of competitive selection mechanism most recently employed by one of the country's most valuable companies. In late 2017, as we mentioned in the prologue, Amazon announced that it would place a second headquarters operation somewhere in North America, creating perhaps around fifty thousand good jobs. A total of 238 cities and regions from all over the United States (and Canada)—irrespective of political inclination—submitted bids, laying out various kinds of welcome carpets, including tax breaks and supportive infrastructure.

Amazon, however, eventually chose two locations that will help it make a presumably bigger profit—partly by receiving the largest possible tax breaks. This is what companies do: they serve the interests of their shareholders, not the public. The result is a zero-sum tax competition that does nothing to raise the wealth of the nation as a whole.

The competition we have in mind would serve the interest of the nation, not individual companies. Places would compete not on the basis of tax breaks but on the basis of their qualifications to become a new technology hub. This would involve demonstrating the proper preconditions for scientific innovation, including research infrastructure, and support for better scientific education, from high school through college. It would involve ensuring sustainable development plans for the area so that we don't just create new congested and high-cost-of-living cities. Places would need to demonstrate partnerships with the private sector that can lead from lab science to product development.

Second, we should share the benefits of innovation more directly with the US taxpayer. For too long, the government has funded basic research—such as digital computers, the internet, and the Human Genome Project—that has essentially become windfall profits for a small number of investors who are able to get in early into enough technology-development projects.[22] The increasing shift in the returns from production toward capital owners (people who own companies, property, and so on, rather than workers), combined with falling effective rates of taxation on those returns to capital, leaves many Americans rightly suspicious of government investments that lead to more profitable firms.

As part of our competitive criteria for areas to attract the additional federal science funding, local governments would need to provide a way for taxpayers to share directly in the upside. For example, local and state government could hold a large, publicly owned parcel of land for development in and around these new research hubs—with the government getting the upside, in higher rents or capital appreciation, as this land becomes increasingly valuable. Profits would be paid out directly to citizens as a cash dividend every year.

We have a great model of how to do this from a relatively conservative state: the Alaska Permanent Fund, which distributes the revenues from natural resources (oil and gas) equally to all state residents. An annual innovation dividend would be paid out in cash terms equally to all Americans, illustrating vividly the returns from the public's investment in advancing science.

Taxpayers take risks all the time, whether they know it or not. Ever since the creation of the American Republic—and much more so since 1940—the federal government has invested in pushing frontiers forward, first in a geographical sense and more recently in terms of technology.

When projects go wrong—like the collapse of solar manufacturer Solyndra, which borrowed more than $500 million from the federal government—there are accusations, investigations, and some attempt to assign blame. The taxpayer has to absorb the losses.

When projects go well—radar, penicillin, jet planes, satellites, the internet, and most recently the Human Genome Project—great fortunes are created, but only for the lucky few. It's time for all Americans to get a serious piece of the upside from accelerated innovation.

A ROAD MAP

The first part of the book focuses on the largely forgotten history of how publicly funded science contributed to victory in World War II and then created the underpinnings for the dynamic American economy of the postwar period. The heroes of this story are not household names, but they can rightly claim a substantial share of the credit for our US postwar economic boom. We then explain how scientific overconfidence, conflicts with politicians, and budgetary concerns inclined the public sector to curtail science funding.

The second part explains the economic case for a major push today on publicly funded research and development. We explain why the private sector systematically underinvests in science. We also show how publicly funded science continues to be innovative and job-creating, albeit at too low a level.

Finally, we bring these lessons to bear on how to rebuild the American growth engine, based on the enormous opportunities for growth outside of coastal megacities. We propose a detailed plan for expanding scientific efforts and ensuring the benefits are broadly shared.

June 1940 represented a moment of deep crisis for the world—and one to which, eventually, the United States responded dramatically. The issues we face today are less obviously about national security but, because they affect the sustainability of our economic well-being, may prove just as profound.

To what extent will the United States create the good jobs of the future? While we hesitate, other countries invest heavily in new science and its applications. We are already being overtaken in key sectors. Respond now or again risk being left in the dust of rival nations.

1

For Our Comfort, Our Security, Our Prosperity

Here wo arc, standing alone. What is going to happen?

—British prime minister Winston Churchill, in conversation with James B. Conant, April 10, 1941[1]

BY 1940, THE UNITED STATES HAD ESTABLISHED ITSELF AS ONE OF THE MOST INNOVATIVE nations on earth—based not so much on scientific leadership as on practical engineering applied to sectors such as automobiles and telecommunications. What Vannevar Bush realized is that innovation of a different magnitude was needed, specifically when it came to the technology that would win the war. For example, in his view, the range and performance of combat aircraft would likely play a decisive role. American fighter planes in 1940, however, were outclassed by those of Germany and Japan.[2]

More broadly, it started to become clear—at least to Bush and his colleagues—that the United States needed to more urgently develop technology that could be applied to war. One obvious response would be for the government to draft scientists and put them to work in its own laboratories, along the lines of the German or Soviet model. The early success of German technology in World War II certainly recommended that model.

Another possibility would be to hand the task directly to private business—but the goal now was national defense, not making profits. Over the previous century, the private sector had racked up impressive achievements, including developing railroads, electricity, and telephones. What was the right way to break loose from the traditional profit-oriented framework of private business while retaining private initiative and the ability to move fast? To understand the strategic design choice faced by Vannevar Bush in 1940—and much of what followed during the war and after—we need to step back briefly into the history of American innovation.

THE RISE OF CORPORATE INNOVATION

The United States of America did not begin as a technologically advanced country. Largely agrarian at the time of independence, the United States was behind the United Kingdom in terms of engineering capabilities not just in 1776 but for at least the next half century. For example, in the building of canals—cutting-edge engineering between 1800 and 1820—Americans routinely relied on imported (mostly British) advice, yet frequently struggled to get it right. American canals leaked at best, and some even had to be completely rebuilt.[3]

American construction techniques eventually improved, however, motivated in large part by the incentive to construct robust means of transportation across, by European standards, very long distances and difficult terrain. From the experience of building in a harsh landscape came important lessons and new opportunities—seen, most clearly, in the development of railroads.

The British developed the first engine that ran on wheels and metal track.[4] Britain also took the lead in building railroads, for which miles of track is one measure of development. In 1830, Britain already had over 125 miles of track, while the United States had only between 23 and 40 miles.[5] Both systems had 7,000 miles in the late 1840s or 1850s. Then the American system grew much larger—reaching 30,000 miles by 1860, while the British system was still only around 13,500 miles in 1869 and, at its peak, 20,000 miles in 1914.[6]

Mileage comparisons might be considered unfair—the United States had more land area and greater distances to cover—but progress in terms of American-built locomotives was just as impressive. The United States imported its first train engines (from the UK) in 1829, but these were quickly found not ideal for American conditions, where it was more difficult to lay track and curves were often sharper. The result was a six-wheeled design (rather than the British four wheels)—and the beginning of a boom in design and production for railroads.[7] Soon Americans were exporting locomotives to the world.

America had become good at practical engineering, long before it led the world in science. Alexis de Tocqueville wrote this of America as he found it in 1831:

In America the purely practical part of the sciences is cultivated admirably, and people attend carefully to the theoretical portion immediately necessary to application; in this way the Americans display a mind that is always clear, free, original, and fertile; but there is almost no one in the United States who gives himself over to the essentially theoretical and abstract portion of human knowledge.[8]

Tocqueville thought this reflected on the essential nature of democracy, but it may just have indicated there was a lot of practical engineering work to do—and the rewards to pure science seemed relatively small or distant in terms of payoffs.

The early American technology development experience was dominated by a few men, largely self-taught and with minimal formal science background. Samuel Morse, a professional painter, invented the telegraph in the 1830s. Cyrus McCormick, a farmer and blacksmith, developed the mechanical reaper in the 1830s (an improvement on his father's design). Isaac Singer, an actor, came up with his own version of the sewing machine in 1851. Charles Goodyear, owner of a hardware store, invented vulcanized rubber in 1844.[9]

The major shift, from the 1870s and particularly during the 1880s, began with electricity—and a more corporate-driven approach to innovation. The main theoretical ideas and experiment-based proofs behind electricity had been established by researchers much earlier, almost entirely in Europe, specifically Germany and the UK. Building on that foundation were brilliant Americans with breakthrough ideas, including Alexander Graham Bell (the telephone, 1876), George Westinghouse (alternating current in the 1880s), and Nikola Tesla (multiple inventions related to electricity in the 1880s). And of course, there was the legendary figure of Thomas Edison, inventor of the light bulb and perhaps the first person to focus his efforts directly on the process and commercialization of invention—with his famous research lab in Menlo Park, New Jersey.

Before Edison, individual inventors, operating alone and with limited resources, had most of the big ideas. After Edison, and following the development of electricity, came the rise of corporate invention, a lot of lawyers, and well-financed patent wars. Corporations, looking for the next wave of invention, became much more interested in science, including hiring scientists and building labs.

Early efforts were hardly auspicious. In 1864, William Franklin Durfee built a Bessemer convertor—a furnace for making steel—in Wyandotte, Michigan. He attached a "steelworks analytical laboratory"— the first industrial lab in the United States and one of the first in the world. His workers were not uniformly in favor of this form of progress. "Those who manned and managed the [Bessemer] converter looked upon the laboratory at first with amazement and then with fear. One dark night they burned the whole thing to the ground."[10]

The first modern corporate R&D lab was arguably that of General Electric, founded in 1900. By 1906, this department had over 100 employees.[11] By 1920, the GE lab employed 301 people, and by 1929, it had a head count of 555.[12]

Research at the Bell telephone companies was consolidated into a separate organization in 1910/11. According to Frank Jewett, who headed this effort—and what became Bell Labs after 1925—the industry had outgrown random invention and also what could be accomplished by engineers alone. Now, in Jewett's assessment, those companies "most obviously dependent on science have organized research laboratories whose sole function it is to search out every nook of the scientific forest for timber that can be used."[13]

By the end of World War I, almost all large industrial corporations had research labs. The Bell companies, International Business Machines (IBM), General Electric, and Westinghouse were early to develop strategies in which their engineers deliberately sought patents for new inventions and used this process to strengthen their market position.[14] There had been just 45,000 American engineers in 1900. This number rose to 230,000 by 1930—of whom 90 percent worked in industry.[15] By 1940, on the eve of war, two-thirds of all science spending was in the hands of the corporate sector.[16]

The American private sector had become a systematically innovative place, with emphasis on understanding and developing whatever knowledge seemed likely to boost corporate profits for incumbents. Research was expensive and conducted by relatively few large firms. In the 1930s, thirteen companies employed one-third of all researchers.[17]

However, investing in basic science—discovery for the sake of discovery—did not make sense as a private-sector priority, and there was no money in it. The private sector was very good at what it was supposed to do: making profits and investing the proceeds in developing new products that seemed likely to generate future profits.

UNIVERSITIES CHALLENGED

In modern America, we have become accustomed to the idea that universities lead the way on basic science. Throughout the pre–World War II period, however, American universities remained small and more focused on teaching than on research. Land-grant colleges, the first of which were created in 1863, were intended to bring improved technology to agriculture and, in a few instances, also to industry. They did so in an applied fashion. But there was little interest in or money for more fundamental research.[18]

The best-funded and most prestigious universities preferred to offer a classical education. The first engineer graduated from Harvard only in 1854, and by 1892, the grand cumulative total of engineering graduates from that college was only 155.[19]

Overall, American universities barely figured in the development of practical technology, relative to industry.[20] As hubs for scientific endeavor, they were dwarfed by efforts in the big European research universities and institutes. The best technical education available to an aspiring young person at the beginning of the twentieth century was without question in Germany, France, or the UK.[21]

Europeans won fourteen Nobel Prizes for chemistry before Theodore Richards of Harvard University won the first for the United States in 1914. The United States did not win another chemistry Nobel until 1932, during which time the Europeans won another fifteen prizes. The American winner in 1932 was Irving Langmuir, of General Electric, who had been educated in part in Germany (he had a PhD from the University of Göttingen).

The pattern was similar for the medicine and physics prizes.[22] Of all the Nobel Prizes for medicine awarded from 1901 through 1932, only two went to researchers based in the United States—both worked at the Rockefeller Institute for Medical Research in New York, and both were born and educated in Europe. In physics, the first native-born American to win a Nobel Prize was Robert Millikan in 1923, the second was Arthur Compton in 1927, and the third was Carl Anderson, who did not win until 1936. By the mid-1930s, the Netherlands had won more physics prizes (four) than had people born in the United States.[23]

ABSENTEE GOVERNMENT

The role of the American government in scientific development and the application of technology before 1940 was consistently small.[24] There was some support for weapon development, such as armories that manufactured guns. But this was all narrowly focused, and the slight increase in intensity that emerged during World War I proved fleeting.[25] The

Great Depression of the 1930s further tightened the already parsimonious government purse strings.

President Roosevelt attempted to organize support for unemployed and underemployed scientists, but in the face of so much other need, this went nowhere. Scientists were also divided—traditionally and still in the 1930s—on whether they wanted government support, with the potential constraints and control this implied.

In 1933, President Roosevelt convened a Science Advisory Board. The group was chaired by Karl Compton who argued for government spending that would help employ engineers and scientists. The initiative quickly went nowhere—spending on science was not a sufficiently high priority. The relationship between leading scientists and FDR's administration slipped to a new low.[26]

CAN YOU SEE ME NOW?

The tide—in terms of government funding for what private industry could not or would not do—began to turn in late August 1940. Sir Henry Tizard arrived in Washington, DC, as head of an expert team bearing information about some of Britain's most important technological discoveries. The Battle of Britain raged through the summer and fall of 1940, with the German Luftwaffe first crippling critical airfields and then switching to the Blitz bombing of civilian areas, including London, Coventry, Birmingham, and other major cities.[27] In this moment of great national desperation, Tizard and a few others persuaded Churchill's government to put aside all conventional notions of secrecy, with the goal of receiving greater material assistance from the United States.[28]

Tizard's mission famously included all its most precious papers and artifacts in a single metal box. Once safely delivered and opened, it revealed impressive technical details on topics as diverse as gun turrets for aircraft, antiaircraft guns, the Kerrison Predictor (an automatic gunfire-control system), armor plate, torpedoes, self-sealing gasoline tanks, and explosives.[29] The British had been working intensely on a myriad set of engineering problems related to war, all of which were now urgent priorities. Tizard's group was authorized to put almost every single card on the table without requesting any reciprocity.[30]

Of all Tizard's offerings, without question the most immediately consequential was a small mechanical device, about the size of a hockey puck: the resonant cavity magnetron. This simple and even elegant piece of equipment created the possibility—with a lot of additional work—of smaller, more powerful, and more accurate radar sets.

In retrospect, what the Americans called Radio Detection and Ranging (RADAR) was developed independently and in secret in at least thirteen countries.[31] The underlying science of radio waves emerged in the late nineteenth century based on pioneering research in Europe.[32] The radio quickly became a wonder of the early twentieth century and was put into wide commercial use during the 1920s. The development of this technology's long-distance communication naturally raised the question: What other applications were possible?

Numerous people noticed the annoying way planes interfered with radio transmissions. A few of the more farsighted wondered: Could this be the basis for actually detecting the location and direction of travel of, for example, a bomber? Researchers in the United States were among the earliest to investigate this question and to propose a workable solution—to bounce radio waves deliberately off distant objects and track carefully what rebounded back.[33] Unfortunately, the American army and navy—the primary potential sources of funding for such work in the United States—did not regard this as a top priority for national defense. The United States, at that time, saw itself as distant from any potential enemies—and far outside the range of aircraft that could carry bombs.

In contrast, from at least the early 1930s, military leaders and top civilian scientists in Britain were increasingly focused on the dangers posed by bombers, with the potential to target large urban areas with conventional explosives or chemical weapons. The speed and effectiveness of aircraft increased significantly during the 1920s—it now took only two hours to fly from Germany to London.[34] And by the 1930s it was clear that German rearmament included building a large air force against which conventional air defenses would be mostly ineffective.

In a 1932 speech, leading British politician Stanley Baldwin expressed the growing fear in a memorable phrase: "The bomber will always get through."[35]

In the early 1930s, none of the existing lines of technology development against the threat of bombing seemed immediately promising. In response, a committee was established, with Henry Tizard in charge.[36] Under Tizard's guidance and with a modest amount of funding, British research teams made surprisingly quick progress, and by 1938, a national radar system had been assembled that could detect initially high-flying aircraft—with extensions soon added to spot any plane that tried to approach the British Isles at low altitude.[37]

But the equipment involved was bulky, and the method of detection—using relatively long-wave or low-frequency radio waves—worked best for roughly establishing the position and bearing of large objects, such as bombers attacking during the day.[38] In both Britain and the United States—and, for that matter, in Germany—researchers were keenly aware of the advantages of both miniaturizing key elements of the technology and making it able to detect much smaller objects, like the periscopes of submarines.

On the American side, prewar radar research was conducted in a fairly low-key manner, characteristic of the time period, but rather quaint when seen from a modern perspective. A significant part of the civilian work was led by Alfred L. Loomis, a lawyer who had taught himself a great deal of modern physics and built a laboratory in his house. It was a big house, the lab was well-equipped, and Loomis was a good scientist. But literally and metaphorically, it was an amateur effort. When the British saw Loomis's work in fall 1940, they were polite, but it was obvious that the Americans were far behind. The Loomis team's accomplishment was modest—essentially a forerunner of the police radar gun.[39]

Still, Loomis was a great networker who was close friends with—and a source of funding for—scientific luminaries such as Ernest Lawrence, winner of the Nobel Prize for physics in 1939, James Conant, chemist and president of Harvard, Karl Compton, president of MIT, and, of course, Vannevar Bush. Bush put Loomis in charge of microwave-related research on the NDRC.

On September 19, 1940, at the Wardman Park hotel in Washington, DC, Tizard's team revealed their breakthrough, the cavity magnetron, which could emit a large amount of power at what was then a very short wavelength.[40] After further technical discussion, which took place at his house in Tuxedo Park, New York, on the weekend of September 28–29, 1940, Loomis fully understood that this technology could turn the tide of war.[41]

While the British had cracked a key piece of the scientific puzzle, a working microwave radar system required much more, including a receiver, a way to handle signals without interference, and overall robustness. Ideally, it also had to fit in the nose of an aircraft. And it obviously had to function effectively under a wide variety of difficult conditions. The British, under siege, did not have the resources necessary to take these next steps. The Americans had scientists and available industrial capacity—but would they take on the work?

Bush strongly believed in delegation, and he trusted Loomis, a bond that been formed over the previous decade, during which time Loomis had risen to prominence as the convener of scientific gatherings and as a generous funder of experiments, increasingly around radio waves.[42] If Loomis and his team said the United States should back this technology, that is what they would do.

Once the decision was taken to back this radar development as fast and as far as it would go, an argument broke out—who exactly should be in charge? For Frank Jewett, president of Bell Labs, there was no question: the project should go to Bell Labs, cooperating perhaps with other bastions of private enterprise.[43]

Bush and Loomis respected Jewett and were themselves no fans of government-led anything; both had built their careers either largely independent of the government (Bush) or keeping ahead of regulation (Loomis's main fortune was made in electricity generation and distribution, the unregulated frontier of the 1920s and 1930s). In his 1970 memoir, Bush was blunt: "Like many a man from New England, I had snorted at the New Deal, and I had been appalled at some of F.D.R.'s political theory and practice."[44]

But Bush was also intensely pragmatic—and not at all ideological in the modern sense of the word. What was needed was not incremental improvement or marginal adjustments; it was fundamental breakthroughs and at great speed. Relying on the private business sector would surely result, in his view, in less than was needed. Seeking profits was fine for incremental change in the civilian economy, but not when the goal was big breakthroughs for military applications. Bush recognized also that this was no time to be hoarding information about what worked and what did not work—sharing knowledge freely and without restriction would result in faster progress but was not in the private sector's interest.

Bush therefore preferred for the project to be based at a university, to more effectively mobilize faculty from around the country.[45] Bush, with Loomis in strong agreement, settled on MIT. Karl Compton was not immediately in agreement, fearing a major disruption to the usual work of his university. But quickly Compton was persuaded that the national interest came first.

It helped that the money was good. Bush contracted directly between the federal government and universities, erring on the side of being generous—paying the "full costs" of these research activities, which included overhead—"the portion of its general expenses properly attributable to the added operation."[46] Fortunately, Bush was able to persuade the House Committee on Appropriations that this was the best way to encourage innovative work.

Bush was also completely clear that the NDRC owned full rights to all inventions developed with its support, although its primary purpose was to help develop more useful good ideas. Unlike the usual situation during peacetime, patents were no impediment to sharing ideas across researchers, irrespective of where they were working.

Bush and his colleagues understood fully the key issue about invention. New ideas benefit the person who has those ideas, but there are also major positive potential effects on others who are pursuing related lines of inquiry. With effective patent pooling under the NDRC, as researchers working on radar—or anything else—witnessed ideas being developed by others, they could more quickly decide to adjust their own direction of work.

With Loomis in charge of the radar microwave committee of the NDRC, the mission was to scale up and apply invention at speeds never previously seen. The effort was launched in mid-October 1940, with plans to hire the first twelve university researchers and arrangements made to contract with private-sector supplies for components.[47]

MIT immediately made ten thousand square feet of lab space available.[48] Loomis then traveled the country's leading scientific outposts, recruiting top talent. He was joined in this effort by Ernest Lawrence from the University of California at Berkeley. Loomis and Lawrence persuaded Lee A. DuBridge, a nuclear physicist at the University of Rochester, to become director. As assistant director, they brought in future Nobel Prize winner Isidor I. Rabi from Columbia, along with Jerrold Zacharias and Norman Ramsey (who had just joined the faculty at the University of Illinois).[49] Luis Alvarez, another future Nobel Prize winner, and Edwin McMillan joined from Berkeley. Lawrence was "so successful in rallying his colleagues to the cause that by November one eminent physicist was joining the staff every day."[50]

The pace of work was remarkable. The first lab meeting was held November 11, 1940, thirty physicists were at work by mid-December, and soon a rudimentary radar system was operating and being tested on the roof of an MIT building. At its peak, the Radiation (Rad) Lab—the code name for this effort—employed nearly four thousand people and designed, by one estimate, half of all the Allied radar systems that were in use by 1945.[51] Among the major achievements were a gun-laying radar and an airborne interception radar (used by night fighters). The lab also developed a separate bombing radar and the first-ever worldwide radio navigation system—known as Long-Range Navigation (LRN or LORAN).[52]

EMBRACING THE FUTURE, EVENTUALLY

Persuading the military to buy some new gadgets was not hard, particularly as rapidly expanding budgets coincided with pressure from the secretary of war to adopt the latest technology. But getting the army and particularly the navy to actually integrate radar and related tools into battlefield decision-making was much harder. Working this out would lay the groundwork for future productive relationships between civilians and the country's military—a major change of mind-set about the inherent usefulness of science and innovation in national defense.

No less a figure than Admiral Ernest J. King, chief of naval operations and commander in chief of the US fleet, played down the importance of radar in 1941: "We want something for this war, not the next one."[53] This reluctance to embrace new technology was not unusual among top officers. The US Army resisted using rockets against German tanks and never adopted an infrared sight developed for its own tanks, even though it was proven to help night vision for sniper rifles. When the NDRC proposed an amphibious truck, the DUKW, "the head of the Service of Supply, said to me [Bush] forcibly that the Army did not want it and would not use it if they got it." The DUKW was developed and proven a great success—for example, landing troops and equipment during the Normandy invasion.[54]

Despite initial military conservatism, science had a lot to offer—as the disaster at Pearl Harbor made apparent. The first wave of attacking Japanese planes was spotted by radar technicians at a range of 132 miles, using US Army mobile SCR-270 long-wave radar sets. With almost an hour in hand, there was time to launch at least some defensive air cover and to get ships under way, but the radar warnings were ignored by the responsible officer.[55] In perfect hindsight, the power of radar—and the destruction caused by ignoring the information that radar systems could provide—should have been evident, but the military was still not fully convinced.

The navy's hesitance to fully embrace all the changes made possible by radar was perhaps most costly in what became known as the Battle of the Atlantic. Convoys—groups of merchant ships with naval escorts—had proven reasonably effective in World War I against submarines. But at the start of World War II, it became evident that the Germans had shifted tactics, including attacking at night, on the surface, and in packs.

The losses to Allied shipping were devastating and unremitting. In June 1942, the Allied fuel supply came under pressure due to U-boat attacks, and there were questions about whether the US Navy could defend even its own Atlantic coastal waters. In late 1942, there was a U-boat focus on northern transatlantic convoys, which lost an average of 26 ships per month. In early 1943, the loss rate for those convoys actually accelerated—reaching 49 ships in March. By the last half of 1942, Germans were building U-boats faster than the Americans, British, and Canadians could sink them.[56]

Shipping losses on this scale convinced the navy that it was time to effectively deploy radar technology—and this helped change the war. Centimeter airborne radar, hot from the Rad Lab, could find submarines on the surface. Sonobuoys and new methods of magnetic detection meant submarines could be tracked more accurately under the waves. The antisubmarine rocket and target-seeking torpedo could then be deployed effectively.

The results were stunning.[57] In forty-four months of war up to May 1943, the Allies sank 192 U-boats; in the next three months—May, June, and July 1943—they sank 100. The ratio of ships sunk to U-boats destroyed shifted dramatically, from 40:1 at its worst to 1:1.[58] More raw materials could now flow into the United States, and American manufactured goods—such as guns, ammunition, vehicles, aircraft, and food—could reach the front largely unimpeded. Radar had demonstrated that new technology was no longer an optional add-on. It had become central to war.

The point was driven home at the Battle of the Bulge in 1944. The Germans attacked under the cover of bad weather, reckoning correctly that lack of visual contact made it hard for conventional artillery to be effective. The Americans, again based on early British ideas, had made great strides with proximity fuses—which exploded shells close to their targets, based on a form of radio frequency sensing (an application of short-range radar). The effect against German ground forces proved devastating. The same technology was also used against enemy planes and V-1 flying bombs; it increased effectiveness of the five-inch antiaircraft batteries by a factor put at "probably about seven."[59]

THE POSTWAR INVENTION BOOM

Vannevar Bush was a master of managing perceptions. He understood firsthand that "engineers" of the day were regarded by senior military personnel as "in all probability a thinly disguised salesman, and hence to be kept at arm's length"—and he insisted that his team be referred to consistently as *scientists*. In one sense, this was accurate, as the people he hired, particularly for the Rad Lab, were actually scientists, mostly physicists.[60]

Realistically, however, most of their wartime efforts were devoted to applications that should more accurately be regarded as engineering—applications of existing knowledge to practical problems—rather than as science, the creation of new knowledge through theory and controlled experiments. Still, their strong training in science served these "engineers" well once they could take their wartime experiences, including with hands-on electronics, back to their labs —and onto inventions such as digital computers and semiconductors.

The postwar invention boom was boosted by the fact that the devices and processes developed under the NDRC (and its successor, the higher-profile and better-funded Office of Scientific Research and Development [OSRD]) were to some extent rough and ready—everyone was in a hurry to make things work and deploy robust versions into combat situations. The flip side was that many interesting problems became more obvious, both in terms of basic science and potential further improvements for products.

For example, the amphibious truck DUKW later became the model for snowmobiles.[61] DDT, a newly developed chemical, found much broader use—beginning in anti-malaria campaigns, it soon spread to become a much more widely used (and arguably overused) pesticide.

As a direct continuation of the government-supported wartime aerospace program, it was the Americans who brought the next generation of jet engine–based flight technologies to scale. It was America, not exhausted and cash-strapped Britain or broken Germany, which proved best positioned to take advantage of the related commercial developments.[62] The early engines for jet planes were developed in the late 1940s and early 1950s, initially for military applications.[63]

In 1953, building on its military-related efforts—including develop-ment of the Boeing KC-135 tanker—Boeing produced its four-engine 707 passenger jet.[64] This was followed by other new products at regular intervals—including the 747 in 1969. By the early 1980s, Boeing was one of the country's leading exporters; in some years, it was sold more overseas (in dollar terms) than any other company.

Of all the wartime science projects, radar can undoubtedly claim the longest list of useful spin-off products.[65] Modern commercial air travel is made possible by hundreds of radar systems across the United States. Much of the useful information in weather reports is based on some form of radar.

There were also more indirect effects. The transistor emerged in part as a consequence of work done on solid-state semiconductor crystals for radio receivers.[66] Cathode ray tubes and memory for digital computers were the immediate descendants of World War II radar systems.

Microwave telephones and early television networks received sig-nificant assistance from radar. Beginning in 1951, television added ultrahigh-frequency (UHF) transmission—carried coast to coast over 107 microwave towers built by AT&T.[67] New antennas—for example, built by RCA—were needed.

Astronomy was transformed by the creation of radio telescopes. Particle accelerators and microwave spectroscopy can also trace their lineage back to the MIT campus—as can the nuclear magnetic reso-nator (the basis for modern magnetic resonance imaging, MRI) and the maser (used in atomic clocks and spacecraft, and forerunner of the laser), for which work Nobel Prizes were awarded in 1952 and 1964, respectively.

And, of course, there is the microwave oven. Raytheon had made magnetron tubes during the war and now needed a new market. The ability of radio waves to heat food was either the result of years of care-ful study or due to a candy bar melting serendipitously, depending on which version of history you prefer.[68] At first, the machines proposed were large and expensive, more appropriate for professional use. Even-tually, the first generally affordable microwave oven appeared in 1967. It was named, descriptively if not appealingly, the Radarange.

Old Washington hands like to emphasize that "personnel is policy"—meaning that who you hire has a major impact on what gets done. But conversely, who gets trained to do what, while working for the government, can have significant impact on what they think about—and invent—later. Judged in those terms, the wartime science effort propelled a generation forward in terms of scientific and industrial achievement. Ten Nobel Prizes can either be traced back to work done at the Rad Lab or were won by people who spent formative years building radar systems.[69]

Most of the postwar top science advisors to government cut their teeth somewhere in the OSRD, most commonly at the Rad Lab. Right through to the Nixon administration, thinking about science policy—and what exactly to support—was shaped by people who had worked alongside Vannevar Bush.

ENDLESS MONEY

It's hard to imagine now, but Bush's research organization had access to essentially unlimited funding. Once the NDRC got under way, Bush saw his major role as managing the relationship with Congress, particularly the appropriations committees.

Initially, Bush suggested to his associates that they might need to spend $5 million per year. In 1942, what had become the OSRD spent $11 million. In 1943, it spent $52.2 million, $86.8 million in 1944, and peaking at $114.5 million in 1945.[70] The combined R&D budgets of the air force, the army, and the navy peaked at $513 million.[71]

Those numbers do not include the Manhattan Engineer District, which built the atomic bomb. Research and development on nuclear weapons was essentially zero in 1940. By 1943, this work cost $77 million, jumping nearly tenfold to $730 million in 1944 and peaking at $859 million in 1945. The Manhattan Project became one of the largest industrial-scientific projects in the history of the world to that date.[72] At its peak, this work employed 130,000 people.[73]

Bush and his colleagues repeatedly stressed that the constraints on their activities were the number of available engineers and scientists—

and they pushed back hard against efforts to draft these specialists into frontline forces. Money, however, was never an issue. The top—and perhaps only—priority was inventing what could be useful and important to the war effort. Ironically, the postwar American commercial success was helped greatly by inventions that emerged from the simplest noncommercial motivation: patriotism and fear of a smart enemy, hell-bent on new applications of scientific knowledge.

NEW FRONTIERS

Civilian physicists had been proven spectacularly right during World War II, not just in their theoretical thinking about hidden power in the universe but also in their ability to harness that power in practical ways. The world had changed, completely and forever. Science and its intelligent applications now trumped everything. The question now was how to harness this idea for the broader social good.

With the war drawing to a close, Bush set himself the task of articulating what should come next—in terms of not just funding for science but how that funding should be structured and supervised. In *Science: The Endless Frontier*, his 1945 report for the president, Bush pulled together the best thinking about what had worked during the war and what could be done next. The wartime effort had focused on mobilizing what was already known, either in terms of specific facts or, more importantly, the skills and abilities of individual scientists. As Bush put it later, "The war effort taught us the power of adequately supported research for our comfort, our security, our prosperity."[74]

The priority task following the war was creating new knowledge. Bush had not changed his pro-free-market beliefs, but he felt that science was a frontier—and the American federal government had always been comfortable expanding frontiers. "It is in keeping also with basic United States policy that the Government should foster the opening of new frontiers and this is the modern way to do it."[75]

Attempting to catch the incipient postwar mood, Bush led off his report not with weapons but with the many potential ways that lives could be saved and improved—the first substantive points in his report are "For the War Against Disease." Bush's statement of the potential impact on health and longevity was not exaggerated: "It is wholly probable that progress in the treatment of cardiovascular disease, renal disease, cancer, and similar refractory diseases will be made as the result of fundamental discoveries in subjects unrelated to those diseases and perhaps entirely unexpected by the investigator."[76]

Industrial research was important, but this would always be of a more applied nature.

> Basic research leads to new knowledge. It provides scientific capital. It creates the fund from which the practical applications of knowledge must be drawn. . . . Today, it is truer than ever that basic research is the pacemaker of technological progress. . . . A nation which depends upon others for its new basic scientific knowledge will be slow in its industrial progress and weak in its competitive position in world trade, regardless of its mechanical skill.[77]

Bush did not advocate continuing the organization of research along the relatively centralized lines of the Rad Lab or the Manhattan Project. The Rad Lab was shut as soon as the war ended. The Manhattan Project was brought more completely under military control—and, understandably, became less oriented to breakthrough ideas and more about incremental adjustments (and nuclear testing). The Atomic Energy Commission was established in 1946.[78]

Moreover, a key constraint was the number of skilled scientists who could be trained—the title of this chapter in *Endless Frontier* is "Renewal of Our Scientific Talent." There was a wartime-induced skills deficit—talented people had not gone to graduate school, because they had been pulled into the armed forces. But more than making up that deficit, the United States needed to train more scientists per year, in particular by broadening the pool of potential students—which meant finding ways for people from lower-income backgrounds to afford higher education.

Bush believed strongly that university-based research, organized through contracts with the federal government, was the way to make progress. These grants should be awarded on a competitive basis to the best scientists. And a relatively strong National Research Foundation with an influential board of directors should run the process. And this funding should extend not just to research projects but to the financing of advanced scientific education—and increasing the number of trained scientists.[79]

Wartime service for young people meant there was a deficit, relative to what otherwise would have been the case, of about 150,000 science and technology students. To increase scientific capacity in a meaningful way, college needed to become more affordable for more people, including through the provision of scholarships.

In 1940, over half of the US adult population had left school with no more than an eighth-grade education; only 6 percent of men and 4 percent of women had completed college.[80] Between 1940 and 1960, college attendance more than doubled—meaning there were an additional two million students enrolled. The number of instructional faculty in higher education increased commensurately from around 110,000 to just over 280,000.[81]

The university-based model paid dividends, as the United States was catapulted to the forefront of global scientific achievement—aided by an influx of talented foreign scientists fleeing either Nazism or Communism. Prior to 1930, ninety Nobel Prizes were awarded for physics, chemistry, and medicine—and the United States had picked up only five (6 percent of the total).[82] In the 1930s, the United States did better, winning ten science Nobel Prizes—or 28 percent of the total.[83]

There was a jump up in the 1940s—the United States won fourteen of thirty prizes awarded. This was the new normal. In subsequent decades, the United States never won less than 49 percent of all the science prizes, and it peaked at 72 percent in the 1990s—a remarkable forty-three out of sixty total prizes.[84]

The United States, long a nation of practical engineers, was becoming a place that valued science and supported scientists—largely because the connections from theory and the laboratory to practical applications were becoming much more apparent. The spread of new technology through more efficient machines and better factory design was accelerated and improved, on balance, by the war effort—reaching a broad range of different activities.

With the removal of wartime controls, the potential productivity gains were obvious. What, however, would be the implications for jobs? Who would gain and who would lose from this surge forward in technology?

MIDDLE-CLASS MIRACLE

In Kurt Vonnegut's first novel, *Player Piano*, published in 1952, automation has become so advanced that workers with only a high school education are not needed to run factories.[85] Managers with higher degrees in engineering are in charge of design and operation. Machines that break down are discarded rather than repaired. Salaries are high for those still working; everyone else gets menial tasks provided—outside of factories—by the government at subsistence wages.[86]

Vonnegut's dystopia articulated the fears of many people who had experienced the 1940s (and the Great Depression of the 1930s) and who could see the transformation of American production through the application of science and science-based engineering. Specifically, what Vonnegut and others anticipated was not that better machines would destroy all jobs but rather that it would make some people—with a great deal of appropriately technical education—more productive, while the need for less-educated people (or any kind of manual work) in factories would decline.

In the terminology of modern economics, this phenomenon is called *skill-biased technological change*. While Vonnegut was obviously dramatizing the effect, a great deal of subsequent research has confirmed that this is part of what happened, over time, after World War II.[87] Automation was a well-established idea that was carried to a new theoretical and practical level during the war, including in the development of systems that controlled the automatic aiming and firing of antiaircraft guns.[88] But, as Vonnegut's story highlights, automation also creates a higher level of demand for skilled labor, as such workers become more productive by working with the new machinery.

If increased demand for skilled labor is the only or predominant change, we would expect the relative wage of skilled people compared to unskilled people—known as the *skill premium*—to increase, perhaps sharply. Some people—perhaps relatively few—would become better off, while most people would not benefit directly (or could actually be worse off, as in Vonnegut's novel).

However, what if the supply of skilled people increases at a pace that at least roughly matches the arrival of machines that make skilled people more productive? In that case, the skill premium may not increase much.[89] Rather, average wages for most of the population would increase—allowing them to afford more goods, buy houses, and perhaps even start to save for retirement or their children's education. There are also important spillover effects to local economies and to wages for all skill levels, as employment in construction and retail sectors increases.[90]

This path—scientific innovation matched by newly skilled workers seeking jobs—proved to be the broadest legacy of the technological breakthroughs of the 1940s. The timing could not have been more propitious, facilitating the rapid switch from wartime to civilian production and making it possible to sustain a high rate of growth through the 1960s. It was only possible, however, because of the commensurate increase in higher education—with a lot more people attending college.

After World War I, discharged veterans received sixty dollars and a ticket home; the result was a great deal of resentment—including a march on Washington in 1932. Taking on board that lesson, the Servicemen's Readjustment Act of 1944—known as the GI Bill of Rights—was designed to ease the transition back into civilian life. "[The GI Bill] was seen as a genuine attempt to thwart a looming social and economic crisis. Some saw inaction as an invitation to another depression."[91]

The GI Bill provided assistance with unemployment insurance and assistance in buying a house.[92] It also provided tuition and other financial support if veterans decided to continue their education.

Veterans accounted for nearly half of all college admissions in 1947. Perhaps the single best indicator for the growing impact of science on the US economy may be the choices made by those veterans.[93] In the official reckoning, 7.5 million veterans took advantage of the legislation;

of them, more than 2 million attended some form of college. Nearly three-quarters of a million people took scientific courses.[94]

Average wages increased steadily from the late 1940s, through the 1950s, and into the 1970s.[95] The skill premium remained at its immediate postwar level, although the labor force as a whole became much more skilled both in terms of years of education and in more specialized technical skills. The number of engineers in the workforce grew rapidly—from about 0.5 percent to 1.5 percent of all employment during the 1940s and 1950s.

At the same time, there was a very real sense that more people were participating in economic gains, certainly compared with the 1930s (when long-term unemployment was a major problem) and even compared with the 1920s. A majority of workers held white-collar jobs as managers, teachers, salespersons, or other office employees. Firms provided implicit long-term employment contracts and good benefits. Long-standing class distinctions began to fade.[96] The number of cars in the United States doubled during the 1950s, from thirty-nine million to seventy-two million—and by 1960, Americans owned more cars than the rest of the world put together. There were eight large shopping centers in the entire country in 1945; by 1960, there were 3,840.[97] More than 3,000 drive-in movie theaters were operational by 1956.[98] The Highway Act of 1956 helped connect the country across interstate roads. Motels sprang up around the country.

The Veterans Administration provided low-cost mortgages to 2.4 million war veterans. Before World War II, around 40 percent of American families owned their own homes; this rose to 62 percent by 1970.

Health indicators also improved, driven in part by improved nutrition but also by medical breakthroughs that had been accelerated by the war—and which were subsequently pushed forward by what became the National Institutes of Health and the National Science Foundation. Antibiotics were, for the first time, readily available. Streptomycin proved, at least initially, to be a wonder drug against tuberculosis. Childhood vaccination reduced or eliminated some previous scourges, such as scarlet fever and diphtheria. In 1939, on the eve of the United States' entry to World War II, life expectancy was 62.1 years for men and 65.4 years for women. Just a decade later, it had risen to 65.2 and 70.7, respectively—an impressive improvement.

Not everyone benefited equally, of course—there is a dark side to economic miracles. The movement of commerce and population to the suburbs meant that some people were left behind in inner cities, without the skills and financial resources needed to remain prosperous. Ongoing racism and sexism meant weaker job opportunities for women and minorities. Access to health care improved, although it remained much better for white Americans than for minorities. But overall, there was broad progress for the newly emergent middle class.

POLITICS OF A NEW GLOBAL ORDER

World War II involved rapid scaling up of American production of military equipment. In four years, the United States built three hundred thousand planes, six hundred thousand jeeps, two million army trucks, and twelve thousand large ships. Aluminum production increased fourfold, and steel production rose nearly four times. Auto manufacturers switched to produce vehicles and components for the military, including nearly four hundred thousand aircraft engines (half of all US production), learning important lessons about reliability along the way.[99]

At their peak, defense-related jobs constituted 40 percent of employment.[100] Most of those government contracts ended abruptly after the surrender of Japan, and mass unemployment seemed entirely possible. Following the end of World War I, when the necessary conversion away from military production was on a significantly smaller scale, unemployment reached 5.2 percent in 1920 and peaked at 11.7 percent in 1921.[101] Unemployment during the worst years of the 1930s was still a recent and traumatic memory for many—measured rates had ranged between 20 and 25 percent.

In 1945, there were 11.43 million people in the armed forces, compared with a total civilian labor force of 53.86 million. Demobilization was rapid. The military was down to 1.59 million people in 1947, while the civilian labor force (age fourteen and older) climbed to over

60 million.[102] Unemployment was practically nonexistent during the war—1.2 percent of the civilian labor force in 1944—and there was a slight rise to 3.9 percent in 1947. Over the next decade, the labor force grew by more than 7 million workers, yet unemployment stayed consistently below 5 percent.[103] How was this possible?

One part of the answer is increased exports, through easier access to markets around the world. US manufacturing companies, based on improved applications of science, created new and improved products for which there was potential demand around the world.[104]

Lowering tariffs had long been a bone of contention in American politics, with significant parts of industry arguing that protectionism (taxes on imports) was essential for prosperity.[105] However, between 1939 and 1945, the world's trading picture changed dramatically.[106] The United States had provided the material goods that its allies needed to fight effectively. With the end of hostilities, the United States moved to provide what was needed for rebuilding—and offered cheap loans to finance those purchases.[107]

US sectors that had an export surplus—exporting more than they imported—were now strongly in favor of more open trade. These included industries that had benefited from the wartime scientific push on electronics, engine design, and better chemistry, including machinery, vehicles, and chemicals.[108] For those sectors, both business leaders and trade unions were not opposed to tariff reductions on goods coming into the United States—if the quid pro quo was increased access for American goods to overseas markets.[109]

The United States helped build a global trading system within which American companies could export first to Europe and Japan, and increasingly to other countries with rising income levels. This open trade strategy worked, in terms of helping sectors that had export and other growth potential. Some of the highest rates of growth from 1947 to 1973—over 6 percent per annum on average—were recorded by electrical machinery and chemicals as well as telephones and other communication services. Rates of productivity growth in those sectors were also among the highest in the nation.[110]

A new trade policy helped promote sectors with potential for global growth. Who gained? At least in the immediate postwar era, a broad swath of the American middle class took a major step forward.

MAKING AMERICA GREAT

The first intense technology-based arms race, 1939–1945, was won by Americans—native born and recent immigrant—in a remarkable come-from-behind fashion, specifically by giving civilian scientists the mandate to invent and to think very far outside what was regarded as reasonable or established practical knowledge. This was not science practiced by lone self-financed inventors, such as had prevailed in the nineteenth century, or by corporations, which had dominated the research-and-development landscape in the early twentieth century. The winning teams in World War II were university-based researchers backed by a vast amount of taxpayer money. This had a major positive impact on the economy and people's jobs.

Much of this postwar impact was unintentional. The priority during the war was just on winning—and on finding ways to make the military effort more meaningful. The United States had stumbled into a new way to organize and finance science, and it quickly found ways to commercialize those new ideas.

After the war, the GI Bill was a stroke of brilliance and luck— strengthening skills for millions of people at just the right time to match the changing nature of machines and organizations. The shift in US trade policy was a logical continuation of the desire to increase the number of good jobs. The United States made goods that people around the world wanted to buy.

World War II called forth collective efforts in an unprecedented manner, with immediate and also long-lasting effects. Existing ideas had been focused onto the war effort, to great effect. There had also been some breaking down of barriers to innovation. The war had challenged long-standing American ideas about the role of government—and how potentially to structure its productive relationship with the private sector. How much of this new model could be sustained?

2

Whatever It Takes

We realize now that progress in technology depends on progress in theory; that the most abstract investigations can lead to the most concrete results; and that the vitality of a scientific community springs from its passion to answer science's most fundamental questions.

—President John F. Kennedy, speech to the National Academy of Sciences, October 22, 1963[1]

ON OCTOBER 4, 1957, THE AMERICAN PUBLIC RECEIVED AN UNPLEASANT SHOCK.[2] THE Soviet Union announced the successful launch of Sputnik—the first ever artificial satellite to orbit the earth. Top US officials knew the Russians were working on a satellite, but no one in Washington expected a successful launch quite so soon. Weighing 185 pounds, the Soviet satellite was both bigger than anticipated and much larger than what the Americans themselves were working on.

Little publicized, the United States had its own satellite program under way, part of which was spearheaded by the navy—which had come a long way in its attitude toward new technology since Admiral King's day. Run by the US Naval Research Laboratory, several test launches in the Vanguard rocket program had gone well. Confident in their response to the Soviets, on December 6, 1957, the navy launched a Vanguard rocket carrying a small satellite. It exploded almost immediately after liftoff.

The country was shaken, and with good reason. The launch of Sputnik and the immediate response—quickly referred to humorously as Kaputnik—made it clear that American efforts had fallen short. Pressure on the Eisenhower administration increased further on November 3, 1957, when the Soviet Union launched another satellite, six times the weight of Sputnik and this time carrying a dog. The American press, naturally, dubbed this Muttnik.[3]

It was bad enough that the Soviet Union had exploded its first atomic bomb in 1949, on its way to closing the nuclear weapons gap with the United States much earlier than expected. Now, for the first time since seizing a leading global role, the United States had fallen behind in a crucial new technology with obvious military and strategic implications. In the press and some parts of the public, the reaction was close to hysteria. Leading politicians were gripped with the idea that there was a "missile gap," with the Soviets in the lead.

President Eisenhower radiated quiet confidence in the days that followed Sputnik, but behind the scenes, he and his advisors became worried. Space mattered. It was hard to say how much, but surely this was a frontier that would be ill-advised to concede to a presumed antagonist. America needed new technology and fast.

FIGHTING OVER THE BUSH MODEL

Despite the undeniable success of the NDRC/OSRD in World War II, by the time of the Sputnik launch, the public-private partnership in research had fallen into some disarray.

From the mid-1940s, Vannevar Bush had argued for a more unified approach to supporting science, recommending that it be structured under a proposed National Research Foundation (NRF). The NRF would have had strong similarities to his wartime OSRD organization, supporting the best people and top-notch science. He wanted, understandably, to continue and build upon the newfound relationship between government and university research.

Bush also wanted more independence from both the president and Congress. The development of expertise and the choice of topics would be buffered from the whims of politicians.[4]

This proposal ran into opposition. President Truman and his advisors balked at the idea of potentially large sums of money not being under the control of the White House. As for Bush himself, in the view of Truman's White House, he had become too powerful and hard to control.[5]

Unfortunately, Bush also antagonized a powerful senator, Harley M. Kilgore of West Virginia. Kilgore, a fan of the New Deal, strongly supported government funding for science—but he wanted more emphasis on economic development through distributing funds around the country. Bush stuck to his more elite-based view—the best scientists should get funding, irrespective of where they worked; of course, this implied more support for the top universities.[6]

Bush actually managed to get his version of the National Research Foundation enshrined in legislation that passed the Senate and the House in 1947. Truman vetoed it.[7] Another three years of negotiation was needed before supporters of the legislation agreed to strengthen presidential authority sufficient to earn a modicum of Truman's support.[8]

While the Bush model may have won the legislative day in principle, opposition along the way from the likes of Kilgore and Truman contributed to scaling back from what Bush and his colleagues had originally thought was needed. In the early 1950s, only limited funding was put behind basic research for the sake of pure pursuit of knowledge—the National Science Foundation received an initial appropriation of $3.5 million in 1952 and $16 million in 1956.[9]

For a broader expansion of government-private sector research cooperation, one further ingredient was needed: a political agreement on what should be the national priority for technology development. Enter Sputnik.

THE PRO-SCIENCE CONSENSUS

Seen from a modern perspective, the political reaction to Sputnik is fascinating. To be sure, there was some partisan jockeying for advantage, but there was also a genuine desire to understand how the Soviets had forged ahead and what could be done to close the gap in satellite-launch capability. Remarkably, a consensus quickly formed across both Democrats and Republicans.

It helped that, by the end of 1957, the scale of the applied science problem was relatively clear: to catch up and potentially gain an edge in space, the United States would need a major push across a wide range of technology. The politics quickly fell into place, helped by long-standing fears of Soviet ambition. Suddenly, there was strong congressional support for more funding—particularly for anything related to missiles.[10]

President Eisenhower had initially downplayed the importance of Sputnik, in part because he felt the United States was making good (secret) progress with rocket technology. But the satellite debate quickly became a broader political fracas centered on the idea that there either was or would soon be a missile gap, with the Soviet Union taking a strong or even unassailable lead. Nikita Khrushchev, the Soviet leader, made provocative statements that continued to put pressure on Eisenhower. "We will bury you" was a phrase that both quickly grabbed attention and stayed with Americans for a long time.[11] From the end of World War II until the early 1950s, the Soviet Union caught up in at least some high-profile technologies, including the atomic bomb, long-range rockets, and satellites.

Democratic politicians piled onto this idea, with plenty of encouragement from elements of the scientific community. Lyndon Johnson, the Senate majority leader, was quick to jump into the fray. The first witness before his "preparedness" investigating committee was physicist Edward Teller, inventor of the hydrogen bomb. Teller argued forcefully that America had fallen behind Soviet science, with profound implications for national security.[12] Vannevar Bush weighed in: "We have been complacent and we have been smug."[13] And even Allen Dulles, head of the CIA, testified in secret that there was a missile gap—with the United States behind by "two to three years."[14]

Faced with his own looming credibility gap on science, Eisenhower went to the top: in a November 1957 speech, he announced that James Killian, president of MIT, would become the first ever presidential science advisor.[15] His next step was to do what Vannevar Bush had been proposing in the wake of World War II: investing heavily in research, while training even more scientists. Beginning in 1956, showing up in the data a little before Sputnik, there was a burst of US activity and a jump in publicly funded research and development, which peaked around 2 percent of gross domestic product (GDP) in 1964.

Meanwhile, the National Defense Education Act of 1958 transformed, among other things, how physics was taught in high school—introducing more advanced mathematics earlier into the curriculum. The NDEA "established the legitimacy of federal funding of higher education and made substantial funds available for low-cost student loans, boosting public and private colleges and universities." There was a particular focus on science, mathematics, and foreign languages.[16]

Federal resources were made available to high schools; enrollment in high school science and math classes increased by 50 percent in some states. Funding began in 1958 and was increased over the next several years. The quality of high school science teaching improved.[17]

In the decade that followed Sputnik, federal funding for research at universities increased by more than four times in inflation-adjusted terms.[18] At universities that granted PhDs, the number of academic research personnel rose from twenty-five thousand to forty-six thousand. Funding for science education, including classrooms and laboratories, also increased dramatically, particularly after the Higher Education Facilities Act of 1963. More than 90 percent of the country's 2,734 colleges and universities received some degree of federal financial support.

TAKE ME TO THE MOON

On October 1, 1958, the National Aeronautics and Space Administration (NASA) opened for business.[19] NASA was created as an independent civilian agency, but very much under the control of the president.

Despite the heated rhetoric, in reality there never was a missile gap. While John F. Kennedy spoke a great deal about the supposed Soviet missile advantage during the 1960 presidential campaign, in office, he decided to turn attention elsewhere, to a more positive role for science and high-profile ways to strengthen national security.[20] The president needed a goal, something that would play well politically—hard enough to grab attention but also doable.

On May 25, 1961, President Kennedy asked Congress to commit to landing a man on the moon by the end of the decade. According to Ted Sorensen, his advisor, Kennedy "sensed that the possibility of putting a man on the moon could galvanize public support for the exploration of space as one of the great human adventures of the twentieth century." It was also rather carefully chosen as a goal that the United States could conceivably reach before the Soviet Union did.[21]

Given the state of technology and the kinds of investments required, there was no way that the private sector could take the lead—this was not a railroad or Thomas Edison–type moment. What the administration needed was a big push on a broad applied science front, fueled by public money while motivating and supporting ingenuity wherever it could be found. The administration needed a really big rocket—and someone who knew how to make this entirely reliable.

Despite all the rapid American technological progress across multiple dimensions during World War II, in 1945, the Germans still had the lead in liquid-fueled long-range missile technology—first with the fairly basic V-1 bomb, which flew more like a plane, and then with the highly sophisticated V-2, the world's first ballistic missile, rising to the edge of space on its deadly and disturbingly accurate trajectory. So in the final days of the war and with the Russian army closing in, the US Operation Paperclip snapped up most of the top German engineers, aiming for an obvious jump start on missile development.[22]

A top German rocket engineer and weapon builder, Wernher von Braun, surrendered to American forces at the very end of World War II. The achievements of his technical team were impressive but also quite horrendous—von Braun had led the work that created the V-2 rocket, which had terrorized British civilians late in the war.[23]

Safely in the United States, von Braun found himself with little to do. In the immediate postwar period, the United States cut military spending sharply, and there was little money for longer-term projects. Von Braun was taken under the umbrella of the US Army Ordnance

Corps while another group, under the US Navy, effectively was given the lead in rocket development. Von Braun was allowed to bring over his team and to develop a relatively small facility in Huntsville, Alabama. Through the early 1950s, there were few resources available—in fact, von Braun busied himself writing a book that advocated the manned exploration of Mars, providing in excruciating detail all the required technical parameters.[24] It was not a best seller.

In the wake of Sputnik, and with the challenge of going to the moon, von Braun became central to the space effort. His Saturn V rocket, which was directly descended from his wartime work, was the technological marvel of the 1960s. To this day, it remains the only system that has lifted people above low-earth orbit. Braun became not just a (controversial) American leading engineer but a subject of public fascination.

He was a star on Disney TV—appearing in a series that promoted Disney attractions, in this case Tomorrowland (part of Disneyland in Anaheim).[25] Less positively, in the 1964 movie, *Dr. Strangelove*, the eponymous character—a scientific weapons expert who seems unbothered by the imminent destruction of the world—is almost certainly modeled on a caricature of von Braun.

None of this mattered, either in the public perception or to the people in charge. The Americans were going to the moon, irrespective of the cost or what needed to be invented to get there.

The Apollo program was expensive, with a total cost almost five times that of the Manhattan Project.[26] The Manhattan Project cost, at its peak, 1 percent of all federal outlays. Apollo, at its peak, comprised 2.2 percent of all federal spending.[27]

This unprecedented expansion in the scientific research enterprise throughout the economy took place even though the government share of the economy—measured in terms of taxes or spending relative to GDP—actually fell between 1958 and 1965.[28] The 1960s R&D boom was not about the government, or even military spending, getting bigger relative to the economy but rather the result of a deliberate effort to shift government resources into research and toward the achievement of some very specific missions, most notably going to the moon.

Much of the increase in research funding can be attributed to the Defense Department—rising from 0.41 percent of GDP to 0.77 percent.[29,30] NASA also became a significant player—with government spending on the development of rockets and related technology rising from almost nothing in the mid-1950s to 0.71 percent of GDP in 1965.

Today, more than sixty-five thousand people work as aerospace engineers, with a mean hourly wage of around fifty-five dollars. Of this category, nearly four thousand work in Huntsville, Alabama—the descendants (in a job-creation sense) of Wernher von Braun's rocket program. This is actually the highest employment level for this category of worker in any metropolitan area.[31] Von Braun's work, in effect, created one of America's earliest high-tech hubs, despite the fact that Alabama was not previously at the forefront of innovation.

IT'S NOT ABOUT TANG

The effects of this increased investment in scientific research, especially when viewed from the perspective of fifty years later, is breathtaking—the United States launched satellites and landed men on the moon, exactly as intended and remarkably on schedule. The military also improved and expanded its stock of missiles; all talk of the missile gap quickly vanished and has never returned. These programs required and involved considerable new knowledge about operating in space, including hypersonic flight, reaction controls for flying above the atmosphere, and piloting techniques for atmospheric reentry.[32] There were also direct improvements in dual-use (military and civilian) technology, including most notably for aircraft design.[33]

To assess the broader impact of NASA, it is important to look at spin-offs, meaning products developed for the space program that turned out to have great uses elsewhere in the economy. There are widely shared "facts" about how NASA helped develop such staples of popular culture as Tang (the orange-flavored drink), Teflon, and Velcro. Unfortunately, these stories are apocryphal; all three items were invented before NASA was created, although the agency did play some role in raising their profile—including by encouraging suppliers to advertise the fact these products were used on Apollo missions.[34]

Nevertheless, reaching space did open up entirely new avenues for scientific investigation. In 2010, the Council for the Advancement of Science Writing offered up its top "50 Science Sagas"—major advances based on research since 1957.[35] From this top fifty, NASA's Deep Space Network (monitoring and measuring distant events) can reasonably claim to have been involved in twenty-two research-based events. Major plausible NASA assists include the discovery of plate tectonics (1961), quasars (1963), and most of everything else we have learned about the universe since 1958.

In addition, NASA created a Technology Transfer Program in 1964, with the explicit goal of promoting broader uses of its ideas.[36] And since the 1970s, when its funding first came under serious pressure, NASA has consistently emphasized the value of civilian spin-offs from its various activities—including highlighting stories through an annual publication (*Spinoff*, published since 1976) and now even with a Tumblr feed.[37] It is hard to find an area of technology development that has not been affected by the NASA enterprise in some fashion.[38] By NASA's own count, at least two thousand products or services have been helped into development and commercialization. Some examples:

- enriched baby food (from life support for Mars missions)
- digital camera sensors (from miniature cameras for interplanetary missions)
- airplane wing designs (the winglets that reduce drag)
- precision GPS (within centimeters)
- memory foam (developed to help counteract effects of acceleration)
- International Search and Rescue System (a personal locator beacon, which uses satellites)
- improvements to truck aerodynamics (reducing fuel consumption by up to 6,800 gallons per vehicle per year)
- shock absorbers for bridges and buildings (successful so far in earthquake-prone regions)
- advanced water filtration

- invisible dental braces (translucent cement, a best seller)
- the DustBuster (portable vacuum cleaner) was the result of a partnership with Black & Decker during the Apollo program
- scratch-resistant, UV-reflective lenses emerged from the coatings created for astronaut helmet visors
- a type of air purifier, specifically an ethylene scrubber that was developed for the International Space Station, slows down the ripening of fruit and the wilting of plants
- there was also a contribution to modern swimsuit designs—although these came not from space but from wind-tunnel testing: specifically, Speedo's LZR Racer, which swimmers wore to the Olympics in 2008 and which was so effective that the rules had to be changed

All these achievements are real, even if dispassionate analysis and hard numbers on the overall rate of return are a bit lacking.[39]

The most important contribution from the broader space effort—including NASA and more military-oriented programs—remains satellites themselves. The first weather and communication relay satellites were launched in 1960; it is hard to imagine the modern world without them.[40] Satellite communications and the Global Positioning System (GPS) are the hidden infrastructure of the modern economy. Many TV signals pass through a satellite at some stage. Satellites are also an essential part of the mobile internet.

This sector has also become a significant part of the US economy, generating a lot of good jobs. Wages in the space industry are on average twice wages elsewhere in the private sector.[41] On December 31, 2016, there were 1,459 operational satellites, of which 594 were operated by US entities.[42] Of all satellites, 35 percent were for commercial communications, 19 percent were for earth observation, and 14 percent were for government communications (with another 6 percent for military surveillance). Between 2012 and 2016, 144 satellites were launched on average each year.

Global revenues of the satellite industry are over $250 billion, of which just under half is generated in the United States, with the largest fraction coming from satellite TV services.[43] There are up to 220 million satellite pay-TV subscribers in the world, with emerging markets as the primary source of growth.[44]

In 2011, total employment in the US "space industry" was estimated by the Organization for Economic Co-operation and Development (OECD) at 170,000 people. By comparison, employment in this sector was 31,000 in Europe and 50,000 in China.[45]

COMPUTE THIS

The main impact of the government's push on scientific research and its applications in the 1940s, 1950s, and 1960s is hiding in plain sight: accelerated development of electronic digital computers.

By 1945, the military had clearly defined problems that would benefit from faster computation—and their tolerance for supporting more fundamental research had increased significantly. Building on impressive wartime results, the Office of Naval Research (ONR) was authorized by Congress in August 1946 with a broad mandate.[46] By the end of 1948, ONR employed one thousand in-house scientists and funded about 40 percent of basic research in the United States, including most of the projects attempting to develop general purpose, stored-program, electronic digital computers.[47]

The first large-scale electronic computers were developed in the UK (not the United States) with the express purpose of helping to break German and Japanese codes during World War II.[48] The initial use of machines for code breaking—including by the US Navy with considerable success from the early 1930s and at Bletchley Park by the British during World War II—used electromechanical analog computers, but by the end of the war, the limitations of this technology had become painfully clear. In early 1942, the Germans modified their Enigma codes—used to communicate with U-boat submarines—in such a way that the computation time needed for code breaking increased dramatically; it now took a month to do what had previously been possible to do in a day.[49] The Allies eventually were able to respond using various work-arounds, including hooking up many electromechanical computers in parallel and getting their hands on a more recent German codebook. Nevertheless, the need for much faster computing had become a first-order matter for national security.

There was also a general realization that the wartime work on radar had developed systems that could handle high electrical pulse rates—a critical element for electronic computers. Immediately after World War II, the military tried repeatedly to get large, established private-sector firms, such as IBM and NCR, to take on the necessary research and development. As Vannevar Bush had anticipated as a general proposition, however, the big established corporate players were not interested.

In the assessment of Kenneth Flamm, a historian of the computer industry, "through the early 1950s the continued reluctance of commercial firms, like IBM and NCR, to invest large sums in risky research-and-development projects with uncertain markets, forced the government to continue sponsoring the new technology. The cold war, with its ensuring technological military competition, heightened government interest."[50]

The next best alternative was to contract out computer development work to academics and industry—with the military providing the cash and taking the risk that the project would not work out. The military had to lead where the private sector was unwilling to tread.

Meanwhile, the Soviet Union conducted a thermonuclear test in 1949, and the Korean War broke out in 1950. There was concern about potential bomber attacks on the United States, so the air force decided to step up funding for a particular computing project: Project Whirlwind, a digital computer project at MIT.[51]

Whirlwind is an interesting case because it speaks to the risks—and nature of potential payoffs—in fundamental research. Initially, funding was provided by the navy, with the goal of developing a flight simulator for pilot training across a wide variety of aircraft. The work went slower than expected, and even the ONR experienced budgetary pressure in the late 1940s.[52] The ONR was happy to hand over the project to the air force, which wanted to develop a system to manage the vast amount of data, mostly from radar looking for enemy bombers.[53] The Whirlwind project contributed several significant breakthroughs in computer technology, including the development of magnetic core memory—a major breakthrough in terms of how to store and access data.[54]

Subsequent development of the SAGE air defense system dramatically impacted the field of computer programming. RAND, an outside contractor, was put in charge of the software effort—estimated to be writing more than a million lines of code—something that was regarded as a monumental challenge at the time when the largest programs involved fewer than fifty thousand lines.[55]

It is estimated that this effort doubled the number of programmers in the United States within a few years, providing as much programmer training as every computer manufacturer combined, multiplied by a factor of four. In addition, between 1963 and 1966, Title 8 of the National Defense Education Act paid for the training of thirty-three thousand computer personnel, at a time when IBM, the biggest computer company, trained ten thousand annually.[56]

Ironically, by the time anti-bomber defense systems were up and running, the development of Soviet missile technology made them largely irrelevant. In the bigger scheme of things, including the competition between the United States and the Soviet Union, the much more important development was that general-purpose digital computers were now well on their way in America.[57] There is no better way to see this than to consider the story of IBM.

INCREASINGLY BIG MACHINES

The rise of International Business Machines was remarkable—and perhaps the first modern role model for technology companies. In 1929, IBM, primarily a manufacturer of punch card machines, employed 4,400 people. It was a relatively small company.[58]

Army and navy intelligence during World War II had used a large number of IBM punch card machines, which were highly efficient peripheral devices.[59] By early 1950, the company had 27,751 employees, making it a large firm but still not an economic behemoth.

The first major IBM move into the transistorized digital computer business was a machine known as Stretch, because it stretched the technical capabilities of the organization. Developed at first for the Los Alamos Scientific Laboratory for use in atomic weapons testing, Stretch was also sold to the National Security Agency.

IBM reportedly did not make money on this early machine, but the knowledge created inside the company led directly to the development and then sale of two hundred IBM 7090s, which were highly profitable—and then to the IBM System 360, which was also a great success. There was, understandably, a close relationship between IBM and its government clients—almost no one in the private sector could afford these enormous and enormously expensive machines.[60] In the 1950s, more than half of IBM's revenues from domestic electronic data processing came from two programs—a guidance computer in the B-52 bomber and air defense.

The government was not just a customer; it was also funding the innovation behind these machines. In 1963, the government paid for 35 percent of IBM's R&D in computing—as well as 50 percent of R&D at Burroughs, and 40 percent at Control Data, both competitors to IBM.[61]

From the SAGE experience, which began with a contract in 1952, IBM developed expertise in producing inexpensive and dependable core memory, as well as printed circuit boards. Total IBM domestic employment in 1955 was thirty-nine thousand, of which seven to eight thousand worked on SAGE.[62]

The lessons learned from working on SAGE were applied to SABRE, its Semi-Automated Business Research Environment. Operational in 1965, this was the first real-time transactions processing system in commercial use, and versions were developed for myriad applications.[63]

IBM's rise continued to be meteoric. Employment grew to 94,912 in 1960, 238,662 in 1970, and 337,119 at the start of 1980.[64] Even more striking: in 1970, the dollar value of IBM shares outstanding (its market capitalization, reflecting expected future profits) was worth 6.8 percent of the entire US stock market—the highest relative valuation of any American company since World War II. In the Fortune 500, a ranking based on revenues, IBM rose from #61 in 1955 to #5 in 1970.[65]

IBM had become one of the largest and most valuable companies in the world.

Did the government support IBM's research or serve more as a buyer of its specialized products? Actually, it did both—and both were essential in encouraging investment in this area. And the same was true of what proved to be the major improvement in the underlying technology—the development of integrated circuits and the associated miniaturization of computer hardware.

MAJOR IMPACT FROM SMALL TRANSISTORS

The transistor was invented at Bell Labs in 1947. Phone companies used a large number of vacuum tubes to alter the flow of electrical current in their systems. Tubes worked well for a long period of time, but they were large, got hot, and were also prone to break. The Bell Labs transformative innovation—assisted in part by wartime work related to radar systems, which needed to be robust—involved creating a component with the same functionality but on a piece of silicon.

In 1956, one of the inventors, William Shockley, moved to the San Jose area and opened a company that attracted a great deal of scientific talent. Within about a year, however, he sufficiently annoyed eight key employees—who left to found Fairchild Semiconductor and to invent, in 1959, the silicon integrated circuit.[66] Multiple transistors could now be created and connected on the same piece of silicon. By 1962, Fairchild could produce an integrated circuit with a dozen transistors; modern computers have billions of transistors on a chip.

This is a terrific story of private-sector innovation—and the most important reason why a microelectronics industry developed in what we now call Silicon Valley. Less emphasized in the popular mythology is the fact that the R&D behind the integrated circuit was largely paid for by the government. In the early period, 1949–1958, about 25 percent of the Bell Labs semiconductor research budget was funded by the military. In 1959, 85 percent of US electronics research was paid for by the federal government—and defense funded nearly half of all semiconductor R&D from the late 1950s to the early 1970s.[67]

The military was the primary customer at first. In the early 1960s, the air force decided to use integrated circuits in the Minuteman II missile; in 1965, these purchases accounted for about one-fifth of sales. Integrated circuits were not used in commercial computers until 1965.[68] NASA and the military were by far the most important clients of the semiconductor transistor business in the early days—their computers needed to be lightweight and tough enough to withstand the effects of acceleration; vacuum tubes were not suitable.[69]

One of the most significant developments of this period was the birth of the Defense Advanced Research Projects Agency (DARPA). DARPA was founded in early 1958, in direct response to Sputnik. DARPA gets a great deal of well-deserved credit for supporting innovation, but seen in the historical context, it was building on the tradition established by the navy and air force—albeit with greater focus on projects with high potential payoffs and greater risks. As one official put it, "If none of our programs fail, we're not stretching far enough"; another said, "If half the people don't respond to a publicly announced challenge saying it's impossible, we haven't set the bar high enough."[70]

Among DARPA's more remarkable achievements: helping to create what became the internet, as well as more broadly supporting the development of computer science departments around the country. DARPA also gets an assist in the development of GPS (through the Transit satellites), speech translation, stealth planes, and gallium arsenide (a high-performance semiconductor).[71] The agency claims contributions to the development of drones and flat-screen displays. The development of artificial limbs has also benefited from DARPA investment.[72]

Almost everything about your computer today—and the way you use it—stems from government funding at the early stages.[73] Strategic support provided by ONR, the air force, and DARPA stands out, including the development of various dimensions of what we now regard as the completely ordinary ways in which we interact with computers, such as the mouse and the graphical user interface (including the funding used by Douglas Engelbart that led to the Mac and Windows operating systems; see Chapter 4).[74] In the 1950s, about eighty different organizations produced computers—the military and defense contractors bought or otherwise paid for almost all of the first machines produced by every single one of these groups.[75]

Much like the period after World War II, the government matched this increase in technological demand with an increase in the supply of skilled workers. The government funded the development of computer science departments primarily through purchasing equipment, funding research through grants, and providing fellowships for graduate students. Between 1981 and 1995, the federal government purchased roughly 65 percent of equipment used in computer science departments.[76] The government also funded the formation of research networks, such as hooking universities up to the Advanced Research Projects Agency Network (ARPANET), which later became the basis for the internet.[77]

At the end of the 1990s, federal funding accounted for about 70 percent of computer science and electrical engineering research accounts at universities.[78] This funding not only produces useful research but has the added benefit of supporting graduate student education. These graduate students often go on to found new companies that are the high-tech backbone of America.

DARPA has also funded some impressive failures, such as the National Aero-Space Plane, an attempt to make a plane that could take off from a runway, fly into space, and then return. Another expensive apparent dead end was the Strategic Computing Initiative, a 1980s effort to create some form of artificial intelligence. Yet even such failures create new knowledge and have an impact over time—the more modern resurgence of AI research, including in self-driving cars, can be traced back to DARPA-funded work.[79]

Moreover, if the United States had not moved first, other countries could have made the early breakthroughs. There was some good work with analog computers in Germany, and some of this continued after the war. The Soviet Union was also early to realize the need for faster computation—thinking along similar military lines as the United States. And the UK had strong early efforts, including its wartime Colossus code-breaking machine and the postwar ACE system, on which Alan Turing, the British World War II math genius, worked. The British fell behind only later during the 1960s when IBM was finally able to convert what it had learned from military work—primarily on the SAGE air defense system—into commercial application, particularly the System 360.[80]

THE MILITARY-INNOVATION COMPLEX

Plenty of things went right with the US wartime scientific push and with the systems that developed subsequently. It is hard to criticize the pace and scale of what was achieved during World War II, and subsequent government-supported developments in computing, aircraft, and medicine are nothing short of amazing.

By 1950, there were 130,000 engineers and scientists "engaged in research and development." The "military research budget" employed nearly half of these people.[81] The military skepticism that had greeted Vannevar Bush in 1940 had completely disappeared. Writing in 1970, Bush himself put it this way: "The obstructionism of military systems, as it existed for a thousand years, ended with the last great war [World War II]. It is far more possible today to maintain a productive collaboration between military men on the one hand and civilian scientists and engineers on the other than it ever was before. The scene is changed. It changed when the atom bomb exploded."[82]

Over the fifty years since 1941, innovation contributed to perhaps as much as half of US economic growth.[83] Some of the effects were immediate, but most took time to show their full effects—there are plenty of lags in how technology develops and affects the far corners of the economy.

For a plausible long-term perspective, look at the US labor market fifty years after Vannevar Bush walked into FDR's office. In 1992, there were 479,000 people working in computer hardware, 366,000 people in communications, 450,000 people in software, 895,000 people in aerospace, and 317,000 people in semiconductors.[84] Another 72,000 people worked in biotech, which at the time was still a young sector. Average pay for employees in these sectors was 60 percent higher than the average for all workers. In all these sectors, there was a long history of public support for research and development, which had proven highly complementary to private efforts.

At the same time, three elements of the public R&D machine that began during World War II must be regarded as storing up potentially difficult issues for the future.

First, the wartime effort was focused on harnessing science to more effectively kill people, including civilians, through bombing and other means. By 1945, Vannevar Bush and his colleagues, to be fair, were emphasizing peaceful uses for new technology, including advancing science to save and improve lives. However, the practice of research remained deeply intertwined with national defense; increasingly, this relationship caused unease in some quarters.

Second, there were relatively few large contractors for the development of military technology, creating potential monopolies or overly cozy relationships with the customer, particularly the Department of Defense. Between 1940 and 1944, the US government placed over $175 billion of prime defense contracts with US corporations; two-thirds of these awards went to only one hundred companies and 20 percent to only five companies.[85] In part, this concentration of opportunity reflected who had existing design and manufacturing capability. It was also partly due to the economies of scale that were realized when particular firms could specialize.

Third, there was a concentration of research funding in a small set of elite universities. Large contracts were handed out to major research universities, such as MIT, Harvard, and Berkeley, without much scrutiny or oversight. MIT was "the largest single recipient of wartime research contracts": $56 million from OSRD—large relative to the $250 million in contracts for universities and even relative to the $1 billion in total contracts received by private industry.[86]

The elitist allocation of large-scale government funding was focused on universities that were leading the pack at the start of the war—but also those that were in the close orbit of Vannevar Bush, Alfred Loomis, James Conant, and a few others. As a source of geographical polarization and potential grievance, this was to have profound consequences in the coming years—limiting the breadth of support for the science sector and ultimately weakening the development of technology.

By the end of his time in office, even Eisenhower famously worried about the potential downside of relying on what he called the military-industrial complex. What if this interest group created an incentive for war or could not think beyond its own self-interest?

Or what if the scientists, with their newfound prestige and funding—and their ability to wrap themselves in the national interest—found themselves in conflict with politicians regarding how new technology would be used?

3

Descent from the Heavens

I am sure that at the end of the world—in the last millisecond of the
Earth's existence—the last human will see what we saw.

—George Kistiakowsky, in reaction to witnessing the
first nuclear bomb explosion, Alamogordo, New Mexico,
on July 16, 1945[1]

IN 1945, SCIENCE WAS RIDING HIGH. SCIENTIFIC INVENTION WAS REGARDED BY AMERI-
cans as prestigious, and scientists were involved at the top levels of
decision-making, including with regard to national security.[2] Particularly
on atomic matters, they were experts with indispensable knowledge.

There was a further surge of support—and government funding—
after Sputnik. In 1960, *Time* named America's scientists as Person of
the Year, and the magazine's tone was one of optimism: "1960 was the
richest of all scientific years and the years ahead must be even more
fruitful."[3] Federal government support for research and development
reached almost 2 percent of GDP in the mid-1960s, at the height of the
Apollo program.

Today, however, the situation is quite different. We spend only about
0.7 percent of GDP on publicly supported science, and scientists now

have less political clout.[4] President Eisenhower responded to the Sputnik crisis by appointing James Killian, president of MIT, as his science advisor; the announcement was well received as a signal that serious thinking would take place behind the scenes.[5] In contrast, President Trump's science advisor was not appointed until eighteen months after his new administration took office.[6]

Science—and scientists—have become controversial and less universally respected. When did this happen and why? Three issues stand out as contributing to the erosion of scientists' access to power and to budgetary dollars after 1945.

The first is that postwar expectations for science—particularly atomic energy—were exaggerated. This is perhaps understandable given the speed with which enormous advances were made in the early 1940s. Still, an essential part of the backdrop is that science failed to deliver as promised.

Even worse, the potential danger of unintended consequences was underemphasized by political leaders and some of their high-profile scientific advisors. The original sin may have been to underestimate the risks associated with radiation, in weapons testing and through accidents, and particularly with regard to handling nuclear waste. Once undermined, public trust in atomic power proved hard to rebuild. This loss of credibility proved contagious. If the government and its technical experts could be wrong about radiation, what else might they be concealing?

The second and more dramatic issue was growing disagreement between scientists and politicians. By the 1960s, some senior scientists were becoming skeptical about how technology was being used in the name of national security. The bombing of North Vietnam was a particularly controversial issue, with politically plugged-in scientists on both sides of the issue and a heated debate behind closed doors.

Matters became more public at the end of the 1960s, under Presidents Johnson and Nixon. These presidents wanted to build high-profile pieces of hardware, in particular a supersonic jet and an antiballistic missile system. Top science advisors—insiders with access to the corridors of power—expressed reservations, and even in some instances helped opponents of the administration win the congressional debate against the proposed systems. Politicians did not soon forget this perceived betrayal, and political leaders control the purse strings.

Finally, the rise of the anti-tax movement reshaped how Americans think about what government should do. In the recurring budget debates since the 1970s, science has been repeatedly squeezed. We still fund science, particularly when there is a potential national security dimension, but at a much lower scale relative to the size of our economy.

Understanding this erosion of political support for science spending matters today. It is not enough to propose specific projects or to create moments of enthusiasm. Government support for research and development has greater effects when it can be sustained.

A VERY BIG BANG

When Vannevar Bush argued for the establishment of the NDRC in mid-1940, the potential power of uranium fission was not yet widely appreciated. There had been steady theoretical advances before 1940, and Ernest Lawrence, a physicist at Berkeley, won the 1939 Nobel Prize for inventing the cyclotron—the first particle accelerator, which created new possibilities for work at the atomic level. Meanwhile, in Europe, progress with some other parts of the basic science was moving fast; the first splitting of the uranium atom took place in Germany in December 1938.

James Conant, president of Harvard, was sent to the UK in early 1941 to investigate further. The British were cagey about what they knew—despite the previous year's Tizard mission, they were not keen to reveal that they now thought an atomic bomb was feasible. Then Frederick Lindemann, Churchill's scientific advisor, privately convinced Conant that an atomic bomb was feasible. And if the British might be close to making it work, could the Germans be far behind?[7]

Vannevar Bush was initially skeptical but quickly became persuaded, in part because of his assessment of German capabilities.[8] Once convinced, Bush—in typical fashion—agreed to organize a major effort, with Conant, Lawrence, and Alfred Loomis helping to bring scientists on board.

In an exception to the rule for almost all other major technology developed under the NDRC/OSRD during the war, the military was formally put in charge of the overall project, with Major General Leslie Groves in command. Even Groves had to concede scientific leadership to a civilian, Robert Oppenheimer.[9] And the scientists, even while secluded at Los Alamos, were not subject to standard military discipline. Invention needed creative space for the inventors.

It also needed money. As a matter of urgent national priority, civilian scientists had been encouraged to spend whatever was necessary to build a viable bomb. This proved to be a large amount of taxpayer money. From 1942 to 1946, the Manhattan Project received over $1.5 billion of funding, with funding in its peak year reaching 0.4 percent of GDP (the same percentage of GDP is about $80 billion today).

The role of scientists as shapers of policy was evident at the highest level. In 1945, President Truman convened what was known as the Interim Committee to advise him on whether to use the atomic bomb against Japan; this group included Bush, James Conant, and Karl Compton among its members. Bush and his colleagues had long argued for scientists to share responsibility at the highest possible level of military strategy, and now they had it.[10]

By the end of July 1945, there was no denying that the world had changed. Either a country would have the most modern science and the latest weapons, or it would not. And the frontier, in terms of the military equipment and how to use it, was now likely to move fast.

GREAT EXPECTATIONS

In the immediate aftermath of World War II, American enthusiasm for the potential of new technology—and the benefits it could bring—was almost unlimited.[11] The atomic bomb had moved from theory to detonation in less than a decade, so who knew what could come next. From the public perspective, the prospects for an atomic age seemed literally incredible.

The academic experts were on board. Nine big-name northeastern universities jointly created Associated Universities Incorporated in 1946.[12] The goal was to manage complex projects, and Brookhaven National Laboratory—for atomic energy research—was their initial project.[13]

Even the atmospheric testing of atomic bombs was almost fashionable at first. Aiming to catch the cultural moment created by the demonstration of power in a nuclear test on Bikini Atoll in the Marshall Islands on July 1, 1946, the bikini design for swimwear was invented (and registered as a trademark) by a Parisian designer, Louis Réard.[14] A leading rival swimsuit, designed by Jacques Heim, was named the Atome.[15]

The political vision was not just about building more effective weapons, at least at the level of political rhetoric. In December 1953, President Eisenhower announced an Atoms for Peace program, which included building nuclear reactors and sharing atomic technology with countries seeking economic development. This program remains controversial in terms of its motivation and impact, but there is no question about the promise behind the idea that atomic power could be useful for purely civilian purposes and with great positive impact.

Atomic power could be harnessed in myriad ways, including to drive vehicles or planes. As late as 1960, the US Air Force still had a nuclear-powered bomber under development.[16] In 1958, one company announced a potential atomic pen, and another raised the possibility of a nuclear-powered car.[17] Nuclear weapons could also be used to dig very large holes—for example, to expand the Panama Canal.[18] There was serious discussion of building atomic engines to power spacecraft; multiple "nuclear thermal rocket" prototype engines were successfully tested in a fifteen-year program that ran into the 1970s.[19]

In the 1950s, the chairman of the Atomic Energy Commission even promised that electricity might soon become effectively free, with implied positive effects for the economy.[20] The idea that atomic power might not be entirely safe rarely came up.

The first domestic US nuclear power plant opened in 1957. The pace of construction stepped up during the 1960s, and thirty-seven plants were in operation by 1973. In retrospect, however, the tide of ideas had started to turn much earlier, with growing public concern about radiation.[21]

RADIATION POISON

In a caustic 1950 volume, *Science Is a Sacred Cow,* Anthony Standen argued that much of the newly acquired prestige of science was at best exaggerated. In his view, this led to overconfidence or even arrogance: "Completely gone is any pretense of inculcating the virtue of reserving judgment until all the facts are in."[22] Harsh words, and very much against the grain of public and professional opinion in that moment. But also prescient—as became vividly illustrated by a key side effect of atomic weaponry and power.

Immediately after the bombing of Hiroshima and Nagasaki, the Japanese authorities reported cases of radiation poisoning—a fact disputed by the American military. Writing in the *New York Times,* with a byline dated September 9, 1946, prominent science writer William L. Laurence claimed to have seen evidence clearly refuting claims that radiation could become a significant cause of death.[23] Senior officers were keen to downplay the idea that radiation would have long-lasting effects on people and places.

The military was wrong about radiation; the effects in these specific instances subsequently proved significantly more negative, including a higher incidence of cancer, birth defects, and—in cases of very high exposure—rapid death.[24] Moreover, the *New York Times* neglected to disclose that Mr. Laurence had been seconded to the US military and was essentially presenting the official views disguised as independent reporting.[25] Laurence was a journalist, not a scientist, but the line between independent expert assessment and the official press line was starting to blur.[26]

Fear of radioactive fallout had spread in the 1950s, particularly as a result of atmospheric nuclear tests, and some prominent scientists had backed the case for a test ban.[27] There were close to 120 nuclear weapons tests in 1958, and in February that year, the issues were brought alive in a dramatic television debate between well-informed experts who strongly disagreed: Edward Teller, inventor of the H-bomb, and Linus Pauling, winner of the 1954 Nobel Prize for chemistry. Teller was a master of rhetoric: "Now let me tell you right here, this *alleged damage* which the small radioactivity is causing by producing cancer and leukemia has *not* been proved, to the best of my knowledge, by *any* kind of decent and clear statistics."[28] He went on to suggest "there *is* the possibility, furthermore, that very small amounts of radioactivity are helpful." In retrospect, he was far too sanguine.[29]

It's hard to say who won that particular debate, which included questions of values and how to think about the Soviet Union. More broadly, however, people became increasingly worried about the unintended consequences of new technology and tended no longer to believe government assurances. The failure to deliver on postwar expectations was becoming a bigger concern.

Political leaders—and the military who worked for them—wanted technology to serve their version of the national purpose. Facts about side effects were inconvenient and brushed aside. To be fair, some scientists had great reservations from the beginning about the way in which nuclear technology was being developed.[30] Others saw the world through more rose-tinted glasses, at least until the broader debate about technology began to shift in the early 1960s.

SILENT SPRING

Silent Spring is a vivid and compelling book. Rachel Carson was a well-established science writer, a marine biologist specializing in explaining phenomena of the sea for broad audiences. *The Sea Around Us* won a National Book Award in 1952, and *The Edge of the Sea*, published in 1955, was also a best seller. But she is remembered primarily for the 1962 publication and subsequent impact of *Silent Spring* on the use and abuse of pesticides in American agriculture.

Carson's critique was not so much of science but rather of the careless way new scientific discoveries were being applied—by firms in the private sector, with government connivance. Drawing a parallel with the insidious and initially invisible effects of radiation, she argued that American communities were being poisoned by the overuse of pesticides, the chemical DDT in particular.[31]

In 1939, Paul Müller, a Swiss scientist, had discovered that DDT was effective in killing insects, including mosquitoes that transmit typhus and malaria. Shipped to the United States in 1942, this insecticide was quickly put into mass production and was used widely by the US military in its operations around the world—beginning with the successful effort to quell an outbreak of typhus in Naples in October 1943. Tests in Italy and Greece, supported by the Rockefeller Foundation, found that malaria incidence could be reduced dramatically.[32]

The chemical industry swung into high gear, and around 1.35 billion pounds of DDT were used in the United States over the next three decades.[33] The US Department of Agriculture (USDA) had some reservations as it became clear that DDT could have adverse effects on animals that were not pests, and from 1957, there were some limitations placed on where DDT could be used. At the same time, however, USDA officials and scientists remained in favor of widespread agricultural use, including for cotton, peanut, and soybean crops.

As Carson pointed out, however, the USDA was slow to recognize the way in which a wide variety of insecticides negatively impacted benign insects, as well as birds and the broader ecosystem. There were also legitimate concerns about the impact on people, including death as a result of acute exposure and possible connections to cancer (this is still disputed for DDT).[34]

Carson was no technophobe; she was well aware of the benefits of technology applied to agriculture. She was also making a profound observation about the development of technology—unintended and unfortunate consequences could easily predominate, and the Department of Agriculture stood accused of encouraging excessive risk taking with human health in pursuit of higher yields.[35] Carson's first *New Yorker* article on this topic emphasized the parallel with radiation.[36]

Carson's arguments were widely embraced by the public, by opinion makers, and even by politicians.[37] There was a strong reaction from the chemical industry—arguing that Carson was exaggerating and even mistaken on key facts. DDT was banned from most uses in the United

States in 1972, although the debate, remarkably, continues more than fifty years later.[38]

Irrespective of how you view the merits of DDT, it is undeniable that *Silent Spring's* impact was felt immediately and profoundly.[39] In the post–World War II American love affair with—and generous funding levels for—science and its applications, Carson sounded a major discordant note.[40] By the mid-1960s, many people, including scientists, were increasingly skeptical about the uses to which science was being put.[41]

The environmental movement emerged energized and with more support from the 1960s, based on multiple legitimate concerns.[42] Among these was the simple and increasingly obvious point that the promise of science had been overstated by people in positions of private-sector and governmental power. And the pursuit of profit meant that important unintended effects, including health effects that might manifest only over time, were ignored or downplayed. Rachel Carson's contribution was just the beginning of a much longer debate about how best to protect or help the environment.

Subsequently, of course, the nuclear accidents at Three Mile Island (1979) and Chernobyl (1986) made the painful point that the civilian benefits of nuclear technology had been overstated (free electricity!) and the risks understated (radioactive waste). Managing these kinds of complex systems also proved harder than the experts had imagined.[43] Between 1977 and 1989, forty reactor construction projects were canceled in the United States.[44] From the late 1970s through 2013, no new reactors were built.[45] Rachel Carson had drawn an even more powerful parallel than she'd realized.

The reaction to *Silent Spring* represented a turning point in popular and political views on the application of new technologies. No longer would citizens automatically accept the word of scientists at face value. The relationship between science, government, and the military was also increasingly called into question.

At the same time, ironically, another divide was opening up that would have an equally damaging impact on publicly supported science—

this time between the scientists and the politicians who provided their funding. There is no better way to convey the breakdown in this relationship than by reviewing the career of George Kistiakowsky.

KISTIAKOWSKY'S JOURNEY

George Kistiakowsky experienced the twentieth century in unique fashion. Born in 1900 in Kiev, Ukraine, he not only had a ringside seat for the Russian Revolution but also briefly joined the ill-fated White Army in its fight against the Bolsheviks.[46]

Following his escape from the Communists, Kistiakowsky completed his education at the University of Berlin, immigrated to the United States while still a young man, joined the faculty of Harvard, and established himself as one of the country's leading chemists. It was no surprise when Vannevar Bush appointed him to head the wartime work of the NDRC on explosives.[47] In October 1943, with the Manhattan Project struggling to figure out how to start a chain reaction, Kistiakowsky was brought in to solve the problem—which he did, to great professional acclaim.[48] Building on this experience and reflecting the growing importance of America's nuclear arsenal, Kistiakowsky was an obvious choice as a next-generation leader on science policy.[49]

Appointed to the Science Advisory Board of the air force chief of staff, Kistiakowsky helped convince the air force to develop intercontinental ballistic missiles (ICBMs), moving them away from reliance on long-range bombers. He was an expert on right-sizing the warhead, including facing down pressure from Vice President Nixon, who wanted to build something bigger, presumably for the symbolism. "Couldn't we afford it?" Nixon reportedly asked. Kistiakowsky and his colleagues prevailed, because the facts and the science mattered.[50]

In 1959, Kistiakowsky became chief science advisor to President Eisenhower—the second person ever to hold that position. Few scientists knew more about how the military worked, and Kistiakowsky had become acutely aware of the potential for mass destruction. Kistiakowsky was influential in assessing the feasibility of US war plans and, in that context, began to suggest setting limits on nuclear testing.[51]

In 1960, Kistiakowsky was concerned about the Soviet missile threat, perhaps more so than was Eisenhower.[52] The more he learned, however, the more Kistiakowsky felt information was being distorted within the decision-making structure. Looking back at age eighty-one, he put it this way: "As I got up higher and higher on the rungs I began to realize that these policies were based on frequently very distorted, sometimes deliberately, intelligence information." The bomber gap, the missile gap, and all the other supposed gaps vis-à-vis the Soviets were greatly exaggerated, at least in his retrospective view.[53]

In 1965, Kistiakowsky was disappointed when it became apparent President Johnson would ignore the recommendations of a task force on preventing the spread of nuclear weapons.[54] The Vietnam War, particularly the bombing of North Vietnam, only increased Kistiakowsky's disquiet. President Kennedy had asked the Presidential Scientific Advisory Committee (PSAC) for ideas on Vietnam, but Johnson seemed much less interested in input.[55]

Matters came to a head in 1966, when Kistiakowsky worked with a group of scientists who attempted to design a barrier of button-sized electronic sensors that could be used to prevent infiltration into South Vietnam. From Kistiakowsky's perspective, this would be an alternative to bombing North Vietnam. Robert McNamara solicited the idea but never seemed fully committed.[56] The air force, once the sensors and related technology were available, seemed to regard it as a complement to—rather than a substitute for—bombing. The scientists themselves were increasingly divided, based in part on how skeptical they were of what the military wanted to do.[57]

Kistiakowsky came to feel that he and his scientific colleagues were being manipulated by the Pentagon to simply justify more bombing, and he severed his government connections.[58] He subsequently became active in the Council for a Livable World, founded by another atomic pioneer working for arms limitations.[59]

Interviewed in 1980, Kistiakowsky expressed his extreme reservations about the military and the way that science had been used in the Cold War. Even inventors of the atomic bomb were turning against what science policy had become—or how it was being used.

POLITICIANS VS. SCIENTISTS

The reservations about Vietnam expressed by Kistiakowsky and other scientific advisors opened a rift that only widened in subsequent years. In David Halberstam's influential assessment, highly qualified people held positions in government during the Vietnam War period and ended up making decisions with deeply unfortunate consequences.[60] Kistiakowsky's career and the fate of science advisors more broadly illustrates an additional dimension of what happened. In the 1940s and 1950s, politicians listened to their scientific advisors, in part because the issues were technical. Could we build a hydrogen bomb, would missiles work, and even should nuclear testing continue to take place aboveground? There remained many technical issues also in the 1960s, and science advice was still welcome, but under President Johnson, and then President Nixon, politics moved to the forefront.[61] When scientific advice collided with what politicians wanted to do, the result was protracted struggle.

That was the case, for example, with the development of supersonic civilian aircraft, originally floated under President Kennedy and pushed forward, despite some expert skepticism, under President Johnson and again under President Nixon. The scientific issue was quite simple—the plane created a sonic boom that was vastly louder than the noise created by a regular jet plane. Residents of Oklahoma City were subjected to this level of sound for six months during 1964, by way of experiment. More than fifteen thousand people filed complaints, and five thousand filed damage claims. Not surprisingly, local residents felt the noise level was unacceptable.

Scientists raised concerns about these side effects, along with the small associated benefits of supersonic planes relative to traditional air travel. Prominent former science advisors spoke against the design in congressional testimony. Russell Train, chairman of the Council on Environmental Quality (under the White House) appeared before the Joint Economic Committee in May 1970 and emphasized the potential issue of stratospheric pollution.[62] Another congressional witness was Richard Garwin, who had been a confidential advisor to the White House on supersonic travel. He stated that supersonic jets would generate airport noise that "is far beyond the maximum acceptable for jet aircraft now."[63]

The US aircraft industry wanted to build the plane, and influential nonscientists in policy circles thought that it would boost US prestige—and match the Concorde, which was developed by the British and the French during this period.[64]

In the end, the opposition scientists prevailed. Funding for the supersonic aircraft was withdrawn, much to the annoyance of the White House and to the delight of Senator Bill Proxmire, who had summoned the scientists to testify. Proxmire felt that the program had been revealed to be nothing more than excessive government support for private business: "We were financing a completely private, commercial enterprise with hundreds of millions of Federal research dollars."[65]

The conflict between independent science and establishment politics came to a further dramatic head under President Nixon, when current and former members of the President's Science Advisory Committee publicly challenged the administration's proposal for antiballistic missile systems—intended to shoot down or divert incoming nuclear warheads (a difficult if not impossible proposition).[66] As the Soviet Union and China built nuclear weapons, pressure had developed for some kind of antiballistic missile defense. Large-scale systems had proven prohibitively expensive and of dubious value, so President Johnson's Defense Department proposed the "lighter" or less comprehensive coverage that could (arguably) be provided by the Sentinel program. By the time Richard Nixon was elected president, Sentinel (rebranded as Safeguard) had become intensely controversial—with people living in "protected" cities taking the view that the system just made them into more prominent targets.

Part of the political pushback came from local people in places like Seattle and suburban Chicago, who became concerned about the risks of nuclear accidents that might be associated with antiballistic missile (ABM) bases. The military initially refused to discuss the details, arguing that much of the information was classified. However, when nuclear physicists weighed in with their negative assessments, the Pentagon was forced into an all-out publicity effort.[67]

Most notable in this fight over ideas was the role of physicists from the Argonne National Laboratory, located near Chicago.[68] In November 1968, despite working for the government, John Erskine, David R. Inglis, and their colleagues took the lead in organizing and disseminating information that was directly counter to what the administration was trying to achieve.

General Alfred Starbird, head of the army's Sentinel program, insisted, "There cannot be an accidental nuclear explosion." George Stanford, one of the Argonne scientists, rebutted this as "a ridiculous statement. . . . They have circumvented a lot of possibilities, but they still have the human and mechanical components to consider."[69] In town hall–type meetings, the physicists prevailed in swinging local opinion against the ABM bases.[70]

Former members of PSAC testified in Congress against the Sentinel program. One senator reportedly remarked that he was "unable to find a former presidential Science Advisor who advocates the deployment of the ABM program."[71]

Nixon initially wanted to the keep the program, but the opposition became too widespread, and Congress declined to fund the proposed version.[72] When Franklin Long, a chemist from Cornell, was proposed to be the next science advisor, President Nixon turned him down—apparently because Long had opposed the ABM program.[73] Soon after that, Nixon eliminated the science advisor position and actually shut down the PSAC.[74] Scientists had won the battle over Sentinel, but their privileged relationship with power was further eroded. Speak truth to authority—and authority will cut your funding.

Killian and Kistiakowsky had been remarkably successful as science advisors, participating in the creation of NASA, improving weapons, and even pushing for arms control.[75] Within the White House, their voices were authoritative, and they were backed by physicists and others who had worked together under Vannevar Bush's World War II effort. It helped that they worked on well-defined technical questions, such as whether to switch from bombers to missiles as a defense priority and how to think about a potential ban on nuclear weapons testing.

By the late 1960s, in contrast, even the strategic defense questions had become complex in political terms and less amenable to technical solutions—this was exactly Kistiakowsky's experience with Vietnam. The change was not that science was becoming harder—inventing the atomic bomb, based only on relatively new theory, was at least as hard as building missiles. But missiles seemed increasingly irrelevant—or an expensive distraction—as attention turned to civil rights and debates about the causes and effects of poverty. At the same time, science was facing a new pressure it hadn't seen in decades: a squeeze on its funding.

PUTTING THE BRAKES ON THE UNIVERSITY GRAVY TRAIN

Perhaps the hardest-hitting critique of the 1960s was also the most lighthearted. In a series of *Science* articles, culminating in *The Politics of Pure Science* (published in 1967), Daniel Greenberg peeled back the mystique of modern science, exposing the same sort of pursuit of subsidy we see in all other industries. Science had virtually unlimited access to funding in the early 1960s, and this generated resentment.

Greenberg created the humorous character of Dr. Grant Swinger, director of the Breakthrough Institute and chairman of the board of the Center for the Absorption of Federal Funds.[76] Among Dr. Swinger's more memorable proposals was the Transcontinental Linear Accelerator (TCLA), designed to run from Berkeley to Cambridge, "to pass through at least 12 states, which means 24 senators and about 100 congressmen could reasonably be expected to support it." The route might even skirt "several congressional districts which went against the administration in the last election."[77]

In retrospect, Greenberg's critique was the beginning of the end for unchecked scientist access to federal funds. Just as concerns about the environmental damage of scientific advancement were gaining traction on the left, concerns about the Bush model of endless subsidies for academically led science were starting to increase. And these concerns found their focus on the other side of the aisle.

On the right of the political spectrum, skepticism about science can perhaps be traced back to the anti-fluoridation messages of the John Birch Society, founded in 1958.[78] Senator Barry Goldwater's election campaign in 1964 can be seen as foreshadowing important Republican messages of the current era, including small government, but there was no evident opposition to science in general and certainly no concern expressed about the application of science to warfare.[79] "Among Goldwater Southerners, even thermonuclear warfare gets identified with regional pride, sentiment, and rancor."[80]

Richard Nixon's position on science was more complex or perhaps just ambiguous. He created the Environmental Protection Agency (EPA), addressing issues raised by the growing environmental movement. But libertarian groups and others on the right had begun to raise questions about whether federally supported research was truly useful. Was this money just being used to support what had become hotbeds of left-wing protest—the universities?

In the account of one key aide (speechwriter and later presidential candidate himself), Pat Buchanan, a turning point for Nixon's 1968 presidential bid came with student unrest in the spring of that year, particularly the occupation of buildings and other actions on the campus of Columbia University. Nixon called this "the first major skirmish in a revolutionary struggle to seize the universities of this country and transform them into sanctuaries for radicals and vehicles for revolutionary political and social goals."[81] Universities—and their government funding—would never be seen in the same way again.

There were campus protests against the military—and against science helping the military—on all manner of campuses, including places previously regarded as elite.[82] In 1966, there were protests against war-related companies, such as Dow Chemical, manufacturer of napalm. Some prominent scientists based in Boston took out a newspaper advertisement opposing the United States' use of chemical weapons, such as the defoliant Agent Orange, in Vietnam; others, including from Columbia University, made the case against antiballistic missile (ABM) systems and sites.[83] There were student protests against classified defense-sponsored research on campus.[84] The Bush model was focused around the university and assumed a tight relationship with the government. As parts of the political establishment became suspicious of university faculty and students—and vice versa—the Bush model became harder to sustain.

The election of 1968 arguably represented the end of the postwar political consensus and the beginning of our modern social and geographic polarization. Attitudes did not shift overnight, but from 1968, the rising narrative was much more anti-government and therefore also against government-supported activities, such as university-based research.[85] Books and reports on how the government wasted taxpayer money became a popular genre. Politicians vied with each other to make fun of federally supported research projects.[86] The federal research budget declined more than 10 percent in inflation-adjusted terms from 1968 to 1971. The percentage of faculty who received federal support fell from 65 percent in 1968 to 57 percent in 1974.[87]

THE PURSE STRINGS TIGHTEN

These political shifts coincided with America's greatest technological achievement to that date—putting a man on the moon in July 1969. But this also meant that the space mission, as defined by President Kennedy, had been accomplished.

At the same time, the United States was facing budgetary pressures at a level not seen since the cost of fighting World War II. The United States spent about $168 billion on direct military operations in Vietnam, 1965–1972, which would be equivalent to over $1 trillion in today's money. Veterans costs and support to the regime in Saigon (until 1975) added significantly to the tab.[88]

At the same time, unlike World War II, the United States was not just trying to restore its preferred world order outside its borders—the country was transforming within its borders as well through the massive Great Society programs of the 1960s. For example, Medicare, created in 1965, provided subsidized medical care to everyone over the age of sixty-five—and by 1970, twenty million Americans were eligible. Mandatory spending—mostly Social Security and Medicare—jumped from 30 percent of all federal spending in 1962 to close to 50 percent in 1975.[89]

Facing these budgetary pressures, President Nixon presided over an overall decline in federally funded R&D spending.[90] From 1967 to 1975, federal support for basic research declined by about 18 percent in inflation-adjusted terms.[91] Most dramatic was the decline in funding for NASA, the darling of the 1960s. This decline ultimately amounted to half a percentage point of GDP ($100 billion in today's money), perhaps the biggest single science cutback of all time. NASA was not alone in experiencing cuts.

In part, this decline was precipitated by pressure from Senator Michael "Mike" Mansfield, majority leader of the Democrats in the Senate. Criticism of the military—including its influence over the economy—had grown during the 1960s, primarily due to the Vietnam War, but also in reaction to what was seen as an excessive buildup of nuclear weapons. Protests grew during 1968, including at the Democratic convention in Chicago, when ten thousand demonstrators had violent confrontations with local police and the National Guard—broadcast live on television.

Reacting to these events, and the pressure to curtail the influence of the military, in 1969, Mansfield proposed a major change in how federal research was structured. His amendment to the Military Authorization Act forbade the Defense Department from using its funds "to carry out any research project or study unless such project or study has a direct and apparent relationship to a specific military function."[92]

Mansfield's view was that up to $311 million in research funding could be switched over to civilian research efforts, as led by the NSF.[93] But the overall effect was that the NSF did not expand, other than taking over some materials research laboratories. The squeeze on federal support for research and development intensified, with the largest declines in physics and chemistry.[94]

The employment impact of publicly funded research spending was mentioned by analysts but largely ignored in the political discussions.[95] There was little or no systematic official consideration given to how knowledge is developed or its value as it moves across sectors of the economy—for military to civilian use or vice versa.

THE REAGAN REVOLUTION

The divergence of interests between politicians and scientists was one major reason for the turn away from public funding of research and development. This was augmented by the new budgetary pressures arising from the Vietnam War and the Great Society. But the US government still had sufficient funds to finance ongoing research commitments. From 1950 to 1974, the United States had never had a deficit of more than 1.5 percent of GDP that was not eliminated within three years.[96] The federal budget deficit grew to 3.3 percent of GDP by 1975, its highest point since World War II, but fell thereafter and was down to 1.6 percent by 1979.

In the same time frame, a new force increased budgetary pressure: the anti-tax movement. While taxes were never popular in the United States, anti-tax sentiment picked up significantly starting in the mid-1970s. The genesis of the anti-tax movement can be traced to California's Proposition 13 in 1978. Proposition 13 was the first of a series of state laws that limit the ability of localities in a state to levy property taxes. Since its passage, nearly forty statewide tax-limiting measures have been passed by voters in eighteen states through the initiative process.[97]

The anti-tax movement reached the federal level with the election of Ronald Reagan in 1980, who ran on a strongly anti-tax platform. A weak economy combined with the largest tax cuts of the postwar period led the deficit to rise to a postwar high of 5.9 percent of GDP by 1983. The deficit averaged almost 4 percent of GDP over the next decade before falling under President Clinton to become a surplus in 1998. By 2002, due partially to another huge round of tax cuts under President George W. Bush, it rose again before peaking at 9.7 percent of GDP in 2009 in the midst of a deep recession.[98] The deficit has since slowly been reduced as the economy recovered, and it is currently projected to be about 3 percent of GDP by 2023.

Ronald Reagan favored more research, with a very specific weapons-development objective.[99] On March 23, 1983, President Reagan announced his Strategic Defense Initiative, creating "a long-term research and development program" with the aim of intercepting enemy missiles—and eliminating the threat they posed to the United States. His project, dubbed "Star Wars" was not about creating new basic science and stands in strong contrast to, for example, the development of the digital computer.[100] Overall Department of Defense spending under Reagan rose from $40.7 billion (0.48 percent of GDP) in 1980 to $76.5 billion (0.7 percent of GDP) in 1987.

However, while public spending on military R&D rose along with the defense budget, by more than 40 percent from 1979 to 1988, public spending on R&D outside the Department of Defense fell by 30 percent. On net, despite the famous Reagan military buildup, total public R&D was basically constant during his presidency.[101]

Particularly striking was reduced support for energy research. Following the Organization of Petroleum Exporting Countries (OPEC) embargo of 1973, atomic energy research was combined with other efforts and placed under the Department of Energy in 1977. Significant funds were expended amounting, at their peak, to about 0.5 percent of federal government spending.[102]

However, federal government–supported energy research fell by almost 50 percent under President Reagan. The threat to national security receded as oil prices came down, in real terms, during the 1980s. In contrast with the Manhattan Project and the Apollo program, the client for energy research was not directly the government but rather the private sector—which was not consistently enthusiastic about this form of government intervention.[103]

By the 1990s, the situation had shifted further against federal funding of science. When Republicans took control of Congress in 1994, they took the opportunity to bring pressure on the EPA and its regulations, including the merits of the underlying science. Led by House Speaker Newt Gingrich, the Republicans also eliminated the Office of Technology Assessment, which had existed since 1972, but which had apparently been too critical of the Star Wars initiative.[104]

The fall of the Berlin Wall in 1989 represented the end of the Soviet threat—and this removed what had been, at least since Sputnik, the major motivation behind a great deal of government support for science. There is no better illustration of this than the debate over the US supercollider facility in the early 1990s. A who's who of physics spoke up in support of the Superconducting Super Collider that was under construction in Texas, which would have been the world's most powerful particle accelerator (by about twenty times) and would have pushed the frontier in terms of potential discoveries for high-energy physics.[105] It was to no avail—Congress canceled the project in October 1993, in part due to large cost overruns. With the Cold War over, the pressure to increase knowledge of nuclear phenomena was less compelling. This time, when scientists ran up against the politicians, the politicians won.

A major supercollider ended up being built at the CERN facility in Switzerland. And the results in terms of new discoveries have been impressive. At the level of pure science, researchers using the supercollider confirmed the existence of the subatomic Higgs boson particle.[106] At a more applied level, a team in New Zealand used technology developed at CERN—in pursuit of the Higgs boson—to produce the first color 3-D x-ray scanner.[107] There is no way to know if this new technology would have been developed in the United States had the supercollider been located here or whether it would lead to a new growth sector, but these are the types of scientific investment risks that the United States took in the 1950s and 1960s and that we no longer take.

Government spending on science experienced a slight renaissance during the Great Recession that began in 2008—because key parts of the Obama stimulus package were focused on investments in science and technology, particularly in the area of clean energy. That resurgence proved short-lived. Beginning in 2011, some politicians, particularly Republicans in the House of Representatives, pushed back hard on the deficit spending. In the subsequent prolonged battle over the proper role of government, publicly funded R&D proved to be very much on the chopping block.

The Budget Control Act of 2011 cut discretionary spending, which includes public R&D financing, by $1.2 trillion over the next decade, with a specific cap for each year. Subsequent budget deals doubled down on this strategy, and the net result has been a large reduction in nondefense discretionary spending, which fell by 15 percent from 2010 to 2014.[108] As a direct result of these budget battles, publicly financed research and development fell from 0.98 percent of GDP in 2008 to 0.71 percent of GDP in 2018.[109]

EMBRACING SCIENCE AGAIN

Think back to the spring of 1940, with Vannevar Bush about to visit the Oval Office. The federal government had a minimal presence in supporting science. The potential relationship between government and academic research seemed fraught with complications. And powerful interests—the US Navy among them—were more than skeptical about the benefits of rapid innovation for national defense (and prosperity).

In the subsequent seventy years, attitudes changed completely. We have embraced technology and science more than any other previous civilization, and we have helped spread those values and this way of organizing the economy around the world. Americans watched *The Jetsons* in the early 1960s, *Star Trek* later in that decade (and again in most decades that followed), *2001: A Space Odyssey* (1968), and of course *Star Wars* (1977) and a lot more science fiction subsequently.[110]

In the early twentieth century, American scientists were seen mostly as conservative, in political terms.[111] This is not surprising; they were prosperous white men.[112] Vannevar Bush and his scientific friends did not generally express positive views about the New Deal. They went to work for FDR and the federal government because they feared the rise of Germany and—correctly—anticipated its science-based approach to war needed to be matched. Almost without exception, they felt more comfortable with Dwight Eisenhower in power.

Since that time, it seems fair to say, scientists have moved to the left and the political spectrum has shifted to the right—in ways that are not favorable to supporting unfettered scientific research and its implications.[113] Over the past few decades, debates about science and its implications have been widespread and sometimes virulent, including the validity of scientists' views on global climate change, as well as a wide range of other issues, such as endangered species, the dangers associated with high levels of dietary sugar and fat, and whether abstinence-only birth control is effective.[114]

The decrease in publicly funded research relative to the size of our economy from the 1970s to the present has been significant. However, while there have been ups and downs, over the same period, total research-and-development spending has not declined, fluctuating since the late 1960s around 2.5 percent of GDP.

The reason is straightforward—as publicly funded research declined relative to the size of the economy, there was an offsetting increase in private-sector research and development. This raises an obvious and important question: If private invention and commercialization can replace or effectively substitute for what was previously funded by the government, is there really a problem?

4

The Limits of Private Research and Development

A discovery in one firm, sector or country can trigger new avenues of research, inspire new research projects or find new applications in other firms, sectors or countries.

—Bronwyn Hall, Jacques Mairesse, and Pierre Mohnen, leading researchers on the economics of R&D[1]

THE WAY NEW PRODUCTS AND INDUSTRIES ARE CREATED IN AMERICA IS SHROUDED IN MYTH. A person has an idea and through grit and determination, perhaps working alone in her garage, brings it to life. She receives the financial support she needs from farsighted investors. This good idea is turned into a product that makes consumers happier, and everyone—the idea generator, employer, investors—becomes rich. The best thing the government can do is get out of the way of the development and commercialization of those ideas.

This myth is based on some impressive examples.[2] Individuals from Thomas Edison to Steve Jobs have shown how individual initiative and private-market financing can create amazing innovations, gigantic companies, and profound impacts on modern life.

At the same time, this myth obscures three key realities about just how new ideas get translated into economic output. The first, as we showed in the earlier chapters, is that the basis for new ideas is often government-funded research. The reason we have breakthroughs like GPS, the internet, and most lifesaving pharmaceuticals is the underlying publicly led or financed research that made the discovery possible.

Second, the fruits of innovation are shared widely—beyond just the inventors. Ironically, in fact, the returns to the original inventor are sometimes quite low. We all know about the incredible wealth of inventors like Steve Jobs, but what about Dan Bricklin, who invented the first spreadsheet program (VisiCalc) in 1979 but who made only $3 million from its sale to Lotus, which went on to make a huge fortune (before the follow-on Microsoft Excel made even more money)? Or Charles Goodyear, who labored in poverty for years to perfect the process for widely useable rubber, discovered it by accident after a decade, and then mistakenly gave away his secret without filing for a patent—leaving him with little but a company named in his honor forty years after his death?[3]

Indeed, accounting for the high risk of failure of new ventures, many high-tech entrepreneurs who are financed by venture capital in the United States would, on average, have done better working in salaried positions than starting their own companies.[4]

And third, there are very good ideas that do not make it into the market because funders do not want to take on the necessary risks. We know about the success stories, but what about the products that didn't make it—or were lost to companies in other nations?

Add this all together and the unfettered private market does not always match up to the mythology. The story of the how America lost the enormous flat-panel display industry is a dramatic illustration of these forces at work.

MISSED OPPORTUNITY: FLAT-PANEL DISPLAYS

One of the most impressive technological advances of the last part of the twentieth century was the development of flat-panel displays. In the 1960s and 1970s, such a technology seemed like something out of science fiction. People watched TV and used the first personal computers with heavy rounded screens that had poor resolution. Today, every type of visual digital interface, from computers to televisions to smart watches, uses some form of flat-panel display technology.

This industry grew tenfold from the mid-1990s to the mid-2000s, and global sales stand currently at $114 billion.[5] Virtually none of the profits from this industry have been earned by US companies, nor do American workers have jobs making its products.[6] Yet US researchers not once but *twice* invented the technologies that led to this industry. In both cases, US research-and-development infrastructure was unable to capture the gains—the profits, good jobs, and exports—from these inventions.

The origin of this story lies with the Radio Corporation of America (RCA). In the early 1960s, RCA researchers such as Richard Williams and George Heilmeier began experimenting with using small electric fields to turn dye colors on and off in a display.[7] This was the beginning of liquid crystal display (LCD). The company hosted a press conference in 1968 to demonstrate the world's first commercial liquid crystal display, a digital clock.[8]

But then RCA transferred Heilmeier's LCD research team to RCA's semiconductor group. The managers of this group deemed liquid crystal study unlikely to lead to anything of use and summarily terminated all research activity for LCDs. The dominant RCA product at the time was the transistor-based cathode ray tube (CRT) television for which RCA had proprietary technology. The semiconductor group seems to have been concerned that development of a rival liquid crystal display technology would undermine the hugely successful and highly profitable CRT television business and the royalties received from licenses.[9]

In 1968, after RCA had already begun scaling back its LCD research business, Japanese broadcast network NHK came to RCA to film its documentary *Companies of the World, Modern Alchemy*. One scene included Heilmeier operating his display. About this time, eager to enter the high-technology electronics business, Japan's Sharp Corporation was aggressively developing a pocket-sized calculator.[10] Wada Tomio was in charge of making displays for Sharp calculators at the time. When he viewed the NHK documentary and learned of LCD, he suggested to Sharp executives that they use it for their calculators. Sharp management went to New Jersey to see the LCD demonstration in person and proposed a cooperative effort with RCA to develop these displays for calculators.

But RCA wasn't interested—due to an unsuccessful effort to diversify into other markets, RCA had begun a severe cost-cutting program. As usual during any cost-cutting exercise, research and development was early to the chopping block. So RCA rejected this proposal, leading Sharp to purchase the patent license from RCA for $3 million—a huge bargain in retrospect.[11]

The timely development of new technology, its incorporation into new products, and the skill and ingenuity of its engineers allowed Sharp to quickly and efficiently gather together the basic technology, and in 1973, Sharp announced the world's first commercial pocket calculator with a liquid crystal display. Many years later, James Tietjen, the director of the David Sarnoff Research Center (formerly RCA Laboratories), while taking in the Sharp Museum's pioneering product displays, summed it up: "LCDs . . . had started in RCA Laboratories, but ended up at Sharp Corporation."[12]

It would be bad enough for the United States if the story ended there—but this loss led to an even bigger failure as this industry modernized. The LCD popularized by Sharp used what was called *passive matrix* technology.[13] An image would be composed of rows and columns of pixels. Complex images would require many columns and rows, which would result in slow data signals. For watches and calculators, the display could just take longer to show the image, but for rapidly changing images, this would not work.

Scientists at the US-based Westinghouse corporation were working on developing an *active matrix* addressing system that would use transistors to open all the pixels at once to more rapidly form brighter, sharper images than the LCD display that had been developed at RCA. The research team was headed by T. Peter Brody, who had written some important technical papers on the subject.

But Westinghouse soon ran into the same type of shortsighted corporate planning that doomed LCDs at RCA. Brody's work was shifted from division to division, and he was only able to survive due to some military contracts from the US Air Force and the Office of Naval Research. By 1972, Brody demonstrated the first active matrix liquid crystal display. However, Westinghouse executives killed the project in the mid-1970s because no division was willing to fund the building of a manufacturing facility.[14]

In response, Brody left the company and quickly moved to start his own firm to commercialize the technology. Over the next two years, he presented his ideas to more than forty venture capitalists and electronics companies. Only one company, 3M, was interested, and in 1980, 3M funded Brody with $1.5 million so he could launch Panelvision, which continued the thin-film transistor research he started at Westinghouse.[15]

In 1984, Brody's company began selling experimental products and lab prototypes. They soon had eighty customers in twelve industry segments, but the scale was too small to turn a profit. The company needed to develop a real manufacturing process and high-volume production capability. This required more capital. Early start-ups in the flat-panel display field needed $30–$200 million to go from research to mass manufacturing.[16]

But investors were not willing to pony up the money because they did not think they could compete with Japan.[17] Here is the key point: some of the major elements of LCD were also used in active matrix technology. Since Japan had taken over production of LCD technologies, once active matrix was discovered, they had the manufacturing scale ready to go for producing the next wave of active matrix displays. This competitive advantage for Japanese companies—and their ability to capture value from a wave of new product creation—left investors hesitant about moving from research into volume production with Panelvision. Without adequate funding, Panelvision failed.[18]

The Japanese developed high-volume production capability for flat-panel displays, then captured a larger and larger market share that allowed them to drop their prices and corner the world market. Although the United States had developed the technology first, American companies did not invest, did not build factories, and did not create jobs. An ironic and depressing coda to the story is that the State of Wisconsin recently spent $4 billion for tax breaks and other spending to attract a flat-screen manufacturing plant for the Taiwanese company Foxconn—jobs that could have been in the United States to start with.

Like many myths, the myth of the private sector innovation machine in the United States has some elements of truth—and misses many elements of reality. There are critical limitations in relying on the private sector to lead innovation-driven growth in the United States. In this chapter, we review those limitations. But first we need to ask: Why does this matter for the US economy? Why should we care about an obscure topic like research and development?

R&D, PRODUCTIVITY, AND THE US STANDARD OF LIVING

From 1947 to 1973, Americans enjoyed an unprecedented rise in the standard of living. Real per capita GDP nearly doubled.[19] On average, families were able to consume almost twice as much per person in 1973 as they were immediately after World War II.[20]

American experience since the 1970s has been quite different. From 1973 through early 2018, real per capita GDP grew by only around 1.7 percent per year on average.[21] At this rate of growth, it takes more than forty years for incomes to double on average—representing a dramatic slowdown.

The living standards of a country are determined, above all, by its level of productivity—how much can be produced, given the available people, buildings, equipment, and resources. Economic growth is, consequently, primarily about increasing productivity.[22]

The fundamental driver of higher productivity is knowledge. This has been true throughout human history—all our big breakthroughs have come from understanding how to do something differently. In the early nineteenth century, British engineers figured out how to put a steam engine on wheels and run it safely on iron tracks. At the very beginning of the twentieth century, two bicycle mechanics from Ohio discovered how to control flight. In the 1950s, building on British and German wartime technology, the science of jet travel and rockets was cracked wide open.

Knowledge comes from two fundamental sources. The first source is *education*. Any advance in knowledge starts from a sufficiently deep understanding of what came before. It is impossible to stand on the shoulders of past giants if you cannot get a ladder to climb past their feet. Education provides that ladder.

The second source is *research*. No matter how much you know about past accomplishments, you need to experiment further if you want to create new discovery. This is what the process of research is all about.

Of course, knowledge itself doesn't put the food on the table or the car in the driveway. What is needed is the process of converting that knowledge into the goods and services that raise our standard of living. And this is where the development enters the picture—as seen in the phrase *research and development*. Research provides the basis for increasing productivity, while development turns it into a reality.

It is for these reasons that research and development are viewed as essential to productivity—and ultimately to economic growth. Governments around the world recognize this problem, and so they protect new ideas with patents. Patents grant a legal monopoly to a firm, which will be upheld by the courts—in return for full disclosure and free use of the technology after the patent expires. Patented inventions in the United States, for example, can be protected by the patenting firm for twenty years from patent application.[23] The goal (historically and in theory) is to protect inventors against investing resources in a new product only to see it stolen by another firm.

Of course, the patent system existed at the time of Thomas Edison—and he took great advantage of the system, accumulating 2,332 patents (1,093 in the United States alone) in his lifetime![24] There are, however, three reasons why, even given the patent system, private companies underinvest in research and development. These are not just theoretical problems but real ones.

THE LIMITS OF PRIVATE R&D #1: SPILLOVERS[25]

When the managers of a firm decide to undertake a research project, they are investing in the future of the firm (no doubt, also with an eye to their own careers). And privately undertaken research and development typically generates a high rate of return for the people involved.

But research and development also creates benefits for other firms and society at large. Other firms can learn from research and development they haven't funded and produce better products of their own— garnering the profits from doing so. So the initial firm is doing much of the investing and only seeing part of the total profits earned. In the jargon of economics, there is a free-rider.

An iconic example is the story of the PARC research facility founded by the Xerox Corporation in 1970. This research organization drew on a talented team of Stanford University computer scientists—many of whom had worked with Douglas Engelbart, the legendary inventor whose insights were inspired by his experience with radar and whose work was largely government funded. These scientists developed an operating system for personal computers that utilized a graphical user interface (GUI).[26] In the 1970s, PCs used what was known as a command line interface, based on what was used for larger mainframe computers— the user had to type out specific commands to execute programs.

With the new GUI system, instead, a computer mouse was used to navigate across a screen. With a click, the user could toggle between windows, print out documents, and do graphical design—a radical concept for personal computers in their early days. Yet by the late 1980s, this was the standard structure of operating systems for personal computers worldwide.

Do any of us own computers that use the Xerox operating system? No, our personal computers typically use operating systems from Apple or Microsoft. This is because Steve Jobs had the foresight to offer Xerox one hundred thousand shares of Apple Stock at the price of $10.50 per share, in return for a chance to learn about this new technology. He considered the technology "revolutionary," later saying, "I remember within ten minutes of seeing the graphical user interface stuff, just knowing that every computer would work this way someday. It was just so obvious."[27]

Jobs was right. What he saw on those visits to PARC became an essential part of the Macintosh computer. By 1988, over one million

Macintoshes had been sold, totaling about $4 billion in sales. Taking a longer view, from 2006 to 2017, the sum of revenue from sales attributed to the Mac products was $228 billion.[28]

And this new GUI technology did not just benefit Apple—it also fundamentally changed the Microsoft operating system (OS) that ran most personal computers. Microsoft struck an initial deal with Jobs's replacement as CEO of Apple, John Sculley, to obtain a royalty-free license to use Apple's technology, which—so the story goes—Sculley thought applied only to the current version of Windows.[29] When Microsoft extended this technology to future versions, Apple sued and lost.[30]

If we add up the money that Microsoft made on its Windows operating system, the original PARC research led to even higher earnings. For example, Microsoft's Windows 7 software was reported to have sold over 450 million copies.[31] At an average price of $120 for the basic OS, Windows 7 would have brought in about $50 billion in revenue.

And the reward for Xerox and PARC? Xerox ended up selling these shares at Apple's initial IPO at $28 a share, so they made a profit of almost $2 million, but that was nothing compared to what Apple got out of the deal.[32] Subsequently, computer science research was abandoned at PARC in the mid-1980s.[33] Xerox undertook the fundamental research and most of the development that changed the PC market forever—and was rewarded on a very modest scale. In effect, Xerox was very good at creating value through innovation but much less effective at realizing that value for itself (and its shareholders).

Research and development creates potential gains for other companies beyond the one doing the initial work. The company making the large upfront investments in new ideas and products frequently does not capture the full value. This is especially true in cases when intellectual property laws do not apply, such as when the innovation is sufficiently groundbreaking to be considered a general idea or an approach that cannot be patented (as with Apple's operating system).

The problem with spillovers from R&D is that these lead to a *free-rider problem:* firms will underinvest in R&D because they don't receive the full benefits of those investments. Xerox PARC devoted significant resources to a research effort that benefited others. Why should that company, or others, take future risks like this if it is possible that they won't be the ones seeing the gain? As Bill Gates reportedly said to Steve Jobs, "[It was] like we both had this rich neighbor named Xerox and I broke into his house to steal the TV set and found out that you had already stolen it."[34]

The story of PARC shows how the research process creates far-flung benefits for others. But once again, a given firm does not care if its scientific discovery benefits other firms—indeed, it would prefer that the discovery *not* benefit its competitors. As a result, the free-rider problem causes them to underinvest in invention and commercialization of new products.

THE LIMITS OF PRIVATE R&D #2: PROPRIETARY PRIVATE RESEARCH

This problem is made even worse by the second issue—the proprietary nature of private research. Companies don't tell others the details when attempted inventions fail or have side effects, resulting in duplicated efforts or in abandoning efforts that would actually be productive. This is illustrated most compellingly in the context of pharmaceutical development.

The pharmaceutical industry in the United States has delivered some of the most amazing medical innovations of the past fifty years. Drugs for treating hypertension, high cholesterol, diabetes, and other chronic illnesses have saved millions of lives, but developing new drugs is expensive—and becoming more so over time, with the typical cost estimated to be in excess of $2.5 billion.[35] The trial-and-error nature of research is the reason for the high cost.[36] Every scientific discovery that becomes a new drug is the result of dozens of steps, from identifying the "target" biological entity (e.g., gene or protein), to finding the right "hit molecule" that interacts with the target and is the building block for a drug that could combat the disease, to three stages of clinical trial with the possibility of failure at each stage. To give a sense of the risks and work involved, once a target has been identified, anywhere from two hundred thousand to more than one million compounds must be screened to identify hits, and only 9.6 percent of the drugs that enter human trials in stage one end up being approved.

What this means is that there is a lot more failure than success in drug development, but most of the information that is made public is on the successes, and the proprietary nature of failures can lead to significant setbacks to the research process—as is illustrated with the case of statins.

Statins are a class of enzyme inhibitors that regulate the pathway that produces cholesterol. In the 1970s, it was understood that high blood cholesterol correlated with coronary heart disease, but it was unclear at that point whether lowering cholesterol could improve health outcomes. While it is clear to us now (based on what we have learned from our experience with statins) that lowering cholesterol is a vital part of improving heart health, this was a highly uncertain proposition in the 1970s.

In 1976, Akira Endo of the Japanese pharmaceutical company Sankyo discovered the first statin, compactin. Around same time, Roy Vagelos of the American pharmaceutical company Merck led a research team searching for such enzyme inhibitors, and in 1978, Vagelos's group discovered lovastatin. Both Sankyo and Merck began clinical trials on their respective compounds. Initial results from both sets of clinical trials were promising; both drugs were reported to be both safe and effective.[37]

In August of 1980, however, Sankyo halted development of compactin in response to toxicology reports. Dogs who received one hundred times the normal dose for two years experienced gastrointestinal lesions that were supposedly interpreted as lymphoma.[38] A month later, Vagelos's group caught wind of this development but did not get the full details. All they heard was a rumor that Sankyo's cholesterol drug had caused tumors in animals and that they had stopped clinical trials in humans. In response, Vagelos immediately halted lovastatin's clinical trials in humans, and lovastatin's development was shelved indefinitely. At the time, Merck had no way of knowing whether compactin's possible toxicity was a result of a shared mechanism with lovastatin, but they were unwilling to take the risk.

In his biography, Vagelos notes, "We couldn't allow anyone to use our compound if there was the slightest possibility it might be carcinogenic.

Even an unsubstantiated rumor was a sufficient basis for making that decision." Vagelos repeatedly reached out to Sankyo to get data from compactin's toxicology reports. Vagelos tried framing this issue as an ethical concern for the well-being of patients exposed to lovastatin, but Sankyo refused to offer any information. Vagelos even offered a business deal in exchange for data, and yet Sankyo executives continued to view the issue as one of corporate competition.[39]

Most assumed this was the end for lovastatin. However, in 1982, doctors from Oregon Health & Science University and the University of Texas at Dallas requested lovastatin for trials in high-risk patients who did not respond to other treatments.[40] The trials were once again successful, so Merck began large-scale clinical trials and toxicology studies in 1984. Lovastatin finally gained approval in 1987.[41] It quickly became successful; Merck's sales of lovastatin peaked at $1.3 billion in 1994.[42]

Today, statins are the largest-selling class of drugs around the world. Some thirty million people worldwide take statins, and statin sales totaled $25 billion in 2005.[43] From the first approval of statins in 1987 through 2008, economists estimate that the value of statins in the United States alone was more than $1 trillion in terms of health improvements.[44] In just 2008, the use of statins prevented an estimated forty thousand deaths, sixty thousand hospitalizations due to heart attacks, and twenty-two thousand hospitalizations due to strokes.

But these benefits did not have to start in 1987. It turns out that there was no evidence that these results for dogs were indicators of true cancer risks, but Merck had no way of knowing this given the private nature of Sankyo's findings.[45] In retrospect, Sankyo may have overreacted—and Merck had no choice but to follow suit. The result was a multiyear delay in this lifesaving drug, potentially causing thousands of excess deaths and billions of lost economic benefits.

This example illustrates what is meant by the spillovers of research and development: there are valuable lessons for other companies that could make discovery much more efficient, but it is in no one company's interests to make those lessons available. They do not get anything from it, and indeed they just make discovery cheaper for their competitors.

THE LIMITS OF PRIVATE R&D #3: DEVELOPMENT LAGS

A third problem with the patent system is that for technologies with long development periods, the period of monopoly by the time the product reaches the market may be fairly short. Pharmaceuticals face such "lags to commercialization" when the clinical trials required to show their value can take many years, such as with potentially lifesaving cancer drugs. But the patent expires twenty years after application—so that by the time the drug comes to market, there isn't much patent protection left.

As a result, the private sector underinvests in the drugs that have the longest development periods.[46] Consider a vivid example: From 2009 to 2014, eight new drugs were approved to treat lung cancer, the leading cause of cancer deaths in the United States. Yet all eight targeted patients with the most advanced form of lung cancer and were approved based on estimated incremental improvements in survival (such as extending life by two months on average). None of the patent applications tackled the more serious issue of long-run treatments of earlier-stage cancers, which might save years rather than months of life—and no drug has ever been produced to actually prevent lung cancer.

Recent research shows that this isn't just about the fact that saving more years of life is harder; it is about the fact that demonstrating success takes more years, allowing fewer years until commercialization. As commercialization lags rise for drug development, private research on those drugs falls. The drugs with such long development lags are almost exclusively funded by public, rather than private, research.

This is a critical issue for the health of the public. If firms did not face such long lags to commercialization, almost one million more years of life would have been gained from more rapid development of lifesaving drugs. Using the method typically used to put a dollar amount on saved years of life, this suggests that over the long run, these commercialization lags cost the United States $2.2 trillion in lost value of life.[47]

A vivid illustration of this issue arose through Pfizer's recent termination of R&D on treatments for Alzheimer's and Parkinson's. The problem wasn't a lack of funds but rather the short effective patent period for such research. According to James Hendrix, director of global science initiatives at the Alzheimer's Association:

> The way our patent laws are set up doesn't work for the protracted studies into Alzheimer's treatment. Trials often take between five and 10 years, sometimes more, before it can be determined if a drug or intervention is working. Patent protection and market exclusivity will likely be expired or nearly expired by that time. The loss of exclusivity makes it difficult for drug companies to justify the costs of the study.[48]

INTO THE VALLEY OF DEATH

While the free-rider problem and spillovers lead to too little research, there is another set of problems in translating research into development and ultimately into economic growth. Research is carried out by technical experts who are excited by discovery. However, the ultimate good that emerges from this process of discovery requires much more than just an excited scientist; it requires the ability to turn that discovery into a new technology, then into a new product, and finally into a sale to consumers. These are steps that go beyond the training and skill level of the basic scientists doing the discovery, and they require *financing*. Taking an idea from the lab to the store is expensive.

In our economy, turning a good idea into a product is exactly what should be financed by private capital. Private capitalists should be able to provide both the funding and expertise to help scientists take their ideas from the laboratory to the marketplace. Indeed, the United States has a successful venture capital (VC) industry with a long and impressive track record of doing so. But this industry has fallen short when it comes to maximizing the entrepreneurial—and economic growth—-potential of new technologies.

The VC industry has been an important player in our economy for decades. Early VC was closely associated with technology companies, so it makes sense that the growth of the VC industry beginning in the early 1970s has become linked to Sand Hill Road, in Menlo Park, California, which hosted firms like Kleiner Perkins Caufield & Byers and Sequoia. Virtually every major player in Silicon Valley received money from a Sand Hill Road firm.[49] In 1973, the National Venture Capital Association (NVCA) was formed. By the early 1990s, nearly half of venture money was going to the West Coast.[50]

The VC industry has been a clear success story in terms of promoting the growth of technology companies in the United States. The examples are legendary; Microsoft, Google, Apple, Amazon, Intel, and many more of the leading companies in the United States were funded at their early stages by venture capital. Sixty percent of all companies who had an initial public offering (IPO) between 1999 and 2009 had venture backing.[51] In 2014, 17 percent of US public corporations had started with VC backing, representing 21 percent of the entire capitalization of publicly traded companies in the country.[52]

That said, the VC industry faces three defining constraints. The first is that the people who run these funds are investing in an exceedingly risky environment. Even after a rigorous process of culling thousands of proposals to the few that get funded, most venture-backed investments fail. Data from a leading venture investing firm show that 8 percent of their investment dollars resulted in more than 70 percent of the overall returns of the portfolio, while 60 percent of the investment dollars were spent on projects that were ultimately terminated below the cost of the investment.[53]

The second is that VCs are ultimately investing in something that is largely out of their control. Venture investors are relying on entrepreneurs to put in the incredibly hard work required to take a product from idea to market. There is a legitimate concern that those who are the best inventors may not be ideally suited to put in that effort. If VCs invest a lot of money in a good idea and the entrepreneur is not dedicated or skilled enough to turn this into a productive company, then the venture capitalists have a failed investment on their hands.

The final constraint is that the pool of investors willing to risk their money on very early-stage enterprises is actually quite limited. Only one-sixth of 1 percent of new start-ups each year get venture backing. The amount of actual capital that is committed to backing venture capital partnerships has typically been around 0.2 percent of the value of the US stock market.[54] In other words, while the $76 billion in venture commitments in 2016 may seem large in absolute dollars, it is tiny compared both to the multitrillion-dollar size of our financial markets and to the requests for start-up funds by hundreds of thousands of firms each year.[55] Venture investments amounted to only 2.5 percent of gross domestic private investment in the United States in 2016.[56]

To attract and disburse these limited dollars, venture capitalists have developed two investing approaches that make sense from their perspective—but that also explain a great deal about the limitations of the existing venture capital industry as a catalyst for economic growth.[57]

The first is to pay entrepreneurs in proportion to the actual commercial success of the product. That is, while VCs can't tell how much effort the entrepreneurs are making, they can use the signal sent by the market as to whether the process was a success. So entrepreneur earnings are not proportional to their effort but rather to their market success.

This strategy makes a great deal of sense for the venture capitalists—but it places a lot of risk on the entrepreneur. The inventor could genuinely put in enormous effort only to, through no fault of their own, have the market not value their contribution. And individuals, with their limited budgets, are not in a good position to bear this risk.

If you look only at the experience of successful entrepreneurs like Mark Zuckerberg or Jeff Bezos, entrepreneurship appears to be a high-return activity, but in reality, most new start-up firms yield no meaningful value to entrepreneurs, and most of the total value to entrepreneurs comes from the tiny fraction of ventures that is wildly successful.[58]

After accounting for risk, the return on starting a company is not high for the typical entrepreneur. A comprehensive study gathered data on the income earned by entrepreneurs and their risk of success and failure. The study concluded that if a worker is well paid and does not have millions of their own assets to put at risk, they will be better off staying at their job than striking out on their own.[59] Consequently, many potential entrepreneurs do not go forward with their ideas because they cannot afford the risk of failure. This poses a major bottleneck to the ability of the private market to promote entrepreneurship.

The second VC approach is to invite investors to put their money in funds that aim to earn high returns within a fixed period of time. These funds are typically structured to have a life of ten years, and venture capitalists ideally like to exit earlier to establish a strong record and to encourage follow-on investments in their subsequent funds. Venture capitalists therefore prefer investing in projects where the commercial viability is established quickly, typically within three to five years.[60] Indeed, the less time that is left before the VC fund ends, the less risk the VC is willing to take.[61]

As a result, the structure of venture funds is not well designed to provide financing for capital-intensive, long-run projects of the type that are often required for major technological advances. Such projects face a problem of going from the idea to demonstration of product viability that is known as the *valley of death:* a range where there are large investments required and the time period can be long before the investor knows for sure that there is a product that can be brought to market.

Projects that are low capital intensity and high technology risk are prime territory for VCs. The fact that VCs need to make many investments to realize a few successes implies they typically invest under $10 million in equity per start-up. Sectors such as information technology in general and software in particular require relatively low levels of initial capital investment and short sales cycles that exhibit general commercial viability quickly. The venture capital model is perfectly suited for such opportunities.

There is much less of a good fit with sectors requiring large capital investments and long investment ramp-ups before sales begin. A particularly strong example is investments in clean energy. Even if new energy technologies work in the lab, it is hard to predict how they will work when scaled up for the real world. Demonstration of commercial viability can be long and expensive—the funds required to prove commercial viability can reach several hundred million dollars over a five- to ten-year period, compared to the much smaller amounts that VCs are used to investing in start-ups.[62]

In fact, there was a large venture push into clean technology start-ups in the first decade of the twentieth century; from 2004 to 2008, the share of first-series VC dollars going to this sector rose from 1.5 percent to 5 percent. Their entry was associated with a burst of innovation in the field. One study found that the large incumbent firms in this sector were more likely to focus on incremental innovations but that the new VC-financed start-ups were associated with more novel and influential innovations. However, VCs quickly turned away from this sector as the recession tightened the money available for financing, and by 2012, the share of VC funding going to clean energy was back to 1.5 percent.[63] In general, when it is easier for venture investors to raise funding, they are more willing to invest in riskier long-run ventures, but this inclination recedes when credit conditions tighten.[64]

Ironically, the short time-horizon problem appears to be getting worse as technology such as Amazon Web Services makes it cheaper to start new companies. VCs are increasingly focused on "spray and pray" models of small funding to companies where they can more quickly determine whether the company will succeed—worsening the valley-of-death problem for capital-intensive start-ups.[65] It is for this reason that experts are pessimistic about the ability of venture investors to fund new technologies that require significant lag times and capital intensity.[66]

The limitations of private VC as a financing model in capital-intensive industries are clearly illustrated in the case of Boston-Power and the production of lithium-ion batteries. The first commercial lithium-ion batteries were released in the early 1990s and have since become the most commonly used type of battery in consumer and home electronics. Lithium-ion batteries are more energy dense and experience less self-discharge (the process by which batteries naturally lose their charge over time) relative to nickel-based batteries, which were prevalent before the 1990s. Today, lithium-ion batteries comprise 37 percent of the global revenue from battery sales and are the dominant battery for portable electronics.[67]

Even with lithium-ion's advantages over older battery technologies, the field remains relatively new, with researchers still pursuing many technological and manufacturing improvements, such as extending battery life span and reducing production costs. Safety has also been a concern, especially following the well-publicized Samsung Galaxy Note 7 exploding-battery incidents in late 2016.[68]

Boston-Power started in 2005 to work on improving lithium-ion technology. The company was a highly touted start-up, with early customers such as computer manufacturer Hewlett-Packard and car manufacturer Saab. It was initially quite successful in raising funds from venture investors; by 2010, Boston-Power had raised $185 million in financing from private sources (as well as from the Swedish government).

But the company needed more to take the next step. They wanted to build a 450,000-square-foot manufacturing facility in Auburn, a small central Massachusetts town, that would have immediately created seven to eight hundred jobs. This would require more funding than the private VCs were willing to provide; as we have described, this type of large-scale manufacturing investment is outside the venture investing wheelhouse. Boston-Power then turned to the federal government but were unable to secure the $100 million grant for which they applied, as government spending in this area was focused on more established companies.[69]

Fortunately for Boston-Power—and unfortunately for the United States—another source of funding was willing to step in: China. Boston-Power raised over $300 million from the Chinese venture firm GSR, as well as in low-interest loans, grants, buildings, and subsidies.[70] Of course, this meant building the new plant in China, not in the United States. Employees in the United States were shed as the move to China took place, and as of 2017, Boston-Power had only fifty employees in the United States and about five hundred in China.[71]

Since moving to China, Boston-Power has continued to receive Chinese government financial support for further development. In December 2014, the company announced it had secured US$290 million in local government financial support to expand its Chinese facilities fivefold.[72] The Chinese government was willing to invest where private US VCs were not, and the result is a growth in manufacturing capacity happening not in central Massachusetts but in China.

PRIVATE R&D IS TOO LOW . . .

The logic of arguments such as R&D spillovers and the valley of death is strong, but do these issues really matter in reality? After all, we have a lot of private research and development in the United States. Indeed, as mentioned at the end of Chapter 3, the decline in public R&D spending over the past several decades has been accompanied by an increase on the private side. Currently, around 70 percent of the R&D in America is business funded.[73] So how do we know that this level of private-sector investment is not ideal?

After all, the returns to private research and development are large. Look no further than the pharmaceutical industry. Its profit margin of almost 20 percent is one of the highest of the world's major industrial sectors.[74] Two-thirds of drug companies saw an increase in their profit margins from 2006 to 2015.[75] Among the largest twenty-five companies, annual average profit margins fluctuated between 15 and 20 percent; for comparison, the annual average profit margin across the largest five hundred global nondrug companies fluctuated between 4 and 9 percent.[76]

More generally, a number of studies show that the economic benefits to R&D investments are large, as measured by the rate of return, or the earnings created per dollar of investment. Company investments in research and development are estimated to have a rate of return of 20–30 percent in the long run, much higher than returns through other forms of investment.[77]

Yet despite these high returns, private industry is not sufficiently investing in the research that will create the technologies of the future—as well as the millions of jobs that would emerge from these new technologies. A perfect example is cell and gene therapy manufacturing, perhaps the most significant breakthrough in the biopharmaceutical sector in recent years.

Cell and gene therapies are new technologies that have the potential to cure diseases previously considered untreatable. Cell therapy involves transplanting live cells into patients to restore lost functionality, while gene therapy involves delivering genetic material into patients to modify the functionality of defective genes. Unlike most other pharmaceuticals, cell and gene therapy treatments are generally onetime treatments, in contrast to drugs that require regular dosing. Additionally, manufacturing for cell and gene therapies is much more involved than for other pharmaceuticals. Whereas a single manufacturing process or platform could produce a wide variety of traditional pharmaceuticals that treat different diseases, cell and gene therapy manufacturing is highly specialized. Not all manufacturing facilities can support the full range of manufacturing processes used, and in general, manufacturing plants for traditional drugs cannot be easily converted into plants that produce cell and gene therapy products.[78]

Unfortunately, the United States is falling significantly short in providing the manufacturing resources needed to turn these genetic breakthroughs into new products. One problem is the enormous start-up costs; the cost of setting up a large-scale cell or gene therapy manufacturing facility can be upward of $200 million, compared with less than $30 million for a similar-scale small-molecule manufacturing facility.[79] Furthermore, a single facility may not be enough. Cell and gene therapy treatments are highly unstable and have extremely short shelf lives (one example, Provenge, has a shelf life of eighteen hours), so decentralized manufacturing at multiple smaller and geographically separate nodes (rather than a single centralized hub) becomes a necessity.[80] These high costs are well beyond the range that is supported by venture capital investors, so start-up drug companies have no way to finance their own capacity.

As a result, some 80 percent of gene and cell therapy companies outsource to contract manufacturing organizations (CMOs), facilities that lease their space to drug companies for testing and development. Existing CMOs are struggling to keep up with demand, however. Wait times at CMOs currently average over sixteen months, and the current shortfall in worldwide cell/gene therapy manufacturing may be about five times the entire current capacity.[81] According to one source,

> drug companies have resorted to buying slots in virus production
> queues years in advance—like buying a nonrefundable airline ticket
> long before your vacation and hoping you can get away when the

time comes. Other firms . . . worried that production at one company will fail . . . buy places in line at two contract companies. Still other biotechs have simply been shut out, unable to get their viruses made.[82]

While CMOs are expanding, they are finding it difficult to do so fast enough in large part because current manufacturing technologies are underdeveloped and referred to by insiders as "outright primitive" and "incredibly labor-intensive."[83] Rather than using closed, sterile bioreactors (standard for most traditional drug manufacturing), current procedures can require technicians to manually transfer materials between open plasticware.[84] Under these modes of production, it is "not possible to achieve significant economies of scale that can support commercial viability as production levels rise."[85]

Moreover, expanding manufacturing access will require substantial coordination and collaboration that is not in the interest of any one manufacturer—or any one VC financier.[86] Due to the high setup costs of the requisite infrastructure, manufacturing platforms are only economical if the fixed costs are spread across multiple products. But doing so requires sharing commercial rights and production information at an unprecedented level. One pharma industry news source concludes that "there is widespread agreement that new financial models to support these therapies will require levels of innovation and stakeholder alignment that have not been tried previously . . . the full range of issues associated with development, production, distribution, administration, and patient monitoring could still deter many companies from advancing promising early stage research and limit their access to capital."[87]

In this example, we have the bitter spot of failure of private R&D: a scale too large to be financed by VCs, and the only potential solution involves incorporating the spillovers from all firms' R&D efforts.

This example of a shortfall in private R&D, despite a high private rate of return, illustrates why there is too little total R&D investment in the United States. What matters is not the private rate of return (what the company makes from its investment) but the *social rate of return:* the economic returns from a given company's investments that incorporate the effects not only on that company but on the economy as a whole.

In the case of cell and gene research and development, that would include the value of a firm's investment in manufacturing capacity not only for their drug but for all the other drugs that might make use of that capacity.

Recent studies have tried to measure the social rate of return. In particular, studies find that an increase in R&D activities by a firm leads directly to more productive R&D by firms that are in a similar technology space. The key idea is that knowledge is transferred between firms when the scientists are exposed to each other—as in the case of Apple learning about graphical user interfaces from their interaction with PARC scientists. These studies confirm that there are enormous spillovers of R&D, with social returns to R&D of more than 50 percent—that is, each dollar invested in R&D yields fifty cents return per year.[88]

If scientific research by one firm has benefits for many others, then it will underinvest relative to what is best for the United States as a whole. RCA, Westinghouse, and Xerox PARC did not put enough money into developing their technology in the past. They considered only the limited return to themselves; the return to the economy as a whole from new ways of displaying images or doing personal computing was not, nor should it have been, part of their decision-making. A similar issue arises with gene and cell therapy development today—small drug companies have no incentive to consider the benefit to other firms from their investment in manufacturing facilities.[89]

. . . AND HEADING IN THE WRONG DIRECTION . . .

There is another problem as well: private R&D is increasingly turning away from basic exploratory scientific research toward more commercially oriented development. Private corporations have always been more focused on product development than basic research, but as of 1987, almost one-third of private R&D was still devoted to basic research. Today, that share has fallen to one-fifth.[90] This means that the private sector is spending less and is less likely to discover the future breakthroughs that will drive economic growth.

The nature of corporate R&D has changed as well, as can be seen by the dramatic decline in publication by company scientists of their research.[91] The publication of basic research was once common and expected for corporate scientists. It led to breakthroughs, like the scanning tunneling microscope that enabled scientists to view the world down to molecules and atoms (invented by two IBM scientists, for which they won the 1986 Nobel Prize in Physics) or the discovery of the cosmic microwave background radiation that provided evidence for the Big Bang (discovered by Bell Labs researchers who won the 1978 Nobel Prize in Physics).[92]

This kind of work has become much less common. Publications in basic research by corporate scientists fell by 60 percent from 1980 to 2006, and the decline continued at least until 2010.[93] This decline is not just because of a shift in economic activity across industries or a lack of start-ups in recent years; it has been the case across all sectors with both new and established firms. Of most concern is that the drop has been most significant for publications considered by experts to be "basic" or "influential."[94]

Perhaps most importantly, the reduction in research appears related to the problem of spillovers discussed earlier. A great way to measure the value of corporate research is by how much it gets cited when firms apply for patents. One important recent study examined how publications by corporate scientists vary based on how valuable it is internally (how much it is cited in their own patents) and how valuable it is externally (how much it is cited by patents of other firms). Unsurprisingly, when research is more valuable internally, more of it gets done. But when rivals cite a firm's research more frequently, then less of it gets done.[95] This is the heart of the difference between private and social returns. Research that benefits other firms is socially valuable, but it will not get done. There is no reason to conduct expensive basic research when it will primarily benefit your competitors.

The results for the corporate production of private research are important. Consider IBM, one of the nation's leading technology companies and a traditional producer of significant research (including the Nobel Prize–winning work cited earlier). Perhaps responding to exactly these pressures, IBM changed its reward system for scientists in 1989, explicitly rewarding scientists for patenting (as opposed to publications). This resulted in a large increase in patenting and a decline in disclosed research by IBM scientists.[96]

. . . WHILE IDEAS ARE GETTING HARDER TO FIND

The wonderful thing about pushing on the research frontier is that the potential for new ideas is essentially endless. Science constantly advances in ways that appear inconceivable from the perspective of the past. In just 150 years, Jules Verne's predictions of electric submarines, video-conferencing, and skywriting, among others, moved from the realm of science fiction to reality.[97] Unfortunately, while the scientific frontier remains vast, the cost of new discoveries is becoming ever-more expensive.

One much-discussed example is what is known as Moore's law, a rule of thumb invented by Gordon Moore, a key figure in the early years of the transistor industry.[98] While publicly funded research and government purchases—particularly for rockets—were important catalysts in the early development of the transistor business, private enterprise subsequently drove a great deal of innovation. In 1965, Gordon Moore predicted that the number of transistors packed onto a computer chip would double approximately every two years. He has proven (roughly) right for half a century.[99] However, the cost of achieving this remarkable progress continues to grow, in the sense that a steadily increasing number of researchers are needed to push Moore's law forward.

The number of researchers required in order to double chip density today is more than eighteen times the number who were needed in the early 1970s. In other words, more and more money needs to be spent just to maintain the same rate of productivity growth over time.

This phenomenon is apparent not just with transistors; an increasing number of researchers work on improving agricultural crop yields, yet the rate of increase in yields is slowing over time. The productivity of research in this area is estimated to be declining by about 6 percent per year.

Improvements in health from new drug discovery similarly require an increasing amount of research and development. Comparing deaths averted due to timely treatment of breast cancer, for example, to the number of relevant research studies, productivity is declining by 7 percent per year.

If we want to continue to grow as a country, we need to increase our investments in discovery. Due to the types of market failures outlined earlier, it is far from clear whether private corporations and our venture capital financing system will be sufficient for what comes next.

THE PROMISE AND LIMITS OF PRIVATE R&D

Research and development conducted by private companies in the United States has grown enormously over the past four decades. We have substantially replaced the publicly funded science that drove our growth after World War II with private research efforts. Such private R&D has shown some impressive results, including high average returns for the corporate sector.

However, despite their enormous impact, these private R&D investments are much too small from a broader perspective. This is not a criticism of any individuals; rather, it is simply a feature of the system. Private companies do not capture the spillovers that their R&D efforts create for other corporations, so private sector executives in established firms underinvest in invention. The venture capital industry, which provides admirable support to some start-ups, is focused on fast-impact industries, such as information technology, and not generally on longer-run and capital-intensive investments like clean energy or new cell and gene therapies.

Leading entrepreneur-philanthropists get this. In recent years, there have been impressive investments in science funded by publicly minded individuals, including Eric Schmidt, Elon Musk, Paul Allen, Bill and Melinda Gates, Mark Zuckerberg, Michael Bloomberg, Jon Meade Huntsman Sr., Eli and Edythe Broad, David H. Koch, Laurene Powell Jobs, and others (including numerous private foundations). The good news is that these people, with a wide variety of political views on other matters, share the assessment that science—including basic research—is of fundamental importance for the future of the United States.

The less good news is that even the wealthiest people on the planet can barely move the needle relative to what the United States previously invested in science. America is, roughly speaking, a $20 trillion economy; 2 percent of our GDP is nearly $400 billion *per year*. Even the richest person in the world has a total stock of wealth of only around $100 billion—a mark broken in early 2018 by Jeff Bezos of Amazon, with Bill Gates and Warren Buffett in close pursuit. If the richest Americans put much of their wealth immediately into science, it would have some impact for a few years, but over the longer run, this would hardly move the needle. Publicly funded investment in research and development is the only approach that could potentially return us to the days when technology-led growth lifted all boats.

However, we should be careful. Private failure is not enough to justify government intervention. Just because the private sector is under-investing does not necessarily imply that the government will make the right investments. What evidence do we have that public R&D can actually fill the gaps we described in this chapter—and as a result deliver higher growth and better jobs to the United States?

5

Public R&D:

Pushing Frontiers and Promoting Growth

[Decoding the human genome sequence] is the most significant undertaking that we have mounted so far in an organized way in all of science. I believe that reading our blueprints, cataloguing our own instruction book, will be judged by history as more significant than even splitting the atom or going to the moon.

> —Francis S. Collins, director of the National Institutes of Health, 1998[1]

IN *SCIENCE: THE ENDLESS FRONTIER,* VANNEVAR BUSH AND COLLEAGUES ARGUED THAT THE possibilities for scientific discovery were literally without limit. The decades since that report appear to have validated his vision. From early work on radar, we have moved to computers and the internet, with innovations in artificial intelligence on the horizon. From early work on penicillin, we have moved to a suite of lifesaving and life-improving drugs, turning most recently to genetically targeted drugs that can extend life even further.

But the fact that the frontier is endless does not mean that it is easy to get there. The cost of exploring the frontier is increasing, and there are strong theoretical and real-world reasons why the private sector will fall short of reaching that frontier. Private companies do not have an incentive to do the path-breaking research that moves the frontier forward for others. Private financiers are not structured to provide the large financial commitments required to innovate in capital-intensive areas like clean energy.

In the decades after World War II, the public sector filled this gap. Public financing of research resulted in scientific breakthroughs that transformed the world while they simultaneously powered US economic growth and created broad opportunities for the American middle class. US economic growth—measured as the increase in GDP per capita—from World War II through the start of the 1970s was around 2.5 percent per year, and the benefits were shared equally throughout the income distribution. Since the late 1960s, a declining public sector role in R&D has coincided with a slowdown in productivity growth and a stagnating standard of living for most Americans. Since 1973, growth in GDP per capita has averaged only about 1.7 percent per year—and the vast majority of those benefits have accrued only to those at the top of the income distribution.

Can a return to a bigger public-sector role in the research-and-development process return us to a higher-productivity path—and create broad-based economic growth and a dynamic job market in the process? In this chapter, we present a variety of evidence, ranging from innovative economic studies to compelling examples, to suggest that the answer is an emphatic *yes*. Scaling up publicly financed science can jump-start the growth engine that powered the postwar US economy, including, crucially, wide participation in the benefits of that growth. There is no better way to see this than with one of the most important public research efforts of the past thirty years: the Human Genome Project.

THE HUMAN GENOME PROJECT

DNA, deoxyribonucleic acid, is passed from adult organisms to their offspring during reproduction and contains all the instructions needed for an organism to develop, survive, and reproduce.[2] Researchers refer to DNA found in the cell's nucleus as *nuclear DNA,* and an organism's complete set of nuclear DNA is called its *genome.*[3]

DNA is made of chemical building blocks called *nucleotides,* which in turn are made of a phosphate group, a sugar group, and one of four types of nitrogen bases: adenine (A), thymine (T), guanine (G), and cytosine (C). The order, or sequence, of these bases determines what biological instructions are contained in a strand of DNA. For example, the sequence ATCGTT might instruct for blue eyes, while ATCGCT might instruct for brown.[4] Sequencing DNA means determining the order—or sequence—of the four bases that make up the DNA molecule.[5] The human genome is made up of over three billion of these genetic combinations, and the sequence tells scientists the kind of genetic information that is carried in a particular DNA segment.[6]

DNA sequencing was developed in the mid-1970s, separately by Frederick Sanger and Walter Gilbert (who later shared the 1980 Nobel Prize in Chemistry for their work); the method developed by Sanger, who was working at the Laboratory of Molecular Biology in Cambridge, UK, on a government-funded research project, became the more widely used approach.[7] Sanger's method involved isolating DNA from a cell and then using that as a template to make copies and eventually figure out the sequence of that DNA. This was a laborious and repetitive process that involved mixing the DNA with other chemicals many times to create a test tube full of different-length DNA strands, then running an electric current through the mixture to separate DNA strands, then "reading" the resulting strands like a multiple-choice answer sheet.[8]

Despite the hard work involved, the results were nothing short of miraculous. Now that scientists had a way to read DNA in normal cells, they could use the same technique to identify *changes* in genes associated with diseases. Discoveries started rolling in, from the discovery of the Huntington's disease gene in 1983 to the gene responsible for cystic fibrosis in 1989. The discovery of these defects raised the tantalizing possibility of potentially making new drugs that target those changes or the faulty molecules they produce.[9]

Sparked by such discoveries, scientists started raising the idea of sequencing all the genes in the human body. The problem was that Sanger's manual method was so time-consuming that sequencing the entire human genome would take over a hundred years.[10] Many scientists thought that the possible discoveries were not worth the time needed to sequence the DNA.

Kathy Weston, researcher at Cancer Research UK around the same time as Sanger, stated, "Many thought 'that's completely stupid'. They didn't think there was anything more they could learn."[11] However, developments in the late 1980s, most notably the introduction of automatic sequencers, which mechanized the repetitive aspects of the sequencing, started to bring down the costs of this enterprise.

The private sector was not initially eager to pursue this project. Walter Gilbert was a Harvard professor, winner of the Nobel Prize for his work on genome sequencing, and a founder of Biogen, an early successful biotechnology company. In 1987, Gilbert announced he would launch a new biotech venture, the Genome Corporation, whose sole purpose would be to "read" the human genome and sell the information it deciphered. "The total human sequence is the grail of human genetics," he declared.[12]

Gilbert aimed to get $10 million in initial funding to get his company going but was unable to line up any financial backing in the first year. Skeptics of the company questioned the economic basis for such a company. They pointed out that once a physical map is in hand a few years from now, anyone wishing to know a particular gene sequence could do the job himself—a restatement of the spillover problem that leads to insufficient private R&D. The venture never took off, and the company folded by 1988.[13]

That might have been the end of the story had the scientific community not managed to convince the US federal government to make this a priority. Starting in 1988, Congress agreed to fund the National Institutes of Health (NIH) for research on the human genome.[14] James Watson, who had won a Nobel Prize for his work on discovering the structure of DNA, became the director of the new National Center for Human Genome Research (NCHGR). The collective effort of the

NIH, NCHGR, the Department of Energy, and their international partners constituted the Human Genome Project.[15] The project officially began in 1990 and was predicted to last fifteen years, with a total cost of $3 billion.

The story of the Human Genome Project (HGP) over the next decade illustrates how research advances in fits and starts. On paper, progress was slow; by February 1999, less than 15 percent of the genome had been sequenced.[16] In fact, the underlying technology for faster and faster automation of sequencing was being developed in the background, spurred on by this government effort.[17]

Some of these developments were made at public research institutions, such as the development of the colony picker—which combined a robot arm with a coupled video device for imaging—at Lawrence Berkeley National Laboratory, and the development of the Base-Finder program, which efficiently processed the vast data collected, at the University of Wisconsin. Other developments came from private companies, such as developments in automatic sequencing by Applied Biosystems.

Most notable among these private companies was Celera, founded by Dr. Craig Venter, formerly a section chief at the NIH. Celera began a competing effort to sequence the human genome in 1999. Leading experts claim that Venter's method would not have succeeded on such a large scale without all the preliminary work done by the HGP—that is, the mapping that was already in the public domain by the late 1990s gave Venter's method the leg up it needed to succeed.[18] But Celera succeeded in putting pressure on the public-sector-led HGP to complete its own preliminary map of the genome in 2003, two years ahead of schedule.[19]

The $3 billion federal investment in the HGP has paid off in an impressive manner. By 2004, the total stock market value of the genomics sector was $28 billion, and most of these firms—75 percent of those publicly traded and 62 percent of ones privately held—were in the United States.[20]

The Battelle Technology Partnership Practice found that economic activity associated with human genome sequencing between 1988 and

2012 amounted, directly and indirectly, to $965 billion. Even counting the federal government's ongoing investments in HGP-related research since 2003, this yields a ratio of economic impact to government spending of 65:1. In 2012 alone, the direct and indirect impact of human genome sequencing created 280,000 jobs and $19 billion in personal income (an average of almost $70,000 per job).[21]

Another way to put it: the genomics-enabled industry sector generated and stimulated nearly $3.9 billion in federal taxes and $2.1 billion in US state and local taxes in 2012. Thus in one year, revenues returned to governments equaled the entire thirteen-year investment in the HGP.[22]

The benefits of the HGP investment do not stop with pharmaceuticals; the spillover effects are much broader. Agriculture and global food security are being significantly enhanced through the application of genomics to plant and livestock improvement—for example, through identifying the right inputs (e.g., nutrient uptake or pest resistance) and outputs (e.g., chemical composition).[23] Genomics is also being applied in the tracing of food contamination and associated pathogenic events. Likewise, commercial enterprises across a series of product categories in biotechnology, biofuels, food processing, drug and vitamin production, and bio-based materials are applying advanced genomic knowledge and technologies to bring to market new and more efficient industrial processes to power the US and global economies.[24] The NIH estimates that the HGP produced nearly $1 trillion in economic growth at the cost of $2 per year per US resident.

THE NIH INNOVATION MACHINE[25]

The Human Genome Project is just one example of the incredible value that has been delivered by public research through the NIH. This government agency has powered the innovations that have dramatically improved the health and length of life of all Americans.

The NIH is the single largest public funder of biomedical research in the world, supplying $37 billion a year in research funding. This accounts for roughly one-quarter of all medical research spending in the

United States.[26] Over 80 percent of the agency's funding is awarded through some fifty thousand competitive grants to three hundred thousand researchers at twenty-five hundred research institutions. The agency also spends approximately 10 percent of its budget on research in its own labs, supplying funding to another six thousand researchers.[27]

The NIH has been largely protected from the vicissitudes of funding that marked many of the other agencies in the history of public R&D in the United States. Agency funding grew rapidly until the late 1960s, fell slightly in the early 1970s, but then grew steadily until the late 2000s; for example, while Department of Defense spending in 2010, as a share of GDP, was only 60 percent of its 1967 value, NIH spending as a share of GDP was 80 percent higher than in 1967. But even the NIH couldn't avoid the large budget cuts of recent years, with funding falling as a share of GDP by about 15 percent from 2010 to 2017. Moreover, the successes of the NIH, along with the ever-increasing costs of discovery in the medical sector discussed in Chapter 4, suggest that funding should be rising even faster.

NIH funding has consistently created both broad and successful research. Organizationally, the agency comprises twenty-seven centers and institutes, ranging from the National Cancer Institute (oldest) to the National Center for Advancing Translational Sciences (newest). Funding from these centers and institutes has supported 153 Nobel laureates and 195 Lasker awardees.[28] In 2016, 115,000 articles acknowledged NIH support. Each R01 grant (the typical investigator-led research proposal) produces 7.36 published research articles on average, and each such article receives 300 citations on average.[29]

Knowledge from this research spreads well beyond the scientific community. For example, NIH funding contributed to research underlying all 210 new drugs approved by the Food and Drug Administration (FDA) between 2010 and 2016. Researchers at MIT have estimated that each additional $10 million in agency funding generates 2.7 additional private-sector patents. Using estimates of the stock market return to additional patents, this suggests that $10 million in NIH funding yields $30.2 million in more value for private firms on the stock market. This is an enormous return to government funding of research.[30]

Undoubtedly, this research produces massive benefits for the economy. One study estimates that NIH basic research funding for drugs produces a 43 percent return on investment. Agency funding also stimulates private research: a dollar increase in basic research funding leads to an additional $8.38 in industry R&D spending over eight years.[31]

More importantly, NIH-funded research consistently improves health and saves lives. In economic terms, research-related gains in average life expectancy between 1970 and 2000 have had an estimated economic value of $95 trillion in the United States alone. To give an example, cancer death rates have dropped by more than 1.5 percent annually for the last fifteen years. Every 1 percent reduction in cancer deaths has a net present value of $500 billion to current and future Americans.[32]

Success stories from public health research funding are not hard to come by. In many cases, NIH-supported research has fundamentally changed our understanding of diseases and options for treatment. For example, the Framingham Heart Study offered many of the early insights into the preventable causes of cardiovascular disease. It began in 1948 as an epidemiological study with five thousand participants in the town of Framingham, Massachusetts. At the time, heart disease would typically only be treated ex post (e.g., after a heart attack). The study was the first to identify cigarette smoking, high blood pressure, high cholesterol, obesity, and diabetes as risk factors associated with heart disease. In doing so, the study demonstrated that preventative measures in medication or lifestyle could significantly improve cardiovascular health. Thanks to this change in approach to treatment, health outcomes associated with cardiovascular disease have improved dramatically. Death rates from heart disease fell 67.5 percent from 1969 to 2013, and associated life expectancy increases between 1970 and 2000 have added $1.6 trillion to national wealth. Seventy years later, the Framingham Heart Study continues and now includes offspring cohorts of children and grandchildren of the original participants.[33]

Other notable medical advances brought forth by NIH research include vaccines that have virtually eliminated diseases. Before a vaccine became available, Haemophilus influenzae type B (Hib) was the leading cause of bacterial meningitis in children. By the mid-1970s, twenty thousand cases of Hib were reported each year, incurring $2 billion in annual medical costs. Over one thousand children died annually from Hib, and thousands more suffered from deafness, seizures, intellectual disability, or brain damage.

In 1968, the NIH funded the first research for developing a Hib vaccine and shortly thereafter funded clinical trials for the vaccine in children. NIH and FDA scientists discovered an improved conjugate vaccine (a vaccine that uses only a specific piece of the germ) in the 1980s, and NIH-funded clinical trials brought the first conjugate vaccine to FDA approval in 1987.[34] Following release of the vaccine, Hib was all but eliminated. Today, Hib incidence is down 99 percent since before vaccines were available. Only forty cases of the disease were reported in the United States in 2009, representing a savings of $3.7 billion in societal costs for the children born that year.[35]

It is important to emphasize that NIH funding leads to new treatments even when the underlying research does not begin with treatments in mind; indeed, more than half of these patents to agency-supported research are for a different disease from the grants they cite.[36] For example, NIH researchers were studying a particular class of enzymes knowns as *Janus kinases* (JAK) when they discovered a mutation in one enzyme that could be used to battle autoimmune disorders. This led to some of the leading treatments in use today to help the 1.5 million Americans with rheumatoid arthritis.[37]

NOT JUST THE NIH: HIGH RETURNS TO MILITARY R&D

The case of the NIH is a compelling one in terms of both economic benefits and improvement in human health. However, health is not the only area where public support for innovation continues to pay huge dividends for economies around the world.

Skepticism abounds regarding the value—for the civilian economy—of military R&D. In the United States, defense-related research and development consistently represents more than half of all government-funded research and development. Tales about wasteful military spending during the Reagan administration became legendary, such as $110 for an electric diode worth $0.04, or $435 for a single claw hammer, or $437 for a measuring tape![38] But what these entertaining anecdotes miss is that alongside this wasteful spending was valuable investment by the Defense Department in research and development.

Recent research by Enrico Moretti, Claudia Steinwender, and John Van Reenen demonstrates this convincingly.[39] They study changes in military R&D across OECD nations over almost a quarter century. They confirm that more public spending increases (crowding in), rather than displacing (crowding out), private research-and-development spending. Each dollar of publicly financed military research-and-development spending leads to $2.50–$5.90 in private R&D. This is a huge effect, showing that—at a minimum—military research is promoting more, not less, private sector innovation—just as is the case for the NIH.

Most importantly for our purposes, they find a large effect on productivity from more research-and-development spending. To put their results in context, they suggest that the rise in US military R&D after 9/11, from 0.45 percent to 0.6 percent of GDP, led to 2 percent faster growth.[40] This is a large effect from a fairly modest change in spending.

In the 1940s and 1950s, there was a positive catalytic effect on the broader economy from military-related research, as we discussed in Chapters 1 and 2. But the benefits continue to this day. Want an illustration? Look at the Roomba currently cleaning floors around the world.

In 1990, three MIT graduates founded iRobot. In 1998, the young company received a research contract from DARPA to develop robots for space exploration and military defense. The resultant PackBot robot was used in Iraq, Afghanistan, and the aftermath of 9/11. But the company's real success came in the nonmilitary sphere, with the release of the Roomba in 2002. The Roomba design came from a robot called Fetch designed in 1997 for the air force.[41] As Colin Angle, the cofounder of iRobot, said, "It was a little weird working on mine-hunting robots and then my next meeting would be about vacuuming. . . . The military business . . . enabled us to learn how to manufacture and sell and distribute these vacuuming robots."[42]

By 2005, the company was trading on the Nasdaq. As of 2012, the company had sold eight million home vacuum robots—compared to five thousand defense/security robots.[43] Ninety percent of revenues for the company come from consumer robots.[44] Currently, the company has sold fifteen million robots and employs one thousand workers in the United States.[45,46] Robot vacuums account for 20 percent of the world-wide vacuum market, and Roomba accounts for 70 percent of robot vacuums.[47] Military R&D paved the way for a successful private sector company that is creating jobs.

PUBLIC FINANCING OF TECHNOLOGY PAYS DIVIDENDS

We have documented the limitations of the VC model and its implications for the US economy. Can the government possibly help? The experience of the Small Business Innovation Research (SBIR) program in the United States, as well as similar programs around the world, suggests that it can.

The SBIR is the largest US federal government spending program supporting private research and development.[48] The SBIR began in 1982 and currently mandates that federal agencies spending more than $100 million annually on external research set aside 3.2 percent of these funds for awards to small businesses. As of 2015, eleven federal agencies participated in the SBIR program, setting aside more than $2 billion each year.

The SBIR program has two phases. Phase I provides grants of $150,000 to fund nine months of proof-of-concept work; phase II awards grants of $1 million two years after phase I to fund later-stage demonstrations. The program is fairly selective, with only about 10 percent of applicants receiving funding. For many small firms, the SBIR "serves as the first place many entrepreneurs involved in technological innovation go to for funding."[49]

Despite its limited budget, the SBIR has been a major success. The SBIR typically supports five to seven times as many early-stage tech start-ups as does private VC, and it has a vigorous and labor-intensive peer-review process that allows for revised proposals, helping early-state technology firms develop their core missions. The SBIR also provides a key signal to the private sector of valuable potential investment in the sectors that venture funds have typically avoided; SBIR winners represent only 3 percent of VC funding recipients in information technology, but 20 percent in life sciences and 10 percent in the energy/industrial sector.[50]

Indeed, the very first SBIR grant recipient was Gary Hendrix, who used the grant to form the software firm Symantec. The SBIR grant allowed Hendrix, who had been the principal investigator of a project at Machine Intelligence Corporation when the company went bankrupt, to continue the project as Symantec. His team was successful, and the project's breakthrough product Q&A would generate $50 million in sales. Hendrix has said that Q&A's development created "the intellectual and commercial pizzaz [sic] to quickly attract $14 million of venture capital and IPO investment along with top-flight people in management, scientists, engineers and marketing." Symantec currently employs over 12,000 employees in over thirty-five countries, of which 6,148 employees were in the Americas (likely most in the United States).[51]

Another notable early success is the telecommunications company Qualcomm, which received funding from SBIR as a start-up with thirty-five employees in 1987—and today has grown to 38,000 employees (of which around 20,000 are in the United States).[52] As cofounder Irwin Jacobs stated before Congress in 2011,

> The value and importance of SBIR funding at a critical point in Qualcomm's earliest days should not be underestimated. Cutting-edge research leads to breakthrough discoveries, but in order for companies to attract private funding, they need support to prove the feasibility of new and often risky and unproven technologies. For Qualcomm, SBIR provided one source of that critical start-up funding. And while it was not the only source of funding for us at the time, it was one of the critical "stamps of approval" that allowed us to successfully pursue sources of private capital.[53]

The success of SBIR is not just confirmed by notable examples but by academic analysis as well.[54] One study found that firms that were awarded grants enjoyed substantially greater employment (a 56 percent increase) and sales growth (a 98 percent boost) than comparable firms that did not win SBIR funding.[55] Another study found that winning a phase I grant led firm patents to rise by at least 30 percent, doubled the chance of receiving VC financing, and doubled the probability of earning positive revenues within two years.[56]

A powerful recent example of the catalytic role of the SBIR is the story of Illumina. Illumina was founded in 1998 to enter into the nascent DNA sequencing market (a market that existed because of the Human Genome Project).[57] As a start-up, Illumina received NIH SBIR funding between 1999 and 2004 to contribute to the development of its genotyping, parallel arrays, and gene expression–profiling technologies—all of which played important roles in Illumina's growth. The SBIR funding was not the only financing received by Illumina, as private VCs also invested in the company. But Dr. Mark Chee, the founder of Illumina, has pointed out that the funding from the NIH SBIR program propelled the development of the company's core technologies at a very early stage, when obtaining funding from private investors would have been difficult.[58] And a case study written for the National Research Council concluded that by "providing flexibility in pursuing projects outside the mainstream of immediate research objectives," SBIR funding "provided a key counter-balance to the tendency to over-focus, which is perhaps inevitable in a small company."[59]

As a result of this SBIR-supported research, Illumina has grown rapidly. As of June 2018, the company has 6,200 employees (of which just under 4,000 are in the United States) and sales of $2.94 billion. It has commercial offices in the United States, Brazil, the UK, Netherlands, China, Singapore, Japan, and Australia.[60]

The SBIR is not alone in government technology programs that have successfully financed new start-ups, but it is relatively unique in its long-run success and sustainability. A natural comparison is with the National Institute of Standards and Technology, an arm of the US Department of Commerce that "works with industry and science to advance innovation and improve quality of life."[61] The NIST was originally established in 1901 to ensure standardization of weights and measures, as well as to be a physical laboratory for the United States; four scientific researchers at the NIST have been awarded Nobel Prizes in Physics for their work on laser coding of atoms.[62]

Over time, the NIST created significant "extramural" programs to promote the translation of science into the economy. The Advanced Technology Partnership (ATP) was introduced in 1981 to increase the competitiveness of US firms by promoting "high risk research with large potential societal and economic benefits."[63] A recent study showed that winning an ATP grant resulted in a higher odds of firm survival fourteen to sixteen years later.[64] Despite this success, the ATP program and a successor NIST program were killed by Congress, and the most recent budget proposal from the Trump administration proposed to cut the NIST itself by 34 percent.[65]

INVESTMENTS THAT LIFT ALL BOATS, NOT JUST THE YACHTS

Today's economic debate in the United States isn't focused only on growth but also on jobs. And the jobs debate raises a major concern with our discussion so far: that faster technological progress will simply mean a quicker path to robots taking our jobs. Will we end up with the *Player Piano* economy envisioned by Kurt Vonnegut, with a few highly skilled employees and everyone else replaced by higher-tech machines?

As we discussed in Chapter 1, this concern turned out to be unfounded in the years after World War II. Rising demand for skills was met by a rapid increase in skilled workers, and the whole economy benefited. In 1947, the typical American family earned $28,491 in 2016 terms. By 1973, this had roughly doubled to $58,539—that is, as the size of the economy increased, the amount earned by the typical family doubled.[66] Real family incomes grew at the same roughly 2.5 percent that the economy (in terms of GDP per capita) grew. The rising tide of productivity-led growth raised all boats—everyone benefited.

And when everyone benefits, inequality falls. In 1947, the richest 20 percent of Americans had 8.5 times as much income as the poorest 20 percent. By 1973, that ratio of top 20 percent to bottom 20 percent had fallen to 7.5.[67]

But over the past forty years, economic growth has become divorced from job creation. The gains from growth have been increasingly focused on a small share of our highest-income earners, and real median household income has stagnated.

By 2016, median family incomes had grown to only $65,063, a 20 percent increase from what it was in 1973[68]—that is, from 1973 to 2018, while average GDP per capita was growing at 1.7 percent per year, real family incomes were growing at 0.4 percent per year! So while the typical family saw 100 percent of the growth (in GDP per capita) before 1973, they have seen only about 25 percent of the growth since then.

Moreover, since the early 1970s, growth in incomes has diverged radically across income groups, with rapidly rising incomes at the top and stagnating incomes for everyone else. This has led to a striking widening in the distribution of incomes. As noted earlier, in 1973, the top 20 percent of Americans had 7.5 times as much income as the bottom 20 percent. By 2016, this gap had risen to 13.3 times—that is, the richest 20 percent of Americans have $13.30 for every dollar that the poorest 20 percent have.[69]

Focusing on the top 20 percent doesn't do justice to the extremes of income inequality growth. The top 1 percent of Americans have seen an even more dramatic turn in their fortunes. From 1945 to 1973, the share of incomes earned by the top 1 percent of Americans fell from 12.5 percent to 9 percent. From 1973 to 2015, the share earned by the top 1 percent rose from 9.5 percent to over 22 percent.[70] From 1993 to 2015, more than half of all the income growth in the United States went to the top 1 percent of the income distribution[71]—that is, if you took all of the growth in US incomes over that entire period, you could divide it into two piles: a slightly larger one going to the top 1 percent of all Americans, and a slightly smaller one going to the other 99 percent.

A boost in public financing of research and development can create jobs not only for PhD scientists but for a much broader swath of Americans—just as was the case with aerospace, electronics, and other industries built on the back of publicly funded research after World War II. Higher productivity doesn't just raise wages for skilled workers but also for all of the less-skilled workers who provide the backbone of the local economy. Recent research has shown that having more highly educated and more productive workers helps everyone; for every 1 percent increase in the productivity of the workforce in a city, the wages of highly skilled workers rise 0.6 percent—and the wages of less-skilled workers rise 1.2 percent![72]

Consider the case of gene and cell therapy discussed in Chapter 4. One bottleneck to further development of this industry is a lack of qualified workers.[73] Solving this bottleneck means making jobs for Americans with specialized skills, but not necessarily a postgraduate or even a bachelor's degree. One industry source reports that "the evidence suggests that . . . [employers] will create an increasing number of specialist manufacturing roles . . . best filled by specialist technicians (that is, by skilled workers who are qualified to below degree level)."[74] Indeed, the Bureau of Labor Statistics projects that the number of jobs for medical and clinical lab technologists and technicians in the United States will grow by 13 percent between 2016 and 2026 (nearly twice the national average of 7 percent), adding 42,700 jobs in the process. These jobs had a median salary of $51,770 in 2017 (37 percent more than the national median) and typically require a professional certificate, associate's degree, or bachelor's degree, depending on the level of skill required.[75]

PUBLIC RESEARCH FUNDING AND JOBS: THE EVIDENCE

The notion that more public research funding will lead to more good jobs is not just a conjecture—it is supported by solid evidence from both the United States and around the world.

A great example of this phenomenon comes from looking at what happened around US universities, which have been the hubs of innovation in the modern knowledge economy. Some of the most successful cities in the United States have emerged around some of our nation's leading educational institutions, such as MIT and Harvard in Cambridge, and Berkeley and Stanford just outside of San Francisco. But the benefits of publicly financed universities are not limited to this small set of cities. National studies show that more university research spending leads to more factory operations locating in the same county as the university and to more jobs in nearby areas.[76]

A particularly interesting study looked at what happened to the local economy when universities were given a financial incentive to commercialize the innovations coming out of their research spending. The Bayh-Dole Act of 1980 gave universities the property rights to innovations developed under federal funding, allowing the universities to benefit from the value of companies developed by their faculty from federal grants. There was a significant rise in university patenting after the Bayh-Dole Act; while only 55 universities had been granted a patent in 1976, 340 universities had been granted at least one patent by 2006.[77]

This study showed that after the Bayh-Dole Act, there was strong economic growth around universities in the very industries that were related to that university's research strength. For example, the University of Texas at Austin had strong electrical engineering and computer science departments before Bayh-Dole and then saw particularly strong growth in those industries after Bayh-Dole. More generally, the study finds that one additional university patent led to a permanent rise in employment of fifteen people.

To confirm that this is not just a peculiarity of a particular study, we looked at data ourselves. In particular, the National Science Foundation collects data each year on public research funding to every university in the United States. We used these data to match universities to the employment and payroll of firms in the same counties as those universities, and we looked at what happens to jobs and pay when the federal government sends more research dollars to universities in a specific county.[78] The results are striking: doubling the amount of university research spending is associated with 1 percent more employment in that county.[79]

Further confirmation that public R&D can create good jobs comes from other countries. The New Zealand government has a program that provides public grants to innovative start-up firms, much like the SBIR (but with actually giving money to the companies rather than loaning it). A study of this program found that among those firms that receive public grant funding, employment growth is 6 percent faster over the next four years than comparable firms that did not receive funding.[80]

One of the most innovative government support programs for R&D in the world is the Finnish Tekes program. Finland differs from the United States in devoting much of its public funding to providing direct R&D subsidies to companies through Tekes. These subsidies generally cover 35–50 percent of the cost of an R&D project and are provided competitively based on factors such as technological promise and collaboration with other firms. A recent study used regional variation in the funding of firms through Tekes to show that those firms that received funding saw much larger increases in employment, with receipt of a grant leading to an 85 percent rise in employment among the mostly small firms receiving these grants. This result is confirmed by another study finding Tekes grants leading to more rapid productivity growth among small- and medium-sized firms.[81]

The study of military research and development across countries discussed earlier also shows that such spending not only creates growth but also increases jobs. In particular, the authors find that a rise in military R&D of $570,000 leads to 270 more jobs outside of research and development itself.

Taken together, we have painted a rosy picture of public research funding as an investment for the United States and around the world. Compelling case studies and many academic analyses suggest that investing in public R&D will benefit our economy. But before rushing headlong into more public investment, two potential limitations are important to note.

THE LOCALIZED BENEFITS OF PUBLIC INVESTMENTS

As highlighted earlier, a major source of social returns that are higher than private returns is the spillover of technological innovations to other sectors. One really interesting finding from this set of studies is that spillovers are *very local*—that is, despite the growing ease of international business, R&D done in one place still appears to benefit other firms in that same place.[82] Some argue that the localization of R&D spillovers is actually increasing over time.[83]

Evidence for the local benefits of university research are particularly striking. In one study, the authors examined the citations included in patent applications and focused in particular on citations to university-based research (including university patents).[84] They found that citations to university research decline sharply as the patent application is filed farther and farther from universities—that is, research coming from universities doesn't disseminate equally worldwide or even countrywide. Rather, research disseminates more rapidly to local companies.

Another important study considered the birth of the biotechnology field, the driver of pharmaceutical innovation in the United States and around the world.[85] This study noted that biotechnology research was being carried out well before the discovery of the basic technique for recombinant DNA in 1973, the foundation for commercial applications of that research. The authors then showed that the places where scientists were doing biotechnology research before commercialization became exactly the places where the new commercial biotechnology sector took off—and where it remains strongest. That is, even though recombinant DNA was a nationally known discovery, it turned into a leading industry only in places where that specific scientific expertise was already established.

This local concentration may be due to more frequent face-to-face interactions between the university researchers and local companies, and as a result, the spillovers of this university research in terms of generating new businesses is fairly localized.[86] Indeed, one study found that university spin-offs are more likely when there is more of a presence of local venture funders.[87]

A terrific case study of this phenomenon involves the location of a proposed large new science center in the UK in 2007.[88] The Diamond Light Source is a synchrotron facility, a circular particle accelerator that produces beams of x-rays, infrared, and ultraviolet light. Such synchrotron light is useful to study small objects, such as molecules and atoms, whose visualization requires light with shorter wavelengths than those available in microscopes. This facility was to cost £380 million, representing the single largest investment in research infrastructure in the modern history of the UK. It was funded primarily by the UK government.

The big question was where to put the Diamond Light Source. The initial plan was to place it near Manchester, where the existing outdated synchrotron was located. However, one of the funders, the Wellcome Trust, suggested that it be built instead in Oxfordshire, 160 miles away, where it could benefit from colocation with Oxford University–based science units. After much controversy, that argument won the day, and the facility was built in Oxfordshire.

The impacts on the locus of research activity were immediate. There was a similar amount of synchrotron-related research in both locations before the plans for the new facility were announced in 2003. Yet after that point, and particularly after the facility opened in 2007, the number of articles related to synchrotron-related research authored by Oxford-based academics grew rapidly, while there was only a moderate increase in research by Manchester-based academics.

So the location of research funding matters. Unfortunately, when it comes to geographic disparities in the United States, government research funding is currently part of the problem, not part of the solution.

One-quarter of federal government R&D spending per capita in 2015 went to two states (Maryland and New Mexico). Five states had more than 5 percent each of public R&D spending per capita (Alabama, Maryland, Massachusetts, New Mexico, and Virginia), while the bottom ten states *combined* had only 4.4 percent of public research spending per capita.

Things were not very different in 1975. In that year, once again, one-quarter of R&D spending went to Maryland and New Mexico. Once again, five states had more than 5 percent of public R&D spending per capita, although the list was somewhat different (Alabama and Virginia being replaced by California and Washington). And once again, the bottom ten states received a tiny share of spending (only 3.5 percent).

Given this distribution, the prospect of simply increasing R&D with no locational restrictions is not likely to be very appealing to the majority of US voters. For example, a $100 billion increase in public spending is $370 per capita in the United States—that is, if the public research funding were distributed equally across states per capita, each state would get $370 for each person in the state. But if instead these dollars were distributed in the same way as existing per capita research spending, this would mean, for example, that the state of Maryland would get $3,150 per resident, the state of New Mexico would get $1,900 per resident, and the state of Massachusetts would get $1,000 per resident. At the same time, Arkansas, Louisiana, Kansas, Kentucky, and South Dakota would all get less than $100 per resident. Taken together, only twelve states would actually take home more than $370 per resident, despite the fact that this is the average for the nation.

PUBLIC R&D IS RISKY—SO FAILURES MUST BE TOLERATED

We have argued that public R&D is a great investment, with huge returns for human health and for the economy. But this is still a risky investment. One study we cited earlier found that there was one patent per two or three NIH studies. So even at its most productive, the typical NIH study will not yield a patent. This is once again a reminder that research and development is a process that does not yield a constant stream of winners but rather a process whereby numerous tries are needed, but when you do hit a winner, it is very valuable. Indeed, the study of the success of SBIR found that the results were driven by the top one-third of the distribution of firms—that is, while many firms got the awards, it was a relatively small subset that showed large benefits.

The goal for publicly funded research is not to have every investment pay out. Rather, the objective should be for the winners to be so successful that overall, the portfolio is highly productive. The problem is that our political debate provides too many opportunities to jump on failures without seeing the big-picture path toward success. The example of Solyndra provides a cautionary tale.

In February 2009, President Obama signed into a law the American Recovery and Reinvestment Act. This law involved about $800 billion in stimulus to help the economy recover from its most significant downturn since the Great Depression. A major target of funding as part of the ARRA was spending on energy efficiency and renewable energy research. The purpose was stimulating the growth of a clean energy sector in the United States to provide jobs in the short term and develop new technologies to combat global warming over the longer term.

As part of this program, the government funded nearly forty new energy projects at a cost of $36 billion.[89] It is too early to fully assess the success of the program, but the progress to date is excellent. So far, borrowers have defaulted on only 2.3 percent of the funds granted as part of the project, and of all the new firms set up as part of the initiative, only 8 percent have gone bankrupt.[90] There are numerous success stories from this financing, such as NRG Solar and MidAmerican Renewables' Agua Caliente photovoltaic solar plant. This project received a $967 million loan guarantee to complete the facility. The power produced by this solar plant can support the energy needs of 230,000 homes at peak capacity and is being sold to Pacific Gas and Electric under a twenty-five-year contract.[91] Over this twenty-five years, this zero-carbon power will avoid the release of 5.5 million metric tons of carbon into the atmosphere, the equivalent of taking forty thousand cars off the road annually.[92] More generally, the first five large solar projects in the United States were funded under this initiative; these projects had been unable to raise sufficient private financing.[93]

But the political focus was all on a failure: Solyndra. This company manufactured thin-film solar cells and was based in Fremont, California. Solyndra had an innovative plan to create new solar panels made out of cylindrical tubes rather than the traditional flat panels, which (the company claimed) allowed the panels to capture significantly more electricity in a given year and did not have to move to track the sun.[94] Solyndra was the first recipient under the ARRA clean energy initiative, receiving a $535 million loan guarantee that it used to build a $750 million factory. It was widely touted as a success story by the administration—but it turned out to be an enormous failure.[95]

This was partly due to factors outside Solyndra's control: there was a massive reduction in the price of silicon that made it impossible to compete with traditionally produced solar panels.[96] And it was partly due to false claims by Solyndra; in 2009, the company told the government that they had firm contracts to sell $2.2 billion worth of solar panels over the next five years, but in reality, those deals were not confirmed. In any case, Solyndra eventually filed for bankruptcy and defaulted on its loans.[97]

This failure was a major focal point of debate over this clean energy initiative. As Fred Upton, Republican from Michigan and Chairman of the House Energy Committee, stated, "Solyndra will be remembered in the history books as a sad hallmark of a newly installed administration that felt it was above the rules, lusting for positive headlines rather than focused on delivering results."[98]

But what was not featured as part of the debate was the fact that the investment in Solyndra represented only 1.5 percent of the total amount invested in this initiative—and that the bulk of the investment was performing well. This overall good news was dominated by the bad news about Solyndra. As one sector analyst said, "Solyndra is a black eye for the program, and that means bad things for the solar industry in the United States."[99]

These types of failures have led to excessive conservatism in US government support for solar energy development. As one expert report concluded, the very low rate of default on government loans for solar technology development suggests that the federal government has been too conservative with these loans. Moreover, existing loans are focused on large-scale projects that are well on their way to success rather than pilot-scale facilities that are most likely to lead to new knowledge generation—but which are also riskier.[100]

The concern about failure is not just manifested in the energy arena. Two public agencies that funded cutting-edge research in the past now seem less willing to take big risks. One review found that NIH grants in recent years are scored much more based on "doability" than on innovation; at the time a grant proposal is submitted, it is typical for two of the three objectives to have been completed.[101] As Nobel laureate Roger Kornberg states, "If the work that you propose isn't virtually certain of success, then it won't be funded."[102]

This conservative view of research risks is even extending to an agency charged with taking big risks, DARPA, which has in recent years shifted to funding research that is near term and less risky.[103] As Don Ingber, a professor of pathology at Harvard, states, "DARPA seems to be shifting to the NIH model—more near-term, more risk-averse."[104]

Successful scientific endeavors involve failure. Recall that the typical venture investment fails; venture capitalists earn the vast majority of their returns on a small share of their investments. If we want the public sector to promote innovation, we cannot hold it to a standard that is so much higher than we do with the private sector. If failure is not an acceptable option, then risks will not be taken. And if risks are not taken, then bold successes will be impossible.

THE PRAGMATIC CASE FOR PUBLIC R&D

The evidence clearly demonstrates the economic benefits of public funding of research and development. It complements and encourages, rather than replaces, private efforts; studies from the United States and throughout the world show that more public financing of research leads to more private R&D, not less.[105] Public funding of research and development leads to more innovation, faster growth, and more jobs.

But public funding of research has not fully delivered on its promise. In particular, spending on public R&D has not fully recognized the gains from local coordination between university researchers and a burgeoning private sector to create economic growth. And to the extent that public spending has been targeted, it has been to those areas of the country that are already doing very well. It's time to improve the model.

6

America:

Lands of Opportunity

We want to find a city that is excited to work with us and where our customers, employees, and the community can all benefit.

—Amazon, official statement on the webpage that announced 20 finalists (out of 238 applicants) in the competition to become the location for its HQ2[1]

AMERICA IS OFTEN CALLED "THE LAND OF OPPORTUNITY," BUT IN RECENT DECADES, THE OPPORtunities have been shrinking—in a geographical sense—as we increasingly rely on a small set of superstar cities located on the coasts to drive our innovation economy. Meanwhile, much of the rest of the country has missed out, as people are unable to move to these economic epicenters because of limited high-priced housing. This lack of mobility has reinforced our nation's divided politics, specifically the splits across regions and also between large cities and smaller towns or rural areas.

America does not have to rely on a small set of superstar cities for growth. There are opportunities for rapid growth around the country that are just waiting to be tapped. Cities outside the superstar centers on the coasts have excellent educational institutions, talented populations, and a high quality of life. They are ready to take their place as growth engines driving the technology-based economy of the future.

Unfortunately, the path to widespread economic opportunity is blocked by the allocation of the public and private infrastructure of research and development. The continued targeting of both early-stage investment dollars from the private sector and of basic research from the federal government to the superstar cities simply reinforce the on-going regional inequity. States are trying to resist these trends through the kinds of tax breaks that Amazon was offered in its recent competition to determine the location of its second headquarters, but that just leads to a race to the bottom, where corporations win and US taxpayers lose.

There is a better way. The federal government has a long history of undertaking place-based policies that target areas around the nation, beginning with support provided to various locations as the frontier moved westward during the nineteenth century. Other contributions include the land-grant colleges that created the modern US educational system, the Tennessee Valley Authority that modernized a large area in the Southern United States, and the distribution of military bases around the nation, which helped share the benefits of the postwar boom.

It's time to update this thinking and apply it to an expansion of research and development that will keep the United States at the forefront of the modern world economy.

SUPERSTAR CITIES PULLING AWAY

While overall rates of growth have slowed in the United States, a set of superstar cities is thriving—and pulling away from the rest of the country.

To see this, we can look at the numbers on average earnings per worker across metropolitan statistical areas (MSAs) in the 48 contiguous US states in 1980 and 2016.[2] These MSAs pick up what is happening in both cities and in their surrounding suburban areas.[3] Using public

RANK	1980			2016		
	Metropolitan Statistical Area (MSA)	State	Average Earnings	Metropolitan Statistical Area (MSA)	State	Average Earnings
1	Bridgeport-Stamford-Norwalk	CT	$54,194	Bridgeport-Stamford-Norwalk	CT	$83,470
2	Flint	MI	$53,463	San Jose–Sunnyvale– Santa Clara	CA	$81,541
3	Detroit-Warren-Dearborn	MI	$53,290	San Francisco–Oakland-Heyward	CA	$76,697
4	Midland	MI	$51,043	Washington-Arlington-Alexandria	DC-MD-VA	$69,890
5	Washington-Arlington-Alexandria	DC-MD-VA	$50,093	Seattle-Tacoma-Bellevue	WA	$65,580
6	Saginaw	MI	$49,469	Boston-Cambridge-Newton	MA	$65,131
7	Midland	TX	$49,319	Trenton	NJ	$64,939
8	Casper	WY	$49,310	New York–Newark–Jersey City	NY-NJ-PA	$64,055
9	Monroe	MI	$49,107	Boulder	CO	$61,161
10	Bremerton-Silverdale	WA	$48,987	Baltimore-Columbia-Towson	MD	$60,418

survey data, we have created a list for both 1980 and 2016 of superstar cities, which we define as the top ten mainland urban areas with highest earnings per worker.

In 1980, five of the top ten MSAs were in Michigan, and a sixth was Casper, Wyoming. These were MSAs whose income derived primarily from manufacturing and natural resource extraction. By 2016, the top ten included Boston, New York, San Francisco, San Jose, and Seattle, which were outside the top ten in 1980; Boston and New York weren't even in the top twenty in 1980.[4] The good jobs today are in information technology, biotechnology, and financial services. None of those previously star Michigan areas make the top ten list today—indeed, they don't even make the top twenty.

There is also an evident shift in prosperity toward the coasts. In 1980, three of the top ten MSAs were on the East or West Coast; by 2016, nine of the top ten were on the coasts.

In addition, there is a widening disparity of incomes between the most prosperous areas and the rest. In 1980, the top ten cities had 30 percent higher earnings per worker than cities elsewhere in the country. By 2016, the top ten MSAs had earnings that were 57 percent higher than elsewhere.

Disparities are also opening up between the very highest-earning cities and those merely doing very well. Average earnings in the top three cities in 1980 were 8 percent higher than average earnings in the rest of the top ten in that year. Average earnings in the top three cities in 2016 were 25 percent higher than the rest of the top ten in that year.

It is the shift to a knowledge-based economy that appears to be driving income divergence across geographic areas.[5] This process creates greater *agglomeration,* meaning the crowding together of similar or related activities. For example, there are over two thousand tech companies in Silicon Valley, which is the densest concentration in the world.[6] The *Economist* identified ninety-nine listed technology companies with market values of over $1 billion in Silicon Valley, which are together worth $2.8 trillion and account for around 6 percent of all corporate America's profits.[7] As another example, the Boston/Cambridge area is home to about one thousand biotech-related businesses, and Kendall Square has the highest concentration of biotech companies in the world.[8]

Agglomeration in the technology economy arises when more talented workers in an area raise the economic returns to other talented workers who are located nearby.[9] For example, recent research shows that inventors are more productive when there is a higher local density of other inventors in their area.[10] Thereby, places that are able to initially attract talent are able to reward additional talented workers at a higher level, leading to a concentration of talent in certain places—while others fall behind.

Agglomeration arises from a number of economic forces.[11] Firms and individuals can share resources ranging from better public transportation (airports and roads) to higher-quality schools to sports arenas. Having more people living in an area with similar skills makes it easier to find workers whose skills match what firms need—and can also help workers find the kind of opportunity they want (in the job market or even in the dating market). Finally, more interactions with a wider set of skilled individuals means more opportunity for learning.

Surprisingly, the concentration of economic activity in superstar cities doesn't seem to be slowing down. The high cost of living in successful cities, along with the reduction in communication barriers brought about by the internet, should—you might think—lead individuals to move out of those cities and into new locations with lower costs of living. Bogged down by their high costs, existing technology hubs might give way to new growth centers.

In fact, the opposite is happening. The success of technology companies depends critically on the entire economic ecosystem around the company so that it is hard to break away from an existing hub. The geographic divergence we have seen recently in the United States reflects the fact that some areas have succeeded in creating ecosystems that foster growth, attracting more skilled workers, and continuing to grow faster.

Well-performing areas look set to do even better.[12] The cities that have the most college graduates are the ones adding college graduates the fastest. The cities with the highest-earning college graduates are the ones where college graduate earnings have been growing the fastest. The cities with high life expectancy are the cities where life expectancy is growing the fastest. Every day, the American landscape splits further and further between the haves and have-nots.

Recall that this trend has been reinforced in an important way by the government; the locations that have been favored by public research spending are by and large the same superstar areas of the country. Seven of the ten highest-earning MSAs are in states that are in the top ten in terms of per capita public R&D.[13] *None* of the top ten—or even the top twenty—highest-paying MSAs are in states that are in the bottom half of spending on public R&D per capita.

THE RENT IS TOO DAMN HIGH

If some cities are doing so much better than others, then why don't more people move there? The United States is a nation with historically high mobility and a history of strong-willed pioneers striking out for new areas in search of riches. There is no secret regarding where the best opportunities are today. Why isn't everyone in their covered wagon heading to those cities?

After all, US history is replete with boomtowns. In 1850, there were thirty thousand people in Chicago; by 1910, there were more than two million residents. However, today, economic booms no longer necessarily lead to burgeoning urban populations. The metro areas offering the highest pay in 2000, such as San Francisco, Seattle, and Boston, have some of the slowest population growth rates in the country, while individuals have flocked to lower pay and less productive metropolitan areas.[14] New York, San Francisco, and San Jose are today smaller, relative to other cities, than they used to be.[15]

The problem with living in booming cities such as San Francisco is quite obvious—they have the highest cost of living. The list of cities where the cost of living is the highest reads very much like the list of cities that have most benefited from the knowledge economy: San Jose, San Francisco, Boston, New York, Washington, DC, Los Angeles, and so on.[16] This high cost of living forms a barrier deterring entry into the city and into its workforce.

The high cost of living in these places is not mostly about the cost of food or other services. A quarter pounder with cheese costs only twice as much in Boston, Massachusetts, as it does in the lowest-wage parts of the country.[17] Rather, the most significant difference is in the cost of housing. Housing expenditures are the single largest element of family budgets, accounting for 40 percent of spending on average.[18] The cost of housing varies a great deal across cities in the United States.

Indeed, the same dispersion that we noted earlier in wages is also present in what folks have to pay for a house. In 1980, families living in the ten highest-earning cities paid $188,880 on average for their homes; in all other cities, house prices averaged $151,050. By 2016, those in the top ten highest-earning cities paid $607,530 for their homes, compared to $222,020 nationally. That is, housing prices in the top cities in 1980 were 25 percent higher than other cities in 1980; by 2016, they were more almost three times as high.[19]

It might not seem surprising that housing is more expensive when everyone wants to move to a city. This simply reflects the basic law of supply and demand. However, housing is much more expensive than it has to be in prosperous cities because of a mechanism interfering with the unfettered operation of the housing market: zoning regulations. Throughout the United States, local regulations restrict the use of land in ways that make it impossible to provide the supply of housing that is required to meet its demand. This means that as areas grow, more and more workers are bidding for a limited set of places to live reasonably close to the cities where the good jobs are located.

For much of US history, local economic booms were matched by local building booms, but this era has ended. For example, in Manhattan, there were thirteen thousand new housing units permitted in 1960 alone, which is nearly two-thirds of the total permitted during the entire decade of the 1990s. The cost of constructing housing does vary somewhat across areas; for example, it is cheaper to build in the flat southwest than the hilly northeast, but this variation is very small relative to the enormous variation in house prices. Local restrictions on constructing housing are the primary driver of house price variations.[20]

The United States is relatively unique in having land use under local control, as opposed to national land-planning agencies in places like the UK and France. The problem this raises is that existing owners have an incentive to restrict housing supply, both to increase the local amenities (such as by having height restrictions on buildings to make the skyline more appealing) and to keep house prices high.

The set of restrictions imposed varies widely, from minimum lot sizes (most Boston suburbs have a minimum lot size of over one acre for the majority of their homes), to maximum heights, to multistage and costly review processes for environmental and other restrictions.[21] While the set of restrictions is complicated, the net effect is to significantly raise home prices and rents. Researchers estimate that in one-sixth of the metropolitan areas in the United States (including most of the highest-earning ones discussed earlier), the prices are at least 25 percent higher than construction costs, and in markets such as Los Angeles and San Francisco, they are twice as high.[22]

Consider in particular the example of Palo Alto, California, the epicenter of Silicon Valley. The technology industry in and around the city has grown spectacularly, but its housing stock has not. Low-slung, single-family housing dominates, even with thousands of students and young employees who might prefer smaller apartments. According to Zillow, single-family homes trade at a median price of $2.6 million, and median rents have climbed from $3,800 in 2011 to $6,000 in 2017.[23] Despite this, Palo Alto leadership has focused on restraining the growth rate of jobs rather than building more housing.[24] In 2017, the city planning commission approved an extension of the city's recent restriction of new office development to no more than fifty thousand square feet per year in an effort to slow development.[25]

Another good example is the suburbs around Boston. The Route 128 corridor that circumscribes Boston's core has long been the site of a cluster of prominent companies, initially focused on computer services and more recently on financial services, management consulting, and biotechnology.[26] In response to the growing industrial cluster, cities and towns in this area aggressively used zoning to maintain the predominance of single-family housing. According to the Fair Housing Center of Greater Boston, the type of development that occurred around Route 128 served to intensify racial segregation in the metropolitan area by excluding lower-income people and people of color from living near good job opportunities. Specifically, zoning tactics like setting minimum lot sizes served "to control density, protect open space and artificially inflate housing prices."[27] Today, towns around Route 128 are among the most expensive in Massachusetts.[28]

Income now flows to a smaller set of cities, but individuals can't afford to move to those cities to take advantage of the opportunities—and therefore get left behind in the places that are not benefiting from the agglomeration economies. Indeed, one recent study estimates that restrictive housing policies cause millions of workers to be "missing" from the most productive cities in the economy. If barriers to housing supply were removed, this study estimates that many more workers could live in these more productive cities; if this reallocation had occurred over the past several decades, the United States as a nation could have grown 50 percent faster in that time.[29]

Moreover, mobility, like everything else in America, has become polarized. Almost half of college graduates move out of their birth states by age thirty, while only 17 percent of high school dropouts do so.[30] This at least partly reflects the fact that higher education leads to higher wages, which leads to a better ability to afford to move to thriving cities, which means even faster wage growth in the future. And as a result, we get a continued divergence between the most and least educated in our society.

At the same time, people living in and around the highest-income cities are spending much longer commuting.[31] In the top ten cities of 1980, 5.4 percent of workers had to spend an hour or more commuting, compared to 3.8 percent nationally. In 2016, 14 percent of commuters in the top ten cities spent more than an hour commuting, while nationally it was less than 6 percent.[32] Meanwhile, in San Francisco, a proposal to build high-density housing close to mass transit is meeting opposition from, among others, environmentalists—who would in other forums likely argue for lower carbon emissions.[33]

BABY EINSTEINS WITHOUT ACCESS TO CAPITAL

One contributor to this ongoing dispersion in economic opportunities is the method of financing innovation. We noted some limits of the venture capital model in Chapter 4. Another problem is that, despite fluid national and international capital markets, VCs like to invest where they are located. This follows naturally from their concern about moral hazard—early-stage investors are more eager to invest when they know the entrepreneurs and can monitor them closely.[34]

Once again, this is a profit-maximizing strategy for investors, but it has the consequence that the early success of VCs in existing superstar cities has led to a concentration of start-up capital in those cities. And this concentration is striking. Twenty-five percent of all VC financing in the United States is concentrated in the San Francisco area, while another 15 percent is in nearby San Jose. Another 10 percent is in the New York area, 10 percent is in Boston, and 5 percent is in LA. This means that two-thirds of all VC financing is focused in five places in our entire nation—and these are the places that are already the epicenters of the knowledge economy.[35]

The result is that new discovery is not being financed in those parts of the country that do not already have successful investors, and this can have long-run implications for polarization.

A vivid illustration of this point is recent research that contrasts the place of birth of individuals who do and do not eventually create patented technologies in the United States. Future inventors grew up in exactly the places where existing inventors are concentrated. In 1980, the rate of patenting in the top twenty cities was about 2.5 times as high as other large cities in the United States. By 2010, it was 6 times as high—that is, the highest-earning cities are also creating new knowledge at a faster rate than other cities in the United States.[36]

This is particularly disturbing because it suggests a strong mechanism for perpetuating the polarized nature of the US labor market. There are undoubtedly many "future Einsteins" born in parts of the country where inventing is not happening—but productive opportunities are lost when there is no mechanism for the discovery of ideas from these parts of the country, nor the financing for the development of these ideas into valuable goods that can create jobs and grow the economy.

ECONOMIC POLARIZATION AFFECTS POLITICAL POLARIZATION

The divergence in economic outcomes between successful technology hubs and those areas of the country that have not kept up with the knowledge economy is striking.[37] But the correlation with growing geographic polarization of our political system is even more profound.[38] In the 2016 election, Hillary Clinton received a 26 percent higher vote share in the fifty most-educated counties in America, while Donald Trump had a 31 percent higher vote share in the fifty least-educated counties.[39] The result is highly educated Democratic areas and less well-educated Republican areas that are having difficulty speaking to each other.

Particularly, the difference in attitudes toward education and science across geographic areas is disturbing. The General Social Survey (GSS) is a data set that has for several decades collected a variety of measures on public attitudes.[40] The data do not identify cities, but they do identify census regions, so we can examine differences in attitudes between the large cities in coastal regions that host most of the superstar cities (the Northeast, Mid-Atlantic, and Pacific coast) and the rest of the country.

The results show some striking differences between the places doing really well and the rest of the country. The superstar areas are significantly more likely to say that "scientific research that advances the frontiers of knowledge is necessary and should be supported by the federal government" and to report that the United States should be spending more money to support scientific research. Perhaps most importantly, residents in these prosperous cities are 25 percent more likely to say that they have great confidence in our educational system![41]

The dispersion in economic outcomes between the coastal big cities and the rest of the country may well widen further. The very factors that led these coastal cities to become superstars can become self-perpetuating. These cities will invest more in education, and this will be supported by a concentrated investment ecosystem. Regional disparities in growth, which used to be self-correcting, may actually continue to widen.

WHO CAN CROWN NEW SUPERSTARS?

Economic activity—and (even more worrisome) economic opportunity—is increasingly concentrated in a set of coastal superstar cities. It does not have to be this way. To visualize the many places in America that want to become the new epicenters of technology-led growth, consider the recent bidding war to attract an investment by Amazon.

On September 7, 2017, Amazon, at that time one of the most valuable companies in the United States, made a striking announcement: it would build a second North American headquarters in addition to its home base in Seattle.[42] The reaction was frenzied. Cities from all across the country raised their hands and made the case that they would be the best place for this new hub of activity. In the end, there were applications from 238 cities in 43 states, the District of Columbia, and Puerto Rico.[43]

These cities ranged in size from Lawrence, Kansas, with fewer than one hundred thousand residents, to suburban New York, with more than twenty million. In terms of racial composition, applicants included Manchester, New Hampshire (more than 90 percent white), and Memphis, Tennessee (nearly 50 percent African American). Amazon's suitors also covered the spectrum in terms of political preferences, from Oakland, California, where 78 percent of the voters supported Democrat Hillary Clinton in the 2016 presidential election, to Pensacola, Florida, where 64 percent of the voters supported Republican Donald Trump in the same contest.

What did all these diverse cities have in common? They wanted the opportunity for economic growth—and the associated jobs—that would come with Amazon's decision.

On January 18, 2018, Amazon announced its twenty finalists. And the distribution was almost as wide as the distribution of applications.[44] Included were politically liberal superstar coastal cities, such as Boston, Philadelphia, Los Angeles, New York, and three near Washington, DC; rising tech hubs such as Austin and Pittsburgh; college towns such as Columbus, Ohio, and Raleigh, North Carolina; and areas with a promising academic base and a low cost of living, such as Nashville, Tennessee.[45]

Each finalist could make a compelling case based on objective facts about their location, from the large number of colleges and world-class airport in Atlanta to the popularity of Denver with millennials, the connection to Latin America of Miami, the central location and low cost of living of Philadelphia, and the cutting edge of artificial intelligence (AI) research (including a major investment by Google) of Toronto.[46] And of course, there were tax breaks. The details are not typically public, but available figures suggest enormous offers of more than $7 billion in tax credits from New Jersey[47] and more than $3 billion in tax breaks and grants, as well as $2 billion in transportation upgrades, from Maryland.[48]

The question that faced Amazon was: Should it choose an existing superstar coastal city? These cities have the advantage of dynamic and rapidly growing economies centered on new technologies and some of the most talented and educated workers in the nation, but they have the downside of long commutes and high housing prices. Is it time for a company like Amazon to help create a new superstar city?

We recently learned the answer, and it is no. On November 12, 2018, Amazon announced that it was splitting its new HQ2 between two superstar cities: New York City and Washington, DC (strictly speaking, Amazon is investing in Northern Virginia, but this is very much part of the DC economic area). Amazon's decision further confirms that agglomeration economies are leading to a continued divergence of the superstar cities from the rest of the country. Indeed, these two cities alone accounted for about half of the net increase in business establishments in the United States between 2007 and 2016.[49] As one expert said, "We look naïve in even raising the question that this could have gone to a different kind of midwestern, heartland place. There wasn't really an alternative."[50]

If we are going to crown some new superstars, the public sector will need to take a stronger role.

WHAT MAKES A SUPERSTAR CITY?

We have discussed the shift of American economic activity and innovation toward a smaller set of superstar cities as a natural consequence of the agglomeration inherent in a knowledge-based economy. Is there some reason why certain cities are destined to become superstars?

Perhaps the most important reason why some cities become superstars is the presence of a highly skilled workforce, especially one with a high level of education. And, no surprise, the cities that have done best economically since 1980 are those with a high share of the population having a college degree.[51] Today, the top ten highest-earning major metro areas in the United States all have a share of the adult population with college degrees of 39 percent or more.[52]

However, by this criteria, there are many other American cities that could have become superstars. Thirty other large metropolitan areas have a population within which at least 39 percent have a college degree. And these metropolitan areas are located in twenty-five different states! By any reasonable standard, there are many places with more than enough highly educated people.

Moreover, while the excellent universities in superstar cities are world famous, including Berkeley, Stanford, Harvard, MIT, and others, there are excellent universities all over the United States.

The ranking of the quality of PhD programs in the sciences provided by the National Research Council (NRC), the research arm of the National Academies of Science, Engineering, and Medicine, provides evidence that this is the case.[53] Not surprisingly, there is a high concentration of top PhD programs in the ten superstar cities: roughly 13 percent of the best programs are found there. But this means that there are dozens of top programs elsewhere in the nation. Seventy-five other cities have a top-twenty program!

High-quality undergraduate institutions are even more widely dispersed around the nation. One measure of undergraduate quality is whether students go on to graduate study, particularly at a highly ranked graduate school. Almost 80 percent of people enrolled in PhD programs—and almost 75 percent of students at top-twenty graduate schools—come from undergraduate schools not in the metropolitan areas of superstar cities.[54] Students can clearly choose from a wide variety of cities outside the superstar areas to obtain a top-notch science education.

If so many cities have at least the educational qualifications to become a superstar city, why did relatively so few emerge? That there is nothing predetermined about which cities become superstars and which do not can be seen in two of the most famous epicenters of technology today. Neither Kendall Square in Cambridge, Massachusetts, nor Seattle, Washington, were clear choices forty years ago.[55]

KENDALL SQUARE: BECOMING THE BIOTECHNOLOGY
CENTER OF THE WORLD

Located in East Cambridge, Kendall Square was the heart of an industrial center from the Civil War through the first half of the twentieth century. Goods ranging from telescope lenses to soap to the once-famous Necco Wafers candy were produced in this area.[56]

By the mid-1940s, however, these factories began closing as companies looked for cheaper labor elsewhere. When soap maker Lever Brothers, which was Cambridge's biggest employer, decided to leave in 1959, the decline of industrial Cambridge was complete. "Kendall Square was a moribund 19th-century district," said Robert Simha, director of planning at MIT. "Companies were sliding away. People were losing jobs. The city was losing income. The few plants that remained, like the vulcanized rubber plant, were smelly and polluted the air."[57]

The town turned to the remaining prominent resident of Kendall Square, MIT, for help. In 1960, the president of MIT announced that the University would purchase the former Lever Brothers site and develop it into office buildings under the moniker Technology Square.[58]

There seemed to be an ideal tenant: the National Aeronautics and Space Administration. Both President John F. Kennedy and his influential brother Senator Ted Kennedy pushed NASA to consider their home state—and specifically Kendall Square—for a proposed scientific campus, intended to develop new electronics systems for manned spaceflight and other programs.[59] The Electronics Research Center (ERC) was set up in Kendall Square in 1964. But the respite was temporary—due to budget cutbacks, President Nixon closed the ERC in 1970.[60]

Kendall Square's decline continued. During the 1970s, the town of Cambridge continued efforts to develop plans, but there was no consensus on what needed to be done in what became known as Nowhere Square. From 1950 to 1980, the number of working-age people living in the Kendall Square area declined from 4,200 to 2,500.

But the seeds of Kendall Square's rebirth were being planted. When future Nobel Prize–winning professor Phillip Sharp of MIT founded Biogen, a business based on recombinant DNA technology, he originally started in Geneva.[61] But he wanted the business to be as close to his lab as possible, so in 1982, he moved the company to a small factory building on Binney Street in Cambridge, not an immediately obvious choice. According to one postdoctoral fellow from the early 1990s: "I remember one of the graduate students in [Phillip Sharp's] lab got assaulted—knifed—on one of the streets that was no more than four, five blocks from where we worked."[62]

Nevertheless, Biogen did well. Over the next decade, other companies followed suit, and the seeds of a biotechnology hub were born. Genzyme moved their headquarters from Boston to Cambridge in 1990, Millennium Pharmaceuticals was founded in Cambridge in 1993, and Amgen was created in 2001.

Naturally enough, established companies—known as Big Pharma—did not want to be excluded from this fast-growing hub. Many of the leading drugs produced by large pharmaceutical companies were coming off patent, and there were no replacements in the pipeline. "So what to do when the goose stops laying the golden eggs?" asks entrepreneur Tim Rowe. "You have to go where the new goose is."[63]

In 2003, the Swiss drugmaker Novartis repurposed the building where Necco Wafers were made—creating a cutting-edge pharmaceutical research center. With more than two thousand employees, Novartis is now Cambridge's largest employer. Other giants, such as Pfizer, AstraZeneca, Amgen, and Baxter, have followed, all opening Kendall Square research centers in recent years.[64]

This geographical concentration of effort reflects a growing appreciation within the pharma sector for the advantage of proximity. "Fifteen years ago, a pharmaceutical company did not want its staff talking to other scientists. That's over," says David Dixon, principal of Boston-based Goody Clancy, an architecture and urban-planning firm commissioned to study Kendall Square. "Now they want to talk to each other. They attend forums, meet at lunch and after work to exchange ideas, and they can do that because they are close together."[65]

This success in biotechnology, ironically, has extended to the other high-tech sectors where Cambridge previously appeared to have fallen behind Silicon Valley or Seattle. Gleaming new research centers for Amazon, Google, and Microsoft are now centerpieces of Kendall Square, and there are hundreds of start-up companies focused on new technologies ranging from information technology to clean energy. And there is more than $14 billion in venture capital under investment in the Kendall Square area alone.[66]

By 2010, the working-age population in the Kendall Square area rose past its 1950 peak and today has 6,200 working-age residents. Landowners, as you would expect, have done very well; from 2000 to 2016 alone, median house values have risen from $338,000 to $586,000 in East Cambridge.[67]

SEATTLE VS. ALBUQUERQUE[68]

Microsoft is closely associated with the rise of Seattle as a technology-development hub, but actually it came very close to building its global brand in Albuquerque, New Mexico, where it was located in its first years. Microsoft's first client was in Albuquerque, and the budding software company prospered in that area—enough so that one of the its cofounders, Bill Gates, dropped out of Harvard to devote himself full-time to the enterprise. By 1978, the company had already more than $1 million in revenues and thirteen full-time employees.

Gates and his cofounder, Paul Allen, missed home—which was Seattle, Washington. So on New Year's Day, 1979, they moved their headquarters to Seattle. Seattle's economy at that time was heavily dependent on old-style manufacturing and lumber. People were leaving by the thousands, and quality of life was declining. Just a few years before Microsoft's move, the *Economist* had labeled Seattle the "city of despair," writing that "the city has become a vast pawn shop, with families selling anything they can do without to get money to buy food and pay rent." Indeed, a giant billboard appeared near the airport saying, "Will the last person leaving SEATTLE—Turn out the lights."

At least on paper, Albuquerque was a more promising location in 1979. The share of the population with a college education was only 5 percent lower than in Seattle, and average wages were similar. Seattle actually had 50 percent more robberies per capita. With its excellent weather and the famous Sandia National Laboratories, Albuquerque had the potential to become a new tech hub.

The call of home trumped these factors; Microsoft moved northwest, and Seattle's high-tech boom followed. Microsoft's presence and rapid growth made Seattle more attractive to other high-tech companies.

When Amazon's founder, Jeff Bezos, hopped in a car in 1994 and drove west (from New York) to his new life as an internet retailer, he chose as his destination not his home city of Albuquerque but instead a place where he had no personal connections—Seattle. By this time, Seattle was a magnet for high-tech activity and had a larger pool of talented tech employees. And it was home to a significant venture capital presence—some of the earliest investments in Amazon came from Seattle-based VCs.

Despite relatively similar initial conditions, the paths of these two cities have diverged radically. From 1980 to 2016, average earnings per worker in Seattle rose by 37 percent in real terms—while earnings grew by only 7 percent in real terms in Albuquerque. Today, the share of the population with a college education is 45 percent higher in Seattle than Albuquerque. Albuquerque's crime rate is now higher than Seattle's, with a murder rate that is more than double.[69] It is not inconceivable that, had things played out differently, *Breaking Bad's* Walter White would have gone from high school teacher to drug kingpin in Seattle, not Albuquerque.

STATE POLICY AND THE RACE TO THE BOTTOM

The large geographic disparities between superstar cities and their counterparts around the country have, not surprisingly, gained the attention of local policy makers, and they are not taking these disparities lying down. There has been a huge increase in development efforts at both the state and local level to try to increase their share of good jobs. Local policy makers know well the stories of places like Kendall Square, Seattle, and others, and they want to create the next superstar cities. But their efforts to redistribute the pie are often self-defeating and end up enriching corporations from the pocket of the taxpayer.

The main tool that states and localities use in their battle to grow is tax breaks for businesses. Measuring the size of these tax breaks is complicated, but a recent comprehensive effort by the researchers at the nonpartisan Upjohn Institute, one of the nation's leading think tanks studying local economies, shows that they add up to more than $45 billion annually. This amounts to 1.42 percent of the profits of businesses in the United States, or 30 percent of the average amount that states and localities actually collect in business taxes.[70]

Goodjobsfirst.org tracks these data and reports on the costs to states of particularly large tax breaks. These include an $8.7 billion deal for Boeing to stay in the state of Washington in 2013 (after a $3.2 billion deal in 2003) and a $5.6 billion deal for Alcoa to remain in New York in 2007. There have been twenty-seven deals, each costing states more than $1 billion since the beginning of the twenty-first century, and the pace is quickening—nineteen of those deals were in 2010 or later.

The most high-profile recent example is the arrangement for Foxconn to move to the state of Wisconsin. The Taiwanese manufacturer had put out word that it was considering a major new plant in the United States in January 2017, and its founder had said that "incentives would be needed to make it happen."[71] Wisconsin reportedly beat out six other states—Indiana, North Carolina, Ohio, Texas, Pennsylvania, and New York—going after the Foxconn plant.[72]

In July 2017, Foxconn agreed to set up a $10 billion plant to manufacture consumer electronics in Wisconsin.[73] The reward was a rich bounty, including $3 billion in state tax breaks, another $753 million in tax incentives from the city and county where the plant was to be built (including buying the land and giving it to Foxconn for free), $400 million in road improvements, and an upgrade to local electricity systems that will cost $140 million.[74] According to Wisconsin's own estimates, it will take until at least 2043 for the state to recoup its lost revenue.[75]

Are these tax breaks a good deal for the citizens of states like Wisconsin? That depends on the answer to two questions. First, to what extent would the companies have come to the locality anyway, even without the tax break? After all, if a firm was going to come to a city anyway and the city gives that firm a tax break, then the tax break hasn't created jobs—it has just lowered tax revenues. If Foxconn had already decided to come to Wisconsin, then all the state did was give away a lot of tax revenues that could have gone to their citizens. Second, if it is true that tax breaks attract firms to a locality, does it actually cause a significant increase in economic development?

The evidence on the first of these questions suggests that businesses are not very sensitive to such tax breaks, at least compared to all the other factors that determine business location decisions. For example, a recent study of tax breaks in Texas found that about 85–90 percent of projects that collected a major state tax break were going to locate in the state anyway.[76]

On the other hand, when businesses settle in an area, they do offer a powerful economic benefit. One particularly interesting study compared cities that won competitions to attract new manufacturing plants relative to other comparable cities that were the finalists in these competitions. They found that the cities that won had much faster growth—including productivity gains to *existing firms*—from winning the competition. In other words, having new businesses around made existing businesses more productive. This is compelling evidence for the agglomeration effects we discussed earlier: having more productive activities in an area makes everyone else around them more productive.[77]

So states face a trade-off. The jobs and higher productivity brought in by new businesses will raise the state tax base so that the state could collect the same revenues even with lower taxes. But if the tax break is too large, it will exceed any gains from the new business. Whether states end up on the right or wrong side of this trade-off is a matter of debate with no clear answer.

But what is clear is that while these tax breaks may or may not be a good deal from the perspective of specific areas, they are a terrible deal from the perspective of the United States as a whole. That is because almost every plant over which states are competing is going to locate in the United States in any case, so the country gains no jobs when a plant chooses one city over another—these would be American jobs anyway. Foxconn was going to build a US plant; it just had to choose where to do it. And nineteen of the twenty finalists for Amazon were in the United States, so those jobs were always likely to end up in the United States regardless of the size of the tax breaks offered to the company.

From a national perspective, these tax policy battles are a zero-sum game. There is a certain set of businesses that are choosing locations, and if those businesses choose one location, they do not choose another. Along the way, this race to the bottom has transferred massive resources from state and local taxpayers to the companies (and shareholders) that can win the competition.

Why do we care? Because state and local taxes are necessary to finance the public spending demands of their residents.[78] Those spending demands do not, of course, decrease when new businesses come to town. Indeed, they may grow, as a larger population and new businesses need more schools, better roads, and increased policing, all of which are funded at the state and local levels.

When one city wins a competition over another, total state and local taxes in the United States fall. State policy may or may not provide net gains to the state, but there are clearly national losses.

Of course, one location may be a better match for new business operations than others. In other words, the agglomeration benefits of new activities—offices, manufacturing plants—will vary across places. It would never make economic sense to randomly choose where to locate a new plant or business. State competition can in theory reveal the best places for plants to locate. States that have the most to gain from a plant will likely offer the best deal, and in return, plants will choose the best places to be. This is the magic of competition.

On the other hand, there are large losses from this destructive tax competition, with local communities perhaps getting a larger base of tax-paying jobs but the nation as a whole losing out from transferring tax revenues to wealthy corporations. What we need is a way to tap into the state-level urge to compete, but in a productive, positive-sum way. In doing so, we can build on a rich American tradition of place-based policies implemented by the federal government.

US HISTORY WITH PLACE-BASED POLICIES

There is no predestination behind which places become superstar cities. Some of the most prosperous and dynamic cities today have been leading urban areas for more than a century (e.g., New York), while others— such as Seattle—were on no one's radar forty years ago.

The difference today is that new top-performing cities do not appear to be emerging organically as they did earlier in US history. As the evidence discussed in this chapter shows, we are no longer a nation of *convergence*, where areas doing well naturally fall back and new areas emerge. Rather, we have become a nation of *divergence*, where a few large urban areas do much better—and better than all other places. The attractiveness of agglomeration—and talented people crowding together—in the knowledge-based economy creates centripetal forces pulling economic activity toward existing superstar cities.

Reversing the great divergence across the United States requires active federal policy. This is neither a radical nor a new concept— federal policies have favored or disfavored areas for hundreds of years, profoundly affecting the shape of our nation. Look no further than the decision of where to locate our nation's capital.[79] As of the late 1780s, Philadelphia seemed destined to be our nation's capital. But the compromise of 1790 instead moved the capital to the new District of Columbia in the underdeveloped Potomac basin, in return for delegates from the South acquiescing to allow the federal government to assume responsibility for some state debts. Today, Washington, DC, has the fourth-highest average earnings of any city in America, in large part due to well-paying government jobs, while Philadelphia ranks sixteenth. This was just the first of many decisions by the federal government, several of which we outline here, that have had profound implications for the regional patterns of growth in the United States.

LAND-GRANT COLLEGES: BUILDING HIGHER EDUCATION IN THE UNITED STATES

The Morrill Act of 1862 granted each state an area of federal land for the purpose of establishing a college. These land-grant colleges were intended to be centers for teaching "agriculture and the mechanic arts."[80] The law did not specify how these plots of land would be assigned; it was up to the state legislatures. As a result, the placement of land-grant colleges in each state was heavily influenced by the local political climate.

For example, Maine was quick to respond to the Morrill Act, with the state legislature first discussing terms of the act in early 1863. Governor Abner Coburn supported giving the grant to an existing institution, and so a committee was appointed to consider the options. In response, the president of Bowdoin College put forward a proposal to become Maine's land-grant college. Bowdoin's proposal appealed to the state on fiscal grounds, promising that Bowdoin was prepared to accept the land grant without the need for any additional expenditures from the state. The committee supported Bowdoin's proposal but faced opposition from farmers who favored establishing an independent institution. Ezekiel Holmes, editor of the *Maine Farmer,* appealed to a desire to keep talent in the rural communities and to maintain the importance of the agricultural sciences. The Bowdoin plan was rejected, and instead the Maine College of Agriculture and the Mechanic Arts (now University of Maine) was established in 1865.[81]

This became a common theme within the state legislatures: representatives from rural areas favored establishing independent institutions, while those from urban areas favored partnerships with existing institutions. These political decisions, while seemingly arbitrary at the time, have had long-term economic impacts on the areas surrounding land-grant colleges. One study found that, after eighty years, land-grant designation increased local population density by 45 percent and increased manufacturing output per worker by 57 percent in the area surrounding a land-grant college.[82] Another study found that in 1990, places with land-grant colleges had more highly educated populations and higher wages for all workers, not just college graduates.[83]

THE TENNESSEE VALLEY AUTHORITY:
BUILDING SOUTHERN ENERGY INFRASTRUCTURE

Perhaps the best twentieth-century example of the federal government explicitly using place-based policies to grow an area is the Tennessee Valley Authority (TVA), created in 1933. A part of the New Deal, the TVA was established to modernize and industrialize a region of the country that was particularly hard hit by the Great Depression. Indeed, in 1930, counties that would later come under the control of the TVA had 33 percent lower average manufacturing wages, 33 percent lower average farm values, and 27 percent lower median house values than the rest of the country. The TVA's mission was to improve navigation, control floods, and produce electricity in the region. Indirectly, the TVA was intended to revitalize the local economy and serve as a model development project.[84] At its peak from 1950 to 1955, there was a huge annual subsidy to that region—one-tenth the size of the entire local economy—but by 1960, the subsidies were gone. The total spent on this project was about $30 billion (measured in today's dollars) over the entire period.[85]

The result of this spending was a complete transformation of the Tennessee valley, including much of Tennessee and portions of many nearby states. During the period of spending, all types of industries grew much more rapidly in this area than in comparable areas around the nation. But even years after the spending ended, manufacturing growth in this area was much higher than in comparable regions. This big push created agglomeration economies that have lasted, allowing this previously backward region to have long-run economic success.[86] Today, the TVA creates an annual economic impact of $11.9 billion and supports 130,000 jobs.[87]

And the political success of the TVA is enduring. Barry Goldwater infamously proposed selling the TVA during an interview with the *Saturday Evening Post,* and incumbent president Lyndon Johnson used this against Goldwater in televised ads during his successful 1964 campaign for reelection.[88] In 2013, President Obama proposed privatizing the TVA but faced opposition from both ends of the political spectrum.[89]

Despite the economic and political success of the TVA, it remains unique—no comparable federal authority exists with such broad control over water resources in any other region. Early proponents meant for the TVA to be just the first of several valley authorities. A bill introduced in 1937 would have created seven additional valley authorities in different regions across the country, and by 1945, ten bills before Congress proposed the creation of new valley authorities. None of these bills ever passed, perhaps in part because of a shift in focus from civilian programs to military buildup following the onset of World War II.[90] The success of the TVA and the lack of comparable investments elsewhere were noted by President Eisenhower in a 1954 letter to the governor of Tennessee, saying, "It is high time that other regions were getting the same opportunities."[91]

Compared to those areas that did not receive additional valley authorities, the Tennessee Valley Authority was transformative for the local economy. Between 1940 and 2000, long-run growth rates were estimated to be 5.3 percent higher for manufacturing employment and 2.5 percent higher for median family income in the TVA region, relative to regions where similar authorities were proposed but never created.[92]

MILITARY BASES: SPREADING THE POSTWAR WEALTH

An important driver of jobs and earnings across areas in the United States in the postwar period was the placement of military bases. The National Conference of State Legislatures recently reviewed the large set of studies that show the economic benefits to communities from having a military base.[93] In 2015, for example, military installations in North Carolina supported 578,000 jobs, $34 billion in personal income, and $66 billion in gross state product. This amounts to roughly 10 percent of the state's overall economy. Specific bases are estimated to have large local footprints; for example, a 2013 study of the Marine Corps Air Ground Combat Center in Twentynine Palms, California, estimated that the center is the main economic driver in the Morongo basin and one of the largest employers in the county, contributing an estimated $1.7 billion annually to the local economy. The installation supports 24,300 jobs, or nearly 77 percent of all employment in the basin, and an estimated 62 percent of the area's economic activity.[94]

Despite their outsized economic impact, the locations chosen for military bases were often based on political advocacy rather than economic impact. This means that the federal government, like it or not, has long been making decisions that drive economic growth—based on winning or losing a military base.

For example, Malmstrom Air Force Base in Great Falls, Montana, owes its existence to local advocacy. In response to the breakout of World War II in Europe, the Great Falls Chamber of Commerce contacted Montana's two senators in 1939 to request consideration for development of a military base near Great Falls.[95] Also in 1939, the Great Falls Airport Commission appealed to Harry H. Woodring, secretary of war, to station an air corps at the existing Great Falls Municipal Airport.[96] Construction of a new base began in 1942, and Great Falls Army Base (now Malmstrom AFB) opened later that year. The base's construction has paid off for the locals; it contributes an estimated economic impact of $360 million annually.[97]

In summary, the notion of having the federal government implement place-based policies is neither new nor radical. Over two centuries, federal policies that have favored some places over others have had dramatic implications for the patterns of economic growth around the United States.

A recent review shows, however, that not all place-based federal policies have paid off.[98] In particular, the Appalachian Regional Commission was a redistribution program established in 1965 to provide highways to underdeveloped areas of the United States; it was associated with a short-run rise in growth in these areas in the 1970s, but this was not long-lived. International evidence is mixed on this front as well.[99] This review concludes that simply spreading money around, rather than focusing on interventions that have high returns in particular places, is an ineffective strategy.

THE PLACES YOU'LL GO

The concentration of economic activity in a limited set of places in the United States isn't preordained. The many areas that could become new hubs of a technologically based economic growth strategy have well-educated populations, strong educational institutions, and the potential for a dynamic local economy.[100] In addition, they have a high quality of life, featuring shorter commutes and more affordable housing than today's superstar cities. To illustrate, we have gathered data on a wide variety of indicators of life across the major metropolitan areas of the United States.

There are 378 major statistical areas in the contiguous United States, defined as cities and adjacent commuting areas with at least fifty thousand inhabitants.[101] For each of these MSAs, we have collected information on three categories of criteria of the type that companies like Amazon, or the government, might use to think about locations for future technology hubs.

First is a sufficient pool of workers to fill the jobs of the future. Retaining and attracting workers is not easy; it requires a diversity of job choices, a large dating pool (i.e., a large number of single people), and enough population to support such amenities as good restaurants and cultural events. The scale of the city does not have to be as big as New York or even Boston, but without at least tens of thousands of local residents, the new area is unlikely to attract and retain the labor required.

Second is a high-quality base of both skill and entrepreneurial spirit, the ingredient that combined with educational attainment to create today's technology centers. These are typically measured in the economics literature by the share of the population with a college degree and the number of patents per capita. But history tells us that a successful tech hub also requires a high-quality university base as well. Universities were the epicenter of the growth in innovation in post–World War II America. We need to maintain our leadership in university education and to more effectively integrate universities into the business community. The relationships between Stanford University and Silicon Valley, or MIT and the Kendall Square biotech hub, set the paradigm. Of course, great universities can be created, and we have seen dramatic improvements in the science and engineering education at a variety of US educational institutions over the past thirty years.[102] That said, a natural starting place in evaluating cities as potential tech hubs is the quality of their existing university science and engineering education.

Quality of life is the third element. The major problem facing existing superstar cities is constraints on real estate that have driven housing prices sky-high. Another issue is how long workers have to commute to their jobs; commuting makes people very unhappy.[103] Finally, one of the key determinants of quality of life is safety, since it goes without saying that areas with high criminal activity are not desirable places to live.

Putting these together, we arrive at a perhaps surprising conclusion given the existing concentration of superstar cities in the United States today: there are dozens of cities that are large *and* have highly educated and entrepreneurial populations, *and* strong educational institutions, *and* a good quality of life.

A great example is Pittsburgh, Pennsylvania. This city of 2.3 million (1.25 million people aged twenty-five to sixty-four) has a highly educated population (35 percent of people twenty-five and older have a college education), is quite entrepreneurial (0.4 patents per worker, more than double the national average), has excellent schools (with fourteen top-twenty science programs, and an average of more than one hundred undergrads per year going to top PhD programs), low house prices (an average of $183,000, below the typical MSA), and low crime rates (twenty-nine violent crimes per ten thousand people, about 10 percent below the national median). One downside with Pittsburgh, however, is the long commute that many people have to endure—only 60 percent of people commute less than a half hour (compared to a national median of 72 percent).

To more systematically compare areas in the United States, we have used the data described here to create a Tech Hub Index System (THIS). The appendix at the end of the book describes THIS, data sources, and construction in more detail, as well as presenting the key data. We created this index in three steps:

- First, we made a list of economic areas in the United States, which included the usual metropolitan statistical areas (MSAs) along with combinations of various MSAs that might reasonably pool their efforts to create a tech hub. For this purpose, we pooled across MSAs that are within one-hour driving time of each other, and where (a) each area by itself is too small but combined they are a sizeable hub, or (b) the areas are complementary—for example, because one area has a large population while the other has an excellent university.

- Second, from this comprehensive US-wide list of individual/combined MSAs, we selected just those economic areas that met three criteria: large enough working age population (at least one hundred thousand people aged twenty-five to sixty-four), sufficiently well-educated (at least 25 percent college graduates), and relatively modest housing prices (average house price less than $265,000).

- Third, we ranked these places by giving one-third weight to three categories: size (population aged twenty-five to sixty-four); education/innovation (equal one-quarter weights within this category to percent college graduates, number of top science graduate programs, number of undergraduates who go on to study at top science graduate programs, and patents per worker); and lifestyle (equal one-third within-category weights to house price, crime rate, and commuting time).[104]

Doing so yielded 102 potential tech hubs around the United States, consisting of 130 cities (since some are combined). These tech hubs are in thirty-six different states, spread geographically across all regions of the country:[105]

- New England: Massachusetts
- Middle Atlantic: New Jersey, New York, and Pennsylvania
- South Atlantic: Florida, Georgia, North Carolina, South Carolina, Virginia, and West Virginia
- East-North Central: Illinois, Indiana, Michigan, Ohio, and Wisconsin
- West-North Central: Iowa, Kansas, Minnesota, Missouri, Nebraska, North Dakota, and South Dakota
- East-South Central: Alabama, Kentucky, Mississippi, and Tennessee
- West-South Central: Arkansas, Louisiana, Oklahoma, and Texas

- Mountain: Arizona, Idaho, New Mexico, and Utah
- Pacific: Oregon and Washington

The only states not on our list have either a relatively small population, or less education, or high housing prices (or more than one element that does not meet our threshold). Of the thirty-six states included, twenty-one have at least three potential research hubs completely or partly in their state, including seven each in Florida, Michigan, and Ohio; six in Alabama and Indiana; and five in Georgia, Missouri, New York, North Carolina, Pennsylvania, Tennessee, and Texas.

Top of the list is Rochester, New York, which is in or near the top quarter of the cities on virtually all criteria, including third in the country in patents per worker, twelfth in undergraduates going to top science programs, and nineteenth in affordable housing. The top ten places in our ranking are mostly located in the industrial Northeast and Midwest, particularly New York (#1 Rochester, #3 Syracuse/Utica-Rome, and #8 Binghamton/Ithaca) and Ohio (#4 Columbus, #6 Cleveland-Elyria, and #9 Cincinnati), as well as Pennsylvania (#2 Pittsburgh), Illinois (#5 Bloomington/Champaign-Urbana), Indiana (#10 Indianapolis-Carmel-Anderson/Lafayette–West Lafayette), and Iowa (#7 Ames/Des Moines–West Des Moines). The next ten (ranked eleven through twenty) expand the geographic scope to include states like Georgia (#13 Atlanta–Sandy Springs–Roswell), Michigan (#11 Grand Rapids–Wyoming), Missouri (#12 St. Louis), Texas (#17 Dallas–Fort Worth–Arlington), and Wisconsin (#18 Appleton/Green Bay/Oshkosh-Neenah). The list then broadens further to include all the regions listed above.

One way to validate our assessment is to compare it to what other evaluators think of the potential of these areas for business growth. We looked at data from two different organizations that track economic development by MSA, although neither is focused on the exact question of where tech hubs could be built. The Kauffman Index of Growth Entrepreneurship provides, for the forty largest MSAs in the United States, a series of indicators about the entrepreneurial environment, such as the rate of start-up growth and small business activity.[106] *Site Selection* magazine reports the number of "corporate facility investment projects" for the top ten cities in three size buckets: population greater than one million; two hundred thousand to one million people; and fewer than two hundred thousand inhabitants.[107]

Our list does not match perfectly with either the Kauffman Foundation or *Site Selection* lists, but the overlap is strong. Ten of our top twenty-five places are ranked in the top forty Growth Entrepreneurship locations by the Kauffman Foundation. Ten of our top twenty-five also appear among the thirty-two cities that *Site Selection* identifies as having had the most new projects in 2017.

To be clear, THIS is only one way to approach the data. We do not in any way mean to imply that cities missing from this list cannot be tech hubs—or that cities on this list automatically would make good tech hubs. Every element of the index is amenable to change over time, with proper government policies and appropriate investment.

For example, our full list contains relatively few places in the Mountain or Pacific regions, reflecting the lack of traditionally highly rated science education in those areas and significantly more dispersed populations. But the US history discussed earlier suggests that high-quality educational institutions can be built. Stanford, today a powerhouse of science and innovation, was for a long time regarded as a less impressive institution[108] The San Jose area postwar tech boom helped the university, a large owner of land, and generated great opportunities for its alumni. Philanthropy and smart hiring helped Stanford to its preeminent position. Plenty of schools in the United States could aspire to the same today.

Our THIS list is meant instead to illustrate the inclusive geographic possibilities that could be associated with a big push on science. These 130 cities have more than eighty million Americans living in or near them! The notion that there is a fixed set of predetermined superstar cities does not fit US history and is not consistent with the data today.

IT'S TIME TO CROWN SOME NEW SUPERSTARS

One of the major advantages of the United States versus many of our international competitors is the size of our country. We have dozens of places with significant concentrations of talent that can be turned into research-and-development centers. Yet we have ended up concentrating both private and public R&D in a lopsided small set of cities that leave most of our vast country unrepresented.

There are many places outside the existing set of superstar cities in the United States that could foster research-led economic growth centers. The bidding for Amazon and the (locally sensible but nationally wasteful) state tax competition for existing companies demonstrate that many locations are ready to take that next step. But the forces of convergence that would naturally push them into the superstar tier simply aren't happening, as the agglomeration forces of the technology economy continue to favor the rich coastal megacities. Spreading success across a broader swath of our country is entirely feasible, but it is also going to require a jump start.

Innovation for Growth

Americans generally recognize inventiveness as one of their nation's competitive strengths. They understand that invention is a powerful engine of economic growth. Yet it gets amazingly little direct attention or funding from product makers, universities, or the government.

—Nathan Myhrvold, cofounder of Intellectual Ventures, one of the top five owners of US patents[1]

THE HISTORY OF SCIENTIFIC RESEARCH, TECHNOLOGY DEVELOPMENT, AND ECONOMIC GROWTH IN the United States gives us three important lessons. First, publicly funded programs—such as the Manhattan Project, the Atomic Energy Commission, the National Institutes of Health, the National Science Foundation, DARPA, and the Apollo missions—took on tasks that the private sector would not or could not tackle.

Second, these programs created technology that boosted growth and generated good jobs for millions of Americans. The United States became the undisputed innovation leader of the world in large part due to these efforts. Almost all our major technological breakthroughs of the past half century or more—including by private-sector companies in the computer, health care, or transportation space—have their roots in those public investments.

Third, these dramatic and high-impact surges in public R&D were, for the most part, not sustained. The economic basis of these programs was compelling, but political support quickly dwindled. Funding for science has repeatedly been seen as excessive and as primarily favoring relatively few highly educated people.

The United States now faces problems that are quite different from 1941 or 1957. German work on the atomic bomb and the development of Soviet missile capability posed very real existential threats. In both instances, American fears may have been exaggerated, but given the available information—and the strong scientific infrastructure of America's enemies—policy makers had good reason to be afraid. Germany developed long-range rockets capable of delivering deadly explosives, and the Soviet Union launched the first-ever satellite. Investing heavily in American technology, along with a commensurate expansion in educational opportunities, made a great deal of sense as a national security response. The strongly positive benefits for the broader economy were, ironically, a side effect.

Today, we again face serious external competition. Europe, Japan, and especially China are investing increasing amounts in science and technology. As a result, the rest of the world is threatening to erase our seventy-year lead in technology creation—and in some cases has already done so. Our more serious problems, however, are internal. Growth over the past several decades has been slow, and the gains that the economy has delivered have been concentrated in the highest-income groups and a few superstar cities. We need to boost our rate of economic growth in a way that creates good jobs, with decent wages, for more people and across the entire country, not just along the booming coasts.

In spring 1940, Vannevar Bush walked into the Oval Office with a half-page proposal that said, in effect: trust the scientists, and we will work out the details. Such an approach would not work today. The relationship between scientists and policy makers has changed irrevocably, and we live in an era of constrained budgets at least when it comes to this kind of endeavor. Politicians—and the public—quite reasonably want greater assurances that they would get value for their money and a broad sharing of benefits.

Rebuilding the American growth-and-jobs machine in an economically sensible and politically sustainable manner requires weaving together three major elements: more support for basic science and related commercial development; emphasis on a national strategy of developing new tech hubs as a cost-effective way to take advantage of local research spillovers and agglomeration; and a funding mechanism that results in direct and transparent returns for all Americans.

For evidence that such a strategy can work, start with Orlando, Florida.

NOT A MICKEY MOUSE STORY

Orlando brings lots of things to mind: amusement rides, fairy castles, and giant mice. Fairly low on the list would be computer simulation. Yet Orlando is not only a destination for family fun, it has also emerged as the world's center of the $5 billion modeling, simulation, and training (MS&T) industry. This industrial cluster is anchored by the University of Central Florida, one of the nation's largest universities, and the Central Florida Research Park (CFRP), which hosts 130 private companies and ten thousand employees.[2]

It was not always this way. The East Orange County area in which both the university and the research park reside was once a sleepy subdivision of Orange County, dominated by Disney.[3] In 1980, East Orange had fewer than 40,000 residents and 17,000 workers. Thirty years later, it had grown sixfold, with more than 220,000 residents and 107,000 workers. This growth had little to do with Disney; the rest of Orange County grew, but at a much slower rate. As a result, East Orange tripled the percentage of jobs it held in the overall county, from only 8 percent to almost 25 percent.

What happened is a modern version of what once made America the most prosperous nation on earth. The federal government, a local university, and the private sector came together to create a dynamic jobs engine.

The story begins with the closing of the Orlando air force base that had been established during World War II. Whenever a military base is scheduled to be closed, there is substantial lobbying to keep it open, which usually fails. The story ended differently for Orlando—thanks to an influential resident with an important connection.

Martin Andersen, the publisher of the *Orlando Sentinel,* got to know a young politician named Lyndon Johnson through a common mentor. Andersen's paper endorsed Johnson during his 1956 and 1960 campaigns for the Democratic Party presidential nomination. During Johnson's 1964 reelection campaign, Andersen organized a motorcade for Johnson during a visit to Orlando. When Johnson offered to reciprocate with a testimonial, Andersen reportedly responded, "What I'd really like, Mr. President, is a military base." After his visit, Johnson called Andersen and reportedly said simply, "I'm sending you a naval base."[4]

Shortly thereafter, Orlando received a terrific gift. The departing air force base was not closed but rather replaced by a new naval base. Part of the new naval base was the Naval Training Device Center (NTDC), whose mission was the development of combat simulation devices.[5]

Coincidentally, the University of Central Florida opened in 1968 as Florida Technological University, with a mission to provide personnel to support the growing space program at the Kennedy Space Center and Cape Canaveral Air Force Station. The university grew and was renamed the University of Central Florida in 1978. A major step was taken in 1980, when University president Trevor Colbourn decided to create a research park connected to the university. At the time, with sky-high interest rates, it was difficult to sell the land near the university for residential purposes. So instead, the CFRP was established and bought slightly more than one thousand acres of land south of its campus for $2,500 per acre. The CFRP was set up as its own authority, financing its growth by issuing special purpose bonds of the type used by airports.[6]

The next step for CFRP was to find an anchor tenant around which the park could build. And they found the perfect anchor with the naval simulation center, which in the early 1980s needed a new building.[7] Colbourn and other business leaders convinced the simulation center to move the few miles from the base to the new CFRP and to construct its new building there instead.

The navy's move turned out to be a motivating force for other companies to locate at the CFRP. An early participant was Perceptronics, a training-simulation company, which arrived in 1987. Today, the park has ten thousand employees, with employment in the park growing at about five hundred employees per year.[8]

The park and the university have a symbiotic relationship as new ideas flow from the university to the park, which functions as a "real-world lab" for testing these ideas. This relationship has paid off for the university as well as the local economy. From 1979 to 2015, the federal grant dollars going to the university rose from $2.5 million to $82 million. And commitments from the state, the private sector, and other university sources followed in step; total research-and-development funding at UCF rose from $3.4 million in 1979 to $188 million in 2016. In 1978, the UCF had an enrollment of ten thousand students; today it is one of the largest universities in the United States, with more than sixty thousand students.[9] In 1982, UCF had no highly ranked science departments; by 2005, its electrical engineering program was in the nation's top twenty.

Meanwhile, entities based at this research park receive more than $1.4 billion in federal financing, mostly from the military but also from the US Geological Survey, US Army Corps of Engineers, and others.[10] But despite the substantial government catalyst, the park is to a large degree a privately funded venture and a centerpiece of the country's computer simulation industry; moreover, about 60 percent of the park workforce is involved in other activities in which the university excels, ranging from lasers and optics to medical devices to computer technology.[11] And not only has the CFRP created jobs, it has created land value as well; the land in CFRP is now worth about $350,000 per acre.[12] The federal government, a budding university, and an entrepreneurial private sector working together have created thousands of jobs and billions of economic value in a place known by many for only citrus and Disney.

The UCF/CFRP relationship is an economic success story in terms of developing, changing, and growing the local economy, but there are three important limits. First, the genesis of this hub was a political favor, which is not the most economically efficient way to allocate federal funds. To create a national initiative, we would recommend a more objective way of allocating research-and-development dollars to the places where they can be productively employed.

Second, the increase in research funding has not led to the development of large homegrown technology companies, due in part to the lack of financing in this area for the transition across the valley of death. A report from the National Venture Capital Association found that Orlando was the forty-sixth-ranked city in the nation in the number of companies receiving deals for financial backing.[13]

The companies in the CFRP have struggled to grow their size and customer base. As a result, the success of the CFRP is still overly tied to the military budget. In September 2013, for example, San Diego–based Cubic Corporation cited US spending reductions as the reason it dismissed an undisclosed number of workers from its 350-employee workforce in Orlando. Two months later, it landed a large new contract worth as much as $112 million to provide simulation training systems for an advanced navy warship, which led to an increase in hiring in Orlando.[14]

Finally, the Orlando area suffers from a lack of the skilled workers required to grow the technology sector. Primary and secondary education in Florida remains quite weak. *US News* ranks Florida fortieth for pre-K through 12 education. Florida ranked forty-third for high school graduation rate, forty-second for math scores, and thirty-second for reading scores.[15] CFRP manager Joe Wallace has been told by companies that for every PhD they hire, they need ten technicians—but that such a pool of talent is not available in the area.[16]

The Orlando example is not an isolated one. The classic example of a place transformed by research enterprise is North Carolina's Research Triangle Park, founded in the 1950s and now the nation's largest research park. More recent examples include the Georgia Research Alliance (GRA). This program devotes state and private resources to recruiting top research talent to Georgia universities and to leverage those researchers for research funding and economic development. The GRA's "eminent scholars" program has recruited dozens of the nation's top scientists to Georgia universities, resulting in $4 billion in outside federal and private investment in Georgia. GRA efforts have led to a portfolio of 180 spin-off companies with more than $660 million in revenue and employment of more than 1,300 professionals.[17]

At the national level, we should build on the example of Orlando— and other places that have become strong hubs—while keeping in mind these shortcomings. The goal is to create a lasting set of successful technology hubs spread more widely around the country.

FUNDING SCIENCE FOR GROWTH

The heart of our proposal for jump-starting America is a substantial federal investment in R&D. If we devote an additional half of one percentage point of GDP to research funding—roughly $100 billion per year—we would return public funding to its level in the 1980s. Based on history and available evidence, this investment would lead to a significant growth boost, arising from more invention and faster productivity growth.[18]

The evidence reviewed in Chapter 5 shows that past expansions of public R&D have been a cost-effective way to increase employment. On the high end, our own regression estimates of the impact of more university R&D funding on jobs suggest that university research spending raises employment at a cost of $28,000 per job, while the study of the New Zealand public R&D program increasing employment implies a cost per job of $29,000.[19] On the lower end, the study of the Finnish Tekes program implies a cost per job of $8,100, while the study of military R&D in Europe suggests a cost per job created of only $2,100. This entire range is quite low, relative to what it costs to create jobs in other contexts. For example, existing estimates of the jobs created by stimulus spending in the Great Recession suggested a cost per job created of about $50,000.[20]

If we conservatively assume that expansions of research and development create one additional job per $25,000 in spending, then an investment of $100 billion per year would create four million good new jobs. This would be a major step toward addressing the shortfall in quality jobs in the United States.

Alternative calculations produce similar numbers. Orlando receives $1.4 billion in government funding for its computer simulation industry. Since 1980, if the East Orange County subdivision had grown at the same rate as the rest of the county, it would have had thirty-eight thousand new jobs. Instead, it added ninety-one thousand new jobs. If we divide the government funding by the number of extra jobs created in East Orange County relative to the rest of the county, we get an estimate of $26,770 per job.

This is just the tip of the iceberg. The really big potential gains come from being at the forefront of the next wave of global superstar technologies. No one knows exactly which technology will be the next blockbuster, but there are plenty of candidates. Being the first to develop radar, jet engines, and the internet was worth a huge amount to the United States in terms of good jobs created and stronger national security.

What we need is a portfolio of high-risk and capital-intensive research and development that can lead to broad-based economic growth by creating high-paying middle-class jobs. We should focus on funding science that looks likely to have a strong return in terms of creating sustainable growth into the future. And the possibilities are indeed endless. In Chapter 8, we highlight promising potential developments in sectors such as synthetic biology, alternative energy, and ocean exploration, but keep in mind these are just a few examples of what may be possible in the near future.

As we noted with the Human Genome Project, a relatively small ($3 billion) federal investment gave birth to an industry that created good jobs for hundreds of thousands of people. But, as we will discuss in the next chapter, other countries are already moving to take advantage of these opportunities. If we want these new jobs to be in the United States, we need to take the lead in developing the technologies.

NOT JUST R, BUT ALSO D: CROSSING THE VALLEY OF DEATH

There is a successful history of organizations such as the military and NIH using government grants to finance research ranging from radar to the human genome. Our initiative for jump-starting America, however, is focused not just on creating knowledge but also on increasing economic growth and the number of good jobs. These additional steps require translating the discoveries made by researchers into products that are valued in the economy.

We reviewed the problem of transforming research into products (pages 98–104), especially the valley of death faced by new ideas in getting from the laboratory to the prototype. We talked about barriers faced by innovative new firms, from economies of scale in manufacturing to a venture capital sector that does not prioritize large-scale and long-term investments.

During World War II, America solved this problem by just having the federal government pay for both the research and product development. Initiatives such as the Rad Lab and the Manhattan Project were not just about the basic science but about taking the ideas all the way to products that the military could implement quickly. Such an approach does not make sense today, because the goal is not the development of weapons per se.

The focus today must be on partnering with, not displacing, the private sector. Recall our discussion of the limitations of the venture capital sector in the United States: limited funds lead them to avoid the valley of death. But the potential problem when the government tries to fill in these missing areas is that it can end up competing with the private sector—and that is a competition the government is bound to lose, in terms of finding the best investments to finance. Private-sector investors have the expertise and the incentives to pick the best investments—so the projects the private sector passes on are likely to be less productive unless government officials start to strong-arm people or hand out bigger firm-specific subsidies.

Entrepreneurship expert Josh Lerner confirms the valuable role of some public initiatives to promote R&D, but he also discusses some compelling examples of failed government initiatives: Malaysia invested in a massive bioscience complex that is now known as the Valley of the Bio-Ghosts, and Norway "squandered much of its oil wealth in the 1970s and 1980s propping up failed ventures and funding ill-conceived new businesses by relatives of parliamentarians and bureaucrats."[21]

Lerner suggests that a better solution is to address head-on the problem of limited capital available to invest in start-up companies, by partnering with private investors to find the best opportunities to fill the valley of death in a way that is likely to yield long-run returns. Public partnerships can increase the compressed time frame of existing venture capitalists that leads them to be unwilling to invest in long-run bets. Our review of the VC sector showed that when capital is more readily available, VCs are willing to fund longer-run, riskier projects—resulting in more innovation. The government can operate strategically in partnership with VCs to loosen those capital constraints.

Experienced venture capitalists could also play an important leadership role in this initiative. The US venture capital sector is the envy of the world—we should be harnessing its strengths.

Crossing the valley of death most effectively means coordinating between scientists, manufacturers, and financiers. And despite the advances in communications technologies of the past thirty years, such collaboration still happens best face-to-face. Research and development yields its highest return, for example, in areas where venture capital is most readily available. Venture investors, however, naturally prefer to locate where there are already a good number of start-ups and potential deals for them to look at—leading to the excessive concentration of VC dollars in just a few cities today. That is why we need a geographic focus for our new investments—through the creation of innovation hubs.

SPREADING THE WEALTH

A long-standing feature of both private tech development and public R&D spending is the focus on a few outstanding locations. Cities like Boston and San Francisco have all the preconditions for science-based success, from world-leading universities to vibrant venture capital communities. Naturally, these places have become hubs for US innovation and the focus of federal government funding as well. This pattern shows no sign of slowing, with the top metro areas pulling further and further away from the rest of the country.

There is a strong economic argument for this research concentration. Public research dollars will be most effective when provided to the scientists with the best ideas. This suggests that research should be allocated nationally through a competition in which the best scientists win. Should those scientists be concentrated in a few cities, so be it.

On the other hand, there may be many high-quality research ideas that are being ignored in other parts of the country because there is less research funding available in those areas. There are certainly restrictions on taking existing ideas to scale because of the limited reach of private venture funding in these places. When it comes to establishing new hotbeds of innovative job growth, we face a chicken-and-egg problem: venture capital investors are reluctant to focus on places without a large existing tech presence, but it is hard to build a tech presence in today's economy without VCs willing to fund the new enterprises.

At the same time, conducting research in the existing small set of coastal locations is unambiguously a lot more expensive than doing the same in lower-cost locations elsewhere in the country. The constraints that local real estate regulations place on property development have costs for research and development, as projects become increasingly expensive to carry out, and it is hard to find affordable places to live for the workers—of all education levels—who are an essential part of the research infrastructure.

A centerpiece of our proposal is to spread the availability of public research funding more broadly across America. Based on existing evidence regarding the complementarity between private and public research, if we expand publicly funded research in new places, private research and development dollars will follow. Places like Orlando—in terms of tech potential—exist all over the United States and are well positioned to become hosts to the next breakthrough technology. Great universities, talented residents, and productive business environments exist alongside reasonable housing costs and a high quality of living all around the country. In Chapter 6, we reviewed the wide variety of places in the United States that meet these conditions.

While there may or may not be some economic costs to redirecting public R&D toward new locations, there are unambiguous political gains. More government funding directed to a small subset of already successful places will be significantly less popular than ensuring that the whole country is represented in any new research initiative. If additional public R&D spending simply follows existing patterns, then most of the country will be left with little to show for a sizeable expansion.

Senator Harley Kilgore had a version of this insight in the late 1940s, but Vannevar Bush pushed back—most likely contributing to the creation of a smaller federal research enterprise than might otherwise have been possible. It would be unwise to ignore the regional pressure for scientific and economic opportunity today. We do too little research and development in America. However, if we want to do more, there needs to be political buy-in. A hypothetical reduction in the efficiency of R&D spending is a small price to pay for a large expansion in the pipeline of new ideas.

However, this won't work if the dollars are spread too thinly either. The agglomeration effects that we discussed earlier are not going away. To capture the benefits of agglomeration, places must create a compelling case for skilled workers, researchers, and investors to locate there. Incremental investments in the research infrastructure of an area are unlikely to have this effect.

What is needed is a big push: a major leap forward that announces to the world that these new locations are ready and qualified to become technology hubs. This means picking winners and not simply succumbing to political pressure to give money to any qualified city. To do so, we need to follow the lesson of Amazon and other successful US companies.

CREATING NEW INNOVATION HUBS THROUGH COMPETITION

Political advantages notwithstanding, there is a huge risk to having Congress and the White House simply pick the next research hubs. The Orlando technology and research center got its beginnings from a political favor by then president Lyndon Johnson, and while it turned out well for this area, relying more generally on political whim and favor would be unwise. While it is desirable to introduce new places in the

United States into the forefront of technology research and development, it only makes sense if those places are ready. Otherwise, this simply becomes a federal transfer program to politically favored areas and does not maximize the potential for economic growth for our nation as a whole.

We recommend spreading research-related dollars wider than the existing superstar cities to which they flow today. At the same time, we want dollars to go to places where they can be employed productively, not just where powerful politicians call home. And we want sufficient investment in areas so that they can get over the hump of agglomeration economies and become a desirable destination for the technologies of the future. We propose to resolve this tension by proceeding exactly as private companies do, through a competitive process.

In a *catalyst competition,* areas would apply to become one of the new hubs. Evaluation criteria should be based on measurable dimensions consistent with the idea that an area could become a new center of discovery and job growth. This is discussed at more length in Chapter 6, and our THIS index provides one illustration of how this might be done, although many variants of this approach are possible.

In addition, places would have to demonstrate substantial local buy-in along several dimensions. One is having pro-growth zoning regulations. If the technology hubs are successful, they will become larger and denser urban areas that are attractive both for businesses and individuals. This raises the risk that we re-create in these new hubs the model of restrictive regulations in the superstar cities that have led to high house prices and slower-than-expected job growth. Areas must have a long-run plan to promote sensible growth that allows sufficient affordable real estate within reasonable commuting distances of the new research centers.

The recent string of natural disasters, such as the experience with Hurricane Harvey in Houston, have highlighted, of course, the perils of zoning regulations that are too loose. Clearly, sensible restrictions are needed. There is a large middle ground between the overly tight zoning restrictions that have made the Bay Area and Boston unaffordable places for many people to live and the overly loose zoning rules that led to environmental disaster in Houston. An advantage of the competition for hubs is that we would encourage areas to look for that sweet spot in their urban planning—or they pass up the chance for this new opportunity for local growth.

Another is having a successful infrastructure plan for building a hub that both promotes basic research and its development into commercial products. This means, for example, having strong transportation networks within the area to facilitate interaction and from the area to key markets where commercialized products might be sold.

The third is a plan for building and sustaining an educational base that can support the growth of a new technology hub. Areas need to show that they can not only support growing demand for skilled jobs but also ensure sufficient supply of workers to take those jobs. In part, this will be university-based; there are many excellent universities around the nation that could be drawn on for this endeavor. But this will also require higher-quality high school, vocational, and local college education to train the workers that will support research scientists in creating the products of tomorrow. We discuss such an approach later (pages 186–188). In competing to be a technology hub, areas will have to show commitment along many dimensions to raising the supply of skills in their area.

Competition between areas to attract new business is hardly novel, and large companies play localities against each other on a regular basis. Amazon used a version of exactly this process in determining where to locate its HQ2. The problem is that the existing competition across states is a zero-sum game that simply transfers to shareholders of major companies much of the gain they bring to a city. States and cities already spend almost $50 billion per year in tax breaks that may or may not make sense for their location, but which leaves the nation as a whole less well off. In contrast, our proposal creates a positive-sum game within which areas benefit from better jobs and higher productivity, while the country as a whole wins from increased innovation.

The federal government already uses a version of this approach, though on a smaller scale. For example, the US Army's recent choice of Austin for its high-tech Futures Command was the result of a process that started with a list of 150 cities and then whittled down to 5—very much along the lines of the Amazon-type corporate location process. Key criteria included distance to people with math and science expertise, as well as private sector (including academic) history of research and development. Naturally, the army also considered quality of life, including the cost of living, and what kind of support was available from local government. The University of Texas reportedly provided space in a downtown office building, making it easier for the army's Futures Command to potentially interact with local technology companies.[22]

USING AN INDEPENDENT COMMISSION

A major issue that will be raised with such a new large commitment is governance. How do we make sure this does not turn into a congressional (or executive branch) boondoggle, with funds handed out as political favors rather than rewarding the most deserving research projects?

We agree that this is a serious issue. It is critical that this new program be administered through a new independent entity that is not part of either the administration or Congress. It should follow the structure of the Base Realignment and Closure (BRAC) Commission, which has, over recent decades, successfully reduced the number of military bases.

The BRAC is an underappreciated mechanism for making the kind of hard decisions that seem to constantly bedevil our paralyzed and polarized Congress. Following the end of the Cold War, the United States realized it had substantial excess military real estate but that it would be hard to shutter this capacity since elected politicians have a strong parochial incentive to keep local bases active. The BRAC process was introduced to address this problem in 1988, with rounds in four subsequent years, the most recent being 2005.

The BRAC Commission consists of nine members appointed by the president. The Department of Defense presents this commission with a list of bases to be closed, and the commission reviews and modifies this list before presenting it to the president. Along the way, there is substantial scope for public input to the process, with the 2005 committee hearing from hundreds of public officials and receiving around two hundred thousand pieces of mail from private citizens. All nonconfidential information and proceedings were provided to the public, and each site on the list had to be visited by at least two members of the commission. If the president approves, the full set of changes goes into effect—unless the entire list is rejected by Congress.

In a world where it is hard to take on entrenched interests, the BRAC Commission was an unqualified success. These rounds resulted in the closure of more than 350 installations that were no longer necessary.

BRAC is our model for the creation of an Innovation Commission (IC) that would make recommendations to Congress for areas that would receive funding to establish the new hubs. The commission would make a recommendation on which Congress could vote up or down, but with a presumption of acceptance. This commission would be fully transparent in all its work. Commissioners would be appointed for a fixed period of time and would be charged with generating a financial return for society as a whole—in the form of an innovation dividend, discussed later. This financial return will provide a clear measure of whether the commission does its job properly.

To remain both politically viable and economically productive, the Innovation Commission has to address head-on the issue of failure. While, as we have shown, there are high returns to science-based investments, there are also high risks. The real benefit comes from a small number of investments yielding extraordinary returns. Recall (from Chapter 4) that even for venture capital investors, who currently get to pick the best bets, a small minority (8 percent) of their investment dollars result in the vast majority of their overall returns, while three-fifths of their projects do not even make back the cost of investment.

If we really aim to improve our existing system for converting good ideas into a more productive economy, we must also recognize that many projects will fail—and the ones that succeed may take a while to do so. Unfortunately, as the example of Solyndra (pages 133–135) shows, our political system provides too many incentives to jump on failures without acknowledging the big-picture path toward success.

A proper means of achieving the balance between long-run risk taking and accountability is to incorporate effective evaluation of the initiative. While we would be investing in projects whose success is only revealed over the long run, constant evaluation and readjustment are possible. The IC must use careful and objective evaluation of performance to adjust how public resources are allocated.

WHAT DOES THE MONEY ACTUALLY GET SPENT ON?

The technology hubs would ultimately propose the most effective mix of spending to maximize the returns in their areas, but their spending would be broadly focused in several categories.

The first is basic research. The United States has a high-quality peer-review mechanism for evaluating and supporting scientific research through organizations such as the NIH and DARPA, and the stories and evidence throughout this book—ranging from lifesaving drugs to the internet—testify to their success. Ongoing peer review would be a central component of allocating new dollars.

The second is development. This importantly includes providing the manufacturing infrastructure to take ideas from the lab to the market. No longer should the United States lose the ability to develop innovative and job-producing technologies to other nations because of a lack of capacity to develop those products. Scaled-up research hubs provide a perfect mechanism for coordinating the manufacturing needs of related projects to overcome problems of economies of scale, as well as for internalizing the spillovers of developing innovative new generalized R&D assets that benefit all producers in the area. One example could be publicly funded manufacturing resources for developing new and innovative drugs, addressing the shortfall that we highlighted with cell and gene therapies. Other examples are highlighted in the next chapter.

The third is financing. As shown in Chapter 5, programs such as the Small Business Innovation Research program have been successful on a fairly modest scale in helping companies cross the valley of death. The government could dramatically increase the size of SBIR-like programs, while partnering with the private sector to ensure that we supplement, and do not displace, private-sector support for innovation.

Fourth, at the early stages of developing technology hubs, spending would be focused on infrastructure. New research hubs require the proper infrastructure to both do basic research and to convert that research to new products. In the competitive proposal stage, hubs need to propose what they would undertake in terms of building research infrastructure, schools, business parks, and other amenities to promote their areas. In addition to building strong infrastructure, this stage has the advantage of employing some workers for whom retraining in technological skills is not cost effective.

Finally, a major target of spending would be on improving technical and scientific education at the educational institutions associated with research hubs.

SUPPLY TO MEET THE DEMAND

As discussed in Chapter 2, the twenty years after World War II was a "Goldilocks" period where both a rise in demand and supply of skills led to a rise in pay throughout the income distribution. A major push on publicly funded research and associated development drove up the demand for skills. At the same time, the expansion of science education in our nation's primary and secondary schools, as well as the availability of low-cost higher education through the GI Bill, raised the supply of skilled workers. Put these developments together and you get the creation of a high-wage middle class built on technological advancement. In the last few decades, however, the rapidly rising demand for skills has not been met with increased supply, leading to rising inequality.

Our plan so far would create the demand for skills, but without an adequate increase in supply, the plan will boost the wages for already-skilled people only, leading to rising inequality. To create genuinely shared prosperity, we need to raise the supply of skills as well. This is an area that has received much more attention than the failure of public research and development, with proposals from groups as disparate as the Brookings Institution, McKinsey & Company, and the Trump administration.[23] Several key ideas stick out as highly practical, politically feasible, and economically important.

Increasing the supply of skills starts with investments before college. The 1958 National Defense Education Act led to a large increase in science education across high schools in the United States. We need to reinvest in the type of skills training for high school students that allows them to succeed through a variety of channels, from technical schools to community colleges and four-year colleges. As noted earlier, as part of the innovation hub competition, areas would have to demonstrate a commitment to skills training starting in high school.

A second step in increasing skills supply is making college education affordable for the middle class. Faced with extreme fiscal pressures, states are raising tuition at the state universities that are main avenues of higher education in the United States. While elite private universities are removing financial barriers through more generous financial aid for some people, their admissions barriers rise exponentially as students from around the nation and the world seek attendance at these institutions.

For many students, college means taking on significant student loan debt to complete their education. The average student graduating a four-year college in the United States today leaves with a debt burden of around $30,000.[24] The student debt load in the United States is more than $1.4 trillion, and the total cost of college each year is over $500 billion.[25] Many individuals who take on these loans go to schools that do not provide productive career opportunities, as witnessed by recent scandals at a set of for-profit universities; many others take large loans to pay for college but never complete the degree that can provide them access to the skilled labor market.[26]

One option to increase skills supply could be financing for students to study in the universities associated with new hubs. This would include expanded access to student loans, as well as targeted grants to students studying at those universities in the types of science fields that provide training for future work in the high-skill economy.[27] Importantly, this should be combined with strong ongoing support for students once they enroll in college, to promote not only college attendance but also completion.

It is imperative to incorporate vocational training as well. It is unrealistic to think that every job that will be created through an initiative such as this will be a high-value-added research job. A larger structure is required to make the research endeavor a successful one, and that larger structure will require a variety of jobs. They will range from semiskilled jobs such as lab technicians to less-skilled jobs such as maintenance staff. The educational plan for the area should incorporate the ability to provide the training that is needed for these jobs as well.

Finally, it is critical that businesses work together to provide the type of general skills training that will benefit entire industries, not just specific businesses. Business investment in training suffers from the same type of spillover problem we discussed with R&D: when businesses train workers, they are providing skills that may be valuable not only to their businesses but to others. As a result, businesses may underinvest in training to avoid paying for skills that workers can just take to other jobs.

Again, cell and gene therapy manufacturing highlights these barriers. For the types of positions that are likely to open up in greater numbers in the near future, college graduates are (according to one expert) "overqualified, but underskilled," suggesting that firms are likely to turn to apprenticeship training. However, demand from a single firm alone would not warrant establishing a large training center. Instead, "it will be necessary to aggregate the demand for apprenticeship training across cell therapy employers so that the number of trainees exceeds the minimum required to make it worthwhile for a provider to offer training, and also to reduce the risk faced by potential training providers."[28]

Public-sector involvement can help fix this underinvestment problem also. One form of such involvement is financing institutions that provide midcareer skills development for workers; as a recent report from the Council of Economic Advisers emphasizes, public education spending peaks at age fifteen and is largely nonexistent after age thirty. There are a host of private and public partnerships for worker skills development that appear successful and could be greatly expanded.[29] Areas bidding to be innovation hubs could propose coordination strategies across businesses and such institutions to provide the type of ongoing training needed for successful skills upgrading.

Remember that this is not just education for the future discovery of new technologies. The higher education sector has been an engine of job growth for decades in the United States, and we should build on that success.[30]

HOW DOES THE MONEY GET RAISED?

A realistic plan must include provisions not only for how the funds get spent but for how they get raised. In particular, an initiative such as this one requires not only politically independent allocation of funds but independent financing as well. If the financing of this initiative is subject to annual political debate, it will cause difficulties.

The danger is that the financing could become a political bargaining chip, which could interfere with the independence of the Innovation Commission. For example, politicians could condition appropriations on selection of particular sites for the innovation, which would interfere with the most productive set of sites being chosen for the project.

In addition, this project represents a long-run investment in select areas around the United States. In return for this financing, these hubs are committing to major structural changes, ranging from zoning law changes to infrastructure development. Cities will be unwilling to make such a commitment if the proposed funding is not fully guaranteed for many years.

As a result, successful implementation of this program would require a onetime, multiyear authorization that would provide independence and financing certainty to the initiative. Congressional approval is needed for each round of hubs, just as it is needed for a round of base closings recommended by the BRAC. But once a round of hubs is authorized, there is no second-guessing or congressional fiddling around the margins.

Moving out of the annual appropriations process will be challenging, but precedents do exist. For example, multiyear appropriations provide that obligated funds are available until some future date; examples include appropriations for military construction, although these typically last about five years. There are also examples of *no-year appropriations*, which are available "until expended," including appropriations for the

Federal Aviation Administration to purchase an aircraft, or appropriations to the AIP (Airport Improvement Program) that provides grants
to public agencies or private entities for public-use airport projects.[31] We
are proposing a scale that is beyond these examples, but the structural
precedents are in place.

ESTABLISHING AN INNOVATION DIVIDEND

The American people have benefited enormously from past public investments in research and development—but nowhere nearly as much
as they could have. The federal government has spent billions of dollars on R&D that has directly led to commercialization of goods from
prescription drugs to cell phone apps that use GPS. The companies
producing these goods have hired millions of workers and paid billions
in taxes, making America richer.

But continuing to rely on such *indirect returns* to public investment is problematic for two reasons. The first is that the returns are
increasingly concentrated in a smaller and smaller set of wealthy entrepreneurs. From the end of World War II through 1970, the share
of GDP going to workers as compensation rose from 54 percent to
over 58 percent, but it has steadily declined since, and it is now back
at its pre–World War II levels. This means that an ever-larger share of
the returns to innovation is going to a smaller share of capitalists. If
the "labor share" had remained at its 1970 level, compensation today
would be $800 billion higher, or $5,000 per person in the US labor
force today.

The second, and related, issue is that the capital owners deriving a
larger and larger share of our national income are paying less and less
tax on that income. The past several decades have seen a large decline in
the effective tax rate paid by corporations on their profits in the United
States.[32] And the recently passed (2017) Trump tax cuts will further
continue this trend by significantly reducing the taxation of corporate
profits and, at least temporarily, high-income individuals.[33]

A key element to the success of our proposal is that US citizens
directly see a return from their investment into science. US taxpayers

are investors in this new initiative, and they should see regular dividends from that investment. So we propose that the returns to this large new public investment accrue more directly to the citizens of the United States through an innovation dividend.

FINANCING THE INNOVATION DIVIDEND: ENRICHING TAXPAYERS, NOT LOCAL LANDLORDS

The innovation hub model we propose will lead to exciting new superstar cities around the country. Individuals and firms will want to move to these cities and to live near the new research hub. And as a result, the price of land around these hubs will rise. As discussed earlier, one feature of a successful proposal to be an innovation hub will be zoning rules that allow for affordable development. But even with such rules in place, there will be a rising value both for companies to be located at the research hub and for individuals to live nearby. We propose that the government own some of the land on which the hub is based—and that the rising rents on this land finance the innovation dividend.

Kendall Square near MIT is a perfect example of the value of technology hub real estate. Boston is a dense urban environment with a large variety of locations in which companies could locate. Yet companies will consistently pay rents that are many multiples of nearby areas to be in Kendall Square; Kendall Square recently passed Midtown Manhattan as the most expensive commercial real estate market in the United States.[34] This is not surprising given the evidence reviewed earlier about the local nature of research spillovers.

But as we discussed in Chapter 6, this real estate was not always so valuable. The rapid rise in rents in this area have benefited real estate developers such as Joel Marcus, chairman and cofounder of Alexandria Real Estate Equities. From the thirty-five buildings it owns in Cambridge, Alexandria brought in $318 million in rental income in 2017—more than triple what it made one decade earlier.[35]

In other words, a lot of the benefit from publicly and privately financed research has accrued to the owners of the local land. Our proposal is that in these new research hubs, those benefits are captured and shared with the taxpayer—through public ownership of the land on which the research hubs sit.

Public ownership of land under the research hub can be accomplished in several ways. The first is by relying on existing, and often underused, government-owned real estate. The US federal government is the largest real estate manager in the nation, with more than 3 billion square feet of buildings owned or leased, as well as 34 million acres of land. Moreover, there remains significant unused capacity in federal buildings—only 79 percent of federal buildings are used at 75–100 percent of capacity.[36] To pick an example that scores highly on our THIS index, for example, Pittsburgh has 8.2 million square feet of federal property, of which 665,000 is underused or unused, as well as more than 1,300 acres of federal land.

We are not proposing to use undeveloped public lands in the western part of the United States—wilderness areas or national forests would not make sense as tech hubs! Our suggestion is about making better use of real estate that has already been developed and that is indisputably available for commercial purposes—for example, as offices or labs. Many of the potential locations for these research hubs have substantial underused federal real estate.

Of course, existing federal real estate holdings may not be sufficiently concentrated to help create dynamic areas that will attract workers and businesses. Local governments who want to apply for hubs may need to use their own real estate or purchase land in the open market through standard transactions. Land swaps between the federal government and local government or even universities should be considered. A prominent example was the recent land swap between the US Department of Transportation and MIT of a valuable fourteen-acre parcel near Kendall Square.[37] MIT paid the federal government $750 million and agreed to create a "vibrant mixed-use site that will benefit MIT's mission and the Cambridge community," including a new federal facility.

Once federal funds start flowing into an area, however, the very conditions that make the area attractive will come under pressure from natural market reactions. The owners of the land targeted for research infrastructure and business development will realize that while that land may not be worth much today, it may be quite valuable in the future. Rational investors will therefore incorporate those expectations into prices. Depending on the timing of announcements, there is a risk that the government will end up paying higher prices for any land on which research hubs would be located, and consequently, there will be lower gains to be distributed to taxpayers. In the worst-case scenario, government funds will have served more to enrich local real estate owners rather than all Americans. Indeed, real estate investors bought up land and buildings in cities considered likely winners in the Amazon HQ2 contest, while others were reported to be raising funds so that they could purchase property as soon as the winner was announced.[38]

For this reason, it is important that communities acquire land before the announcement of a hub investment. This is what Amazon did in 2018, buying the real estate it needed before revealing its HQ2 choices. More broadly, when applying to the competition, areas should be encouraged to demonstrate the political and legal feasibility of providing publicly owned land for research, development, and commercialization.

The government should also explore innovative lease structures that are *performance-related*. One disadvantage of trying to capture returns through a fixed payment mechanism such as leases, compared to holding equity, is that it is not nearly as flexible and responsive to company performance. A five-year lease to a company that becomes incredibly successful will still pay at the initial lease rate, whereas the value of equity holdings in the company would rise rapidly.

The government could instead offer initially lower lease rates that are linked to company performance; the government then shares the risk—and the returns—of the enterprise. This allows the government to share in some of the upside created by the hubs, while providing some insurance for firms that might not able to cover high rents in the early stages of their ventures.

This is not a particularly new or radical idea—in fact, such a lease structure has long been a feature of retail leases.[39] What would be new would be extending this beyond leases that are a function of retail sales to leases that are a function of firm growth—that is, the rental rate could be tied to the measures of success such as sales, employment, profitability, or market value.

Moreover, by tying the government's return to the success of local companies, it provides a further mechanism to ensure that the government doesn't engage in cronyism by giving prime spots to favorite companies that are not productive or synergistic with the existing firms in the area. Doing so could lower the earnings in the area broadly, leading to a noticeable reduction in the revenues flowing in to finance the innovation dividend. Over time, the dividend promise provides a natural check on government malfeasance.

DISTRIBUTING THE DIVIDEND

The returns on government holdings of land would go into a national endowment fund. The resources in this fund would be immediately distributed to all Americans through an innovation dividend, a flat per capita check each year—with everyone receiving an equal dollar amount.[40] This innovation dividend idea draws directly on one of the most successful redistribution programs in the United States, the Alaska Permanent Fund.

In Alaska, leases and royalties for oil exploration and the creation of the massive Trans-Alaska Pipeline System added up to almost $1 billion in the early 1970s—and was just as quickly spent by the state legislature.[41] Alaskans voted in 1976 by a margin of 2–1 to amend the constitution to put at least 25 percent of oil revenues into a dedicated fund called the Alaska Permanent Fund.[42]

The Alaska Permanent Fund Corporation (APFC) is managed by a board of trustees and currently manages about $60 billion in assets. One of the key factors in its success has been an annual dividend that is paid to every man, woman, and child who is resident in Alaska (residents must reapply every year to establish their residency). There is remarkably little fraud, with only 0.03 percent of applications viewed as ineligible. The dividend each year amounts to roughly 10 percent of the net income earned by the APFC during the year.[43] Since 1982, the fund has paid out

$40,000 per resident of the state. The dividend in 2016 was $1,022; it peaked in 2015 at $2,072.[44]

This payment provides a way to ensure that all Alaskans benefit equally from oil revenues and has the advantage of lifting state residents out of poverty; one 2016 study found that the dividend annually lifts 15,000–25,000 Alaskans out of poverty.[45] Indeed, the dividend may be one reason that Alaska is the most equal state in the nation in terms of income distribution.[46]

Alaska is one of the most strongly Republican states in the country. Their state congressional delegation is consistently highly conservative and votes against many government spending initiatives, yet this government payment is highly popular. Moreover, this model has spread to one of the most liberal states in the United States: California. California's Global Warming Solutions Act, also known as Assembly Bill (AB) 32, requires all power plants, natural gas distributers, and other large industries that emit greenhouse gases to pay a fee based on the amount they pollute. The fees are then redistributed to individuals in the state as a "credit" on utility bills. Anyone who is an electricity or natural gas bill customer can receive this "credit," which is essentially a reduction in the utility bill. The distribution varies slightly by electricity provider, but it is typically a similar amount for every electricity user.[47]

The success of programs like this in states as disparate as Alaska and California suggests that a similar structure could draw bipartisan support in distributing the returns from the government investment in scientific research.

TIME TO MOVE

The enormous rise in public financing of research and development during and after World War II transformed our nation, creating the new products on which our modern economy was built and generating economic opportunities for all. The subsequent falloff in public funding contributed to slower productivity growth and reduced opportunities for most Americans. This should not be surprising given the economics of R&D. The private sector is unlikely through its own profit-seeking behavior to finance enough research to capture the broader social benefits of new ideas, especially those expensive and risky ventures that create industries and jobs.

To jump-start America, we need to return to the model of public-sector leadership in research and development that marked the postwar period. We have provided here the outline of a plan for doing so. Obviously, turning this outline into actual legislation would raise a wide variety of more detailed logistical hurdles, but we view this as a roadmap toward a feasible plan to return the government to its leadership role in promoting technology-led growth in the United States.

The Central Florida Research Park illustrates some of the principles that we have in mind with our proposal—but also some of the limitations. There is a lack of investment capital for firms in the CFRP, resulting in fewer large homegrown employers. And there is a skills deficit that keeps companies from finding the skilled labor they would need to grow. This is why we need to build on and improve models such as the Orlando model—combining innovative R&D infrastructure with sufficient funding and with the supply of skilled employees that are needed to fill the jobs of the future. And we need to do this soon—because other countries are already there.

8

Big Science and the Industries of the Future:

If Not Us, Then Who?

Big Science is an inevitable stage in the development of science and, for better or for worse, it is here to stay.

—Alvin M. Weinberg, 1961[1]

IN SPRING 1929, PHYSICS PROFESSOR ERNEST LAWRENCE HAD AN IDEA.[2] RESEARCHERS HAD deduced that if particles could be charged with enough energy, they could be used to break apart atoms, revealing a great deal about the nature of matter. However, generating enough energy—up to ten million volts—in a single shot was proving difficult. What if, Lawrence conjectured, energy was applied in a series of cumulative steps while the particles were accelerating in a controlled manner around a circular apparatus?

Lawrence's accelerator was a simple yet brilliant idea, providing the foundation for many breakthroughs—including work that contributed to the development of the atomic bomb. Within a decade, Lawrence was an acknowledged leader of American science and winner of the Nobel Prize. At first, however, his cyclotron was hard to fund.

Not all experts were convinced that Lawrence's idea would work, and his early results were inconclusive at best. To prove his method, Lawrence needed to build a bigger machine, with stronger magnets, and the requisite hardware was beyond the budget available through his employer, the University of California at Berkeley. Lawrence had a rising reputation, and other schools were trying to hire him, so Berkeley went all out—over the objections of some faculty—and offered him $700 in support for his lab (worth about $10,000 today). This was nowhere near enough.

Lawrence became a scientific entrepreneur, in the sense that he pitched the value of his apparatus to anyone who could be a potential source of funds. This was the 1930s, so government funding was not really an option, and universities had relatively little cash of their own to invest in such ventures. Companies were, naturally, not at all interested in supporting a project that appeared so far from potential commercial application.

Fortunately, private foundations were willing to put up some capital. A local foundation—created to promote science by a former member of the Berkeley faculty—provided early support, and the Rockefeller Foundation was also generous.[3] Lawrence's successful experiments not only changed how physicists thought about the composition of atoms, they also demonstrated that the age of Big Science had arrived.

Previously, big breakthroughs in empirical physics had been possible with relatively few resources. Marie Curie won two Nobel Prizes working from a small studio in central Paris. Ernest Rutherford completely transformed physics—and won his own Nobel—in a modest lab with only two assistants. Even Lawrence himself started out with just one helper.

By the time Lawrence reached his pinnacle, however, hundreds of people were involved in his scientific ventures. The Manhattan Project, in many ways descended from and inspired by Lawrence's work, employed more than one hundred thousand people in all capacities. As we discussed in Chapter 4, today pushing the scientific frontier forward becomes ever-more expensive while remaining essential for economic growth and good jobs.

The question now is: Where exactly should we invest our public dollars, with a view to generating new technologies that will create good jobs? The United States is a big country, and there is an argument for supporting as much science as possible—with a large, diversified portfolio, we are more likely to generate a larger number of winners. Still, the available dollars will never be unlimited—and choices need to be made.

Ernest Lawrence had great impact on science and subsequent technology development for three reasons—all of which were picked up on by his friend Vannevar Bush in the subsequent wartime push. First, work on ideas where the field is in flux—physics in the 1920s was full of controversies about the structure of atoms.

Second, put your money where it can make a difference—such as experiments that will definitely decide big questions and open the door to further work. The British work on radar created exactly this opportunity in 1940—the cavity magnetron opened the door, and the Americans walked through to great effect.

Third, pay attention to what other countries are supporting, particularly when governments elsewhere see themselves as competing with the United States, either militarily or through economic means. It was justifiable fear of efforts by other nations that motivated first the Manhattan Project and then the all-out efforts that followed Sputnik.

Where do we find these opportunities—and this competitive pressure—today? In our assessment, there are many possible avenues for productive advancement, and we wrote this book specifically to encourage further debate about exactly where to put our (hopefully expanded) science dollars going forward.

To promote that discussion, here are three areas that are worth further consideration. This is not intended to be an exhaustive—or even a long—list but rather some suggestive illustrations of where science may be heading. We have deliberately picked examples for which there are relatively clear—although perhaps not uncontroversial—measures of how the United States is doing relative to other countries also seeking to be at the forefront of technology development. Our goal is to focus attention on what we might lose to other nations if the United States retreats to the sidelines in innovative areas such as these.

SYNTHETIC BIOLOGY

Malaria is one of the deadliest infectious diseases in the world. In 2016, there were 216 million malaria cases that led to 440,000 deaths; two-thirds of those dying were children under the age of five.[4] The Centers for Disease Control and Prevention (CDC) estimate the economic costs of malaria to be at least $12 billion per year, and some economists argue that malaria is responsible for a "growth penalty" of up to 1.3 percent per year in some African countries.[5]

Fortunately, malaria can be effectively treated using the drug artemisinin. Artemisinin is taken orally over several days and kills the plasmodium parasites that cause malaria.[6] The availability of this drug has greatly increased the odds of survival for people hit with the most stubborn strains of the disease and is a major reason why the number of malaria-related deaths has fallen by more than half in the last decade.[7]

Unfortunately, artemisinin is produced naturally only by the Chinese sweet wormwood plant and only in tiny amounts, with lead times of at least eighteen months—so that farmers must predict needs for their plants more than a year in advance. As a result, supply has been erratic, with rapidly rising and falling prices of this critical medicine—for example, the price tripled from 2003 to 2005.[8]

Coming to the rescue is the potential of an important new scientific frontier—synthetic biology. With funding from private philanthropists, scientists took the complicated metabolic pathway from this rare plant and replicated it into yeast—so that the drug can now be produced on command. This pathway was licensed by a team of researchers affiliated with UC Berkeley and the California Institute of Quantitative Biomedical Research to the pharmaceutical manufacturer Sanofi, which agreed to produce and supply the drug at cost to patients with malaria in the developing world, thus stabilizing the market for this lifesaving drug.[9] As of May 2015, fifteen million treatments have been made available to African nations severely challenged by malaria outbreaks.[10]

This lifesaving example illustrates the leading edge of the potential for synthetic biology, which can be broadly defined as "design, construction, and characterization of improved or novel biological systems using engineering design principles."[11] Within medicine alone, there is the potential for new minimally invasive tests for cancer (such as urine tests that use nanoparticles designed to interact with cancer cells and release easily detected synthetic biomarkers), treatment for traumatic brain injuries (through noninvasive methods of stimulating brain circuits), and fighting infection (through modifying a cell's activity to initiate or shut off production of a protein).[12] This list does not include a wide variety of applications outside of the health arena.

For example, synthetic biology holds promise for feeding the world's population in a more sustainable fashion.[13] Animal food products can be produced without animal involvement; current projects include making a substance that has the same molecular identity as cow's milk, but without involving cows.[14] According to one assessment, cellular agriculture can also make food products specifically tailored to human needs, such as "nutrient-packed foods with a longer shelf life, meat with lower saturated fat, lactose-free milk, cholesterol-free eggs."[15] Some bacteria can help protect crops against drought by increasing water-use efficiency and reducing the need for chemical fertilizers.[16]

Another priority area is energy production. Scientists at the Lawrence Berkeley National Laboratory at UC Berkeley created a process of artificial photosynthesis in April 2015. The system can "capture carbon dioxide emissions from fossil fuels before they are released into the atmosphere and convert them into fuels, pharmaceuticals, plastics, and other valuable products."[17]

Synthetic biology techniques can also change the way that we create essential materials. Synthetic biology has enabled the construction of a gene that encodes the same amino acid sequence as the rubber plant enzyme, allowing for more renewable development of rubber.[18] Other companies are working on developing renewable bio-based acrylic that can produce a comparable product to petroleum-based acrylic but with a 75 percent reduction in greenhouse gas emissions.[19] And recent research in bioplastics focuses on generation sources using algae and modified methanobacteria to create materials that have similar characteristics to petroleum-based plastics.[20] A petroleum-based plastic water bottle can take one thousand years to biodegrade, and the United States might be adding as much as 380,000 tons of plastic bottles to landfills per year.[21] One prototype of an algae bottle takes about a week to shrink down when emptied and left in the open air.[22]

According to a recent USDA study, there are already 2,250 certified bio-based products on the market today. And the economic opportunities in this space are enormous. The USDA estimates that bioeconomy opportunities could lead to $369 billion in economic activity, four million new jobs, and three hundred million fewer gallons of petroleum required per year.[23]

The origins of what became synthetic biology lie in studies from the early 1960s on assembling new systems for regulating body function from molecular components.[24] But the real growth in the field began in the twenty-first century, with a shift toward practical applications in both medicine and other areas.[25]

The US government has been a major funder of advances in synthetic biology, investing $820 million in synthetic biology research from 2008 to 2014.[26] For example, a leading funder of research in this area was the National Science Foundation (NSF), through its Synthetic Biology Engineering Research Center (Synberc). Synberc was a multi-institutional research center, and its key members included faculty from leading academic institutions as well as industrial leaders in the field. The mission of the organization was to develop the foundational understanding and technology of biological solutions, to train a new cadre of engineers who specialize in synthetic biology, and to engage policy makers and the public about the responsible advancement of synthetic biology. The NSF provided almost $138 million in support to this initiative over the 2006–2016 period.[27]

The program appears to have been a major success. As of April 2015, Synberc had produced "364 papers in peer-reviewed journals, 88 patent applications (9 patents awarded, 5 licenses issued), 71 graduated PhDs, 8 start-up companies, and $88.6 million direct associated project funding."[28] Synberc was one of the main supporters for the iGEM

(International Genetically Engineered Machine) competition, a global synthetic biology education program for undergraduate students. Synberc partnered with the private sector; its industrial advisory board (IAB) included 29 established and start-up companies.[29]

Yet Synberc was planned as only a ten-year commitment, and in 2013, its funding began to decrease. Working with the private Alfred P. Sloan Foundation, the NSF hired a biotechnology firm that concluded that funding for the program must not only continue but should increase.[30] Congress did not follow this recommendation, and Synberc was replaced at a much lower level of funding—with the new Engineering Biology Research Consortium that is funded at just over $1 million over three years.[31]

Just as the United States is backing off, other countries are charging forward. The UK specifically has funded nearly $165 million in synthetic biology research since 2005. Japan is very active in the field as well, with a large number of companies, research centers, and universities active in the area.[32]

Then there is China. When Peking University scored its first victory at the iGEM competition in 2007, it led to the government establishing the Key Laboratory of Synthetic Biology. Since its founding in 2008, this laboratory has grown to more than sixty research scientists and seventy graduate students, and there are now thirteen research institutions in China focusing on synthetic biology.[33] From 2008 to 2016, the government has spent over 250 million yuan (US$38 million) on synthetic biology projects. A Ministry of Science and Technology representative said, "Synthetic biology has become an area of continuous investments by [the Ministry of Science and Technology] in China. In the upcoming years, 2–3 large . . . projects will be initiated every year . . . which has demonstrated that synthetic biology has been taken as [strategic] importance for the nation."

So while the United States started with a commanding lead in synthetic biology, other nations are catching up. When the iGEM competition was started by the NSF in 2006, there were 37 teams participating, 19 of which were from the United States. By 2018, there were 343 team entries, including 79 from the United States, 6 from Japan, 14 from the

UK, 16 from Germany, 10 from France, 18 from Canada, 9 from Taiwan—and 103 from China![34]

More generally, a recent report concludes that spending by other countries, particularly in Asia, threatens to erode US leadership in medical R&D.[35] "In 2004, US spending for medical R&D was 57 percent of the global total. By 2014, the US share of the global total had fallen to 44 percent, with Asia . . . increasing investment by 9.4 percent per year." In 2015, the *Journal of the American Medical Association* wrote that if current trends continue, China will overtake the United States as the global leader in medical R&D in the next ten years. China already has a greater share of the global science and technology workforce and of patents than the United States. Just when we need more funding of medical science, the US commitment to medical R&D is falling—as noted in Chapter 5, NIH research spending as a share of GDP fell by 15 percent from 2010 to 2017.

For example, consider a case we highlighted earlier: cell and gene therapy manufacturing. In Chapter 4, we discussed the problem of underprovision by the private sector of the manufacturing resources needed to move this sector forward. In Chapter 5, we discussed the well-paid jobs that are waiting to be created in this sector. Yet the United States currently lacks organization and collaboration surrounding advanced therapy manufacturing at the scale that is found in other countries.[36] The US private sector is making rapid progress in this area, but it is being slowed by these manufacturing bottlenecks.

In contrast, Canada's Center for Commercialization of Regenerative Medicine (CCRM) aims to offer direct aid to bring cell and gene therapies to market. Since its founding in 2011, CCRM has secured over C$90 million (US$69 million) in funding.[37] As an example, CCRM recently partnered with St. Louis–based Affigen to assist in developing a manufacturing platform for its lymphoma and leukemia treatments. CCRM also plans to open a manufacturing facility for cell and gene therapy materials in 2018.[38] The UK has a similar center in Cell and Gene Therapy Catapult, a government-funded consortium established in 2012 at a cost of £90 million (US$140 million).[39] CGT Catapult has already built a £60 million (US$95 million) manufacturing center "to accelerate growth of the industry in the UK" and has plans for more, hoping to attract investment to the country as a whole.[40]

HYDROGEN POWER—AND A NUCLEAR COMEBACK?

Driving is the primary mode of transportation in the United States and uses most of the 19.7 million barrels of oil consumed daily.[41] Much of that oil comes from other countries; about 2.9 billion barrels of oil, valued at $141.9 billion, were imported in 2017—amounting to 0.7 percent of GDP.[42] All this driving has dire implications for the environment as well; driving accounts for 28 percent of the manmade CO_2 emissions in the United States.[43]

It does not have to be this way. In theory, the role of oil as an "energy carrier" could be played by other substances that are plentiful in our environment, such as hydrogen, methane, methanol, or even ammonia.[44] For example, we know today that hydrogen fuel cell electric vehicles (FCEV) can readily reduce emissions by 30 percent relative to gasoline-powered engines using existing technology.[45]

Hydrogen-powered vehicles are not a new idea; the first vehicle was developed in 1991, and by the early 1990s, many automakers were investing in research in the area.[46] Given the high cost of manufacturing the fuel cells at that time, as well as the rapid development of electric vehicles, FCEVs were left behind.[47] But in recent years, lowered production costs have allowed hydrogen-powered fuel cells to make a comeback, given that they have more range, faster refueling, and better performance in the cold than electric vehicles.[48] Senior VP of Honda (one of the three major carmakers producing hydrogen fuel cell cars) Mike Accavitti said in 2013, "Innovation has reached a point that allows a more commercially viable fuel cell vehicle to be mass-produced."[49]

The future of such vehicles faces two key barriers. The first is that to use hydrogen as fuel, it must be extracted from compounds like water and methane. Naturally, any extraction process uses energy. Steam reforming is currently the most-used method of extracting hydrogen. It combines high-temperature steam with natural gas to extract hydrogen. But the real gains could come from the fact that hydrogen could be produced by carbon-free sources—which would allow for carbon-free travel. Emissions could be reduced by up to 90 percent using hydrogen produced by low-carbon energy sources like wind, solar, or nuclear.[50]

The second is the free-rider problem we encountered earlier: to make hydrogen-powered travel attractive, there must be sufficient access to hydrogen refilling stations. No company wants to invest in these filling stations if there is no guarantee they will be used, and no one wants to travel in hydrogen-powered cars if there is no way to fill them up.

The stakes here are enormous. If the United States were at the leading edge of developing this technology, the results for our economy could be transformative. A 2008 report from the Department of Energy (DoE) suggested that by 2050, a hydrogen-based power sector could create 675,000 new jobs and reduce oil imports by $370 billion a year, or 1 percent of projected GDP.[51] Even at this early stage, in the northeastern United States alone, the hydrogen and fuel cell supply chain contributed more than 6,550 jobs and approximately $620 million in labor income.[52]

The US government recognized the importance of hydrogen and made major public research investments in this area. DoE funding for this area rose from $147 million in 2004 to $267 million in 2008, but it has been steadily falling since, with funding of only $101 million in FY 2017—even as the need for such investments is as important as ever.[53]

US investments are falling just as they are rising elsewhere. The UK announced a £35 million (US$45 million) investment to encourage the use of ultralow emissions cars and motorbikes. A six-year, €100 million (US$106 million) project was launched by the EU in 2016, adding 1,230 FCEVs and 20 hydrogen refueling stations to the European network.[54] In 2014, Japan's Environment Ministry launched a ¥3 billion (US$27 million) power-to-fuel project to convert excess renewables into hydrogen for later use in transport.[55]

There is some effort to improve the hydrogen economy infrastructure in the United States, but so far only at a very modest level. California is leading the nation in funding and building hydrogen fueling stations for FCEVs, and it has proposed to have one hundred such stations by 2025.[56]

This pales in comparison to what is happening in other nations. By 2030, Germany is expected to build up to 1,000 hydrogen fueling stations, allowing good coverage for the estimated car fleet of 1.8 million vehicles, representing around 216,000 tons of hydrogen demand. France also has a substantial program.[57]

Japan is massively subsidizing both hydrogen vehicles and refueling stations, particularly in Tokyo, home of the 2020 Olympics. In the spring of 2016, then Tokyo governor Yoichi Masuzoe declared, "The 1964 Tokyo Olympics left the Shinkansen high-speed train system as its legacy. The upcoming Olympics will leave a hydrogen society as its legacy."[58]

Again, of course, there is China. China invested $40 million in research on fuel cell technologies in the 2001–2005 period, and growth since has been rapid. In 2004, the Beijing Hydrogen Park was promoted and funded by both the federal and Beijing municipal government.[59] The first hydrogen refueling station was set up there in 2006 for the demonstration of FCEV bus commercialization in China in 2006. Beijing SinoHytec, BP, and Beijing Tongfang are the project stakeholders. The park has a research-and-development center, a hydrogen refueling station, a fuel cell vehicle garage, and a maintenance workshop.

China has now more than four hundred patents related to fuel cells, ranging from catalysts to systems integration. As of 2010, there were more than sixty institutions and companies working on hydrogen fuel cell technologies.[60] In October 2017, the first commercial hydrogen tram was built in China. It emits only water, can be refilled in fifteen minutes, and can do three fifteen-kilometer round trips along a key commuter line per refill at a maximum speed of seventy kilometers per hour.[61] In December 2017, another hydrogen fuel cell industry park was announced. It will be built in Wuhan with an investment of 11.5 billion yuan (about US$1.7 billion) from a Shenzhen-based tech company.[62]

One way to supercharge the environmental benefits of hydrogen power would be to massively expand the supply of carbon-free electricity. And one method for doing so that may be making a comeback is nuclear energy, due to dramatic innovations in safety available through high-temperature gas-cooled reactors (HTGR). An HTGR uses inert helium coolant (which can never corrode or explode the way water, steam, and hydrogen can), fuel that is tolerant of much higher temperatures than traditional nuclear fuel, and a large reactor vessel that can passively conduct heat away from the core during accidents (the basis of this design's claim to be "passively safe").[63]

The Energy Policy Act of 2005 included authorization for an ambitious research program in the United States to develop an HTGR. Researchers at Idaho National Laboratory (INL) completed a series of studies of different chemical and fuel production processes driven by heat from HTGRs, identifying many promising options.[64] However, the US Department of Energy substantially scaled back the scope of and funding for the program in 2011.[65]

Meanwhile, China is rapidly improving its industrial capacity to build, operate, and potentially export nuclear reactors, and its research programs are testing out all the promising options for new reactor technologies. While the United States was scaling back its HTGR program in 2011, China was pushing ahead with the construction of a small, experimental HTGR at Tsinghua University and preparing for the construction of a larger, two-reactor HTGR in Shandong Province. Construction on this two-reactor demonstration plant was completed in 2017, and the plant was expected to begin providing electricity to the grid before the end of 2018.[66]

China also signed an agreement in 2015 with the US start-up TerraPower, founded by Bill Gates in 2006, to build a fast neutron reactor by 2025. Fast neutron reactors were originally developed by the US Atomic Energy Commission starting in the 1950s, and they produce significant amounts of plutonium as they operate, which has the potential to substantially increase the world's overall supply of nuclear fuel.[67]

THE SEA

A significant portion of world economic growth has its foundation in the discovery of new frontiers. These discoveries have been dramatic and have covered much of the known world. But there is still one vast unexplored part of our world: the deep sea.

The United States, as of 2014, spends 160 times as much exploring space as it does exploring the oceans.[68] Experts suggest that this disparity is irrational considering that "the ocean already provides us with about half the oxygen we breathe, is our single largest source of protein, has a wealth of mineral resources, and provides key ingredients for pharmaceuticals."[69] Further exploration of the oceans would both increase our access to vital natural resources and could produce path-breaking discoveries in biodiversity. Yet after being an early leader in exploring the oceans, we are falling behind.

Deep water and ultra-deep water (five thousand feet of water depth and beyond) is recognized as one of the last remaining areas of the world where oil and natural gas resources remain to be discovered and produced.[70] Yet a more important potential benefit of deepwater exploration is deep-sea mining, which can extract valuable metals and elements from the seafloor. One such valuable element is cobalt, which has numerous applications in chemical and high-technology industries for such products as lithium-ion batteries, electric vehicles, photovoltaic cells, superconductors, and advanced laser systems. Cobalt demand has been growing rapidly, and in 2017 alone, the price for cobalt more than doubled due to increased demand and instability in the Democratic Republic of the Congo, which supplies over two-thirds of the global cobalt supply.[71]

Deep-sea exploration contracts have already been approved for cobalt, as well as other increasingly expensive elements with high-tech and industrial applications like nickel, copper, and manganese.[72] All these elements can be found in nodules that litter the seafloor; nodules in the Clarion-Clipperton Fracture Zone, a Europe-sized area of the Pacific Ocean, could produce enough nickel and cobalt to match or exceed current land-based reserves.[73]

Additionally, deep-sea nodules could yield rare earth element (REE) discoveries.[74] REEs are a set of elements that have many important applications in modern technology for which there is no equal substitute; they are critical in the production of rechargeable batteries, computer and phone displays, and wind turbines and hybrid cars. These elements are not necessarily rare in general but are found in low abundance using current mining techniques, and an increasing demand for these elements is straining supply.[75]

China currently produces 80 percent of the world's rare earth element supply, giving it immense bargaining power.[76] This power is readily apparent in the market; when China's government decided to restrict exports of these elements in 2011, prices spiked.[77] Neodymium, a REE necessary for a range of products, including headphones and hybrid electric cars, saw a price increase from $42 to $283 per kilogram; samarium, crucial to the manufacture of missiles, climbed to more than $146 per kilogram, up from $18.50 a year earlier.[78]

Deep-sea mining would be an effective way to obtain a large amount of rare earth elements; in one specific section of the ocean floor, "one square kilometer could meet a fifth of the world's annual consumption of rare metals."[79]

And these minerals may just be the tip of the iceberg. The area from six thousand to eleven thousand meters down, known as the *hadal zone*, is one of the least explored regions on Earth. The zones are hot spots for high microbial activity because they receive an unusually high flux of organic matter made up of animal carcasses and sinking algae originating from the surrounding shallower seabeds.[80] For example, a compound found in the deep-sea sponge *Discodermia dissoluta* has shown potential in combating lung and breast cancer.[81] A report from the National Oceanic and Atmospheric Administration in 2000 explained that new exploration into the deep sea has discovered hundreds of new marine species and entirely new ecosystems, and "the benefit attributed to these advances has been enormous; for example, a new industry, marine biotechnology, has shown impressive returns. Understanding biodiversity of the oceans is critical to sustaining their immense global economic value."[82]

As with most modern technologies, deep-sea exploration was initially dominated by the United States—driven by government funding and academic science. Exploration has been carried out both by remote-operated vehicles (ROVs, unmanned vehicles with instrumentation that can collect samples while connected by a cable) and human-occupied vehicles (HOVs).[83] Much of the innovation in this space has occurred at the Woods Hole Oceanographic Institute (WHOI) on Cape Cod, Massachusetts. This institute was founded before World War II based on funding from the Rockefeller Foundation but since the 1950s has relied heavily on government funding.[84]

Thanks to this funding, for years the United States was the leader in exploring the deep sea. The HOV *Alvin* achieved depths of 4,500 meters in 1964 and had improved to 6,500 meters by 2013. And on May 31, 2009, the ROV *Nereus* dove 10,902 meters to explore the Mariana Trench in the western Pacific Ocean—making it the world's deepest-diving vehicle.[85]

As in so many areas, we have not kept up. A signal event was the explosion of the *Nereus* in May 2014, due to extreme pressure. Researchers hoped that Woods Hole would build a replacement vehicle to continue exploring the hadal zone, but the institute decided that the insurance money from the project would be better spent on less-risky projects.[86]

Instead, China has taken the lead. China's first ROV was built in 1994 and had a depth of only 1,000 meters, yet by 2016, the ROV *Haidou-1* had reached a depth of 10,767 meters, much deeper than any functional US ROV. A project, Development of a Manned Deep Submersible, now named *Jiaolong*, was formally started in 2003, with primary funding from the private sector.[87] On June 27, 2012, the *Jiaolong*, with two oceanauts, reached a depth of 7,062 meters in the Mariana Trench in the western Pacific Ocean, deeper than any existing US-based human-occupied vehicle.

China plans to expand their deepwater exploration and build a new mother ship for *Jiaolong* that will increase its capability in surveying and researching the deep sea. Construction should be finished in 2019, and China will begin a new global deep-sea scientific exploration mission with its *Jiaolong* manned deep-sea submersible starting in 2020.[88] Over the next five years, China plans to also build one crewed and one uncrewed submersible, each of which can reach depths of 11,000 meters, which would set the new record. China also plans to put three maritime satellites in place to improve maritime research.[89]

China's largest mining company was granted an exploration license for the deposits in the southwest Indian Ocean in 2017. The Chinese

Ocean Mineral Resources R&D Association has a trial mining system due to deploy in 2020 to recover nodules from the South China Sea. The seabed crawler is currently being built, and *Jiaolong* represents the beginning of the creation of larger vessels that will be needed to handle larger amounts of sample.[90]

THE US LEAD SLIPS AWAY

The stories of synthetic biology, hydrogen power, and deep-sea exploration reflect broader trends. The United States led the world in science innovation for decades, but in area after area, we are potentially falling behind in leadership of scientific discovery.

Although spending on research and development dramatically declined beginning in the late 1960s, the United States was still the world leader in the early 1980s, when we began to get internationally comparable R&D spending figures.[91] In 1981, the United States still spent more than 1 percent of GDP on public R&D, and total R&D spending amounted to 2.3 percent of GDP. These were both the highest proportions in the world. Few countries were even close.[92] The United States had been so far ahead of the world that even with substantial declines we were still the world leaders.

This changed dramatically over the next thirty-five years. Today, nine countries spend a higher share of GDP on public R&D. Seven countries now spend a higher share of their GDP on total R&D (public plus private) than does the United States. These changes in national priorities have real consequences.

For example, Austria (total R&D is 3 percent of GDP, while government R&D spending is 1 percent of GDP), Denmark (3 percent total, 0.87 percent government), Finland (2.9 percent total, 0.84 percent government), Korea (4.2 percent total, 1 percent government), and Switzerland (3.4 percent total, 0.83 percent government) all exceed our spending both in total and at the government level. These countries are smaller than the United States, so perhaps their research enterprise is less likely to challenge American leadership. China, on the other hand, is large and putting increasing resources behind science.

Chinese higher education was decimated as a result of the Cultural Revolution from 1966 to 1976, but during the 1990s and 2000s, the country took a major step forward in science and engineering—with an expansion of university education as a primary catalyst. From 1990 to 2010, Chinese enrollment in higher education rose eightfold, rising from 6 percent to 17 percent of total world higher educational enrollment.[93] From 1990 to 2010, the number of college graduates rose from 300,000 to nearly 3 million.

For comparison, the rise in Soviet higher education that caused great concern in the United States during the Sputnik era was an increase from 800,000 graduates in 1940 to 2.2 million in 1959.[94] Ultimately, the Soviet economic threat proved exaggerated, primarily because the country concentrated on producing weapons and never really had a market economy. China is different—it is a market economy, albeit with a large role for the government. More scientists and more engineers will add up over time to more innovation—including in areas that are directly competitive with what the United States is trying to do.

The rise in Chinese higher education is somewhat bifurcated. On the one hand, nearly half of Chinese undergraduates enroll in two- to three-year-degree programs with greater occupational training and less academic content than traditional baccalaureates. On the other hand, masters and PhDs have increased nearly *fifteenfold* from 1990 to 2010. In 1990, China graduated only 5–7 percent as many science and engineering PhDs as the United States—whereas by 2010, China (28,000 PhDs) had surpassed the United States (24,500). Chinese universities remain of a lower quality than their US counterparts, but the gap is closing: in 2003, China had only ten universities in the top five hundred in the world, and today they have thirty-two.[95]

China is not just satisfied with building its educational infrastructure; it is recruiting hard from abroad. The Chinese Thousand Talents Program is intended to recruit professors under age fifty-five from prestigious foreign institutions. Upon coming to China, the awardees are given leadership positions in universities or R&D institutes, significant research support, high wages and benefits, and even guaranteed admission to top schools for their children and jobs for their spouses.[96]

Currently in its tenth year, the program has recruited more than 2,600 people in medicine, computer science, applied industrial technologies, and other fields. According to a US national intelligence officer for military issues, "Beijing also has employed Western-trained returnees to implement important changes in its science, engineering and math curricula that foster greater creativity and applied skills at China's top-tier universities."[97]

The OECD reports that over the past decade alone, Chinese R&D has risen from 1.3 percent of GDP to 2.1 percent. The reported government R&D spending has grown from 0.34 percent of GDP to 0.44 percent of GDP, and this almost certainly understates the government's contribution to R&D in China, due to intertwined government and private ownership (and control) of companies.[98]

And there are tangible measures to show that this investment is paying off in terms of scientific advancement. In 1990, China produced only 1.2 percent of the world's scientific research papers, while the United States produced 32.5 percent. By 2016, China had passed the United States, publishing more than 426,000 studies, compared to 409,000 studies by the United States. The average quality of these research studies (measured by citations from other scientists) quadrupled over this period in China, while falling slightly in the United States.[99]

Moreover, China is making the very public commitment to building the future—while the United States has become more hesitant in this endeavor over the past several decades. In a speech to open the National People's Congress on March 5, 2016, Li Keqiang, the premier of the State Council of China, gave a broad-brush overview of the central government's draft plan for economic development during the thirteenth five-year plan, which runs from 2016 to 2020. Major elements include boosting science spending, which will rise 9.1 percent this year to 271 billion yuan (US$41 billion), reducing bureaucratic barriers for scientists and improving environmental protection while curbing carbon emissions and other pollutants. The plan is to increase R&D spending to 2.5 percent of GDP by 2020, about the same level as the United States today.[100]

TECHNOLOGY LEADERSHIP PROMOTES ECONOMIC GROWTH

Why should we care which country makes new discoveries? Ultimately, technological development benefits the world as a whole. Who cares if the Chinese make new discoveries?

We have already covered two reasons extensively: economic growth and good jobs. Economic growth in a nation is increasingly a function of the production of new ideas and the transformation of those ideas into products that consumers value. The United States used to be the world leader in both production and transformation, and it showed. We no longer are, and it is showing.

Moving first also means setting the standards—and setting the standards can mean creating the jobs that come with them. This is illustrated by the evolution of cellular communication standards. In each generation of wireless communication, economic benefits have flowed to the global leader.

The modern wireless industry began with the launch of the second-generation (2G) standard by Finland in 1991. This new system allowed for digital encryption of conversations as well as the use of data services (beginning with SMS messages). How did a small country like Finland develop this leadership in a nascent technology? Unsurprisingly (for readers of the earlier chapters), it was due to public-sector research-and-development leadership.

As discussed in Chapter 5, the Tekes program in Finland provides subsidies on a competitive basis to R&D projects, and its success is well documented. Indeed, many credit Tekes with leading the transformation of the Finnish economy from one based on natural resource exports to one based on technology—and telecommunications in particular.

Tekes was established in 1983 and immediately began supporting semiconductor and IT companies whose products could aid in telecom sector growth. Tekes' funding was instrumental in helping Finland's telecom companies with this shift from analog to digital technology. And leading the way was its partnership with Nokia. Nokia, originally founded in 1865, began as a pulp mill, eventually branching out into rubber and cables as well. It moved into telecom in the late 1970s, and by the late 1980s, much of the Finnish telecom industry had merged into Nokia.

About one-third of Tekes' funding was directed to companies in the information and communications industry. In the early 1980s, Tekes was funding about 15 percent of Nokia's total R&D expenditures. Tekes' funding to the Nokia Research Center continued during a recession in 1990, allowing research to continue even during the economic downturn.[101]

And the results were spectacular. The Research Institute of the Finnish Economy estimates that Nokia contributed 25 percent of Finland's growth between 1998 and 2007, a period that Finland's finance minister called an "economic miracle."[102] At the height of its success in 2000, Nokia produced 21 percent of Finnish exports and accounted for 20 percent of its corporate tax revenue.[103]

Meanwhile, US companies suffered. Telecommunications leaders Lucent and Alcatel both suffered rapid declines in employment from the late 1990s through the early 2000s. One expert report blames the decline on the companies' inability to make headway into the 2G market, which could have been prevented had the United States been a 2G leader.[104]

But standards moved on—and Finland, and Europe more generally, lost its leadership. Newer 3G standards were dominated by Japan, and Europe's inability to adopt 3G fast enough is estimated to have cost it hundreds of thousands of jobs.[105] The United States played a much larger leadership role in 4G standards. By the time 4G was introduced, Europe had lost almost its entire market share for mobile phones.[106] Indeed, Japan, which gained large market share from leading the way on 3G, fell back again with the introduction of 4G. Most Japanese corporations exited the handset business, and their early lead in mobile internet services evaporated.

A report published in 2018 estimated that US 4G leadership created "$125 billion in revenue to American companies that could have gone elsewhere if the US hadn't seized 4G leadership. This $125 billion is comprised of international revenue from end-user payments to device manufacturers and resellers, app and content stores, and device component suppliers."[107]

And the next wave of standards, 5G, is on the horizon—with new competition from China. The first group to develop 5G will most likely have intellectual property rights written into the standards, which has clear monetary benefits. Additionally, there will be a security advantage for the first mover, since they will understand better the system's potential vulnerabilities.[108] China was not involved in 2G and 3G and had only a 7 percent share of the 4G market. In contrast, China has invested substantial resources in 5G research since 2009, and estimates suggest they may control a substantial share of the 5G market.[109]

INTELLECTUAL PROPERTY, THE ENVIRONMENT, AND ETHICS

There are also issues beyond measured economic growth that should concern us as technology moves forward. Even the examples presented earlier raise some controversial issues. One lesson of the 1960s and 1970s is that ignoring these issues is a recipe for losing public support of technological advance. At the same time, simply ceding the frontier to other nations means letting them take the lead in a way that might not serve the interests or preferences of our citizens.

One such concern was highlighted on March 24, 2018, when President Trump announced a set of trade sanctions on China because of alleged piracy of US intellectual property. This move was panned by public policy experts from both sides of the aisle as being an ineffective response to the problem at hand and having negative repercussions for the world economy.[110] At the same time, there are legitimate concerns for our nation about both Chinese piracy and pressure on US companies to transfer technology to China.

A much more effective response would be to ensure that the United States is the world leader not just in generating ideas but in commercializing them. As we showed earlier with the development of the flat-screen television panel (pages 86–90), the problem was less Japanese infringement on the patent and more their technological infrastructure to rapidly take advantage of infringement. By not only developing the new technologies but leading the world in commercializing them, we do the most to protect our intellectual property. And this is consistent with US history not only as scientists but as practical engineers in turning good ideas into dominant businesses.

Another important concern is the environmental impact of technological advancement—the very concern that initially led many in America to turn against public science. Even though the frontier of technological advancement has changed from the time of *Silent Spring*, these issues remain paramount. This is an obvious concern with the re-emergence of nuclear generation as a source of energy. But it goes well beyond that.

Consider the serious environmental implications of deep-sea mining. It is possible that the immense sediment plumes that could be generated by mining the deep sea could temporarily choke off the oxygen supply over large areas, decreasing available sunlight for photosynthesis and causing long-term effects on biological productivity.[111] Moreover, the deep sea plays a central role in fighting climate change by storing carbon produced by human activities. The deep sea has already absorbed a quarter of the carbon released from human activity. It would be ironic—and a disaster—if, in an effort to obtain the rare earth elements to power our rechargeable batteries, we ended up worsening climate change.[112]

In principle, such mining activities are regulated by the International Seabed Authority (ISA)—but only more than two hundred kilometers from each country's coasts.[113] The ISA provides strict guidelines for the sort of ecological data that prospective miners must collect along seabeds and is currently working on the development of regulations on the exploitation of mineral resources. However, individual countries are still free to choose their own regulatory approaches to seabed mining.[114] Powerful international companies could take advantage of the lax or nonexistent review and enforcement capabilities in many small island nations of the Pacific Ocean—precisely where seabed mineral deposits are thought to be highly concentrated.

It is therefore up to the countries from which these companies operate to help impose restrictions, which allow exploration in a fashion that balances economic gains against environmental damage. If the United States does want to lead on sustainable harvesting of natural resources, it is critical that we become leaders in the technology of harvesting— with strong safeguards with regard to sustainability and potential adverse side effects.

Similarly, as we move forward with synthetic biological solutions to our looming world food shortage, we face rising public concerns over genetically modified organisms (GMOs). From a 2016 Pew survey, 39 percent of US adults believed GMO foods were worse for health than the alternative, while 10 percent said GMO foods were better for health, and 48 percent said neither better nor worse.[115] However, a 2015 Pew study found that 88 percent of American Association for the Advancement of Science (AAAS) scientists said GMO-derived foods were safe to consume, and the world's largest science and public health organizations, including the World Health Organization, American Medical Association, National Academy of Sciences, and Royal Society, have all publicly stated that consuming foods containing ingredients from GMO crops is not riskier than foods derived from conventional plant techniques.[116]

Resolving these differences in a way that protects the public interest while allowing the United States to lead on this scientific frontier (and capture the associated economic opportunities) requires a rigorous and open debate. But if we sit by while other countries take the lead in these technologies, the opportunities for meaningful debate and productive resolution will pass us by.

A related concern is in the broader area of ethics, which arises naturally in the context of synthetic biology. The next several years will likely be formative in setting the rules of the road for emerging synthetic biology research, and the shaping of synthetic biology governance will be dominated by the nations and their experts who are at the leading edge of technology development. This is because formal regulations or standards usually lag well behind the development of new technologies.

Synthetic biology could have significant negative consequences if it develops in an inappropriate fashion. For example, scientists have proposed to change the DNA of mosquitoes to make them resistant to the malaria parasite, thereby reducing the threat of this deadly disease. But they also need to consider whether this technology could be misapplied or result in a consequential accident should the genes spread to other species or cause other unintended effects.[117]

Another contentious application of synthetic biology that will require careful planning and safety standards is human germ line editing, wherein modifications to sperm or egg DNA would not be applied to just one person but to all their progeny. Tension over what is acceptable to pursue has already come up for germ line editing, after a Chinese research group reported that they used genetic techniques to modify human embryos. There are at least four additional research groups in China known to be pursuing gene editing in human embryos.[118]

Once again, these are thorny issues, but if the United States wants a seat at the table in resolving them, we need to be the scientific leaders, not followers. And if we want to lead, we need to heed a lesson that other countries have learned well: the benefits of coordinated research centers.

HOW OTHER COUNTRIES HAVE MOVED FORWARD: THE RESEARCH PARK STRATEGY

As Asian economies developed their technology sectors, they looked to the United States' successes in areas like Silicon Valley and Route 128 as models. Their conclusion was that the key to success is a research park strategy—and in particular colocating manufacturing with research.

Over the past several decades, these parks have been helpful in driving both technological advancement and economic growth in some Asian economies. Ironically, we have come full circle, and it may be time to look to this model as we think about renewing our technology leadership. In this section, we review some of the more prominent examples that the United States could draw on in creating our own updated version of a research park strategy.[119]

Taiwan

One of us teaches in the Morris and Sophie Chang Building at MIT. The funding for this building was donated by MIT graduate Morris

Chang, who may be considered the father of the semiconductor industry in Taiwan. If Chang is the father, then Hsinchu Science Park (HSP) is the birthplace.

HSP, established in 1980, was Taiwan's first government-sponsored science park. It was run by the National Science Council of the Ministry of Economic Affairs (MOEA) as a collaboration between universities, industry, and the government. It is proximate to the two leading research universities in Taiwan—National Tsing Hua University and National Chiao Tung University. The government purchased the land on which the park resided and has invested US$2 billion in software and hardware facilities. In addition, investments in HSP receive large corporate tax breaks, coinvestment opportunities from the government, and government grants.

The results have been impressive. In 1983, the park had 37 firms. By 2016, there were 487 companies with combined sales equal to about 6 percent of the entire Taiwanese economy. Employment at the park is 2.3 percent of national employment, yet the park is estimated to contribute to 15 percent of GDP. Patents in HSP in 2010 accounted for more than two-fifths of total patents for the nation of Taiwan. Two-thirds of employees in HSP have a university degree or higher, while the ratio is only 7 percent for the broader manufacturing sector; to help supply HSP with skilled workers, on-the-job training and internships for university students are available.

The clear leader of the park is the semiconductor industry, which accounts for roughly 75 percent of the sales made by companies in the park. Indeed, the semiconductor industry has powered the growth of Taiwan as an export-led economy. With annual sales exceeding US$70 billion last year, the semiconductor industry accounts for about 40 percent of exports.[120] Taiwan officials argue that semiconductors will keep Taiwan's estimated US$131 billion high-tech industry strong despite competition from China and elsewhere.[121]

Two points about the development of HSP provide important lessons. The first is the link from R&D to production. When HSP was first conceived, it was intended as a high-tech park focused on R&D work, but much of the success of the park has been through associated manufacturing; as one source says, "Were it not for the manufacturing activities, HSP could not have achieved scale economies needed to set the agglomeration process in motion."[122] R&D and technology development account for 40 percent of employment in the park, with production, manufacturing, advertising, and other employment accounting for the other 60 percent.

Second, the notion that this park would become semiconductor focused was not preordained. When HSP was founded, it was focused on six main high-tech industries: semiconductors, computers and peripherals, communications, photo-electronics, precision machinery, and biotechnology. At founding, the companies were spread broadly in terms of activities, yet the winner quickly became apparent. This may reflect the stronger international ties of this industry than the others in HSP, including the return of Morris Chang from a leading position in the US electronics industry to Taiwan.[123]

This is important because it highlights the fact that not every bet has to win. From 1990 to 2016, sales in the non-semiconductor industries in the park have grown more than fivefold, which is impressive but not that different from overall GDP growth (which was 380 percent). Meanwhile, semiconductor sales have risen fifty-two-fold, which is astonishing. R&D is risky, and many bets do not work out—but the ones that do can carry the day.

Singapore

The island nation of Singapore has not always been a leader in biotechnology. When the country laid out its National Technology Plan in 1985, it devoted only a half page out of fifty-seven pages to the "Medical and Health Care Industry." Even as late as 1993, a high-level white paper in Singapore suggested that research in the medical sector "generally does not yield any financial returns, even over the long term."

However, the 1997/98 Asian financial crisis saw a large and sudden drop-off in the number of foreign patients (mostly Malaysian and Indonesian Chinese) who traditionally patronized Singapore's private hospitals, and the hospital industry decided that medical research was critical to their survival. A new emphasis was put on cultivating the physician-researcher, who would spend up to 75 percent of her time "at the bench," and the remainder "at the bedside" of the patient, where she would translate research into experimental procedures.[124]

The importance of this area was confirmed by the response of Singapore to the severe acute respiratory syndrome (SARS) epidemic in 2003. The virology laboratory at Singapore General Hospital worked on tissue sampling and preliminary analysis, while the Genome Institute of Singapore began to sequence the SARS genome in 2003.[125] The scientific developments were followed closely by the media and general public, and as one account noted, "By the end of it, no one in Singapore could doubt the relevance of cutting-edge medical research to local health. Besides the economic imperative, such research now seemed necessary insurance toward national (including economic) survival. While the SARS crisis lasted only two months, it permanently elevated public consciousness of communal health and embodiment."[126]

This timing was critical because it corresponded to the early stages of Biopolis, Singapore's research park based around medical technology. The park was conceived as a hub to encourage collaboration between major biotechnology companies and public research institutions. Phase I of Biopolis consisted of a S$500 million (S$ denotes Singapore dollars; equivalent to US$364 million), 185,000-square-meter, seven-building complex. Additional phases over the past decade have almost doubled that size. Biopolis now consists of five research institutes under the government's Biomedical Research Council, focusing on bioinformatics, bioprocessing technology, genomics, bioengineering and nanotechnology, and molecular and cell biology.

The park is proximate to the National University of Singapore (NUS), the oldest and largest public university in Singapore, with enrollment of about thirty-six thousand students. The R&D budget for NUS more than tripled from 2003 to 2007, as Biopolis was growing. NUS accounts for about half of the training of research scientists and engineers and of peer-reviewed science-and-technology publications in the country.

The park has seen explosive growth since its founding. The number of research staff housed at Biopolis grew by 250 percent from 2002 to 2011 to over 5,000.[127] Almost forty corporate research labs are situated in Biopolis, and many leading biopharmaceutical companies engage in public-private partnerships within the research park. The park is the epicenter of the growth of the biomedical sciences (BMS) industry, which has become a major contributor to the country's economy. BMS manufacturing output increased by nearly fivefold from S$6 billion (US$4.4 billion) in 2000 to S$29.4 billion (US$21.4 billion) in 2012. During the same period, employment grew by more than twofold from 6,000 to 15,700. The industry now contributes nearly 25 percent of the total value added to the overall manufacturing sector of Singapore.[128]

The success of Biopolis in scientific terms is undeniable. *Scientific American* publishes its "worldVIEWguide," which provides a global biotechnology perspective and ranks each country based on specific metrics. This ranking started in 2009.[129] Singapore has finished in the top ten in every year since 2009 and has finished in the top five every year except 2011. Singapore went from fifth in 2015 to second, behind only the United States (a nation that has nearly sixty times the population), in 2016.[130]

A more directly concerning measure of success from the US perspective is that a major investor in Biopolis is an iconic US company, Procter & Gamble. P&G, a household name in home and personal care, invested S$250 million (US$180 million) to build a mega innovation center in Biopolis in 2011.[131] P&G noted the proximity of Biopolis to Asian markets as one motivation for the move, but they also emphasized the focus on research funding in Singapore, in particular through the Agency for Science, Technology, and Research (A*STAR), which promotes mission-oriented research that advances scientific discovery and technological innovation.

James Kaw, the P&G Singapore Innovation Center director, emphasized the agglomeration benefits of Biopolis, highlighting that being at Biopolis makes it easy for him and his colleagues to meet key managers of A*STAR and their scientific leadership to discuss collaboration ideas. "We like our proximity to the Executive Directors of the different labs," says Mr. Kaw. "We can quickly go to the labs to talk to them."[132]

Singapore plans to pursue this approach further. In early 2016, Prime Minister Lee Hsien Loong, chairman of the Research, Innovation, and Enterprise Council (RIEC), announced an 18 percent increase in the nation's 2016–2020 research budget over the previous five-year budget—to 1 percent of the country's gross domestic product, a percentage on par with that of other industrialized countries. The S$13.5 billion (US$9.7 billion) in funding includes a budget increase of more than 50 percent for emerging research, innovation, and enterprise activities. In addition, the National University of Singapore opened a S$25 million (US$18 billion) synthetic biology center on September 30, 2015, and Rockefeller University plant molecular biologist Nam-Hai Chua announced plans to move his research—exploring plant RNA's impact on drought tolerance—to Singapore's Temasek Life Sciences Laboratory.[133]

China

Taiwan and Singapore are small countries, measured in terms of population or GDP relative to the United States (or as a share of the world economy). However, to see that such an approach can work in a larger country, look no further than China. While the definition of a research park is not entirely homogenous, China is currently estimated to have fifty-four "science and technology industrial parks," totaling sixty thousand companies with eight million employees. These parks contributed 7 percent of China's GDP and close to 50 percent of all China's R&D spending.[134] China's national R&D strategy is structured around these parks.[135]

The research park strategy starts with Zhongguancun in Beijing. The park was the brainchild of Chunxian Chen, a former scientist in the Chinese Academy of Sciences (CAS). Soon after economic reform began in 1978, Chen, along with ten fellow CAS researchers, took academic tours of the United States. He later summarized his visits of Silicon Valley and Route 128 outside Boston at a conference of the Beijing Plasma Association on October 23, 1980. He reasoned that "the density of professional talents in Zhongguancun was not less than the areas of Boston and Silicon Valley."[136] Indeed, in the early 1980s, there were approximately sixty key universities and colleges and two hundred scientific research institutes in Beijing, including Peking University and Tsinghua University, China's top two universities.

The park started slowly, but an early success emerged when Chen's fellow researchers at the CAS started a business, Lenovo, in 1984. CAS provided them with the initial capital of US$24,000 and the company was started in Zhongguancun.[137] Today, the company employs fifty-five thousand, with revenue of US$43 billion.[138]

By 1986, there were one hundred start-ups in Zhongguancun, and the government approved the establishment of Zhongguancun as an experimental zone for the development of high and new technology. And the growth thereafter was exponential. Today, the park covers more than 100 square kilometers and is estimated to house 20,000 companies with 250,000 employees.[139] Nearly half of the Chinese firms listed on the NASDAQ are based in ZGC, and Expert Market ranked Beijing's Zhongguancun as #1 for "world's tech hubs" in 2017, citing its favorable climate for early-stage funding and the city's affordable cost of living.[140,141]

The success of Zhongguancun led to the development of the national Torch Project of the State Science and Technology Commission in 1988. Its purpose was to construct the science-and-technology industry parks to incubate new start-ups in Zhongguancun in particular and in China in general. The state hoped that by building science parks, the R&D institutes, universities, and start-ups could work together closely to commercialize the innovation that rolled out of national science and technology projects. This project has driven the fifty-four research parks now found throughout China.

These parks are not just in large cities. Consider the park in Hefei in Anhui Province. This historically agricultural area was transformed when the University of Science and Technology of China (USTC) relocated its campus from Beijing to Hefei. The USTC is the only mainland university with two national laboratories, and it has as many designated "key laboratories" as do Peking University and Tsinghua University in Beijing, despite having half as many students—and has the highest percentage of alumni elected to the CAS and the Chinese Academy of Engineering.[142]

The Hefei research park was established at the start of the 1990s and has grown enormously. From 1997 through 2015, the number of firms in the Hefei industrial zone (including the park) has risen from just over one hundred to over one thousand, and the number of employees in the Hefei metro area more than doubled from 2.27 million in 1998 to 5.3 million in 2016.[143]

And the growth of Hefei, centered on this research park, has been impressive. The Hefei population doubled from 1990 to 2000, and then again from 2000 to 2010, making it the fastest-growing metro area in China. GDP per capita has grown fourfold from 2006 to 2017, compared to less than tripling in Beijing in the same period.[144]

Canada

Other nations are also focusing their research efforts into concentrated research parks as well. Returning to the case of Amazon, it is worth reflecting on a notable inclusion in the list of finalists: Toronto. This is no mere effort by Amazon to seem inclusive of our neighbor to the north. Rather, it reflects the dramatic growth of Toronto as a technology hub—supported by the efforts of the Ontario government.

A primary source of support is the MaRS (Medical and Related Sciences) Discovery District. MaRS is a not-for-profit corporation that provides research and lab facilities for start-ups, as well as venture capital resources for funding commercialization of innovation.[145] The 1.5 million–square-foot project was developed in two phases. Phase I began in 2000 and consisted of the construction of three new buildings of office space and labs, as well as the retrofitting of the Toronto General Hospital into the MaRS Centre.[146] The federal government of Canada provided an unknown amount of loans for this project, and the province of Ontario loaned C$55 million (US$37 million) to help with land acquisition, construction, and operation. Phase I was completed in 2005 and was quickly at full capacity (and making a profit from rental revenue) when MaRS decided to launch phase II. Phase II consisted of a new West Tower that would be fully privately financed, but in which the government agreed to house two provincial agencies.

Construction began in 2008, but after C$90 million (US$60 million) had been spent, private financing dried up due to the financial crisis. The Ontario government swung into action and, by 2015, had provided C$395 million (US$265 million) in loans.

And the government has been rewarded. MaRS was supposed to repay C$290 million (US$195 million) by 2019, but actually did so in 2017.[147] The building is now fully leased thanks to the arrival of major players such as Facebook, Airbnb, and IBM, as well as twenty-eight Canadian start-ups. According to MaRS's numbers, the building generates C$20 million (US$13 million) per year in rental revenue. An assessment of MaRS's economic impact was done by the Centre for Spatial Economics, which estimates that 6,662 jobs have been created with MaRS.[148]

The fact that a foreign city would even be on the list to be considered by the most valuable company in the United States is notable. The fact that, along objective criteria, Toronto would have been a terrific choice is worrisome.

WHO WINS THE GOOD JOBS?

The United States was an early investor in Big Science, as much by luck as strategy. The development of experimental physics coincided with an influx of foreign talent, primarily a consequence of the rise of Hitler in Germany. When the US government decided to back scientists, led by Vannevar Bush, the goal was urgent national defense.

These investments paid great economic dividends, and the entire venture scaled up effectively in response to the perceived Soviet threat. Combined with broader access to more education after World War II, the effects on the American middle class were positive and long-lasting.

Since the 1970s, however, America has lost interest in backing science on the previous scale. The shift to private-sector research and development has been at best a partial replacement. Private sector companies are not often interested in fully funding ideas that benefit other firms. In other cases, these companies do not have the resources to make the large-scale investments required to do cutting-edge research.

The venture capital financing system is impressive but focuses primarily on backing ideas that can be commercialized easily and with relatively little capital. Increasingly, this approach generates relatively few good jobs in the United States.

This retreat from the scientific frontier will only continue as current fiscal pressures bear down on the federal discretionary budget that includes US science. An aging population and rising medical costs imply an ever-rising commitment to mandatory social insurance programs like Medicare and Social Security, while the willingness of politicians to propose higher taxes remains quite limited. Last in line are discretionary programs such as research funding, as witnessed by a steady decline in such support after the short-lived boost in the late 2000s.

At the same time, the general trend of technology development continues. Other countries, including China, have taken note and are stepping into the gap that American hesitation has created. These countries will increasingly capture the good jobs that are associated with technology creation, and they are also more likely to set the rules for critical regulatory and ethical issues that arise with new technologies.

It is not too late to reverse this trend. A major push now on public funding for science could tip the balance in multiple fields and generate millions of good jobs.

The United States is in a terrific position to do so for many reasons, ranging from sufficient long-term investors to a higher education system that is by far the best in the world. Perhaps most significantly, we have tremendous geographic diversity that we can use to our advantage.

The previous section described research parks in other nations—but we can go further. The next phase is perhaps not research parks but rather broader research hubs that cover large areas and encourage the emergence of new superstar cities. In a nation as spacious and diverse as the United States, there is no need to force everyone to be in the same building or park, so long as they are close enough to benefit from the agglomeration that comes with the knowledge economy.

Creating a new role for the US federal government will require a major financial commitment, but the returns can be spectacular. We have suggested a commitment of $100 billion a year, which would take us less than halfway back to our peak of public research-and-development spending (relative to the size of our economy) but would likely be enough to propel us back to our world leadership position.

Such spending should create roughly four million good jobs and share growth opportunities across our whole nation. Scaling this spending up or down would increase or lower the effects commensurately, but we caution that if the effort is not a major one, it will not benefit from the geographic benefits of successful research hubs.

It seems odd to say that America is struggling when we remain one of the world's richest nations. But public opinion and political expression clearly show that many Americans are—with good reason—not happy with their own prospects. We need to make the major commitments to broad-based growth that will create a new American future. We need to jump-start all of America.

Appendix:

102 Places for Jump-Starting America

AMERICA HAS MANY TALENTED PEOPLE, SPREAD OUT ACROSS A LARGE GEOGRAPHIC AREA. IN this appendix, we describe one way to measure the relative potential for various places to develop as technology hubs. What we propose here is far from being the only approach to measuring the strengths and weaknesses of particular locations. This is a suggestive exercise intended both to illustrate the enormous opportunity that already exists in all corners of our nation and to help start a more detailed conversation on whether, where, and how to jump-start the creation of more good jobs.

We use data on 378 metropolitan statistical areas (MSAs, which represent cities and the associated commuting communities) in the contiguous 48 states.[1] Appendix Table A1 summarizes our eight component measures, sources, and notes on construction.

The American Community Survey (ACS), conducted by the Census Bureau, is the largest annual survey of households in the United

---

Notes to this appendix can be found on p. 242.

States and collects a rich array of demographic and economic information. The Census Bureau makes data available at various geographical levels through the National Historical Geographic Information System (NHGIS).[2] From this, we download variables at the MSA level. The ACS is largest at decennial years, when there is a census sample. House price data are not available for all MSAs in non-decennial years, so we use the latest available comprehensive values, which are for 2010.[3] For commuting time, we measure the number of workers who report commuting less than thirty minutes to work as a share of all commuters.

For information on university quality at the graduate and undergraduate level, we use a 2005 survey carried out by the National

APPENDIX TABLE A1

MEASURE	SOURCE	CONSTRUCTION NOTES
Population age 25–64	American Community Survey, 2016 data	Taken directly from source
College share	American Community Survey, 2016 data	Share of population, age 25+, with a college or postgraduate degree
Top twenty graduate science departments	National Academy of Sciences, 2005 Survey	Number of science and social science programs ranked in the top twenty in 2005 survey
Number of undergraduates going to top-twenty programs	National Science Foundation's Survey of Doctorate Recipients, 2005–2015	Number of undergraduates who subsequently graduated from a top-twenty PhD program, in total over 2005–2015
Patents per worker	Forman, Goldfarb, and Greenstein (2016), 2010 data	Number of patents per employee
House price	American Community Survey, 2010	Average house price
Crime rate	Federal Bureau of Investigations, Uniform Crime Reporting, 2016	Violent crimes per 10,000 persons
Commuting time	American Community Survey, 2016	Share of commuters who travel less than 30 minutes on average to work

Academy of Sciences.[4] This survey uses a broad set of measures to rank the quality of graduate programs at US universities. We use these rankings to create an indicator for top-twenty programs in each field, and then we count how many such programs exist at every university in each MSA.[5]

To measure the quality of undergraduate education, we use a survey of graduating PhD students collected by the National Science Foundation each year through its National Center for Science and Engineering Statistics (NCSES). This Survey of Doctorate Recipients (SDR) has been fielded since 1973, and it includes a variety of information about doctoral graduates, including where they previously received an undergraduate degree. We provided an official at the NSF with a file containing information on the top twenty graduate programs in each field (as described in the preceding paragraph), and he matched that to their survey.[6] He then identified the undergraduate institution for each student graduating from a top-twenty PhD program over the 2005–2015 period. We counted the number of such students receiving an undergraduate degree from each county in the United States. We aggregated those data to the MSA level.[7]

Patent data were provided to us by Shane Greenstein, as used in his paper with Chris Forman and Avi Goldfarb.[8] They collected the number of patents granted by the US Patent and Trademark Office (USPTO), and from this set, they measure the number of new patents each year (*year* here is defined as year of application, due to delays in granting patents). We use 2010 values, as these are the most recent that they had available. We normalized this by the number of workers in each MSA (using data from the ACS, this time for 2010), as this measures the entrepreneurial nature of the workforce.

Crime data are from the FBI's Uniform Crime Reports (UCR) system.[9] We gathered data on violent crimes for every MSA in 2016 and then normalized by population. Violent crime includes murder, rape, robbery, and aggravated assault.

MSAs are a construct of statistical convenience. In thinking about potential technology hubs, it may make sense to combine MSAs. For example, Des Moines and Ames, Iowa, are fifty minutes apart. Des Moines is significantly larger, but Ames has a more highly educated population, high-quality educational institutions, and a higher rate of patenting. By combining them in our data, we create a technology hub that is both large and has strong educational attainment. Using this logic, we created twenty-four pairs of cities and two "triangles" where combining three MSAs seemed appropriate.[10]

We do not claim to have considered all possible combinations. Many MSAs are within an hour of other MSAs and could be combined in various ways apart from our efforts. We also did this work only at the level of MSAs. There may well be combinations of smaller cities or nearby non-MSA areas that create economic development areas with sufficient population, high-quality educational infrastructure, and a good quality of life. We look forward to hearing more about this from readers.

As described in the text, we created our Technology Hub Index System (THIS) by first selecting a set of places in the United States that have—as we define it—sufficiently high population, educational attainment, and quality of life. For population, we choose MSAs with more than one hundred thousand workers age twenty-five to sixty-four. For average education, we choose a college-educated share of the twenty-five-year-old and older population that is greater than 25 percent (this is about 12 percent below the mean national rate of 27.9 percent for this variable). Our cutoff for mean house price is below $265,000, which is about 14 percent above the mean house price of $232,222 in 2010.[11]

The results of this exercise are shown in Appendix Table A2, in which places are listed in order of their overall THIS ranking. The table has columns for:

- MSA name
- Overall THIS ranking

- Ranking for total population (one-third weight in THIS)
- Ranking for each of four education measures (overall education ranking has one-third weight in THIS)
  - » Share of college graduates (one-quarter weight in overall education ranking)
  - » Number of top-twenty graduate programs (one-quarter weight in overall education ranking)
  - » Number of undergraduates going to top-twenty PhD programs (one-quarter weight in overall education ranking)
  - » Patents per worker (one-quarter weight in overall education ranking)
- Ranking for each of three lifestyle measures (overall lifestyle ranking has one-third weight in THIS)
  - » Average house price (one-third weight in overall lifestyle ranking)
  - » Violent crime rate (one-third weight in overall lifestyle ranking)
  - » Share of workers commuting less than 30 minutes to work (one-third weight in overall lifestyle ranking)

The list in Appendix Table A2 is comprised of large urban areas from thirty-six states. States that are excluded are largely due to high house prices (California, Connecticut, Colorado, Maryland, New Hampshire, and Rhode Island), insufficient population in the largest cities (Delaware, Maine, Montana, Vermont, and Wyoming), or insufficient education according to our criteria (Nevada). Of course, all such variables can be changed in the long run, with sufficient local political will.

Appendix Table A2

LOCATION NAME	OVERALL RANKING	RANKING BY SIZE	RANKING BY EDUCATION CATEGORIES				RANKING BY LIFESTYLE CATEGORIES			GROUP OF MORE THAN ONE MSA?
		Population 25–64	Percent College Grad	Top Science Grad Programs	Top Science Under-graduates	Patents Per Worker	Average House Price	Violent Crimes Per Capita	Commute Less Than 30 Min	
Rochester, NY	1	26	30	24	12	3	19	28	35	No
Pittsburgh, PA	2	10	23	7	5	30	35	37	93	No
Syracuse/Utica-Rome, NY	3	29	64	24	22	44	9	33	27	Yes
Columbus, OH	4	15	18	7	11	48	71	34	74	No
Bloomington/Champaign-Urbana, IL	5	73	2	3	4	19	24	22	6	Yes
Cleveland-Elyria, OH	6	16	53	18	10	25	33	49	83	No
Ames/Des Moines-West Des Moines, IA	7	44	7	18	19	21	61	35	18	Yes
Binghamton/Ithaca, NY	8	80	22	4	1	7	10	13	7	Yes
Cincinnati, OH-KY-IN	9	13	33	46	26	22	56	26	80	No
Indianapolis-Carmel-Anderson/Lafayette-West Lafayette, IN	10	11	29	5	8	27	46	90	76	Yes
Grand Rapids-Wyoming, MI	11	27	40	46	32	31	47	41	33	No
St. Louis, MO-IL	12	6	26	14	14	45	66	68	89	No
Atlanta-Sandy Springs-Roswell, GA	13	3	9	6	6	37	98	65	102	No

Akron/Canton-Massillon, OH	14	25	75	46	50	17	16	29	57	Yes
Buffalo-Cheektowaga-Niagara Falls, NY	15	24	41	30	36	53	20	69	38	
Albany-Schenectady-Troy, NY	16	33	11	22	20	5	82	30	70	No
Dallas-Fort Worth-Arlington, TX	17	1	28	30	34	28	95	45	99	No
Appleton/Green Bay/Oshkosh-Neenah, WI	18	42	82	46	47	46	37	4	15	Yes
Dayton, OH	19	40	83	46	51	35	5	31	34	No
Cedar Rapids/Iowa City, IA	20	70	8	24	24	15	65	12	17	Yes
Houston-The Woodlands-Sugar Land, TX	21	2	37	15	16	24	96	89	101	No
Janesville-Beloit/Madison, WI	22	38	3	1	2	12	99	96	40	Yes
Tucson, AZ	23	31	38	12	18	9	68	70	77	No
Detroit-Warren-Dearborn, MI	24	4	52	46	50	6	48	86	97	No
Omaha-Council Bluffs, NE-IA	25	30	20	46	69	78	54	55	20	No
Kansas City, MO-KS	26	14	16	40	73	34	70	76	73	No
Milwaukee-Waukesha-West Allis/Racine, WI	27	17	31	30	33	26	81	94	64	Yes
Lexington-Fayette, KY	28	58	12	16	28	32	79	25	42	No
Battle Creek/Kalamazoo-Portage, MI	29	68	59	40	40	52	13	6	23	Yes
Ann Arbor/Jackson, MI	30	60	1	1	3	2	94	47	67	Yes
Lansing-East Lansing, MI	31	67	27	10	17	69	12	67	24	No
Charlotte-Concord-Gastonia, NC-SC	32	7	24	46	42	62	93	59	94	No
Oklahoma City, OK	33=	19	58	46	45	85	43	71	56	No

LOCATION NAME	OVERALL RANKING	RANKING BY SIZE	RANKING BY EDUCATION CATEGORIES				RANKING BY LIFESTYLE CATEGORIES			GROUP OF MORE THAN ONE MSA?
		Population 25–64	Percent College Grad	Top Science Grad Programs	Top Science Under-graduates	Patents Per Worker	Average House Price	Violent Crimes Per Capita	Commute Less Than 30 Min	
Logan/Ogden-Clearfield, UT-ID	33=	45	42	30	52	42	101	1	41	Yes
Tampa-St. Petersburg-Clearwater, FL	35	5	66	40	47	64	75	56	95	No
Allentown-Bethlehem-Easton, PA-NJ	36	36	70	46	29	20	78	7	88	No
Greenville-Anderson-Mauldin, SC	37	34	69	30	30	11	50	83	65	No
Bloomington/Columbus, IN	38	97	13	12	23	10	51	11	10	Yes
Greensboro-High Point, NC	39	41	72	46	54	57	29	43	45	No
Lawrence/Manhattan/Topeka, KS	40	72	15	18	21	76	42	40	21	Yes
Boise City, ID	41=	46	43	46	81	4	88	14	47	No
San Antonio-New Braunfels, TX	41=	9	77	46	44	71	58	62	92	No
Harrisburg-Carlisle, PA	43	53	36	46	53	36	63	20	50	No
Knoxville, TN	44=	35	63	30	39	40	64	58	68	No
Niles-Benton Harbor/South Bend-Mishawaka, IN-MI	44=	64	88	40	25	23	18	52	30	Yes
Wichita, KS	46	48	48	46	89	60	8	84	11	No
Tulsa, OK	47	28	84	46	83	66	27	72	39	No

48	Lincoln, NE	83	4	22	33	56	60	38	9	No
49	Blacksburg-Christiansburg-Radford/Roanoke, VA	62	67	11	13	29	73	9	85	Yes
50	Orlando-Kissimmee-Sanford, FL	8	46	30	57	67	91	79	100	No
51	Louisville/Jefferson County, KY-IN	22	73	40	~5	70	55	63	75	No
52	Columbia/Jefferson City, MO	81	19	24	~5	79	40	39	13	Yes
53	Clarksville/Nashville-Davidson-Murfreesboro-Franklin, TN-KY	12	35	24	~7	84	102	92	98	Yes
54	Toledo, OH	51	87	46	5~	51	6	91	25	No
55	Fort Wayne, IN	71	86	46	9~	41	2	15	26	No
56	Memphis, TN-MS-AR	20	81	46	7~	59	25	102	81	No
57	College Station-Bryan, TX	98	21	9	1~	50	67	32	3	No
58	Peoria, IL	77	79	46	7~	16	15	44	19	No
59	Fayetteville-Springdale-Rogers, AR-MO	59	47	46	64	82	57	27	32	No
60	Springfield, MA	50	44	18	7	63	92	78	60	No
61	Birmingham-Hoover, AL	23	55	30	61	93	52	88	91	No
62	Albuquerque, NM	32	39	46	55	33	84	101	69	No
63=	New Orleans-Metairie, LA	21	61	30	31	90	89	82	87	No
63=	Winston-Salem, NC	47	93	40	49	58	38	66	55	No
65	Erie, PA	87	76	46	68	43	11	18	16	No
66	Columbia, SC	39	34	46	57	81	32	93	82	No
67	Asheville, NC	65	32	46	82	74	83	8	36	No
68	Gainesville, FL	92	10	16	9	18	53	87	46	No

LOCATION NAME	OVERALL RANKING	RANKING BY SIZE	RANKING BY EDUCATION CATEGORIES				RANKING BY LIFESTYLE CATEGORIES			GROUP OF MORE THAN ONE MSA?
		Population 25–64	Percent College Grad	Top Science Grad Programs	Top Science Under-graduates	Patents Per Worker	Average House Price	Violent Crimes Per Capita	Commute Less Than 30 Min	
Huntsville, AL	69	63	14	46	78	14	69	73	59	No
Fargo, ND-MN	70	95	6	46	56	49	80	23	1	No
Lancaster, PA	71	57	102	46	46	47	87	3	66	No
Davenport-Moline-Rock Island, IA-IL	72	76	94	46	76	54	14	54	14	No
Idaho Falls/Pocatello, ID	73	100	56	46	93	38	30	5	8	Yes
Spokane-Spokane Valley, WA	74=	56	60	46	65	61	86	42	48	No
Jacksonville, FL	74=	18	50	46	88	80	90	80	96	No
Rochester, MN	76	99	17	46	101	1	76	2	22	No
Baton Rouge, LA	77	37	89	24	42	89	62	81	86	No
Palm Bay-Melbourne-Titusville, FL	78=	54	62	30	77	13	72	75	78	No
Eugene, OR	78=	79	68	46	41	55	100	17	12	No
Jackson, MS	80	52	57	46	80	99	34	53	79	No
Auburn-Opelika/Columbus, GA-AL	81	66	65	46	62	88	31	60	49	Yes
Little Rock-North Little Rock-Conway, AR	82	43	49	46	79	94	45	99	63	No
Greenville/New Bern, NC	83	86	74	46	84	77	21	21	31	Yes
Decatur/Springfield, IL	84	82	51	46	95	73	3	97	5	Yes

Morgantown/Wheeling, WV-OH	85	85	96	46	63	83	7	24	53	Yes
Duluth, MN-WI	86	88	101	46	67	86	26	16	28	No
Lubbock, TX	87	84	54	46	66	92	17	100	2	No
Tallahassee, FL	88	78	5	46	36	68	59	98	58	No
Midland/Saginaw, MI	89	91	95	46	100	8	1	74	37	Yes
Daphne-Fairhope-Foley/Mobile, AL	90	49	99	46	92	96	36	51	90	Yes
Sioux Falls, SD	91	93	25	46	97	65	77	46	4	No
Springfield, MO	92	69	92	46	72	97	22	85	43	No
Kennewick-Richland, WA	93	89	98	46	101	39	74	10	29	No
Montgomery, AL	94	75	71	46	85	100	28	61	61	No
Pensacola-Ferry Pass-Brent, FL	95	61	85	46	93	87	44	77	72	No
Chattanooga, TN-GA	96	55	97	46	86	91	41	95	71	No
Lynchburg, VA	97	94	91	46	84	72	49	19	62	No
Johnson City, TN	98	101	100	46	89	75	23	36	54	No
Savannah, GA	99=	74	45	46	98	95	85	50	84	No
Tuscaloosa, AL	99=	96	78	46	70	98	39	57	51	No
Warner Robins, GA	101	102	90	46	99	102	4	48	44	No
Atlantic City-Hammonton, NJ	102	90	80	46	87	101	97	64	52	No

A slash (/) indicates that two or more MSAs were combined in a single row.

Hyphens between city names indicate that those cities are part of the same MSA. Hyphens between two-letter state abbreviations indicate all states in the MSA (or combined MSAs) in that row.

Note that some cities have an MSA, as defined by the Office of Management and Budget, that includes more than one state.

NOTES TO APPENDIX

1. The Office of Management and Budget defines both metropolitan and micropolitan statistical areas. "The general concept of a metropolitan statistical area is that of an area containing a large population nucleus and adjacent communities that have a high degree of integration with that nucleus." Office of Management and Budget, "2010 Standards for Delineating Metropolitan and Micropolitan Statistical Areas," *Federal Register* 75, no. 123 (June 28, 2010): 37246–37252, https://www.gpo.gov/fdsys/pkg/FR-2010-06-28/pdf/2010-15605.pdf.

2. Anyone wishing to use these data should start on this webpage: National Historical Geographic Information System, https://www.nhgis.org.

3. In 2010, the country was in the midst of a housing crisis, so this affected housing prices. However, the crisis was still nationwide at that stage, so we think using data from this year is reasonable. Of course, we encourage people to use alternative measures when these become available (e.g., after the 2020 census).

4. National Academy of Sciences et al., *A Data-Based Assessment of Research-Doctorate Programs in the United States* (Washington, DC: National Academy of Sciences, 2010), https://www.nap.edu/rdp/docs/report_brief.pdf.

5. There are a number of rankings provided in this report. We use the "mean R rank," based on research quality.

6. We are extremely grateful to Darius Singpurwalla for his endless patience with our repeated requests for data.

7. Our summary name for this measure is *quality of undergraduate education,* but of course our specific measure emphasizes quality of preparation for further study in science and other quantitative studies. We think this gets at the kinds of skills helpful in forming tech hubs.

8. Chris Forman, Avi Goldfarb, and Shane Greenstein, "Agglomeration of Invention in the Bay Area: Not Just ICT," *American Economic Review Papers and Proceedings* 106, no. 5 (2016): 146–151.

9. These data are available online through this page: FBI Uniform Crime Reporting, https://ucr.fbi.gov/ucr.

10. We did this using Google Maps. Apologies to anyone living in a place who does not wish to cooperate with neighbors in another MSA or who regards that other MSA as simply too far away. Our list was constructed so as to make places look better—erring on the side of encouraging positive thinking about economic development potential. We welcome the creation of alternative lists or suggestions with modifications for our criteria.

11. We chose these values below/above the mean to allow for some noise in the measurement of the variables and some room for short-term modest changes in these variables.

Acknowledgments

This book represents a major departure from both of our areas of previous research. As a result, we leaned more than usual on a large set of subject experts who generously devoted time to bringing us up to speed on the key issues. These colleagues and friends answered countless annoying questions as we rode freely on their expertise to develop our own.

We are particularly indebted to our MIT colleagues Daron Acemoglu and David Autor. This project grew out of a set of conversations between the four of us in early 2017 about future directions for US economic policy. Without their insights and motivating conversations, this book would not exist. And without their ongoing support and willingness to help us shape our arguments, the book would be much weaker.

Other economists at MIT played a critical role in this book as well. John Van Reenen was perhaps the single person we most pestered with questions, and he was gracious in his thoughtful responses, including working with his coauthor, Claudia Steinwender, on helpful calculations using their data on military R&D. Heidi Williams generously shared her insights on medical R&D. Pierre Azoulay, Danielle Li, Antoinette Schoar, and Scott Stern at the Sloan School at MIT provided thoughtful insights about the economics of R&D and entrepreneurship. Bill Wheaton helped us understand local land-use restrictions and how we might best incorporate real estate policy into our proposal. Paul Joskow and Dick Schmalensee kindly read the entire early manuscript and provided valuable comments throughout, and in particular on energy policy. And once again, David Autor was a constant source of information about the labor market implications of our arguments.

The basic structure of the book benefited from a series of motivating conversations with other researchers as well. Danny Weitzner told us to start with Vannevar Bush, and Andy Lippman suggested that we read about Tuxedo Park. Ed Glaeser provided a valuable set of insights on how to think about local economic policies. Adam Jaffe was a great source of insight on the economics of R&D, and he and his coauthor, Trinh Le, generously performed calculations using their New Zealand data on implied cost per job. Enrico Moretti helped educate us on the economics of local labor markets and on how his research related to our own; his classic book on economic divergence in the United States was a particular inspiration for our own work. Larry Summers provided a critical assessment of the policy issues raised by our proposal. Andy Wu generously shared his knowledge of the economics of venture capital. Phil Budden and Fiona Murray shared their details of their own related work. We also had helpful discussions with (and useful facts from) Robin Brooks, Erik Brynjolfsson, Claude Canizares, Mark Cymrot, Stefano D'LaVigna, Gary Gensler, Amy Glasmeier, Bronwyn Hall, Bob Hall, Chad Jones, Dennis Kelleher, James Kwak, Josh Lerner, Ernie Moniz, Ed Roberts, Jonathan Ruane, and Daniel Wilson.

A variety of other economists helped provide us data or literature reviews at critical points throughout the production process. We are grateful to Rena Conti for discussing the economics of drug development, to Gabriel Chodorow-Reich for helping explain the link between stimulus spending and jobs, to Dave Donaldson for explaining how trade impacts inequality, to Shane Greenstein for sharing patent data, to Michael Greenstone and Richard Hornbeck for providing leads on land and housing values over time, to Sara Heller for helping us find crime data, to Matthew Kahn and Siqi Kheng for helping us understand Chinese research parks, to Jerold Kayden for explaining the legal aspects of eminent domain, to Josh Krieger for providing valuable examples of the stop-and-start nature of medical research, to Frank Levy for providing a review of local economic development policies, to Jim Poterba for providing information on capital market valuation, to Elias Einio to providing interpretation of his work on the SBIR, and to Christina Patterson for providing data on labor shares.

One wonderful feature of being at a place like MIT is that we could draw on a series of technical experts outside economics who patiently explained to us both the basics and cutting edge of the science involved in our discussions. We are in particular grateful to Gigi Hirsch, Jacqueline Wolfrum, and Stacy Springs for helping us understand the process of biomedical innovation and R&D, and for suggesting the example of cellular therapy manufacturing. Eric Lander was a great source of insight on medical R&D as well. William Lehr provided helpful context on the telecommunications industry, John Heywood helped us better understand the potential role of hydrogen-powered vehicles, Thomas Peacock provided valuable background on deep-sea exploration, and Bill Bonvillian encouraged us to think harder about science policy.

Others outside of academic economics provided valuable support as well. Al Link provided insights about research parks in the United States and around the world. Al Fitzpayne and Bruce Reed helped us think through the policy challenges inherent in our proposal, particularly around budgeting. Joe Wallace graciously agreed to meet with us and explain the genesis of the Central Florida Research Park that became such a central example in the book. We owe a particular debt of gratitude to Darius Singpurwalla at the NSF, who helped us construct our data sets on graduate and undergraduate science departments. We are also grateful to Rob Atkinson, Mitch Horowitz, Karen Mills, and Steve Merrill for helpful conversations and insights.

Frances Kaplan, librarian of the California Historical Society, was most gracious in providing access to old maps and to fascinating early regional and Stanford publications.

We also benefited from numerous conversations with other subject matter experts in the science that we so briefly cover here. Eric Althoff motivated us to think about the synthetic biology, and he, John Cumbers, and Rina Singh provided helpful background.

We were pleasantly surprised with the substantial set of valuable comments that we received on an early draft of the book. Many thanks to Eric Althoff, Bill Bonvillian, John Cumbers, Mark Cymrot, Greg Dreifus, Shane Greenstein, Andrea Gruber, Yasheng Huang, Chad Jones, Paul Joskow, Valerie Karplus, Robert Langer, Chap Lawson, Josh Lerner, Bruce Levine, Enrico Moretti, Dan Pomeroy, Ramana Nanda, Philip Reilly, Ed Roberts, Jonathan Ruane, David Saltzman, David Siegel, Dick Schmalensee, Stacy Springs, Jean Tirole, Steve Weisman, Danny Weitzner, Bill Wheaton, David Williams, Heidi Williams, Jaqueline Wolfrum, and Andy Wu for reading the manuscript in part or in full under a tight deadline for comments!

Most important, of course, was the talented and dedicated set of research assistants who gathered the material that forms 90 percent of this book. Yet another benefit of being at MIT is that we could draw on such a skilled and hardworking set of undergraduates, MBA, and PhD students. Tiffany Li, William Kretschmer, Shreyas Matha, and Olivia Zhao all worked over many months, both part- and full-time, to answer our every request, no matter how difficult, obscure, or even ridiculous. We also received excellent assistance at various points from Chris Balaam, John Beatty, Maria Botchkova, Ziv Cohen, Manuel Favela, Amy Kim, Stephanie Li, Louis Liss, Nehal Mehta, Bhavik Nagda, Spencer Pantoja, Maya Perl, Simran Vaidya, and Stephen Yang. Karti Subramanian was outstanding in the formative stages of the project. Lindsey Bennett and John Friedman helped us think about what readers needed to see (and saved us from many slips along the way). In the final stretch, we came to fully appreciate Daniel Curtis's great attention to detail. If there are remaining errors related to physics in this book, it is because we neglected to pay sufficient attention to Daniel's patient explanations.

Of course we are grateful to our brilliant assistants, Nikhil Basavappa, Michelle Fiorenza, and Beata Shuster, for making sure the bills got paid and the trains ran on time!

We also benefited from working with a terrific team of professionals in turning this idea into a reality. A. J. Wilson was really helpful at the formative stages. Rafe Sagalyn provided invaluable assistance in shaping the vision of this book and then connecting us with PublicAffairs as a publishing partner. John Mahaney was a patient and perceptive editor, bringing a long list of insights while also respecting our expertise. Clive Priddle strongly supported the idea of a detailed appendix, with numbers and names. We really appreciate the efforts of Josie Unwin and Lindsay Fradkoff in helping us think about how to present the book, as well as the hard work (and patience) of Michelle Welsh-Horst and her colleagues in the editing process. We owe special thanks to Linda Mark and Amy Kim for making the map happen on a tight deadline.

Finally, the greatest sacrifice in an endeavor like this is made by family members who have to put up with our distraction and commitment to a project that they have heard enough of by now! We are grateful to our wives, Andrea and Mary, and to our children—Rachel, Jack, and Ava; and Celia and Lucie—for putting up with us during this process!

Jon Gruber and Simon Johnson
MIT, November 2018

Notes

PROLOGUE

1. Many of these bids are not fully public. However, from criteria in Amazon's initial requests for proposal and published news reports, it is fair to say that most bids include such elements.

2. "Remarks by President Trump on the Economy," White House, July 27, 2018, https://www.whitehouse.gov/briefings-statements/remarks-president-trump-economy.

3. Amazon also announced that more than five thousand jobs with an average wage of over $150,000 would be created in Nashville, Tennessee, but these will be in an "Operations Center of Excellence" and are not likely to pay as much as the HQ2 jobs going to Northern Virginia and New York. Day One Staff, "Amazon Selects New York City and Northern Virginia for New Headquarters," Day One, November 13, 2018, https://blog.aboutamazon.com/company-news/amazon-selects-new-york-city-and-northern-virginia-for-new-headquarters.

INTRODUCTION TO THE PAPERBACK EDITION

1. See, for example, Ro Khanna, Jonathan Gruber, and Matt Hourihan, "It's Time to Fund America's Investments in the Future," *The Hill*, September 12, 2022, thehill.com/opinion/congress-blog/3639400-its-time-to-fund-americas-investments-in-the-future/.

INTRODUCTION

1. Vannevar Bush, *Science: The Endless Frontier* (Washington, DC: United States Government Printing Office, 1945), p. 19.

2. Details on US army preparation are from Rick Atkinson, *An Army at Dawn* (New York: Henry Holt, 2002), pp. 8–9.

3. Remarkably, these profound problems "did not come to light until the war was well along." These quotes are from Samuel Elliot Morrison, *History of US Naval Operations in World War II, Volume IV, Coral Sea, Midway and Submarine Actions* (Boston: Little, Brown, 1949), pp. 191, 222.

4. Paul Kennedy, *Engineers of Victory: The Problem Solvers Who Turned the Tide in the Second World War* (New York: Random House, 2013).

5. From the *New York Times* obituary for Vannevar Bush: "He directed the work of 30,000 men throughout the country and had over-all responsibility for developing such sophisticated new weapons as radar, the proximity fuze, fire control mechanisms, amphibious vehicles and ultimately the atomic bomb—devices that overnight revolutionized the concept of war." And "The mass production of sulfa drugs and penicillin was achieved by the O.S.R.D." Robert Reinhold, "Dr. Vannevar Bush Is Dead at 84," *New York Times*, June 30, 1974, http://www.nytimes .com/1974/06/30/archives/dr-vannevar-bush-is-dead-at-84-dr-vannevar-bush -who-marshaled.html.

6. Vannevar Bush, *Pieces of the Action* (New York: William Morrow, 1970), pp. 31–32.

7. According to his *New York Times* obituary: "It is estimated that two-thirds of all the physicists in the United States were working for Dr. Bush." Reinhold, "Dr. Vannevar Bush is Dead."

8. These data are from table 1 on p. 80 of Bush, *Science: The Endless Frontier,* calculated by dividing government (federal and state) spending on scientific research (the fifth column) by national income (the second column).

9. Over the years, experts have argued repeatedly about how best to think about and organize the relationship between the development of basic science and applications for commercial use. Bush's own writings suggest that he was a pragmatic inventor who saw pervasive spillover effects from more basic research. This is what we mean by the Bush model described later.

10. "It [the scientific war effort] put penicillin at our service, as could have been done ten years before had there been ample effort, and thus introduced the wide range of antibiotics." Bush, *Pieces of the Action,* p. 8.

11. Terry Sharrer, "The Discovery of Streptomycin," *Scientist,* August 2007, https://www.the-scientist.com/?articles.view/articleNo/25252/title/The-discovery -of-streptomycin/.

12. Bush, *Pieces of the Action,* p. 8.

13. "Out of it [the wartime science effort] came the conquest of malaria, a temporary conquest, it is true, for the lower organisms which prey upon us exhibit agility in evading our chemicals," Bush, *Pieces of the Action,* p. 8. Part of the subsequent resurgence of malaria was due to the development of DDT-resistant mosquitoes. There were also difficulties sustaining anti-mosquito campaigns in some parts of the world.

14. See Bush's *Pieces of the Action,* pp. 43–49, for further discussion on how medical research was brought under his committee's jurisdiction, initially against

his recommendation. Bush was rarely opposed to taking on new tasks but had concerns about the specific politics surrounding medicine.

15. Interestingly, Vannevar Bush's wartime committee did not directly provide the decisive push for computing. Pitched on the idea by a former MIT colleague during the war, Bush felt—most likely correctly—the technology was not at a stage where it could have immediate impact on the war effort.

16. From the National Science Foundation's Science & Engineering Indicators 2018, Chapter 4, figure 4-3, "Ratio of U.S. R&D to gross domestic product, by roles of federal, business, and other nonfederal funding for R&D: 1953–2015," https://nsf.gov/statistics/2018/nsb20181/figures. The peak for federally funded R&D was 1.86 percent of GDP in 1964. The most recent data point in this series, for 2015, is 0.67 percent of GDP.

17. Real GDP was just over $2 trillion in 1947 and $5.7 trillion in 1973, for a compound annual average growth rate of just under 4 percent. Real GDP is from the Bureau of Economic Analysis historical data, accessed through the St. Louis Fed's FRED economic database: for levels, "Real Gross Domestic Product (GDPCA)," FRED Economic Data, updated July 27, 2018, https://fred.stlouisfed. org/series/GDPCA; and for annual growth rates, "Real Gross Domestic Product (A191RL1A225NBEA)," FRED Economic Data, updated July 27, 2018, https:// fred.stlouisfed.org/graph/?id=A191RL1A225NBEA,#0.

18. For longer time periods, slightly different starting or ending dates do not change the averages much. Changing the dates can affect averages over shorter periods, but the general conclusion stands: growth in the size of the American economy has slowed down.

19. "An Update to the Economic Outlook: 2018 to 2028," Congressional Budget Office, August 13, 2018, https://www.cbo.gov/publication/54318.

20. From 1920 to 1970, output per hour grew by 2.82 percent per annum on average in the United States. From 1970 to 2014, this measure of productivity growth declined to just 1.62 percent. As Robert Gordon argues in *The Rise and Fall of American Growth* (Princeton, NJ: Princeton University Press, 2016), most of the decline is due to slower growth in total factor productivity, "the best proxy available for the underlying effect of innovation and technological change on economic growth" (p. 16, figure 1-2 and surrounding text). Gordon argues that the 1920–1970 period was special, representing the effects of major technologies that were invented earlier, before World War II, and which took time to have their effects.

21. In one recent estimate, the GDP of Silicon Valley is around $235 billion. This is an impressive number and larger than the economies of some countries, but total GDP of the United States is close to $20 trillion. https:// cityscene.org/the-silicon-valley-economy-surpasses-the-gdp-of-many-nations / (website discontinued).

22. This point is made by Mariana Mazzucato in *The Entrepreneurial State*, revised ed. (New York: Public Affairs, 2015).

CHAPTER 1: FOR OUR COMFORT, OUR SECURITY, OUR PROSPERITY

1. Jennet Conant, *Man of the Hour: James B. Conant, Warrior Scientist* (New York: Simon & Schuster, 2017), p. 221. Conant was president of Harvard, visiting London to assess British technology and to build potential cooperation, on behalf of Bush's OSRD. He went on to be responsible for overseeing the development of the atomic bomb.

2. Bush was vice chairman and then chairman of the National Advisory Committee for Aeronautics, and his fears proved well-founded. "The Lockheed P-38, Bell P-39, Curtiss P-40, Grumman F4F, and Brewster Buffalo were the most modern U.S. Army and Navy fighters in the active inventory when the war started. Yet, with the exception of the P-38—which was available in only very small numbers at the beginning of the war—these fighters were generally outclassed by the leading Japanese and German fighters against which they had to fight. None of these fighters—except for the P-38—remained in production by the later stages of the war." "As a result, the Japanese essentially retained air superiority in most theaters until the P-38 Lightning, F4U Corsair, and F6F Hellcat began entering service in significant numbers in 1943." Mark Lorell, *The US Combat Aircraft Industry, 1909-2000* (Santa Monica, CA: RAND Corporation, 2003), https://www.rand.org/content/dam/rand/pubs/monograph_reports/2005/MR1696.pdf, p. 57.

3. Elting E. Morison, *From Know-How to Nowhere: The Development of American Technology* (New York: Basic Books, 1974).

4. A direct descendant from the steam engines that pumped water out of coal mines and horse-drawn wagons that moved coal along inclined planes.

5. Estimate for Britain is from Dan Bogart, Leigh Shaw-Taylor, and Xuesheng You, "The Development of the Railway Network in Britain 1825–1911," Cambridge Group for the History of Population and Social Structure, https://www.campop.geog.cam.ac.uk/research/projects/transport/onlineatlas/railways.pdf. US numbers are from table 1 in E. R. Wicker, "Railroad Investment before the Civil War," in *Trends in the American Economy in the Nineteenth Century* (Princeton, NJ: Princeton University Press, 1960).

6. "British Railways," *Encyclopedia Britannica*, https://www.britannica.com/topic/British-Railways.

7. Morison, *From Know-How to Nowhere*.

8. "Why the Americans Apply Themselves to the Practice of the Sciences Rather than to the Theory," in *Democracy in America*, vol. 2, trans. and ed. Harvey C. Mansfield and Debra Winthrop (Chicago: University of Chicago, 2000).

9. This paragraph and the next paragraph are based on Morison, *From Know-How to Nowhere*.

10. As reported in Morison, *From Know-How to Nowhere*, p. 108.

11. Details in this paragraph are from Morison, *From Know-How to Nowhere*, pp. 129–131.

12. David F. Noble, *America by Design: Science, Technology, and the Rise of Corporate Capitalism* (Oxford, UK: Oxford University Press, 1979), p. 114.

13. Noble, *America by Design*, p. 121.

14. Noble, *America by Design*, pp. 11–12. The chemical industry, which developed slightly later, followed a similar approach.

15. Noble, *America by Design*, p. 39. The 1930 number of engineers was only 0.5 percent of workers in industry.

16. Vannevar Bush, *Science: The Endless Frontier* (Washington, DC: United States Government Printing Office, 1945), p. 80. The earliest data for government science spending in this source are from 1923, and the university spending series starts in 1930.

17. Noble, *America by Design*, p. 120.

18. On the history and development of US higher education and its relationship to research, see Jonathan R. Cole, *The Great American University* (New York: Public Affairs, 2009).

19. Noble, *America by Design*, p. 22.

20. In the early twentieth century, there were twenty-six members of the Association of American Universities "and perhaps a dozen other aspirants." The primary activity was teaching undergraduates and even the American elite universities were "no match for Cambridge or Berlin." Hugh Davis Graham and Nancy Diamond, *The Rise of American Research Universities: Elites and Challengers in the Postwar Era* (Baltimore: Johns Hopkins University Press, 1997), p. 20.

21. Vannevar Bush, *Pieces of the Action* (New York: William Morrow, 1970), p. 115: "When I was just starting in as an engineer, they [Germany] had led the world."

22. To be clear, prior to World War II, there were some physics prize winners who did their award-winning work abroad but who lived or worked in the United States at some point in their life. Ferdinand Braun, who won in 1909, arrived in the United states during World War I to testify about a patent and was detained due to his German citizenship. He died while detained in 1917. Albert Einstein, who won the physics prize in 1921, came to the United States in the early 1930s in response to the rise of the Nazis. James Franck won his prize in 1925. He came to the United States and worked as a professor from 1935. Franck returned to West Germany at the end of his life. Frenchman Jean Baptiste Perrin won the physics prize in 192 . He came to the United States in 1940 after the Germans invaded France. In 1936, Austrian Victor Hess won the physics prize. He worked in the United States both before and after he won, but his prize-winning work was done in Austria.

23. US-born scientists Clinton Davisson and Ernest Lawrence won in 1937 and 1939, respectively.

24. A. Hunter Dupree, *Science in the Federal Government: A History of Policies and Activities* (Baltimore: Johns Hopkins University Press, 1986).

25. The National Academy of Sciences was established during the Civil War, and the National Research Council was added in 1916. Neither had much immediate effect on the military effort. See Dupree, *Science in the Federal Government*.

26. G. Pascal Zachary, *Endless Frontier* (Cambridge, MA: MIT Press, 1999), pp. 65–66.

27. "In the twelve months from June 1940 to June 1941 our civilian casualties were 43,381 killed and 50,856 seriously injured, a total of 94,237." Winston Churchill, *The Grand Alliance: The Second World War*, vol. 3 (Boston: Houghton Mifflin, 1950), p. 42.

28. American public opinion at the time remained strongly in favor of neutrality. The official State Department history sums up the situation: "Overall, the Neutrality Acts [of 1935, 1937, and 1939] represented a compromise whereby the United States Government accommodated the isolationist sentiment of the American public, but still retained some ability to interact with the world." https://history.state.gov/milestones/1921-1936/neutrality-acts. President Franklin Delano Roosevelt was sympathetic to the British cause, but it had previously proven hard to entice the United States to share technological insights that could assist the war effort. For example, the British wanted access to the Norden bombsight, which they understood would greatly improve the precision of high-altitude bombing. The Americans were concerned that this could fall into the hands of the Germans—for example, if a plane were shot down—and refused to share this technology until much later.

29. Stephen Phelps, "Minutes of the First Meeting of the British Technical Mission to the USA," in *The Tizard Mission* (Yardley, PA: Westholme, 2009), pp. 295–298.

30. With the exception only of the British jet engine program and what the navy had learned about German magnetic mines. Phelps, *The Tizard Mission*.

31. Raymond C. Watson Jr., *Radar Origins Worldwide* (Bloomington, IN: Trafford, 2009). Of these thirteen countries, at least seven were in the running to deploy workable systems, but the British got there first—at least with regard to full-scale deployment for air defense.

32. The essential work on radio was carried out by James Clerk Maxwell (a Scottish scientist at King's College in London) in the 1860s and Heinrich Rudolf Hertz (at the University of Karlsruhe in Germany) in the late 1880s. Major breakthroughs in terms of applications came from Guglielmo Marconi (an Italian who worked initially in the UK) and others.

33. In September 1922, A. Hoyt Taylor and Leo C. Young made some of the earliest discoveries while working at the Naval Aircraft Radio Laboratory in Washington, DC. Samuel E. Morrison, *The Battle of the Atlantic, September 1939–May 1943* (Annapolis, MD: Naval Institute Press, 1947), pp. 8–9, 225.

34. In 1932, the average speed of US civilian planes, operating on long distance routes, was 110 MPH; by 1940, this speed had increased to 155 MPH.

Ronald Miller and David Sawers, *The Technical Development of Modern Aviation* (New York: Praeger, 1970), p. 211.

35. Baldwin was prime minister of Britain both before and after he made this statement.

36. Tizard was head of Imperial College, a leading engineering school. He was actually a chemist, not a physicist, but he knew how to run a committee. It helped that he had previously been an aircraft researcher who had flown military planes. Tizard also knew how to manage the relationship between civilian scientists and military hierarchy—as well as with the civil service.

37. The early inventive work was funded in a rather haphazard way. Winston Churchill's favorite scientist, Frederick Lindemann, also preferred rather more esoteric forms of air defense—including dropping bombs on parachutes in front of oncoming bombers.

38. For attacks during the day, it was sufficient for ground-based controllers to direct interceptor planes close enough to see their targets. Early on, however, Tizard and his colleagues recognized that guiding fighters at night would require much more precision—and almost certainly involve aircraft-mounted radar.

39. Jennet Conant, *Tuxedo Park* (New York: Simon & Schuster, 2002) provides a fascinating biography of Loomis, as well as a history of his involvement with radar.

40. Conant, *Tuxedo Park*, says this meeting was on September 11, but Robert Buderi, *The Invention That Changed the World* (New York: Simon & Schuster, 1996), says September 19.

41. Conant, *Tuxedo Park*, pp. 189–192.

42. It helped that Loomis had direct access to Henry Stimson, the secretary of war. In fact, they were cousins, and Loomis had long advised Stimson on his personal finances, as well as on the future of technology from an investor's perspective. Bush's team had a consistently better relationship with the army, overseen by Stimson, than with the secretary of the navy and some powerful admirals. Bush, *Pieces of the Action*, p. 50.

43. Buderi, *Invention That Changed the World*, p. 45. Jewett was brought on board in a meeting on October 16, 1940, in Bush's office. Compton was persuaded on October 17.

44. Bush, *Pieces of the Action*, p. 45.

45. Reflecting on the wartime radar effort as a whole, according to Bush, "Scientific personnel became so scarce they even took in biologists and made radar experts out of them." Ibid., p. 138.

46. Ibid., p. 38.

47. The key meeting was again at Tuxedo Park on the weekend of October 12–13, 1940, with Ernest Lawrence now in attendance. The following Monday, Loomis invited companies to bid (and build) equipment that was obviously already needed. There were just a handful of suppliers, with the work divided up among

them: Bell (the magnetron), GE (the magnet), RCA (pulse modulator, cathode ray tubes, and power supply), and Sperry (parabolic reflectors and scanning gear). Westinghouse later contracted for antennas and Bendix for the power supply that would run off an aircraft engine. Buderi, *Invention That Changed the World*, p. 44; Conant, *Tuxedo Park*, p. 201.

48. Conant, *Tuxedo Park*, pp. 197–198. The lab space was made available on October 17 (Buderi, *Invention That Changed the World*, p. 45).

49. "MIT Radiation Laboratory," Lincoln Laboratory, https://www.ll.mit.edu/about/History/RadLab.html.

50. By coincidence, at the end of October, MIT hosted a major annual conference on applied nuclear physics, with six hundred people attending. Loomis turned this effectively into a job fair. By the end of the conference, more than two dozen people had been hired. Conant, *Tuxedo Park*, pp. 202–203.

51. Buderi, *Invention That Changed the World*, p. 50, puts employment at the Rad Lab in summer 1945 at 3,897 people and the annual budget at $43.2 million; this was up from first year numbers of 30–40 employees and a budget of $815,000. The entire OSRD budget in fiscal year 1944/45 was $113.5 million; this does not include the Manhattan Project. In his postwar plans for a new agency to support science, Bush proposed to spend $33.5 million initially, rising to $122.5 million after five years (Zachary, *Endless Frontier*, p. 249)—implying a scale roughly similar to the OSRD at its pinnacle.

52. Buderi, *Invention That Changed the World*, pp. 155–165.

53. Buderi, *Invention That Changed the World*, p. 143. King reportedly said this in spring 1941.

54. Bush, *Pieces of the Action*, pp. 99, 104 on tanks and DUKW, respectively.

55. See Investigation of the Pearl Harbor Attack: Report of the Joint Committee on the Investigation of the Pearl Harbor Attack (Washington, DC: Government Printing Office, July 20, 1946), pp. 140–142. "The maximum distance radar could pick up approaching planes was approximately 130 miles" (p. 129). The actual distance of the attacking force when first detected was 132 miles (p. 152). The lack of preparation and integration with radar was profound—it would have taken four hours to prepare the US Army planes properly for the attack (p. 129).

56. Samuel E. Morrison, *The Atlantic Battle Won, May 1943–May 1945* (Annapolis, MD: Naval Institute Press, 1953), pp. 8–9.

57. This shift was not only about technological miracles but also about designing a new system that applied the technology effectively. This system involved creating a new organizational structure, in this case the Tenth Fleet, in which naval officers and civilian engineers could cooperate without the previous constraints. See Ladislas Farago, *The Tenth Fleet* (New York: Drum, 1986).

58. "The tide turned abruptly in 1943. It could have changed much earlier." Bush, *Pieces of the Action*, p. 88.

59. Bush, *Pieces of the Action*, p. 109.

60. The hiring at the Rad Lab was handled by the director Lee DuBridge. Bush felt DuBridge hired too many physicists relative to engineers. DuBridge retorted, after the Rad Lab success had become clear, "You see we did not need the engineers." Bush replied, according to his account, "Hell, any self-respecting physicist can become an engineer in a year or two if he puts his mind to it" (Bush, *Pieces of the Action*, p. 138). Paul Kennedy, *Engineers of Victory: The Problem Solvers Who Turned the Tide in the Second World War* (New York: Random House, 2013) makes the case that engineering work had a major impact on the war outcome.

61. Bush, *Pieces of the Action*, p. 106.

62. The first jet engine with the performance necessary for a potential commercial jet airliner was the British Rolls-Royce Avon available by 1949/1950. The first American commercial jet engine was the Pratt & Whitney J57 available in 1952/1953.

63. The four most important early engines were the Pratt and Whitney J57, the Rolls-Royce Avon, the Rolls-Royce Conway, and the General Electric J79 (Miller and Sawers, *Technical Development of Modern Aviation*, p. 161).

64. Ibid., pp. 156–157.

65. This list is based on Buderi, *Invention That Changed the World*, pp. 15–16.

66. There was a prewar research agenda at Bell Labs (vacuum tubes were major part of phone systems) and the notion of a semiconductor was first demonstrated in 1940 (Michael Riordan and Lillian Hoddeson, *Crystal Fire: The Invention of the Transistor and the Birth of the Information Age* [New York: W. W. Norton, 1997], p. 88). These researchers and related resources were diverted into the war effort, including on radar and to help the navy—William Shockley, for example, became a consultant to various parts of the military. These experiences contributed to how the research team approached what became transistors after the war (Riordan and Hoddeson, *Crystal Fire*). We discuss the development of the transistor further in the next chapter.

67. Evan Ackerman, "When 82 TV Channels Was More Than Enough," IEEE Spectrum, January 29, 2016, https://spectrum.ieee.org/tech-history/cyberspace /when-82-tv-channels-was-more-than-enough.

68. Evan Ackerman, "A Brief History of the Microwave Oven," IEEE Spectrum, September 30, 2016, https://spectrum.ieee.org/tech-history/space-age/a -brief-history-of-the-microwave-oven.

69. Buderi, *Invention That Changed the World*, p. 48. The only person to win a Nobel Prize for work done at the Rad Lab was Edwin McMillan, who won the chemistry prize in 1951. Thomas R. Cech (chemistry, 1989), Sidney Altman (chemistry, 1989), Mario J. Molina (chemistry, 1995), Felix Bloch (physics, 1952), E. M. Purcell (physics, 1952), Charles H. Townes (physics, 1964), Julian Schwinger (physics, 1965), Luis Alvarez (physics, 1968), and Norman Ramsey (physics, 1989) all won for work they did after their time at the Rad Lab. Isidor Isaac Rabi won the physics prize in 1944 for work that he did in 1939.

70. *The First Annual Report of the National Science Foundation, 1950–51* (Washington, DC: US Government Printing Office, n.d.), p. 31, which has data on federal expenditures for research and development from 1940 through 1950. Correcting for inflation during the war is very difficult, as prices were controlled and the availability of some goods was limited. Still, these nominal figures convey the broad picture.

71. The three services had combined R&D budgets of only $26.4 million in fiscal year 1940 (*First Annual Report of the National Science Foundation*, p. 31).

72. One estimate is that radar cost perhaps 50 percent more than the Manhattan Project. Watson, *Radar Origins Worldwide*, p. 3. This seems high, but there is no question that the development of radar was a major research and industrial endeavor, comparable in scale to the Manhattan Project.

73. "Manhattan Project," CTBTO Preparatory Commission, https://www.ctbto.org/nuclear-testing/history-of-nuclear-testing/manhattan-project/.

74. Bush, *Pieces of the Action*, p. 8.

75. Vannevar Bush, *Science: The Endless Frontier* (Washington, DC: United States Government Printing Office, 1945), p. 8.

76. Bush, *Science*, p. 14.

77. Ibid., p. 19.

78. Officially, the development of both nuclear weapons and power generation came under the authority of the Atomic Energy Commission (https://www.energy.gov/sites/prod/files/AEC%20History.pdf). The commission became controversial for the development of the hydrogen bomb, the investigation of Robert Oppenheimer, and perhaps most of all for the way it oversaw the approval and building of nuclear power stations. Daniel Ford's *Cult of the Atom: The Secret Papers of the Atomic Energy Commission* (New York: Simon and Schuster, 1982) is a hard-hitting critique.

79. Bush, *Science*, p. 7.

80. National Center for Education Statistics, *120 Years of American Education: A Statistical Portrait* (Washington, DC: US Department of Education, 1993), https://nces.ed.gov/pubs93/93442.pdf, p. 7.

81. Ibid., table 23.

82. We count US winners as people who were American by birth or were only associated with American universities/organizations at the time of their win. Our source is biographical information published by the Nobel Foundation.

83. There were two individuals who did their work in Germany (the 1933 physics prize winner and 1938 chemistry winner), although they were not German during this period. They are included in the German total here.

84. From 2010 to 2017, the United States won only 47 percent of the scientific Nobel Prizes.

85. In fiction, the first postwar articulation of the dangers posed by automation—in fact, directly from the development of cybernetics during the 1940s—may have been Vonnegut's *Player Piano*. But the dark side of inventions already existed

as a theme, at least since the work of H. G. Wells; a uranium-based hand grenade features in his 1914 novel, *The World Set Free*.

86. Kurt Vonnegut, *Player Piano* (New York: Dial Press, 2006). Consequently, there is a high degree of inequality in the America of Vonnegut's imagination— very different from what transpired in the 1950s, although not so different from what we face today.

87. The impact of new technology on wages depends on the details of exactly what that technology does. In the early years of the nineteenth-century Industrial Revolution, machines replaced the labor of skilled artisans—and tended to lower their wages. From the early twentieth century, however, technological changes, including the use of electricity in factories, became complementary to skilled labor. Now the efforts of unskilled people could be replaced by machines, but this in turn could create jobs managing the machines, the broader business enterprise, and the surrounding social enterprise—hence the expansion of white-collar jobs. For a full historical analysis, see Claudia Goldin and Lawrence F. Katz, *The Race Between Education and Technology* (Cambridge, MA: Harvard University Press, 2008).

88. Seminal contributions were made by Norbert Wiener, whose work on antiaircraft guns led him to invent what became known as cybernetics, a branch of information theory and a forerunner of artificial intelligence. Wiener published a relatively technical volume, *Cybernetics: Or Control and Communication in the Animal and the Machine*, in 1948, and then a more popular book, *The Human Use of Human Beings*, in 1950. Vonnegut refers to this thinking in *Player Piano*. Wiener's wartime work was supported by the NDRC/OSRD.

89. This is the pretax skill premium (i.e., not including the effect of taxation and any redistributive programs).

90. Enrico Moretti makes this important point in his study of city growth, *The New Geography of Jobs* (New York: Mariner Books, 2013).

91. "Education and Training; History and Timeline," US Department of Veterans Affairs, https://www.benefits.va.gov/gibill/history.asp.

92. Thomas K. McCraw, *American Business Since 1920: How It Worked*, 2nd ed. (Hoboken, NJ: Wiley-Blackwell, 2009), p. 89. "The 1944 GI Bill provided returning veterans with money for college, businesses and home mortgages. Suddenly, millions of servicemen were able to afford homes of their own for the first time. As a result, residential construction jumped from 114,000 new homes in 1944 to 1.7 million in 1950. In 1947, William Levitt turned 4,000 acres of Long Island, New York, potato farms into the then largest privately planned housing project in American history. With 30 houses built in assembly-line fashion every day—each with a tree in the front yard—the American subdivision was born." Claire Suddath, "The Middle Class," *Time*, February 27, 2009, http://content.time.com/time/nation/article/0,8599,1882147,00.html.

93. The official title of this legislation was Public Law 346.

94. Alan T. Waterman, introduction to *Science: The Endless Frontier*, by Vannevar Bush (Alexandria, VA: National Science Foundation, 1960), p. xvi. This edition

appeared to mark the tenth anniversary of the NSF—and the fifteenth anniversary of the report. In a foreword, Bush endorses Waterman's "effective summary of the extent to which the recommendations of *Science: The Endless Frontier* have been realized." Waterman goes on to say, "About two million veterans of the Korean conflict received similar educational opportunities under the Veterans Readjustment Assistance Act of 1952. Engineering, medical, dental, and scientific fields attracted about a quarter million of these."

95. Brad Plumer, "Here's Where Wages Have Been Stagnating Since the 1970s," *Washington Post,* March 21, 2013, https://www.washingtonpost.com/news /wonk/wp/2013/03/21/heres-where-wages-have-been-stagnating-since-1970 /?utm_term=.f7ed8963af35.

96. "The Postwar Economy: 1945–1960," University of Groningen, http:// www.let.rug.nl/usa/outlines/history-1994/postwar-america/the-postwar -economy-1945-1960.php.

97. Ibid.

98. Shmoop Editorial Team, "Society in the 1950s," Shmoop University, last updated November 8, 2011, https://www.shmoop.com/1950s/society.html.

99. McCraw, *American Business Since 1920,* p. 65: "American industrial mobilization as a whole was brilliantly successful. Without question it was the key to victory over Japan, and it was the single most important element in the Allied triumph on the Western Front in Europe."

100. Ibid., p. 75.

101. *Historical Statistics of the United States: Colonial Times to 1970, Bicentennial Edition, Part 1* (Washington, DC: US Bureau of the Census, 1975), https://fraser .stlouisfed.org/files/docs/publications/histstatus/hstat1970_cen_1975_v1.pdf.

102. Some women who entered the workforce during the war were no longer employed and not looking for work in the immediate postwar years. Still, many of them did want to work—and this was part of the labor force expansion.

103. These data are from *Historical Statistics of the United States: Colonial Times to 1970, Bicentennial Edition, Part 2* (Washington, DC: US Bureau of the Census, 1975), "Series D 1–10, Labor Force and its Components: 1900 to 1947"; annual average; data from 1948 are in "Series D 11-25, Labor Force Status of the Population: 1870 to 1970"; the labor force is slightly lower as it is for ages sixteen and higher in this series. Unemployment was 4.4 percent in 1955, reaching 6.8 percent in 1958 ("Series D 85–86")—higher than during the war but much lower than the 20–25 percent rates experienced during the Great Depression. https://fraser .stlouisfed.org/files/docs/publications/histstatus/hstat1970_cen_1975_v2.pdf.

104. Synthetic rubber is a good example. The shift from natural to synthetic rubber (a petroleum by-product) was overseen by Bush's NDRC, and most US rubber products were synthetic by 1945. Before the war, the United States was the largest importer of rubber in the world; after the war, it became a major exporter (McCraw, *American Business Since 1920,* pp. 64–65). James Conant, chemistry professor, Harvard's president, and key confidant of Vannevar Bush, provided scientific oversight.

105. "Since the late nineteenth century, the Democrats had associated high tariffs with monopoly profits for the rich and low tariffs with low prices for goods consumed by the average citizen. Furthermore, they maintained that low US tariffs encouraged low foreign tariffs and thus indirectly stimulated increases in US exports, especially agricultural goods." And "thus, over 80 percent of the Democrats voting in the House of Representatives supported the party's position on extending the trade agreements program during the 1940s and 1950s." Robert Baldwin, "The Changing Nature of US Trade Policy Since World War II," in *The Structure and Evolution of Recent US Trade Policy*, ed. Robert E. Baldwin and Anne O. Krueger (Chicago: University of Chicago Press, 1984), http://www.nber.org/chapters/c5828.pdf.

106. During the interwar years, the US share of world exports fluctuated between 12 and 16 percent; it was 15.3 percent in 1938. In 1948, the situation was transformed: US exports now comprised 30.5 percent of world exports. For manufactured goods, the change was just as dramatic. Among the ten largest industrial countries, in 1928 and 1938, the US share of manufacturing exports was 21 percent. In 1952, the US export share of manufactures was 35 percent. Baldwin, *The Structure and Evolution*, p. 8.

107. The Truman administration launched the Marshall Plan, which provided loans to Europe and oversaw the creation of the International Bank for Reconstruction and Development (the World Bank) and the International Monetary Fund with the same initial primary purpose. Subsequently, "Eisenhower and his main advisors within the administration and in Congress believed—like earlier Democratic administrations—that trade liberalization was an important foreign policy instrument for strengthening the 'free world' against communism" (Ibid., p. 12).

108. Ibid., p. 8.

109. For example, the AFL-CIO changed its view on the desirability of liberal trade policy only in the 1960s, in the face of increasing imports relative to market size in "wool and man-made textiles and apparel, footwear, automobiles, steel, and electrical consumer goods, such as television sets, radios, and phonographs" (Ibid., p. 13).

110. Frank Gollop and Dale Jorgenson, "U.S. Productivity Growth by Industry, 1947–93," in *New Developments in Productivity Measurement*, ed. John W. Kendrick and Beatrice N. Vaccara (Chicago: University of Chicago Press, 1980), pp. 15–136, table 1.29.

CHAPTER 2: WHATEVER IT TAKES

1. John F. Kennedy, "Science as a Guide of Public Policy," in *The Burden and the Glory*, ed. Allan Nevins (New York: Harper & Row, 1964), p. 264.

2. The launch was on October 5, local time (in Kazakhstan). The news reached Washington, DC, on Friday evening, October 4, 1957.

3. William I. Hitchcock, *The Age of Eisenhower* (New York: Simon & Schuster, 2018), p. 379. The first dog in space died after a few hours; subsequently, the Soviet authorities decided to bring orbiting dogs back home safely—and did: https://www.theguardian.com/artanddesign/2014/sep/02/soviet-space-dogs.

4. Bush insisted that it was essential to have the president of the NRF picked by its board of directors, not by the president. No one in the White House found that idea appealing.

5. G. Pascal Zachary, *Endless Frontier* (Cambridge, MA: MIT Press, 1999), pp. 246–260, 300–309.

6. More generally, Bush saw himself as supporting government funding but resisting government control. Kilgore did not have an issue with government control. Zachary, *Endless Frontier*, pp. 253–254.

7. Item 1858 was a pocket veto of S.526, 79th Cong. (1945), https://www.senate.gov/reference/Legislation/Vetoes/Presidents/TrumanH.pdf.

8. The NSF was established by an act of Congress on May 10, 1950. The director of the NSF was appointed by the president, subject to confirmation by the Senate.

9. These amounts are for the fiscal year indicated. For fiscal year 1960, the NSF's "total adjusted appropriation" was $154.8 million. From Alan T. Waterman, introduction to *Science: The Endless Frontier*, by Vannevar Bush (Alexandria, VA: National Science Foundation, 1960), p. xxiv. Waterman was director of the NSF in 1960.

10. Hitchcock, *Eisenhower*, p. 379. Compounding the pressure was the Gaither report, presented to the National Security Council on November 7, 1957: the United States needed to spend an extra $4 billion per year to defend against surprise attacks, on top of the $38 billion per year already being spent (pp. 379–380).

11. Khrushchev first made this statement in November 1956 at the Polish embassy in Moscow.

12. Johnson was Senate majority leader; he organized these hearings as chairman of the Preparedness Subcommittee of the Senate Armed Services Committee. Teller does not mention this testimony in his memoir, but his general position at this time is clear—the United States needed to do more and to spend more to stay up with the Soviets.

13. Hitchcock, *Eisenhower*, p. 383.

14. Ibid., p. 380, quoting a National Intelligence Estimate that projected Soviet capabilities from 1957 to 1962. The *Gaither Report*, presented to the White House in November 1957, had also expressed concern about the missile gap.

15. Killian had previously chaired a 1955 panel, which found that long-range missiles were now an essential part of American defense. During World War II, Killian had effectively been the chief operating officer of MIT, providing well-received support to the Rad Lab and broader wartime scientific effort. Interestingly, Killian himself was not a scientist; he had previously run *Technology Review*, an MIT publication, but he had earned the confidence of scientists. And as he disarmingly points out in his memoir, President Eisenhower was really bringing on board

the image of MIT—and the wartime achievements of the OSRD and broader scientific community.

16. From a legislative perspective, federal support for education had been proposed previously but without effect. The Sputnik crisis broke the logjam. "Sputnik Spurs Passage of the National Defense Education Act," US Senate, October 4, 1957, https://www.senate.gov/artandhistory/history/minute/Sputnik_Spurs _Passage_of_National_Defense_Education_Act.htm.

17. Cornelia Dean, "When Science Suddenly Mattered, in Space and in Class," *New York Times*, September 25, 2007, https://www.nytimes.com/2007/09/25 /science/space/25educ.html.

18. From $254 million to $1.57 billion in nominal dollars. Hugh Davis Graham and Nancy Diamond, *The Rise of American Research Universities: Elites and Challengers in the Postwar Era* (Baltimore: Johns Hopkins University Press, 1997), p. 47. Other details in this paragraph are from pp. 47–48 of this source.

19. "60 Years Ago, Eisenhower Proposes NASA to Congress," April 2, 2018, NASA, https://www.nasa.gov/feature/60-years-ago-eisenhower-proposes -nasa-to-congress.

20. McGeorge Bundy, *Danger and Survival* (New York: Random House, 1988), p. 352: "McNamara discovered within weeks that there was no discernible missile gap," and "the eventual force of 1,000 Minutemen, 656 Polaris missiles on submarines, and some 500 bombers was about the same as what Eisenhower had planned." Bundy was national security advisor from January 1961 to February 1966.

21. Ted Sorensen, *Counselor: A Life at the Edge of History* (New York: Harper, 2008). The quote is from p. 336, and the assessment of the administration's thinking is on pp. 334–336.

22. Annie Jacobsen, *Operation Paperclip: The Secret Intelligence Program that Brought Nazi Scientists to America* (New York: Little, Brown, 2014).

23. Although his culpability in this was always denied by von Braun, V-2 production made use of concentration camp labor. Von Braun's biographical details are drawn from Michael J. Neufeld, *Von Braun: Dreamer of Space, Engineer of War* (New York: Vintage Books, 2007).

24. Wernher von Braun, *The Mars Project* (Champaign: University of Illinois Press, 1991).

25. David Merriman Scott and Richard Jurek, *Marketing the Moon: The Selling of the Apollo Lunar Program* (Cambridge, MA: MIT Press, 2014), chap. 1.

26. "In 2008 dollars, the cumulative cost of the Manhattan project over 5 fiscal years was approximately $22 billion; of the Apollo program over 14 fiscal years, approximately $98 billion; of post-oil shock energy R&D efforts over 35 fiscal years, $118 billion." Deborah D. Stine, *The Manhattan Project, the Apollo Program, and Federal Energy Technology R&D Programs: A Comparative Analysis* (Washington, DC: Congressional Research Service, 2009), https://fas.org/sgp/crs/misc /RL34645.pdf.

27. Ibid.

28. "Table 1.2, Summary of Receipts, Outlays, and Surpluses or Deficits (-) as Percentages of GDP: 1930–2023," Office of Budget and Management Historical Tables, https://www.whitehouse.gov/omb/historical-tables/.

29. *NASA Sounding Rockets, 1958–1968: A Historical Summary,* NASA SP-4401 (Washington, DC: NASA, 1971), https://history.nasa.gov/SP-4401.pdf.

30. "Historical Trends in R&D," American Association for the Advancement of Science, https://www.aaas.org/programs/r-d-budget-and-policy/historical-trends-federal-rd.

31. "Occupational Employment and Wages, May 2017," Bureau of Labor Statistics, https://www.bls.gov/oes/current/oes172011.htm.

32. These were all achievements of the X-15, a 1959–1968 joint program between NASA, the navy, and the private sector (North American Aviation, now part of Boeing); "NASA Exploration and Innovation Lead to New Discoveries," NASA, https://spinoff.nasa.gov/Spinoff2008/pdf/timeline_08.pdf.

33. This includes structural integrity technology; see John A. Alic, Lewis M. Branscomb, Harvey Brooks, Ashton B. Carter, and Gerald L. Epstein, *Beyond Spinoff: Military and Commercial Technologies in a Changing World, Harvard Business School Press* (Brighton, MA: Harvard Business School Press, 1992), p. 38. The Boeing 707 was a spin-off from the Dash-80 prototype, a four-jet swept-wing design developed to provide aerial refueling for the air force.

34. Tang was developed in 1957, the invention of Teflon dates from 1938, and Velcro was created by George de Maestral in the 1940s. Alic et al., *Beyond Spinoff,* p. 57. NASA agrees; see "Are Tang, Teflon, and Velcro NASA Spinoffs?," NASA, https://www.nasa.gov/offices/ipp/home/myth_tang.html.

35. "50 Science Sagas for 50 Years," Council for the Advancement of Science Writing, http://www.casw.org/casw/article/50-science-sagas-50-years#1950s.

36. "About Spinoff," NASA Spinoff, https://spinoff.nasa.gov/about.html.

37. On NASA's Tumblr feed, https://nasa.tumblr.com/, posted October 9, 2015.

38. Jeremy Hsu, "Space Shuttle's Legacy: More Tech Spinoffs Than Apollo Era," July 19, 2011, https://www.space.com/12344-nasa-space-shuttle-program-technology-spinoffs.html.

39. The earliest studies of NASA's impact, conducted in the early 1960s, are among the most systematic and impressive. An analysis conducted by the University of Denver Research Institute, published in 1963, looked at the impact of "spin-off from missile and space programs" on thirty-three separate areas of technology. The most common impact was "stimulation of basic and applied research," but they also found evidence of product improvement and new product development, although they did not put a dollar value on anything specific. For some recent materials, see this page: "STMD: Technology Transfer," NASA, https://www.nasa.gov/directorates/spacetech/techtransfer.

40. These were Television Infrared Observation Satellite, TIROS 1, and ECHO, respectively.

41. Dan Freyer, *Liftoff: Careers in Satellite, the World's First and Most Successful Space Industry* (New York: Society of Satellite Professionals International, 2010), https://www.aem.umn.edu/teaching/undergraduate/advising_guide/Liftoff_Satellite_Careers.pdf, p. 11.

42. Ibid, p. 8.

43. In 2016, the US satellite industry had revenues of $110.3 billion, while the non-US industry had revenues of $150.2 billion.

44. Of global revenues for satellite TV, 41 percent are earned in the United States. *State of the Satellite Industry Report* (Alexandria, VA: Bryce Space and Technology, 2017), https://www.sia.org/wp-content/uploads/2017/07/SIA-SSIR-2017.pdf.

45. *The Space Economy at a Glance 2011* (Paris: OCED, 2011), https://www.oecd.org/sti/futures/space/48301203.pdf.

46. The US Naval Research Laboratory was created in 1923; https://www.onr.navy.mil/en/About-ONR/History, building on work begun during World War I. The ONR has a webpage on the Nobel prize-winners it has supported: https://www.onr.navy.mil/About-ONR/History/Nobels.

47. Kenneth Flamm, *Creating the Computer* (Washington, DC: Brookings Institution, 1988), pp. 42–43, 54. The National Science Foundation was intended to support basic research, "but because computer science did not mature as a separate academic discipline until the mid-1960s, the foundation largely excluded computer research from support in the first decades after the birth of the computer. Fortunately for the U.S. computer, however, the military establishment guaranteed support to the industry for the sake of national security" (Flamm, p. 78).

48. Important precursors included differential analyzers—electromechanical machines for solving particular kinds of differential equations (e.g., useful in ballistics). Vannevar Bush was a leader in this field while at MIT.

49. Flamm, *Creating the Computer*, p. 37.

50. Ibid., p. 75.

51. Ibid., p. 55. Whirlwind was not the first modern large-scale digital computer—that distinction arguably belongs to a British machine invented during World War II to assist with code breaking.

52. See Robert Buderi, *The Invention That Changed the World* (New York: Simon & Schuster, 1996), Chapter 17, on Jay Forrester and Project Whirlwind; also Martin Campbell-Kelly, *Computer: A History of the Information Machine* (New York: Routledge, 2013).

53. The air force, created in 1907, was immediately focused not just on airplane design but also on computational systems that could support air defense, in particular by integrating and processing the information received from myriad radar systems.

54. Magnetic core used material developed in Germany and brought back to the United States—by the military—after the war (Flamm, *Creating the Computer*, pp. 15, 58).

55. RAND, short for **R**esearch **AN**d **D**evelopment, was a public policy group originally set up by the US Air Force. Nathan L. Ensmenger, *The Computer Boys Take Over: Computers, Programmers, and the Politics of Technical Expertise* (Cambridge, MA: MIT Press, 2010).

56. Ibid. Computer programming was not initially regarded as highly skilled work.

57. Buderi, *Invention That Changed The World*, and Flamm, *Creating the Computer*, p. 56. "SAGE was essentially the first wide-area computer network, the first extensive digital data communications system, the first real-time transaction processing system. Concepts developed for its operation formed the base on which time-sharing and computer networks were later developed" (Flamm, *Creating the Computer*, p. 89).

58. Employment data from *Moody's Manual of Investments*; available through Mergent.

59. Flamm, *Creating the Computer*, p. 41.

60. Alic et al., *Beyond Spinoff*, pp. 67–68.

61. National Research Council and Computer Science and Telecommunications Board, *Funding a Revolution: Government Support for Computing Research* (Washington, DC: National Academies Press, 1999, p. 59.

62. Flamm, *Creating the Computer*, pp. 87–89.

63. Ibid., p. 89.

64. General Motors, for long the definition of an industrial giant, employed 288,286 people in 1929.

65. IBM was for a long time the most highly ranked tech company: #8 in 1980, #4 in 1990, #6 in 2000, and still #10 in 2005.

66. "Jean Hoerni at Fairchild developed the planar transistor then Jack Kilby at Texas Instruments and Robert Noyce at Fairchild developed the integrated circuit." "The Transistor and the Integrated Circuit," Design Automation Conference, https://dac.com/blog/post/transistor-and-integrated-circuit.

67. The numbers in this paragraph are from Flamm, *Creating the Computer*, pp. 16, 18.

68. Ibid.

69. Integrated circuits, weather forecasting, highway grooves that reduce tire hydroplaning, and ways to measure air pollution are striking examples in the first edition of NASA's *Spinoff* publication: Neil P. Ruzic, *Spinoff 1976: A Bicentennial Report* (Washington, DC: NASA, 1976), https://spinoff.nasa.gov/back_issues_archives/1976.pdf.

70. DARPA quotes in this and the preceding paragraph are from *Innovation at DARPA* (Arlington, VA: DARPA, 2011), https://www.darpa.mil/attachments/DARPA_Innovation_2016.pdf, p. 6.

71. "DARPA's many important achievements have included seminal roles in the development of the Internet (initially known as Arpanet), stealth aircraft, miniaturized GPS technologies, unmanned aerial vehicles, flat-screen displays, and

the brain-computer interface work that is making it possible for subjects to use their thoughts to move artificial limbs"; *Innovation at DARPA*. On Agent Orange: "Inside DARPA, The Pentagon Agency Whose Technology Has 'Changed the World,'" NPR, March 28, 2017, https://www.npr.org/2017/03/28/521779864 /inside-darpa-the-pentagon-agency-whose-technology-has-changed-the-world. See also the list in *New Scientist:* Duncan Graham-Rowe, "Fifty Years of DARPA: Hits, Misses and Ones to Watch," *New Scientist,* May 15, 2008, https://www .newscientist.com/article/dn13907-fifty-years-of-darpa-hits-misses-and-ones-to -watch/.

72. Not all DARPA innovations have been so positive for human and economic development—the agency also helped invent Agent Orange, a chemical defoliant used in the Vietnam War, which proved highly toxic.

73. Table 3-1 in Flamm, *Creating the Computer,* pp. 76–77, offers a comprehensive list of government support for early computer development.

74. In its earliest days, DARPA had a positive impact on general purpose time-sharing operating systems, as well as on computer networks.

75. Flamm, *Creating the Computer,* p. 79.

76. National Research Council, *Funding a Revolution,* p. 74.

77. Ibid., p. 77.

78. Ibid., p. 68.

79. "Inside DARPA," NPR.

80. About 20 percent of all IBM employees worked on SAGE at its peak.

81. Writing in the mid-1990s, the president's Council of Economic Advisers said, "R&D spending by industry is highly concentrated in the United States—eight industries account for more than 80 percent of the total—and the top two, aircraft and communications equipment, are closely related to defense." *Economic Report of the President: 1995* (Washington, DC: United States Government Printing Office, 1995), https://www.presidency.ucsb.edu/sites/default /files/books/presidential-documents-archive-guidebook/the-economic-report -of-the-president-truman-1947-obama-2017/1995.pdf.

82. Vannevar Bush, *Pieces of the Action* (New York: William Morrow, 1970), p. 31. Admiral William D. Leahy, the president's chief of staff and top military adviser, represented the old-school military view perfectly at the end of a briefing for President Truman in April 1945, in which the president was informed of the existence of the atomic bomb. "This is the biggest fool thing we have ever done. The bomb will never go off, and I speak as an expert in explosives." The quote is as reported by President Truman in his memoir *1945: Year of Decisions* (Old Saybrook, CT: William S. Konecky Associates, 1999), p. 11.

83. This was the assessment of President Clinton's Council of Economic Advisers: "Technology and Economic Growth: Producing Real Results for the American," White House, November 8, 1995, https://clintonwhitehouse2.archives .gov/WH/EOP/OSTP/html/techgrow.html#1. This assessment was produced as part of an argument with congressional Republicans, who were seeking to cut

nonmilitary R&D spending. More specifically, what the CEA found (based on Bureau of Labor Statistics data) was that "investment in [public and private] R&D contributed about 0.2 percentage point to the growth of productivity between 1963 and 1992, with essentially no difference before and after 1972"—although, as they pointed out, this is likely an underestimate of the contribution primarily due to measurement issues, including for productivity in the service sector. Trend productivity growth was 0.9 percent per year from 1978 to 1987 and 1.2 percent per year from 1988 to 1994. *Economic Report of the President: 1995.*

84. The total civilian labor force in the early 1990s was just over 125 million people, and employment was around 117 million, https://www.bls.gov/web/empsit /cps_charts.pdf. Nothing in terms of job creation lasts forever, and from the early 1990s, employment in the computer and electronic products industry, as measured by the Bureau of Labor Statistics, fell from just under 2 million to 1.1 million, https://www.pbs.org/newshour/economy/rise-fall-u-s-corporations. Of course, employment in other technology-related business—including in and around the internet—boomed during that same period of time.

85. "Between 1940 and 1944 the US government placed $175.066 billion of prime defence contracts with US corporations. Two-thirds of these awards went to only 100 companies and 20% to only five companies leading to charges that the prime contractors were favoured." Fred R. Kaen, "World War II Prime Defence Contractors: Were They Favored?," *Journal of Business History* 53 (2011). Kaen, looking just at stock prices, argues the contractors were not favored. Zachary, *Endless Frontier,* reports that one-third of all "war orders" went to ten companies— some of which lent executives to the government (pp. 248–249).

86. Flamm, *Creating the Computer,* p. 55.

CHAPTER 3: DESCENT FROM THE HEAVENS

1. AP, "G.B. Kistiakowsky Is Dead at 82; Bomb Pioneer Sought Nuclear Ban," *New York Times,* December 8, 1982, http://www.nytimes.com/1982/12 /08/obituaries/gb-kistiakowsky-is-dead-at-82-bomb-pioneer-sought-nuclear -ban.html.

2. The general occupation of scientist received one of the highest prestige ratings in a March 1947 survey, just behind US Supreme Court justice and physician. In 1947, 51 percent of respondents did not know what they thought of nuclear physicists specifically. By June 1963, the Don't Know category was down to 10 percent. In that survey, 70 percent of people thought the reputation of nuclear physicist was Excellent; 23 percent thought it was Good, and only 2 percent thought it was Below Average or Poor. By way of comparison, the percent viewing the prestige of economist as Excellent was only 20 percent in 1963. Robert E. Hodge, Paul M. Siegel, and Peter H. Rossi, "Occupational Prestige in the United States, 1925–63," *American Journal of Sociology* 70, no. 3 (1964): 286–302, table 1, p. 290.

3. "U.S. Scientists: 1960," Person of the Year: A Photo History, *Time*, http://content.time.com/time/specials/packages/article/0,28804,2019712_2019703_2019661,00.html.

4. According to the National Science Board's Science & Engineering Indicators 2018, federal spending on R&D was 0.67 percent of GDP in 2015, the latest year for which data are available; see figure 4-3, "Ratio of U.S. R&D to gross domestic product, by roles of federal, business, and other nonfederal funding for R&D: 1953–2015," from https://nsf.gov/statistics/2018/nsb20181/figures.

5. "In its reaction to my appointment, the press was almost unanimously favorable." James R. Killian Jr., *Sputnik, Scientists, and Eisenhower: A Memoir of the First Special Assistant to the President for Science and Technology* (Cambridge, MA: MIT Press, 1977), p. 31.

6. Umair Irfan, "Trump Finally Picked a Science Adviser," *Vox*, August 1, 2018, https://www.vox.com/2018/8/1/17639314/trump-science-adviser-kelvin-droegemeier-ostp.

7. At the end of the war, the US Alsos mission established that "the Germans had no bombs or prototypes, no working reactors or stockpiles of plutonium and uranium-235, no community of scientists with bomb-making expertise who might work for the Russians." There had been an atomic bomb program from 1939 (three years before the Americans got started), but it was scaled back in 1942. Thomas Powers, "The Private Heisenberg and the Absent Bomb," *New York Times Review of Books*, December 22, 2016, http://www.nybooks.com/articles/2016/12/22/private-heisenberg-absent-bomb/.

8. "But the overriding consideration was this: I had great respect for German science. If a bomb were possible, if it turned out to have enormous power, the result in the hands of Hitler might indeed enable him to enslave the world. It was essential to get there first, if an all-out American effort could accomplish the difficult task." Vannevar Bush, *Pieces of the Action* (New York: William Morrow, 1970) p. 59.

9. Later, Groves put it this way: "So when I say that *we* [the military leaders at Los Alamos] *were responsible for the scientific decisions,* I am not saying that we were extremely able nuclear physicists, because actually we were not. We were what might be termed 'thoroughly practical nuclear physicists.'" This quote is from Groves's testimony regarding Oppenheimer's security clearance, held before the Atomic Energy Commission in 1954. It appears in Edward Teller, introduction to *Now It Can Be Told: The Story of the Manhattan Project*, by Leslie Groves (Cambridge, MA: Da Capo Press, 1983), p. vi. Italics are as they appear in the book.

10. Bush's falling out with Truman, discussed in Chapter 2, happened subsequently.

11. The US government published the broad outlines of its nuclear program, in carefully edited form, in 1945: Henry D. Smyth, *Atomic Energy for Military Purposes: A General Account of the Scientific Research That Went Into the Making of Atomic Bombs* (Princeton, NJ: Princeton University Press, 1945). The preface by the author is dated July 1945, with amendments dated September 1, 1945; General Groves's

foreword is dated August 1945. The intent to develop peaceful civilian applications was already apparent, although precisely what this would entail remained vague.

12. The universities were Columbia University, Cornell University, Harvard University, Johns Hopkins University, Massachusetts Institute of Technology, University of Pennsylvania, Princeton University, University of Rochester, and Yale University. Philip Morse, the director of this new lab, was a polymath. An important figure in ASWORG (the navy's anti-submarine group) during the war, he also founded the field of operations research along the way; his textbook, Philip Morse and George E. Kimball, *Methods of Operation Research* (n.p.: Andesite Press, 2015), is a must-read for anyone interested in how to use data to solve real-world problems. Professor Isidor Isaac Rabi, 1944 Nobel Prize winner and a senior person at the Rad Lab, was also involved. See William L. Laurence, "Atomic Laboratory on Long Island to Be a Mighty Research Center," *New York Times,* March 1, 1947, https://timesmachine.nytimes.com/timesmachine/1947/03/01/88763292.pdf, and the *New York Times* obituary for Morse: "Philip McCord Morse, Physicist," *New York Times,* September 13, 1985, https://www.nytimes.com/1985/09/13/us /philip-mccord-morse-physicist.html.

13. AUI has helped to create and manage other projects, including the National Radio Astronomy Observatory: "Our Story," Associated Universities, https://www.aui.edu/our-story/. From Article 1 of its charter: "To constitute an agency through which universities and other research organizations will be enabled to cooperate with one another, with governments and with other organizations toward the development of scientific knowledge in the fields." "Article 1: The Corporation's Purpose," Associated Universities, https://www.aui.edu/charter-by -laws/article-1-corporations-purpose/.

14. According to his wife, "he named the swimsuit a bikini, thinking of the nuclear explosions at Bikini Atoll around that time." From Reuters, "Louis Reard Engineer, Dies: Designed the Bikini in 1946," *New York Times,* September 18, 1984, http://www.nytimes.com/1984/09/18/obituaries/louis-reard-engineer-dies-designed-the-bikini-in-1946.html. These designs did not really catch on until the 1960s, aided by the arrival of Lycra from 1964: Sylvia Rubin, "Fashion Shocker of '46: The Naked Belly Button / But the Bikini Wasn't a Hit Until Sixties," *San Francisco Chronicle,* July 2, 2006, https://www.sfgate.com /news/article/Fashion-shocker-of-46-the-naked-belly-button-2493673.php.

15. On how the atomic bomb changed popular culture, see "How the Bomb Changed Everything," BBC, July 2, 2015, http://www.bbc.com/culture/story /20150702-how-the-bomb-changed-everything. Wonder gave way to fear, but not immediately. The United States dropped a total of twenty-three nuclear bombs on Bikini Atoll. Eleanor Ainge Roy, "'Quite Odd': Coral and Fish Thrive on Bikini Atoll 70 Years After Nuclear Tests," *Guardian,* July 15, 2017, https://www.theguardian.com/world/2017/jul/15/quite-odd-coral-and-fish -thrive-on-bikini-atoll-70-years-after-nuclear-tests.

16. The Aircraft Nuclear Propulsion program was canceled in 1961, because "the atomic airplane showed little military promise." "Reason for Abandonment," *New York Times*, November 7, 1961. The navy did, of course, develop nuclear-powered submarines—followed by aircraft carriers and other vessels.

17. "The Atomic Pen's design called for a tiny packet of radioactive isotopes, which would heat the ink to produce a selectable range of line densities. Perhaps understandably, no production units were ever made." Evan Ackerman, "A Radioactive Pen in Your Pocket? Sure!," IEEE Spectrum, October 28, 2016, https://spectrum.ieee.org/tech-history/heroic-failures/a-radioactive-pen-in-your-pocket-sure. The Nucleon, a nuclear-powered car, was a concept unveiled by Ford.

18. Alexis Madrigal, "7 (Crazy) Civilian Uses for Nuclear Bombs," *Wired*, April 10, 2009, https://www.wired.com/2009/04/yourfriendatom/. Edward Teller made the famous remark about nuclear explosions being used to dig holes; he was only partly being humorous.

19. Richard D. Lyons, "End of Rocket Project Produces Space Age Ghost Town," *New York Times*, March 26, 1972, https://timesmachine.nytimes.com/timesmachine/1972/03/26/90711148.pdf.

20. There is debate about what exactly Lewis Strauss, the chairman of the Atomic Energy Commission, was thinking when he said, in 1954, that electricity would become too cheap to meter, but he did make the free electricity statement. "'Too Cheap to Meter': A History of the Phrase," US Nuclear Regulatory Commission, June 3, 2016, https://public-blog.nrc-gateway.gov/2016/06/03/too-cheap-to-meter-a-history-of-the-phrase/.

21. Glenn Seaborg, one of the country's most influential scientists, was still optimistic about the potential for atomic power in 1970, when his book *Man and Atom* appeared. In retrospect, resistance to building nuclear power plants was only increasing. Seaborg chaired the Atomic Energy Commission (1961–1970); previously, he'd helped discover plutonium and nine other elements and won the Nobel Prize. "Glenn Seaborg," *Economist*, March 4, 1999, https://www.economist.com/node/188956.

22. Anthony Standen, *Science Is a Sacred Cow* (New York: E. P. Dutton, 1950), p. 79. He was writing, as a chemist, specifically about the teaching of chemistry. But his book also makes this general point about what was then modern science. Wolfgang Saxon wrote, "Mr. Standen's point was that scientists, and especially teachers of science, tended to have inflated egos, certain of their superior wisdom and virtue. In reality, he asserted, they are mostly dull and pompous and should be laughed at now and then. Unfortunately in his view, the general public stood in awe of them even when they talked Latinized nonsense," from "Anthony Standen Is Dead at 86; Chemist Who Deflated Pomposity," *New York Times*, June 25, 1993, http://www.nytimes.com/1993/06/25/obituaries/anthony-standen-is-dead-at-86-chemist-who-deflated-pomposity.html.

23. William L. Laurence, "U.S. Atom Bomb Site Belies Tokyo Tales," *New York Times,* September 9, 1945. The message was conveyed by the subheading: "That Blast, Not Radiation, Took Toll."

24. On the long-term effects of radiation, see "Children of the Atomic Bomb," Asian American Studies Center, http://www.aasc.ucla.edu/cab/index.html, based on the work of Dr. James N. Yamazaki, lead physician of the US Atomic Bomb Medical Team in 1949, "studying the effects of nuclear bombing on children in Nagasaki, Japan."

25. Laurence was a distinguished science writer who won two Pulitzer Prizes and cofounded the National Association of Science Writers. He witnessed the Alamogordo (a.k.a. Trinity) nuclear test on July 16, 1945, and flew on the August 9 mission that dropped an atomic bomb on Nagasaki. His military affiliation was not mentioned in a long and otherwise informative obituary in the *New York Times:* "William Laurence, Ex-Science Writer for The Times, Dies," *New York Times,* March 19, 1977, https://www.nytimes.com/1977/03/19/archives /william-laurence-exscience-writer-for-the-times-dies-william-l.html. Laurence's employment during the war by the military is recognized and discussed in detail in General Leslie M. Groves's memoir, *Now It Can Be Told,* originally published in 1962: "It seemed desirable for security reasons, as well as easier for the employer, to have Laurence continue on the payroll of the New York Times, but with his expenses to be covered by the MED [the Manhattan Engineering District, i.e., the atomic bomb project]," p. 326.

26. "Beginning in April 1945, Mr. Laurence was secretly seconded by The Times to the War Department on the request of Maj. Gen. Leslie R. Groves, commander of the atomic bomb project." David W. Dunlap, "1945 Witnessing the A-Bomb, but Forbidden to File," *New York Times,* August 6, 2015, https://www.nytimes.com /times-insider/2015/08/06/1945-witnessing-the-a-bomb-but-forbidden-to-file/.

27. Kelly Moore, *Disrupting Science: Social Movements, American Scientists, and the Politics of the Military 1945-1975* (Princeton, NJ: Princeton University Press, 2013).

28. Melinda Gormley and Melissae Fellet, "When Science Doesn't Have a Simple Answer," *Slate,* July 29, 2015, http://www.slate.com/articles/technology/ future_tense/2015/07/the_cold_war_pauling_teller_debate_on_nuclear_testing_ shows_the_role_scientists.html.

29. According to the Environmental Protection Agency, "Exposure to low levels of radiation encountered in the environment does not cause immediate health effects, but is a minor contributor to our overall cancer risk." EPA, "Radiation Health Effects," https://www.epa.gov/radiation/radiation-health-effects.

30. *The Bulletin of the Atomic Scientists* was founded by physicists aiming to "educate the public to the necessity for a civilian-controlled program of atomic energy free of unreasonable security restrictions." Daniel J. Kevles, *The Physicists: The History of a Scientific Community in Modern America* (Cambridge, MA: Harvard University Press, 1971), p. 351.

31. *DDT* is short for *dichloro-diphenyl-trichloro-ethane;* it was patented in 1940 by Paul Müller, a Swiss chemist, who won the 1948 Nobel Prize in Physiology or Medicine for this work. Scaling-up of production and widespread use against mosquitoes was organized in large part by Vannevar Bush's OSRD/NDRC.

32. "Award Ceremony Speech," Nobel Prize, https://www.nobelprize.org/prizes/medicine/1948/ceremony-speech/.

33. "DDT Regulatory History: A Brief Survey (to 1975)," EPA, https://archive.epa.gov/epa/aboutepa/ddt-regulatory-history-brief-survey-1975.html.

34. Kate Wong, "DDT Debate," *Scientific American,* December 4, 2000, https://www.scientificamerican.com/article/ddt-debate/.

35. Again, this was not a new point—many people have repeated versions at least since Mary Shelley's *Frankenstein,* the ultimate scientific nightmare, published in 1818, before industrialized science had really taken off. Edward Tenner's *Why Things Bite Back: Technology and the Revenge of Unintended Consequences* (New York: Vintage, 1997) provides an entertaining if sobering history of unintended consequences since 1900.

36. "Many man-made chemicals act in much the same way as radiation; they lie long in the soil, and enter into living organisms, passing from one to another. Or they may travel mysteriously by underground streams, emerging to combine, through the alchemy of air and sunlight, into new forms, which kill vegetation, sicken cattle, and work unknown harm on those who drink from once pure wells." Rachel Carson, "Silent Spring-I," *New Yorker,* June 16, 1962, https://www.newyorker.com/magazine/1962/06/16.

37. "In 1972, EPA issued a cancellation order for DDT based on its adverse environmental effects, such as those to wildlife, as well as its potential human health risks. Since then, studies have continued, and a relationship between DDT exposure and reproductive effects in humans is suspected, based on studies in animals. In addition, some animals exposed to DDT in studies developed liver tumors. As a result, today, DDT is classified as a probable human carcinogen by U.S. and international authorities." The Stockholm convention on persistent organic pollutants bans DDT, with the limited and specific exception of malaria control. "DDT—A Brief History and Status," EPA, https://www.epa.gov/ingredients-used-pesticide-products/ddt-brief-history-and-status.

38. See, for example, this online exhibition: Mark Stoll, "The Personal Attacks on Rachel Carson as a Woman Scientist," Environment and Society Portal, 2012, http://www.environmentandsociety.org/exhibitions/silent-spring/personal-attacks-rachel-carson.

39. According to the Environmental Protection Agency, "The publication in 1962 of Rachel Carson's *Silent Spring* stimulated widespread public concern over the dangers of improper pesticide use and the need for better pesticide controls." "DDT—A Brief History and Status," EPA.

40. Carson's impact on Europe was more limited or perhaps just delayed. See Mark Stoll, "Why Europe Responded Differently from the United States,"

Environment and Society Portal, 2012, http://www.environmentandsociety.org /exhibitions/silent-spring/why-europe-responded-differently-united-states.

41. For a detailed assessment of how these concerns spread, see Moore, *Disrupting Science.*

42. "'Silent Spring'was more than a study of the effects of synthetic pesticides; it was an indictment of the late 1950s." Eliza Griswold, "How 'Silent Spring' Ignited the Environmental Movement," *New York Times,* September 23, 2012, http://www.nytimes.com/2012/09/23/magazine/how-silent-spring-ignited -the-environmental-movement.html. While some pro-environment groups such as the Audubon Society have been around for a long time, a wave of new organizations arose from the late 1960s, including the Union of Concerned Scientists and Friends of the Earth in 1969, the Natural Resources Defense Council in 1970, and Greenpeace in 1971.

43. This point is made by Charles Perrow, *Normal Accidents: Living with High-Risk Technologies* (Princeton, NJ: Princeton University Press, 1999). Perrow leads with the case of Three Mile Island and refers to the peril of atomic energy throughout his book, although his point is much broader.

44. See the interactive graphic at "Global Nuclear Power Database," Bulletin of the Atomic Scientists, https://thebulletin.org/global-nuclear-power-database; the number of annual construction starts peaked in 1976 at forty-four (of which twelve were later abandoned).

45. "Almost all the US nuclear generating capacity comes from reactors built between 1967 and 1990. Until 2013 there had been no new construction starts since 1977, largely because for a number of years gas generation was considered more economically attractive and because construction schedules during the 1970s and 1980s had frequently been extended by opposition, compounded by heightened safety fears following the Three Mile Island accident in 1979." "Nuclear Power in the USA,"World Nuclear Associated, updated October 2018, http://www .world-nuclear.org/information-library/country-profiles/countries-t-z/usa-nuclear -power.aspx. About 20 percent of US electricity is generated from nuclear power.

46. "Manhattan Project Spotlight: George and Vera Kistiakowsky," Atomic Heritage Foundation, October 15, 2014, https://www.atomicheritage.org/article /manhattan-project-spotlight-george-and-vera-kistiakowsky.

47. Interviewed by Richard Rhodes, historian of the atomic bomb, in 1980: "But then Oppenheimer and Groves started urging [James] Conant, because they did not have confidence in Neddermeyer, that they needed me over there because I was supposed to be the number one civilian explosives expert, with these new-fangled ideas about precision instruments—explosives position instruments. And so I said all right, this is war time, and although I'm a civilian, I obeyed the orders of my boss Conant." "George Kistiakowsky's Interview," Voices of the Manhattan Project, https://www.manhattanprojectvoices.org/oral -histories/george-kistiakowskys-interview. Neddermeyer was the Manhattan Project expert on detonation. Conant was president of Harvard, right-hand man

to Bush during the war, and top of the scientific hierarchy overseeing the atomic bomb project.

48. Kistiakowsky himself was quite modest about the accomplishment. See "George Kistiakowsky's Interview," Voices of the Manhattan Project.

49. As he put it later, "For many years, well into the mid 1950s, I saw myself as a technical expert being available to policy makers to put the policies into effect." Ibid.

50. "There were three points that were of great importance, our committee concluded. And von Neumann was the leader in it. The warhead could be cut down to somewhere like a thousand pounds and still be of the order of a megaton explosive yield. The size of the missile could be cut down to a third of what old Air Force missiles promised to be. And incidentally that size was the same as the Soviet size of the SS-6, which was then used to launch satellites in space in 1957–58." Ibid.

51. Kistiakowsky's diary makes it clear that he was close to or involved in decision-making at the highest level, including with regular access to the president. He was also seen as relatively nonpartisan and did not participate in Richard Nixon's 1960 election campaign. George B. Kistiakowsky, *A Scientist at the White House: The Private Diary of President Eisenhower's Special Assistant for Science and Technology* (Cambridge, MA: Harvard University Press, Cambridge, 1976).

52. This is according to McGeorge Bundy, *Danger and Survival* (New York: Random House, 1988). Photographs obtained by a U-2 spy plane contributed to a reassessment—the CIA revised down its estimates of long-range missiles to 35 for mid-1960 and 140–200 by mid-1961 (p. 343). At least by early 1961, when Kennedy took office and Bundy became national security advisor, there was no missile gap.

53. "George Kistiakowsky's Interview," Voices of the Manhattan Project.

54. Gregg Herken, *Cardinal Choices* (Stanford, CA: Stanford University Press, 2000), says that the report was "suppressed" (p. 150).

55. Herken, *Cardinal Choices*, p. 150.

56. Ibid. McNamara's thinking is also discussed in David Halberstam, *The Best and the Brightest* (New York: Ballantine Books, 1993), p. 630.

57. A group of scientific advisors known as the Jasons became proponents of the air force bombing approach. By the early 1960s, the Jasons comprised about forty young physicists, who met each summer to consider Pentagon-related problems. Increasingly, however, there was friction between the Jasons and an older set of scientific advisors, known as the Cambridge group (which included Kistiakowsky), who questioned the morality and strategic wisdom of bombing. Herken, *Cardinal Choices*, p. 153.

58. Ibid., p. 155.

59. Leo Szilard, a Hungarian émigré, cofounded Council for a Livable World in 1962. Szilard, first to conceive the notion of a nuclear chain reaction, was a strong voice favoring the development of the atomic bomb, based on his conviction

that the Germans were likely to develop this capability soon. He persuaded Albert Einstein to write to President Roosevelt about this issue.

60. Halberstam, *The Best and the Brightest.*

61. "However disenchantment grew as the Vietnam War continued, and the politicos in the White House—not least, Lyndon Johnson—began to lose confidence in the White House science structure." Guy Stever, *In War and Peace* (Washington, DC: Joseph Henry Press, 2002), p. 205.

62. Joel Primack and Frank von Hippel, *Advice and Dissent: Scientists in the Political Arena* (New York: Basic Books, 1974), p. 22.

63. Ibid.

64. Concorde had the same sonic boom issue and therefore only reached supersonic speeds over water. It was not a commercial success, and maintenance became an issue. After a fatal crash in 2000, all Concordes were withdrawn from service.

65. Martin Tolchin, "The Perplexing Mr. Proxmire," *New York Times,* May 28, 1978, https://www.nytimes.com/1978/05/28/archives/the-perplexing-mr-proxmire-with-new-york-facing-bankruptcy-by-hands.html.

66. Stever, *In War and Peace,* p. 203. Congressional testimony opposing administration policy annoyed the White House.

67. Naturally, there were scientists on both sides of this (and every other) issue. One survey found that 62 percent of scientists were completely opposed to ABMs in general, while 22 percent completely favored these systems; others had more intermediate views. Anne Hessing Cahn, *Eggheads and Warheads: Scientists and the ABM, Science and Public Policy Program* (Cambridge, MA: Department of Political Science and Center for International Studies, MIT, 1971).

68. Argonne National Laboratory grew out of work on the Manhattan Project by physicists at the University of Chicago: "About Argonne," Argonne National Laboratory, https://www.anl.gov/argonne-national-laboratory. The labs were initially under the Atomic Energy Commission and are now part of the Department of Energy, which was created in 1977.

69. Both quotes in the paragraph are from Primack and von Hippel, *Advice and Dissent,* p. 186.

70. Ibid., pp. 183–187.

71. The quote is from Stever, *In War and Peace,* p. 203. See also Herken, *Cardinal Choices,* pp. 166–183.

72. The Nixon administration changed its plans and received funding for two ABM sites that would defend Minuteman missile launch bases in Montana and North Dakota. In 1972, the United States and the Soviet Union agreed to limit ABM deployment. Primack and von Hippel, *Advice and Dissent,* pp. 190–191.

73. Bruce L. R. Smith, *The Advisers: Scientists in the Policy Process* (Washington, DC: Brookings Institution, 1992), p. 171.

74. President Eisenhower created the position of president's science advisor in 1957; he also created the President's Science Advisory Council, or PSAC (there had been a council under Truman, but lower profile). The staff of the science ad-

visor became, in 1962, the Office of Science and Technology (OST). Nixon abolished PSAC and OST in 1973 and transferred some of the responsibilities of the science advisor to the director of the National Science Foundation. Primack and von Hippel, *Advice and Dissent*, p. 289.

75. This was the assessment of Stever, *In War and Peace*, pp. 202–203. As head of the National Science Foundation, Stever witnessed firsthand the Nixon White House turn against its scientific advisors. In Stever's assessment, the role of the presidential science advisor began to decline when McGeorge Bundy built up the National Security Council under President Kennedy (p. 204).

76. Jim Austin, "Dr. Grant Swinger," *Science*, September 30, 2010, http://blogs .sciencemag.org/sciencecareers/2010/09/dr-grant-swinge.html.

77. D. S. Greenberg, "1965: Herewith, a Conversation with the Mythical Grant Swinger, Head of Breakthrough Institute," *Science*, http://science .sciencemag.org/content/147/3653/29.

78. In its modern materials, the society itself disputes that this campaign was ever a major focus of its activities. "Myths vs Facts," John Birch Society, https:// www.jbs.org/about-jbs/myths-vs-facts.

79. "Barry Goldwater for President 1964 Campaign Brochure," 4President Corporation, http://www.4president.org/brochures/goldwater1964brochure.htm.

80. Rancor here presumably means an assertive foreign policy. Richard H. Rovere, "The Campaign: Goldwater," *New Yorker*, October 3, 1964, https://www .newyorker.com/magazine/1964/10/03/the-campaign-goldwater.

81. Patrick J. Buchanan, "With Nixon in '68: The Year America Came Apart," *Wall Street Journal*, April 5, 2018, https://www.wsj.com/articles/with -nixon-in-68-the-year-america-came-apart-1522937732.

82. The beginning was the 1965 "teach-in," with panel discussions on the war held on more than 120 campuses. Moore, *Disrupting Science*, p. 133.

83. Ibid., pp. 133–134.

84. MIT was an epicenter for such protests. Ibid., p. 140.

85. John Sides, "How Did the Dramatic Election of 1968 Change US Politics? This New Book Explains," *Washington Post*, May 25, 2016, https://www .washingtonpost.com/news/monkey-cage/wp/2016/05/25/how-did-the-1968 -election-change-u-s-politics-so-dramatically-this-new-book-explains/?utm_term =.2f90228ccb9d.

86. Nell Greenfieldboyce, "'Shrimp on a Treadmill': The Politics of 'Silly' Studies," NPR, August 23, 2011, https://www.npr.org/2011/08/23/139852035 /shrimp-on-a-treadmill-the-politics-of-silly-studies.

87. Hugh Davis Graham and Nancy Diamond, *The Rise of American Research Universities: Elites and Challengers in the Postwar Era* (Baltimore: Johns Hopkins University Press, 1997), p. 88.

88. Alan Rohn, "How Much Did The Vietnam War Cost?," Vietnam War, updated April 6, 2016, https://thevietnamwar.info/how-much-vietnam-war -cost/.

89. Figure 1, "Mandatory Outlays Before Offsetting Receipts as a Percentage of Total Outlays (FY1962–FY2025)," from Mindy R. Levit, D. Andrew Austin, and Jeffrey M. Stupak, *Mandatory Spending Since 1962* (Washington, DC: Congressional Research Service, 2016), https://fas.org/sgp/crs/misc/RL33074.pdf.

90. And a broader decline in military spending: "Between 1968 and 1971, defense-related employment in the private sector declined by more than 1 million." *Engineering and Scientific Manpower: Recommendations for the Seventies* (Washington, DC: National Academy of Engineering, 1973), https://www.nap.edu/download/20514.

91. Stever, *In War and Peace*, p. 202: "In constant dollars it [overall federal support for basic research] went from $1.7 billion in 1967 to $1.4 billion. Most fields— aside from some areas of biology, engineering, and oceanography—declined, with the sharpest cuts in the physical sciences, especially physics and chemistry."

92. "The Mansfield Amendment," National Science Board, https://www.nsf.gov/nsb/documents/2000/nsb00215/nsb50/1970/mansfield.html. The amendment was later repealed, but its intent remained influential.

93. Ibid. This amendment should not be confused with another famous Mansfield amendment, which aimed in 1971 to reduce US forces deployed in Europe.

94. Stever, *In War and Peace*, p. 202. Stever was director of the National Science Foundation at this time. He asked for $675 million for 1974 and reports that he received $640 million. There was a short-lived boost in energy-related research after the oil crisis of 1973: Alexis C. Madrigal, "Moondoggle: The Forgotten Opposition to the Apollo Program," *Atlantic*, September 12, 2012, https://www.theatlantic.com/technology/archive/2012/09/moondoggle-the-forgotten-opposition-to-the-apollo-program/262254/.

95. The National Research Council suggested there was a potential oversupply of engineers and scientists. See *Engineering and Scientific Manpower*.

96. Data from Jonathan Gruber, *Public Finance and Public Policy*, 6th ed. (New York: Macmillan, 2019).

97. Ibid.

98. Ibid.

99. Stever, *In War and Peace*, discusses the historical and political context on pp. 258–261. Edward Teller pushed hard for a more modern antiballistic missile (ABM) program.

100. Reagan may not have consulted fully with his own top officials before announcing the Star Wars initiative: Caspar Weinberger, the defense secretary, was reportedly "slack-jawed hearing Reagan announce they were going to build this system." "The same thing with the DARPA director, the same thing with the Pentagon's chief technologist. They were just in shock." "Inside DARPA," NPR.

101. As a percent of GDP, from 1979 to 1988, total R&D spending went from 1.07 percent of GDP in 1979 to 1.08 percent in 1988; military R&D went from 0.48 percent to 0.67 percent, and nonmilitary fell from 0.59 percent to 0.41 percent.

102. Deborah D. Stine, *The Manhattan Project, the Apollo Program, and Federal Energy Technology R&D Programs: A Comparative Analysis* (Washington, DC: Congressional Research Service, 2009), https://fas.org/sgp/crs/misc/RL34645.pdf.

103. Ibid.

104. See the discussion in Stever, *In War and Peace*, p. 262. He chaired a committee convened by the OTA at the request of Congress. Their report was not opposed to research on the issue but was skeptical that the United States would be able to defend itself effectively against the Soviet Union in this fashion; see *Office of Technology Assessment, US Congress, Ballistic Missile Defense Technologies* (Washington DC: US Government Printing Office, 1985). For more on the demise of OTA, see Jathan Sadowski, "The Much-Needed and Sane Congressional Office That Gingrich Killed Off and We Need Back," *Atlantic*, October 26, 2012, https://www.theatlantic.com/technology/archive/2012/10/the-much-needed-and-sane-congressional-office-that-gingrich-killed-off-and-we-need-back/264160/.

105. David Appell, "The Supercollider That Never Was," *Scientific American*, October 15, 2013, https://www.scientificamerican.com/article/the-supercollider-that-never-was/.

106. "The Higgs Boson," CERN, https://home.cern/topics/higgs-boson. Two scientists shared the 2013 Nobel Prize in physics for this discovery.

107. Athena Yenko, "World's First Colored Human X-Ray Applies CERN Technology Used in Search of 'God Particle,'" *Tech Times*, July 13, 2018, https://www.techtimes.com/articles/232239/20180713/world-s-first-colored-human-x-ray-applies-cern-technology-used-in-search-of-god-particle.htm.

108. Gruber, *Public Finance and Public Policy*.

109. The size of this decline depends on exactly which start and end year you use. However, there is no question that—with the exception of the short-lived stimulus period (federal R&D was 1.12 percent of GDP in 2009)—there was a real squeeze on federal R&D spending from the early 2000s to the post-Obama period.

110. Watching TV shows is not necessarily the same as supporting government spending. During the 1960s, between 45 and 60 percent of Americans thought the government was spending too much on space. Support eventually increased after the event. In 1979, only 47 percent of Americans thought it was worth landing on the moon, but by 1989, support was up to 77 percent. Madrigal, "Moondoggle."

111. Some scientists did become more left-wing during the 1930s, generally when they struggled to find work opportunities or funding for their research. Peter J. Kuznick, *Beyond the Laboratory: Scientists as Political Activists in 1930's America* (Chicago: University of Chicago Press, 1997).

112. Francie Diep, "When Did Science Become Apolitical?," *Pacific Standard*, March 13, 2017, https://psmag.com/news/when-did-science-become-apolitical.

113. Erik M. Conway and Naomi Oreskes, "Why Conservatives Turned Against Science," *Chronicle of Higher Education*, November 5, 2012, https://www.chronicle.com/article/The-Conservative-Turn-Against/135488. One recent poll

found that only 6 percent of scientists are Republicans; Puneet Opal, "The Danger of Making Science Political," *Atlantic,* January 19, 2013, https://www.theatlantic .com/health/archive/2013/01/the-danger-of-making-science-political/267327/.

114. Chris C. Mooney, *The Republican War on Science* (New York: Basic Books, 2005).

CHAPTER 4: THE LIMITS OF PRIVATE RESEARCH AND DEVELOPMENT

1. Bronwyn Hall, Jacques Mairesse, and Pierre Mohnen, "Measuring the Returns to R&D," in *Handbook of the Economics of Innovation,* vol. 1, ed. Bronwyn Hall and Nathan Rosenberg (Amsterdam: North-Holland, 2010).

2. Steve Jobs and Steve Wozniak did actually start Apple in their family garages. Earlier, Bill Hewlett and David Packard started their company in a garage behind the rooms they were renting.

3. John Steele Gordon and Michael Maiello, "Pioneers Die Broke," *Forbes,* December 23, 2012, https://www.forbes.com/forbes/2002/1223/258.html#6366 c40666e6.

4. Robert E. Hall and Susan E. Woodward, "The Burden of the Nondiversifiable Risk of Entrepreneurship," *American Economic Review* 100, no. 3 (2010): 1163–1194.

5. "Global Market Demand for Flat Panel Displays (FPD) from 2000 to 2020 (in Billion U.S. Dollars)," Statista, https://www.statista.com/statistics/530497 /worldwide-flat-panel-display-market-demand/.

6. As of the mid-1990s, the top ten suppliers of LCDs were in Asia, and there were no US high-volume producers. Sheila Galatowitsch, "Emerging US Flat Panel Display Industry Embraces Automation," *Solid State Technology,* https:// electroiq.com/1996/09/emerging-us-flat-panel-display-industry-embraces -automation/. Of the top thirty-nine LCD manufacturers listed in *Wikipedia,* only three are US based. "List of liquid-crystal-display manufacturers," *Wikipedia,* https://en.wikipedia.org/wiki/List_of_liquid-crystal-display_manufacturers.

7. Robert H. Chen, *Liquid Crystal Displays: Fundamental Physics and Technology* (Hoboken, NJ: John Wiley and Sons, 2011), p. 213. This section draws heavily on Chen's book, but the outline of the story is confirmed elsewhere (e.g., see Benjamin Gross, *The TVs of Tomorrow: How RCA's Flat-Screen Dreams Led to the First LCDs* [Chicago: University of Chicago Press, 2018]). Summary at Benjamin Gross, "How RCA Lost the LCD," IEEE Spectrum, November 1, 2012, https:// spectrum.ieee.org/tech-history/heroic-failures/how-rca-lost-the-lcd.

8. Chen, *Liquid Crystal Displays,* p. 214.

9. Ibid., p. 215.

10. Ibid., p. 216.

11. Ibid.; Joseph A. Castellano, *Liquid Gold: The Story of Liquid Crystal Displays and the Creation of an Industry* (Singapore: World Scientific, 2005), p. 84; Gross, *The TVs of Tomorrow,* p. 202.

12. Chen, *Liquid Crystal Displays*, p. 217.

13. Ibid., p. 256.

14. Ibid.

15. "T. Peter Brody Papers," Philadelphia Area Consortium of Special Collections Libraries, http://dla.library.upenn.edu/cocoon/dla/pacscl/ead.html?sort=date_added_sort%20desc&showall=sort&id=PACSCL_HML_2532&.

16. Finley Colville, "Korean Capital Equipment Suppliers Target US$15 Billion PV Opportunity," Inter PV, http://www.interpv.net/market/market_view.asp?idx=465&part_code=04.

17. Richard Florida and David Browdy, "The Invention That Got Away," *Technology Review* 94, no. 6 (1991). The Japanese company Seiko had entered the US market and infringed on Westinghouse's patents for active-matrix displays. The International Trade Commission encouraged Panelvision to bring suit. The company started this process in motion, alerting Seiko of a potential lawsuit. But the suit was ultimately viewed as not fruitful given Japan's large lead in the technology.

18. The *New York Times* reported similar stories in Andrew Pollack, "US Project Hobbled by Japan's Lead," *New York Times*, December 18, 1990, http://www.nytimes.com/1990/12/18/business/us-project-hobbled-by-japan-s-lead.html?pagewanted=all. Brody tried again with a new company called Magnascreen in 1988. It received interest from larger companies but faltered when these companies were not willing to help build a factory to produce large volumes of flat-panel displays. Neither, ultimately, were venture capitalists willing to provide the funding needed to increase manufacturing to a level that could compete with Japanese companies. Government funding arrived, but it was too late to make a difference— and not enough to matter relative to the established scale of competitors. DARPA awarded Magnascreen a $7.8 million contract in 1988 and, in the budget for 1994, DARPA was given an appropriation of $75 million to spend on high-definition television displays. It was too little; estimates suggest that Japanese investment for LCD manufacturing in 1994/1995 was $4.5 billion. Rick Jurgens, "Don't Try to Catch Up with Japanese Flat Panel Makers," *Christian Science Monitor*, May 3, 1994, https://www.csmonitor.com/1994/0503/03091.html. "The Domestic Flat Panel Display Industry: Cause for Concern?" in *Flat Panel Displays in Perspective* (Washington, DC: US Government Printing Office, 1995), https://www.princeton.edu/~ota/disk1/1995/9520/952004.PDF.

19. Real per capita GDP was $14,203 in the first quarter of 1947 and $26,718 in the first quarter of 1973, a ratio of 1.88 (or an overall increase of 88 percent).

20. There are a number of ways to measure economic growth, but a useful metric for measuring economic growth is comparing the size of the economy in per capita real terms by taking inflation out of the equation. (An economy with twice as many goods but twice as many people isn't richer from the perspective of any given individual.) Data for this paragraph and the next from the FRED database maintained by the St. Louis Fed. "Real Gross Domestic Product Per Capita," FRED Economic Data, https://fred.stlouisfed.org/series/A939RX0Q048SBEA.

21. We calculate this compound average annual growth using the quarterly GDP per capita series, from Q1 1973 to Q1 2018, using data from "Real gross domestic product per capita (A939RX0Q048SBEA),"FRED Economic Data, https://fred.stlouisfed.org/graph/?id=A939RX0Q048SBEA. The equivalent growth rate from Q1 1947 to Q2 1973 was 2.46 percent per annum. Choosing slightly different starting and ending dates does not change the conclusion that there has been a slowdown in the growth of GDP per capita.

22. There is some debate about exactly how best to measure economic growth—for example, when completely new products arrive, such as smartphones. Still, the general point holds—the key to sustained economic growth is to increase productivity.

23. Patent terms available at "2701 Patent Term [R-07.2015]," US Patent and Trademark Office, https://www.uspto.gov/web/offices/pac/mpep/s2701.html.

24. "List of Edison patents," *Wikipedia*, https://en.wikipedia.org/wiki/List_of_Edison_patents.

25. Note that when we use the term *spillovers*, we are referring to two separate phenomena: value creation and value capture. Spillovers in value creation are technical/engineering in nature and occur when a firm's discovery creates general knowledge that other firms can use to innovate (perhaps trying to solve very different problems), thus creating their own new products. Spillovers in value capture are financial and occur when one firm's discovery ends up yielding profits for other firms. This is an important distinction among specialists, but for ease of discussion—and because it does not affect our general point—we group the two together here.

26. Douglas Engelbart, "Workstation History and the Augmented Knowledge Workshop," Doug Engelbart Institute, December 5, 1985, https://www.dougengelbart.org/pubs/augment-101931.html. John Markoff, *What the Dormouse Said: How the Sixties Counterculture Shaped the Personal Computer Industry* (New York: Penguin, 2005).

27. Jeffrey S. Young, *Steve Jobs: The Journey Is the Reward* (New York: Lynx Books, 1988), p. 174. Michael Hiltzik, *Dealers of Lightning* (Collingdale, PA: Diane Publishing Company, 1999), p. 342.

28. "Apple Computer Inc.," Encyclopedia.com, https://www.encyclopedia.com/social-sciences-and-law/economics-business-and-labor/businesses-and-occupations/apple-computer-inc.

29. Apple didn't fight back initially because "while who was right legally was debatable, we couldn't afford to sue the only company developing successful software for Macintosh at a still turbulent time." Brit Hume, "Apple Appears to Be Fighting IBM by Taking On Microsoft," *Washington Post,* April 4, 1988, https://www.washingtonpost.com/archive/business/1988/04/04/apple-appears-to-be-fighting-ibm-by-taking-on-microsoft/ed882313-dd2a-4bc7-b1f5-06394ea93093/?noredirect=on&utm_term=.bff2d1e4712f.

30. John C. Dvorak, "Sorting Out Fact from Fiction in the Apple-Microsoft Lawsuit," *PC Magazine,* 1988, p. 36.

31. Chris Velazco, "Microsoft Sold 450 Million Copies of Windows 7," *TechCrunch,* September 13, 2011, https://techcrunch.com/2011/09/13/microsoft -sold-450-million-copies-of-windows-7/.

32. What if Xerox had never sold its Apple shares? Given the various splits in Apple stock since that date, one share of Apple stock at its IPO is equivalent to fifty-six shares today. As of February 6, 2018, the price of an Apple share is $163.03. So Xerox would be holding 5.6 million shares at $163.03 per share, or $914 million worth of Apple stock. A lot of money, but still small relative to the ultimate value of what Jobs discovered.

33. Hiltzik, *Dealers of Lightning,* p. 387.

34. Andy Hertzfeld, "A Rich Neighbor Named Xerox," Folklore, November 1983, https://www.folklore.org/StoryView.py?story=A_Rich_Neighbor_Named _Xerox.txt.

35. Rick Mullin, "Cost to Develop New Pharmaceutical Drug Now Exceeds $2.5B," *Scientific American,* November 24, 2014, https://www.scientificamerican .com/article/cost-to-develop-new-pharmaceutical drug-now-exceeds-2-5b/.

36. This section summarizes the excellent discussion of early-stage research in James P. Hughes, Stephen Rees, S. Barrett Kalindjian, and Karen L. Philpott, "Principles of Early Drug Discovery," *British Journal of Pharmacology* 162, no. 6 (2011), https://www.ncbi.nlm.nih.gov/pubmed/21091654.

37. P. Roy Vagelos and Louis Galambos, *Medicine, Science, and Merck* (Cambridge, UK: Cambridge University Press, 2004), pp. 133–151. Akira Endo, "A Historical Perspective on the Discovery of Statins," *Proceedings of the Japan Academy Series B, Physical and Biological Sciences* 86, no. 5 (2010).

38. Endo, "A Historical Perspective." Thomas P. Stossel, "The Discovery of Statins," *Cell* 134, no. 6 (2008), https://www.sciencedirect.com/science/article/pii /S0092867408011276.

39. Vagelos and Galambos, *Medicine, Science, and Merck.*

40. In July 1982, the FDA approved Merck providing lovastatin to Roger Illingsworth (OHSU) and Scott Grundy / David Billheimer (UT SW Medical Center). Specifically, Merck did not have approval from the FDA, but approval was granted to the researchers. Conditions of these approvals allowed the researchers to see Merck's drug master file on lovastatin. See: Scott M. Grundy, "History of Statins," https://knightadrc.wustl.edu/Education/PDFs/Berg2012Slides/Grundy .pdf. A brief circulated by the FDA suggests that despite Merck's withdrawal from lovastatin research, the FDA was still very interested in developing statins. See Suzanne White Junod, "Statins: A Success Story Involving FDA, Academia and Industry," *Update,* March–April 2007, https://www.fda.gov/downloads /AboutFDA/History/ProductRegulation/UCM593497.pdf.

41. Endo, "A Historical Perspective."

42. "Merck, Bristol-Myers Want to Sell Cholesterol Medicines Over the Counter," *Courier,* December 11, 2004, https://wcfcourier.com/business/local/merck-bristol-myers-want-to-sell-cholesterol-medicines-over-the/article_3681ea5a-58d7-5558-97f7-d8446b950e50.html.

43. Endo, "A Historical Perspective."

44. David C. Grabowski, Darius N. Lakdawalla, Dana P. Goldman, Michael Eber, Larry Z. Liu, Tamer Abdelgawad, Andreas Kuznik, Michael E. Chernew, and Tomas Philipson, "The Large Social Value Resulting from Use of Statins Warrants Steps to Improve Adherence and Broaden Treatment," *Health Affairs* 31, no. 1 (2012), https://www.healthaffairs.org/doi/pdf/10.1377/hlthaff.2011.1120.

45. Stossel, "The Discovery of Statins."

46. This paragraph summarizes the results from Eric Budish, Benjamin N. Roin, and Heidi Williams, "Do Firms Underinvest in Long-Term Research? Evidence from Cancer Clinical Trials," *American Economic Review* 105, no. 7 (2015): pp. 2044–2085.

47. Ibid. In particular, for the 2003 cohort of US cancer patients, the value of lost life was $89 billion. Taking the present value over all future cohorts yields the figure of $2.2 trillion.

48. Nicole Goodkind, "Pfizer Ends Funding for Alzheimer's, Parkinson's Research," *Newsweek,* January 13, 2018, https://www.newsweek.com/alzheimers-parkinsons-tax-cuts-pfizer-research-780163.

49. "Venture Capital: Sand Hill Road Rules the Valley," *Bloomberg,* December 4, 2014, https://www.bloomberg.com/news/articles/2014-12-04/venture-capital-sand-hill-road-rules-silicon-valley.

50. Paul Gompers, "The Rise and Fall of Venture Capital," *Business and Economic History* 23, no. 2 (1994), https://www.thebhc.org/sites/default/files/beh/BEHprint/v023n2/p0001-p0026.pdf.

51. Steven Kaplan and Josh Lerner, "It Ain't Broke: The Past, Present, and Future of Venture Capital," *Journal of Applied Corporate Finance* 22, no. 2 (2010).

52. Will Gornall and Ilya A. Strebulaev, "The Economic Impact of Venture Capital: Evidence from Public Companies" (research paper no. 15-55, Stanford Graduate School of Business Stanford, CA, 2015), https://papers.ssrn.com/sol3/papers.cfm?abstract_id=2681841.

53. Shikhar Ghosh and Ramana Nanda, "Venture Capital Investment in the Clean Energy Sector" (working paper #11-020, Harvard Business School, Boston, MA, 2010), https://papers.ssrn.com/sol3/papers.cfm?abstract_id=1669445.

54. Kaplan and Lerner, "It Ain't Broke."

55. Bryan Borzykowski, "US Venture Capital Investments Down, But Global Inflows Rise," RocketSpace, February 6, 2017, https://www.rocketspace.com/tech-startups/united-states-venture-capital-investments-down.

56. Data from FRED shows gross private domestic investment of $3,057 billion in 2016. See "Gross Private Domestic Investment," FRED Economic Data, https://fred.stlouisfed.org/graph/?id=GPDIA.

57. This discussion summarizes the material in Hall and Woodward, "Burden of the Nondiversifiable Risk."

58. Hall and Woodward find that 68 percent of start-ups yield no meaningful value to entrepreneurs and that a "large fraction of the total value to entrepreneurs arises from the tiny fraction of startups that deliver hundreds of millions of dollars of exit value to the entrepreneurs." A report from the *Wall Street Journal* in 2012 finds that three out of four start-ups fail. Deborah Gage, "The Venture Capital Secret: 3 Out of 4 Start-Ups Fail," *Wall Street Journal*, September 20, 2012, https://www.wsj.com/articles/SB10000872396390443720204578004980476429190.

59. Hall and Woodward, "Burden of the Nondiversifiable Risk."

60. Venture funders will invest in stages, with relatively small investments initially, but then in ever-increasing investments as they learn more from ongoing company performance. Ramana Nanda, Ken Younge, and Lee Fleming, "Innovation and Entrepreneurship in Renewable Energy," in *The Changing Frontier: Rethinking Science and Innovation Policy*, ed. Adam Jaffe and Benjamin Jones (Chicago: University of Chicago Press), 2015.

61. Relative to companies selected in the first year of a fund, companies that are selected in year four or five are 10 percent older, are 5 percent more likely to be at a later stage of their development, and have received 6 percent more rounds of financing at the time of the investment. For companies that are selected beyond that year, these differences reach 21 percent, 12 percent, and 19 percent. Jean-Noël Barrot, "Investor Horizon and the Life Cycle of Innovative Firms: Evidence from Venture Capital," *Management Science* 63, no. 9 (2016).

62. Nanda, Younge, and Fleming, "Innovation and Entrepreneurship."

63. Ibid.

64. Ramana Nanda and Matthew Rhodes-Kropf, "Investment Cycles and Startup Innovation," *Journal of Financial Economics* 110, no. 2 (2013).

65. "We turn next to showing how this fall in the cost of starting businesses impacted the way in which VCs managed their portfolios. We show that in sectors impacted by the technological shock, VCs responded by providing a little funding and limited governance to an increased number of start-ups, which they were more likely to abandon after the initial round of funding. The number of initial investments made per year by VCs in treated sectors nearly doubled from the pre- to the post-period, without a commensurate increase in follow-on investments, and VCs making initial investments in treated sectors were less likely to take a board seat following the technological shock." Michael Ewens, Ramana Nanda, and Matthew Rhodes-Kropf, "Cost of Experimentation and the Evolution of Venture Capital," *Journal of Financial Economics* 128, no. 3 (2018).

66. Ghosh and Nanda, "Venture Capital Investment."

67. "BU-103: Global Battery Markets," Battery University, http://batteryuniversity.com/index.php/learn/article/global_battery_markets.

68. J. V. Chamary, "Why Are Samsung's Galaxy Note 7 Phones Exploding?," *Forbes*, September 4, 2016, https://www.forbes.com/sites/jvchamary/2016/09/04/samsung-note7-battery/.

69. "A Massachusetts Green Energy Company Heads for China," WBUR 90.9, October 19, 2011, http://www.wbur.org/hereandnow/2011/10/19/energy-china-battery.

70. GSR is not explicitly a government fund, but it is well-connected enough that it can help local governments arrange subsidies packages to attract companies. "When it enters into a deal, GSR does more than invest its own money. It taps its contacts in government in China and at other investment entities to pile on their money too." Jeffrey Ball, "Silicon Valley's New Power Player: China," *Fortune*, December 4, 2015, http://fortune.com/china-clean-tech-silicon-valley/.

71. Eric Wesoff, "Boston-Power Aims to Rival Tesla with Gigawatt Battery Factories," GTM, January 8, 2015, https://www.greentechmedia.com/articles/read/boston-power-aims-to-rival-tesla-with-gigawatt-battery-factories.

72. Boston Power, "Local Chinese Governments Give Financial Support to Leading US Electric Vehicle Battery Company," PR Newswire, December 22, 2014, https://www.prnewswire.com/news-releases/local-chinese-governments-give-financial-support-to-leading-us-electric-vehicle-battery-company-300013108.html.

73. Stephen Merrill, *Righting the Research Imbalance* (Durham, NC: Duke University Center for Innovation Policy, 2018), https://law.duke.edu/sites/default/files/centers/cip/CIP-White-Paper_Righting-the-Research-Imbalance.pdf.

74. Alex Kacik, "Drug Prices Rise as Pharma Prices Soar," *Modern Healthcare*, December 28, 2017, http://www.modernhealthcare.com/article/20171228/NEWS/171229930.

75. *Drug Industry: Profits, Research and Development Spending, and Merger and Acquisition Deals* (Washington, DC: US Government Accountability Office 2017), https://www.gao.gov/assets/690/688472.pdf.

76. Ibid.

77. *Rates of Return to Investment in Science and Innovation* (London: Frontier Economics, 2014), https://assets.publishing.service.gov.uk/government/uploads/system/uploads/attachment_data/file/333006/bis-14-990-rates-of-return-to-investment-in-science-and-innovation-revised-final-report.pdf. For other capital investments, the long run rate of return is on the order of 9 percent. Sarah Osborne and Bonnie A. Retus, "Returns for Domestic Nonfinancial Business," *Survey of Current Business* 96, no. 12 (2016), https://bea.gov/scb/pdf/2016/12%20December/1216_returns_for_domestic_nonfinancial_business.pdf.

78. "Manufacturing Challenges for Cell and Gene Therapies," Cell and Gene Therapy Catapult, February 21, 2017, https://ct.catapult.org.uk/news-media/general-news/manufacturing-challenges-cell-and-gene-therapies.

79. Ralf Otto, Alberto Santagostino, and Ulf Schrader, "Rapid Growth in Bio-pharma: Challenges and Opportunities," McKinsey & Company, December 2014, https://www.mckinsey.com/industries/pharmaceuticals-and-medical-products /our-insights/rapid-growth-in-biopharma. This study reports manufacturing setup costs of $200 million–$500 million. These costs have been falling recently, with Amgen's new state-of-the-art facility in Rhode Island expected to cost about $200 million: "Amgen Breaks Ground on Next-Generation Biomanufacturing Plant in Rhode Island," Amgen, July 31, 2018, https://www.amgen.com/media/news -releases/2018/07/amgen-breaks-ground-on-next-generation-biomanufacturing -plant-in-rhode-island/.

80. Peter Olagunju, Rodney Rietze, and Dieter Hauwaerts, "Meeting the Cell Therapy Cost Challenge with Automation," Invetech, February 21, 2017, https://www.invetechgroup.com/insights/2017/02/meeting-the-cell-therapy-cost -challenge-with-automation/. Provenge (sipuleucel-T) is a prescription medicine that is used to treat certain patients with advanced prostate cancer.

81. Ronald Rader, "Cell and Gene Therapies: Industry Faces Potential Ca-pacity Shortages," *Genetic Engineering and Biotechnology News* 37, no. 20 (2017), https://www.genengnews.com/gen-articles/cell-and-gene-therapies-industry -faces-potential-capacity-shortages/6203.

82. Gina Kolata, "Gene Therapy Hits a Peculiar Roadblock: A Virus Short-age," *New York Times,* November 27, 2017, https://www.nytimes.com/2017/11/27 /health/gene-therapy-virus-shortage.html.

83. Rader, "Cell and Gene Therapies."

84. Ibid.

85. Lev Gervolin and Walter Colasante, "Building New Business Models to Support High-Cost Cell and Gene Therapies," *Pharma Letter,* June 13, 2018, https://www.thepharmaletter.com/article/building-new-business-models-to -support-high-cost-cell-and-gene-therapies.

86. For an expanded analysis focused on one type of manufacturing, see Wil-liam B. Bonvillian, "Advanced Manufacturing: A New Policy Challenge," *Annals of Science and Technology Policy* 1, no. 1 (2017): 1–131.

87. Ibid. Richard P. Harrison, Steven Ruck, Qasim A. Rafiq, and Nicholas Medcalf, "Decentralised Manufacturing of Cell and Gene Therapy Products: Learning from Other Healthcare Sectors," *Biotechnology Advances* 36, no. 6 (2018).

88. Nicholas Bloom, Mark Schankerman, and John Van Reenen, "Identifying Technology Spillovers and Product Market Rivalry," *Econometrica* 81, no. 4 (2013): 1347–1393.

89. We continue to combine two economic concepts. Research on the social rate of return refers to the technical aspect of value creation—the fact that the domain knowledge generated by one firm can be used by other firms to inno-vate. The problem for Xerox and others under discussion here was one of value capture (i.e., they were not the ones who received the enormous returns from

their new inventions). In either case, the problem that arises is the same: since firms know that they will not experience the full return from their investments, they underinvest relative to what would be optimal from a broader society-wide perspective.

90. Merrill, *Righting the Research Imbalance.*

91. Ashish Arora, Sharon Belenzon, and Lia Sheer, "Back to Basics: Why Do Firms Invest in Research?" (working paper #23187, National Bureau of Economic Research, Cambridge, MA, 2017).

92. Arno Penzias and Robert Wilson, "The Large Horn Antenna and the Discovery of Cosmic Microwave Background Radiation," APS Physics, https://www.aps.org/programs/outreach/history/historicsites/penziaswilson.cfm. "Scanning Tunneling Microscope," IBM, http://www-03.ibm.com/ibm/history/ibm100/us/en/icons/microscope/.

93. "Congressional Briefing," Duke Law, https://law.duke.edu/innovationpolicy/congressionalbriefing/.

94. Ashish Arora, Sharon Belenzon, and Andrea Patacconi, "The Decline of Science in Corporate R&D," *Strategic Management Journal* 39, no. 1 (2018).

95. Arora, Belenzon, and Sheer, "Back to Basics."

96. Arora, Belenzon, and Patacconi, "The Decline of Science."

97. "8 Jules Verne Inventions That Came True (Pictures)," *National Geographic,* February 8, 2011, https://news.nationalgeographic.com/news/2011/02/pictures/110208-jules-verne-google-doodle-183rd-birthday-anniversary/.

98. The points about transistors and the increasing cost of productivity improvements are drawn from Nicholas Bloom, Charles Jones, John Van Reenen, and Michael Webb, "Are Ideas Getting Harder to Find?" (working paper #23782, National Bureau of Economic Research, Cambridge, MA, September 2017).

99. Tom Simonite, "Moore's Law Is Dead. Now What?," *MIT Technology Review,* May 13, 2016, https://www.technologyreview.com/s/601441/moores-law-is-dead-now-what/. "Moore's Law is named after Intel cofounder Gordon Moore. He observed in 1965 that transistors were shrinking so fast that every year twice as many could fit onto a chip, and in 1975 adjusted the pace to a doubling every two years."

CHAPTER 5: PUBLIC R&D

1. From interview on *NOVA: Cracking the Code of Life,* May 23, 1998.

2. "Deoxyribonucleic Acid (DNA)," National Human Genome Research Institute, June 16, 2015, https://www.genome.gov/25520880/.

3. Besides the DNA located in the nucleus, humans and other complex organisms also have a small amount of DNA in cell structures known as *mitochondria.* Mitochondria generate the energy the cell needs to function properly.

4. "Deoxyribonucleic Acid (DNA)," National Human Genome Research Institute.

5. "What Is DNA?," US National Library of Medicine, September 4, 2018, https://ghr.nlm.nih.gov/primer/basics/dna.

6. "DNA Sequencing," National Human Genome Research Institute, December 18, 2015, https://www.genome.gov/10001177/dna-sequencing-fact-sheet/.

7. "About the Laboratory of Molecular Biology," Medical Research Council Laboratory of Molecular Biology, http://www2.mrc-lmb.cam.ac.uk/about-lmb/.

8. Misha Gajewski, "Everything You Really Need to Know About DNA Sequencing," Cancer Research UK, April 25, 2016, https://scienceblog.cancerresearchuk.org/2016/04/25/everything-you-really-need-to-know-about-dna-sequencing/.

9. Ibid.

10. Leroy E. Hood, Michael W. Hunkapiller, and Lloyd M. Smith, "Automated DNA Sequencing and Analysis of the Human Genome," *Genomics* 1, no. 3 (1987), https://ac.els-cdn.com/0888754387900462/1-s2.0-0888754387900462-main.pdf?_tid=b131add0-f579-11e7-8189-00000aab0f02&acdnat=1515529047_30f88c264b77e65317f652c6a58df911.

11. Gajewski, "Everything You Really Need."

12. Robert Kanigel, "The Genome Project," *New York Times*, December 13, 1987, https://www.nytimes.com/1987/12/13/magazine/the-genome-project z.html.

13. Kevin Davies, "Kevin Ulmer—The Sisyphus of Sequencing," *Bio IT World*, September 28, 2010, http://www.bio-itworld.com/2010/issues/sept-oct/ulmer.html.

14. HGP first appeared in Reagan's 1988 budget approved by Congress. One of the main advocates for HGP's inclusion in the budget was Senator Peter Domenici, a Republican from New Mexico. Domenici, who apparently described himself as a "sucker for big science," advocated for the Human Genome Project—for example, by introducing a bill in July 1987 to create a federal advisory board and government-university-industry consortium for mapping and sequencing the human genome. Domenici chaired the Senate Committee on Energy and Natural Resources and the Budget Committee, both of which were highly important in setting the Department of Energy budget. Charles DeLisi, director of the DOE's Health and Environmental Research Programs from 1985 to 1987, was the main figure to propose and defend his plans for the HGP in front of Congress. In 2001, DeLisi received the Presidential Citizens Medal for his role in launching the project. Mark Oswald, "Team Was First for Sen. Domenici," *Albuquerque Journal*, September 16, 2017, https://www.abqjournal.com/1064853/team-was-first-for-sen-pete-domenici.html. Jeffrey Mervis, "Human Genome Bill Sponsor Pulls Back, Shifts Tactics," *Scientist*, August 10, 1987, https://www.the-scientist.com/news/human-genome-bill-sponsor-pulls-back-shifts-tactics-63548.

15. The project was very computationally intensive, and the national laboratories of the Department of Energy had the computing resources available. The NCHGR became the National Human Genome Research Institute (NHGRI) in 1997 and was part of the NIH.

16. Gajewski, "Everything You Really Need."

17. The sequencing process can be broken down into several steps. To meet the HGP's challenging goals, scientists were able to improve current technologies and develop new technologies, especially through automation. For example, the "front end" molecular biology step where samples are prepped has benefited from automated robotic samples. The "back end" computer analysis step, which involves designing software packages to analyze results, must also be flexible enough to adapt to different approaches taken in preceding steps. So while all these steps are being individually improved, the overall genome sequencing progress may not appear that impressive. But put all those improved technologies all together and the entire sequencing process has become much more efficient than it once was. Michael C. Giddings, Jessica Severin, Michael Westphall, Jiazhen Wu, and Lloyd M. Smith, "A Software System for Data Analysis in Automated DNA Sequencing," *Genome Research* 8 (1998): 644–665, https://genome.cshlp.org/content/8/6/644.long.

18. Katerina Sideri, *Bioproperty, Biomedicine and Deliberative Governance* (New York: Routledge, 2016), p. 114.

19. A truce between the NIH and Celera was negotiated in 2000, and in February 2001, both the NIH and Celera published draft maps of the genome. For the next two years, Celera was able to protect the genes they had sequenced—but that the NIH had not yet sequenced—with a form of intellectual property. But by 2003, the entire map had been made public, so Celera's intellectual property effectively expired. Celera's intellectual property rights during the 2001–2003 period slowed down follow-on scientific research and product development relative to having the data freely available in the public domain. Specifically, there was significantly less development of downstream scientific research and medical product development for genes that were held with Celera's intellectual property, relative to genes sequenced by the public effort in the same year. The reduction in subsequent scientific research and product development was on the order of 20–30 percent. Heidi Williams, "Intellectual Property Rights and Innovation: Evidence from the Human Genome," *Journal of Political Economy* 121, no. 1 (2013).

20. Ilse R. Wiechers, Noah C. Perin, and Robert Cook-Deegan, "The Emergence of Commercial Genomics: Analysis of the Rise of a Biotechnology Subsector During the Human Genome Project, 1990 to 2004," *Genome Medicine* 5, no. 9 (2013), https://www.ncbi.nlm.nih.gov/pmc/articles/PMC3971346/.

21. *The Impact of Genomics on the U.S. Economy* (Columbus, OH: Battelle Memorial Institute, 2013), https://web.ornl.gov/sci/techresources/Human_Genome/publicat/2013BattelleReportImpact-of-Genomics-on-the-US-Economy.pdf.

22. Ibid.

23. We recognize the controversy over genetic modification of our food supply. Indeed, this type of issue further heightens the importance of being the innovator in an area so that the United States can help set the rules of the road. We discuss this further in Chapter 8.

24. Simon Tripp and Martin Grueber, *Economic Impact of the Human Genome Project* (Columbus, OH: Battelle Memorial Institute, 2011), https://www.battelle .org/docs/default-source/misc/battelle-2011-misc-economic-impact-human -genome-project.pdf.

25. Full disclosure for this section: one of us (Jonathan) has had NIH support for much of his career!

26. Hamilton Moses, David H. M. Matheson, Sarah Cairns-Smith, Benjamin P. George, Chase Palisch, and F. Ray Dorsey, "The Anatomy of Medical Research: US and International Comparisons," *Journal of the American Medical Association* 313, no. 2 (2015), https://www.ncbi.nlm.nih.gov/pubmed/25585329.

27. "What We Do: Budget," National Institutes of Health, April 11, 2018, https://www.nih.gov/about-nih/what-we-do/budget.

28. Awarded annually since 1945, the Lasker Awards recognize major contributions to medical science or individuals who have performed public service on behalf of medicine.

29. Pierre Azoulay, Joshua S. Graff Zivin, Danielle Li, and Bhaven N. Sampat, "Public R&D Investments and Private Sector Patenting: Evidence from NIH Funding Rules," *Review of Economic Studies* 86, no. 1 (2019): 117–152.

30. Ibid.

31. Andrew A. Toole, "Does Public Scientific Research Complement Private Investment in Research and Development in the Pharmaceutical Industry?," *Journal of Law and Economics* 50, no. 1 (2007).

32. "Impact of NIH Research: Our Society," National Institutes of Health, May 1, 2018, https://www.nih.gov/about-nih/what-we-do/impact-nih-research /our-society.

33. *The Framingham Heart Study: Laying the Foundation for Preventative Health Care* (Bethesda, MD: National Institutes of Health, n.d.), https://www.nih.gov /sites/default/files/about-nih/impact/framingham-heart-study.pdf.

34. "Vaccine Types," US Department of Health & Human Services, https:// www.vaccines.gov/basics/types/index.html.

35. *Childhood Hib Vaccines: Nearly Eliminating the Threat of Bacterial Meningitis* (Bethesda, MD: National Institutes of Health, n.d.), https://www.nih.gov/sites /default/files/about-nih/impact/childhood-hib-vaccines-case-study.pdf.

36. "Impact of NIH Research: Our Knowledge," National Institutes of Health, May 8, 2018, https://www.nih.gov/about-nih/what-we-do/impact-nih-research /our-knowledge.

37. The full impact of the JAK research remains at the research frontier: at the start of 2016, a dozen other compounds that target JAKs were in clinical trials for treatment of various autoimmune diseases. *Understanding Immune Cells*

and Inflammation: Opening New Treatment Avenues for Rheumatoid Arthritis and Other Conditions (Bethesda, MD: National Institutes of Health, n.d.), https://www.nih.gov/sites/default/files/about-nih/impact/immune-cells-inflammation-case-study.pdf.

38. James Barron, "High Cost of Military Parts," *New York Times,* September 1, 1983, https://www.nytimes.com/1983/09/01/business/high-cost-of-military-parts.html.

39. Enrico Moretti, Claudia Steinwender, and John Van Reenen, "The Intellectual Spoils of War?: Defense R&D, Productivity and Spillovers" (working paper, 2016), https://eml.berkeley.edu/~moretti/military.pdf.

40. That's 2 percent, not two percentage points (i.e., from 2 percent per year to 2.04 percent per year).

41. Peter Warren Singer, *Wired for War: The Robotics Revolution and Conflict in the Twenty-First Century* (New York: Penguin, 2009), pp. 21–29.

42. Brian Heater, "How Baby Dolls, Mine Sweepers and Mars Rovers Led iRobot to the Roomba," *TechCrunch,* March 8, 2017, https://techcrunch.com/2017/03/08/colin-angle-interview/.

43. Craig Smith, "10 Interesting iRobot Statistics and Facts," DMR, September 7, 2018, https://expandedramblings.com/index.php/irobot-statistics-facts/.

44. Aditya Kaul, "iRobot Doubles Down on Consumer Robots by Selling Military Unit," Tractica, February 11, 2016, https://www.tractica.com/automation-robotics/irobot-doubles-down-on-consumer-robots-by-selling-military-unit/.

45. "iRobot Corporation," United States Securities and Exchange Commission, February 16, 2018, https://www.sec.gov/Archives/edgar/data/1159167/000115916718000004/irbt-12302017x10k.htm.

46. "iRobot Reports Strong Second-Quarter Financial Results," PR Newswire, July 25, 2017, https://www.prnewswire.com/news-releases/irobot-reports-strong-second-quarter-financial-results-300494007.html.

47. Darrell Etherington, "iRobot Says 20 Percent of the World's Vacuums Are Now Robots," *TechCrunch,* November 7, 2016, https://techcrunch.com/2016/11/07/irobot-says-20-percent-of-the-worlds-vacuums-are-now-robots/.

48. Description of the SBIR program comes from Josh Lerner, "The Government as Venture Capitalist: The Long-Run Impact of the SBIR Program," *Journal of Business* 72, no. 3 (1999), and Sabrina Howell, "Financing Innovation: Evidence from R&D Grants," *American Economic Review* 107, no. 4 (2017).

49. Mariana Mazzucato, "Innovation, the State and Patient Capital," *Political Quarterly* 86, no. S1 (2015): 98–118.

50. Matthew Keller and Fred Block, "Explaining the Transformation in the US Innovation System: The Impact of a Small Government Program," *Socio-Economic Review* 11 (2013): 629–656.

51. "Symantec Recognized By Small Business Administration," SBIR, March 3, 2011, https://www.sbir.gov/success-story/symantec-recognized-small-business-administration. Employment numbers for 2017 are from the 2017 Corporate

Responsibility Report (Mountain View, CA: Symantec, 2017), https://www
.symantec.com/content/dam/symantec/docs/reports/2017-corporate-responsibility
-report-en.pdf, p.13.

52. "Qualcomm Inducted into SBIR Hall of Fame," SBIR, March 15, 2011,
https://www.sbir.gov/success-story/qualcomm-inducted-sbir-hall-fame. "The
Small Business Technology Council" (white paper, Small Business Technology
Council, Washington, DC, January 19, 2017), http://sbtc.org/wp-content/uploads
/2017/01/SBTC-SBIR-White-Paper-2017.pdf. *SBIR/STTR Program* (Washington, DC: US Department of the Navy, n.d.), https://www.navysbir.com/docs
/Navy-SBIR-Economic_Impact.pdf. "QUALCOMM Incorporated," United
States Securities and Exchange Commission, November 1, 2017, https://www
.sec.gov/Archives/edgar/data/804328/000123445217000190/qcom10-k2017
.htm. Estimate of US employment is based on "fifty-two percent of its workforce is based in the U.S.," from Mike Freeman, "Qualcomm Sheds 1,231 San
Diego Workers in Latest Restructuring," *San Diego Union-Tribune*, April 19,
2018, https://www.sandiegouniontribune.com/business/technology/sd-fi-layoff
-number-20180419-story.html.

53. "Statement by Dr. Irwin Mark Jacobs Prepared for the Hearing on Reau-
thorization of the SBIR and STTR Programs," United States Senate, February 17,
2011,https://www.sbc.senate.gov/public/_cache/files/4/8/4878f6aa-114e-495a-9fea
-03ab2a21cf9c/78A77C01862D1DAD0B9A5CDCF5DEB9B4.testimony-jacobs
.pdf.

54. The SBIR is not without its critics, many of whom focus on the fact that
the SBIR doesn't do enough to facilitate the pathway from R&D to commercialization and instead creates SBIR "mills" that "live off SBIR awards." On the
flip side, there are some scientists who criticize SBIR because they fear SBIR
commercialization-focused funds will be expanded at the expense of funds for basic
science. *National Research Council (US) Committee for Capitalizing on Science, Technology, and Innovation: An Assessment of the Small Business Innovation Research Program* (Washington, DC: National Academies Press, 2008). Eugenie Samuel Reich,
"US Research Firms Put Under Pressure to Sell," *Nature*, July 9, 2013, https://
www.nature.com/news/us-research-firms-put-under-pressure-to-sell-1.13354.
Jeffrey Mervis, "U.S. Research Groups Going to War Again over Small Business
Funding," *Science*, May 18, 2016, http://www.sciencemag.org/news/2016/05/us
-research-groups-going-war-again-over-small-business-funding.

55. Lerner, "The Government as Venture Capitalist." Scott Wallsten's study
from this era does not support the positive effects documented by Lerner; see Scott
Wallsten, "The Effects of Government-Industry R&D Programs on Private R&D:
The Case of the Small Business Innovation Research Program," *RAND Journal of
Economics* 31, no. 1 (2000): 82–100.

56. Sabrina Howell, "Financing Innovation: Evidence from R&D Grants,"
American Economic Review 107, no. 4 (2017): 1136–1164. On the other hand, those
firms that continue on to phase II are largely those who were not able to obtain VC

financing and were therefore weaker candidates so that there was little effect on phase II. This suggests that the main effect of the SBIR grants is through promoting prototyping—developing proofs of concept that can be used to attract further financing.

57. "Visionary David Walt," Tufts Tech Transfer, http://techtransfer.tufts.edu /visionary-david-walt/.

58. "Illumina Inducted into U.S. SBA Hall of Fame," Illumina, January 23, 2017, https://www.illumina.com/company/news-center/feature-articles/illumina -inducted-into-u-s—small-business-administration-hall-o.html.

59. "Case Studies," Appendix D, in *An Assessment of the SBIR Program at the National Institutes of Health* (Washington, DC: National Academies Press, 2009).

60. "#1250 Illumina," *Forbes*, June 2018, https://www.forbes.com/companies /illumina/. "Illumina Fact Sheet," Illumina, https://www.illumina.com/company /about-us/fact-sheet.html. US employees estimate from "Illumina," Great Place to Work, http://reviews.greatplacetowork.com/illumina-inc (a source that is hard to verify independently).

61. National Institute of Standards and Technology, https://www.nist.gov.

62. Ibid.

63. Daniel Smith, Maryann Feldman, and Gary Anderson, "The Longer Term Effects of Federal Subsidies on Firm Survival: Evidence from the Advanced Technology Program," *Journal of Technology Transfer* 43, no. 3 (2018): 593–614.

64. Ibid.

65. A newer program of public subsidization of R&D is the National Network for Manufacturing Innovation program, or Manufacturing USA, introduced under the Obama administration in 2014. This initiative aims to promote private-public partnerships focused on manufacturing innovation and engaging universities, as well as to coordinate federal resources and programs to overcome barriers to scaling up new technologies and products. The federal government provides financial resources, which are matched by private industry in a collaborative arrangement with: universities; federal laboratories; and federal, state, and local governments. Federal investments are modest, at around $100 million nationally, with about 2:1 matching from the private sector. As of 2016, there were eight established localities for the program, with 753 members. This program is too new to have been evaluated, but its budget is also under attack, with a proposed cut this year from $25 million to $15 million.

66. "Chartbook of Social Inequality: Real Mean and Median Income, Families and Individuals, 1947–2012, and Households, 1967–2012," Russell Sage Foundation, https://www.russellsage.org/sites/all/files/chartbook/Income%20and %20Earnings.pdf. Data updated to 2016 dollars using CPI.

67. "Historical Income Tables: Families," United States Census Bureau, August 10, 2017, https://www.census.gov/data/tables/time-series/demo/income-poverty /historical-income-families.html.

68. "Chartbook of Social Inequality," Russell Sage Foundation. Data updated to 2016 dollars using CPI.

69. "Historical Income Tables: Families," United States Census Bureau.

70. "Chartbook of Social Inequality," Russell Sage Foundation. Data updated to 2016 dollars using CPI.

71. Emmanuel Saez, "Striking It Richer: The Evolution of Top Incomes in the United States (Updated with 2015 Preliminary Estimates)," Econometrics Laboratory, University of California–Berkeley, June 30, 2016, https://eml.berkeley .edu/~saez/saez-UStopincomes-2015.pdf.

72. Richard Hornbeck and Enrico Moretti, "Who Gains When a City Has a Productivity Spurt?" (working paper #24661, National Bureau of Economic Research, Cambridge, MA, September 2018).

73. As one industry source states, "As the industry matures and begins to commercialize products, the highest growth in skills and knowledge demand will not be in this highly expert group but increasingly in competent technicians or operators capable of reliably running routine manufacturing operations." "Outputs from the Advanced Therapies Manufacturing Task-force (People, Skills and Training sub-team)," UK Bioindustry Association, https://www.bioindustry.org /uploads/assets/uploaded/dbf72953-f3c0-40d8-885744ccff307348.pdf.

74. Paul Lewis, "How to Create Skills for an Emerging Industry: The Case of Technician Skills and Training in Cell Therapy," Social Science Research Network, January 2017; http://www.gatsby.org.uk/uploads/education/reports/pdf/paul -lewis-cell-therapy-jan2017.pdf.

75. "Medical and Clinical Laboratory Technologists and Technicians," Bureau of Labor Statistics, June 1, 2018, https://www.bls.gov/ooh/healthcare/medical -and-clinical-laboratory-technologists-and-technicians.htm.

76. Douglas Woodward, Octavio Figueiredo, and Paulo Guimaraes, "Beyond the Silicon Valley: University R&D and High-Technology Location," *Journal of Urban Economics* vol. 60 (2006); Bruce A. Kirchhoff, Scott L. Newbert, Iftekhar Hasan, and Catherine Armington, "The Influence of University R & D Expenditures on New Business Formations and Employment Growth," *Entrepreneurship Theory and Practice* 31, no. 4 (2007).

77. It is difficult to say whether this reflected more patentable research or just a stronger effort by universities to patent existing research, but at least one study suggests that Bayh-Dole led to higher-quality innovation. Naomi Hausman, "University Innovation, Local Economic Growth, and Entrepreneurship" (working paper #CES-WP-12-10, US Census Bureau Center for Economic Studies, Suitland, MD, 2012).

78. In particular, we estimate a model of change in the natural logarithm of the ratio of employment to working-age population on the change in the natural logarithm of the ratio of university research funding to working-age population. The regression is weighted by area population.

79. We cannot, of course, prove that the university research funding was heading to places that would not have grown for other reasons, but we can include county-specific trends in the model to show that these were not simply places that were growing more quickly even absent the university funding.

80. Adam Jaffe and Trinh Le, "The Impact of R&D Subsidization on Innovation: A Study of New Zealand Firms" (working paper #21479, National Bureau of Economic Research, Cambridge, MA, August 2015).

81. Elias Einio, "R&D Subsidies and Company Performance: Evidence from Geographic Variation in Government Funding Based on the ERDF Population-Density Rule," *Review of Economics and Statistics* 96 no. 4 (2014): 710–728. Hannu Piekkola, "Public Funding of R&D and Growth: Firm-Level Evidence from Finland," *Economics of Innovation and New Technology* 16, no. 3 (2007): 195–210.

82. Adam B. Jaffe, Manuel Trajtenberg, and Rebecca Henderson, "Geographic Localization of Knowledge Spillovers as Evidenced by Patent Citations," *Quarterly Journal of Economics* 108, no. 3 (1993). Neil Bania, Lindsay N. Calkins, and Douglas R. Dalenberg, "The Effects of Regional Science and Technology Policy on the Geographic Distribution of Industrial R&D Laboratories," *Journal of Regional Science* 32, no. 2 (1992). Thomas Döring and Jan Schnellenbach, "What Do We Know About Geographical Knowledge Spillovers and Regional Growth?: A Survey of the Literature," *Regional Studies* 40, no. 3 (2006).

83. Jung Won Sonn and Michael Storper, "The Increasing Importance of Geographical Proximity in Knowledge Production: An Analysis of US Patent Citations, 1975–1997," *Environment and Planning A: Economy and Space* 40, no. 5 (2008).

84. Sharon Belenzon and Mark Schankerman, "Spreading the Word: Geography, Policy, and Knowledge Spillovers," *Review of Economics and Statistics* 95, no. 3 (2013).

85. Lynne Zucker, Michael Darby, and Marilynn Brewer, "Intellectual Human Capital and the Birth of U.S. Biotechnology Enterprises," *American Economic Review* 88, no. 1 (1998): 290–306.

86. Woodward, Figueiredo, and Guimaraes, "Beyond the Silicon Valley." Recent confirmation of this effect comes from a study that shows that the introduction of low-cost airline routes increased collaboration among chemists at either end of the route. Christian Catalini, Christian Fons-Rosen, and Patrick Gaule, "How Do Transportation Costs Shape Collaboration?" (working paper #24780, National Bureau of Economic Research, Cambridge, MA, 2018).

87. Gil Avnimelech and Maryann Feldman, "The Stickiness of University Spin-Offs: A Study of Formal and Informal Spin-Offs and Their Location from 124 US Academic Institutions," *International Journal of Technology Management* 68, nos. 1–2 (2015): 122–149.

88. Christian Helmers and Henry G. Overman, "My Precious! The Location and Diffusion of Scientific Research: Evidence from the Synchrotron Diamond

Light Source," *Economic Journal* 127, no. 604 (2017), http://onlinelibrary.wiley
.com/doi/10.1111/ecoj.12387/full.

89. D'Angelo Gore, "Obama's Solyndra Problem," FactCheck.org, October
7, 2011, https://www.factcheck.org/wp-content/cache/wp-rocket/www.factcheck
.org/2011/10/obamas-solyndra-problem/index.html_gzip.

90. Jeff Brady, "After Solyndra Loss, U.S. Energy Loan Program Turning a
Profit," NPR, November 13, 2014, https://www.npr.org/2014/11/13/363572151
/after-solyndra-loss-u-s-energy-loan-program-turning-a-profit. Steve Hargreaves,
"Obama's Alternative Energy Bankruptcies," CNN Money, October 22, 2012,
https://money.cnn.com/2012/10/22/news/economy/obama-energy-bankruptcies
/index.html.

91. "NRG Energy and MidAmerican Solar Complete Agua Caliente, the
World's Largest Fully-Operational Solar Photovoltaic Facility," *Business Wire*,
April 29, 2014, https://www.businesswire.com/news/home/20140429005803/en
/NRG-Energy-MidAmerican-Solar-Complete-Agua-Caliente.

92. *Agua Caliente Solar Project* (Carlsbad, CA: NRG Energy, 2011), http://
assets.fiercemarkets.net/public/sites/energy/reports/aguasolarreport.pdf.

93. "FACT SHEET: The Recovery Act Made the Largest Single Investment in
Clean Energy in History, Driving the Deployment of Clean Energy, Promoting Energy Efficiency, and Supporting Manufacturing," White House Office of the Press
Secretary, February 25, 2016, https://obamawhitehouse.archives.gov/the-press-office
/2016/02/25/fact-sheet-recovery-act-made-largest-single-investment-clean-energy.

94. Steve Hargreaves, "Seven Things You Should Know About Solyndra,"
CNN Money, June 6, 2012, https://money.cnn.com/2012/06/06/technology
/solyndra/index.htm?iid=EL.

95. $535 million loan and $750 million factory. Carol D. Leonnig, "Chu
Takes Responsibility for a Loan Deal That Put More Taxpayer Money at Risk
in Solyndra," *Washington Post*, September 29, 2011, https://www.washingtonpost
.com/politics/chu-takes-responsibility-for-a-loan-deal-that-put-more-taxpayer
-money-at-risk-in-solyndra/2011/09/29/gIQArdYQ8K_story.html?utm_term
=.ddca86f1f1e7.

96. Hargreaves, "Seven Things."

97. Carol Leonnig, Joe Stephens, Sisi Wei, and Amanda Zamora, "Solyndra
Scandal Timeline," *Washington Post*, December 2011, http://www.washingtonpost
.com/wp-srv/special/politics/solyndra-scandal-timeline/?noredirect=on. Carol D.
Leonnig, "Top Leaders of Solyndra Solar Panel Company Repeatedly Misled Federal Officials, Investigation Finds," *Washington Post*, August 26, 2015, https://www
.washingtonpost.com/news/federal-eye/wp/2015/08/26/top-leaders-of-solyndra
-solar-panel-company-repeatedly-misled-federal-officials-investigation-finds
/?utm_term=.9bbdcc0692e8.

98. "Committee Releases Extensive Report Detailing Findings of Solyndra Saga," House Energy and Commerce Committee, August 2, 2012, https://

energycommerce.house.gov/news/committee-releases-extensive-report-detailing
-findings-solyndra-saga/.

99. Matthew L. Wald, "Solar Firm Aided by Federal Loans Shuts Doors," *New York Times,* August 31, 2011, https://www.nytimes.com/2011/09/01/business /energy-environment/solyndra-solar-firm-aided-by-federal-loans-shuts-doors .html.

100. MIT Energy Initiative, *The Future of Solar Energy* (Cambridge, MA: MIT, 2015).

101. Paula Stephan, "The Endless Frontier: Reaping What Bush Sowed," in *The Changing Frontier: Rethinking Science and Innovation Policy,* ed. Adam Jaffe and Benjamin Jones (Chicago: University of Chicago Press, 2015).

102. Ibid., p. 354.

103. Ibid.

104. David Ignatius, "The Ideas Engine Needs a Tuneup," *Washington Post,* June 3, 2007.

105. For Germany, see Matthias Almus and Dirk Czarnitzki, "The Effects of Public R&D Subsidies on Firms' Innovation Activities: The Case of Eastern Germany," *Journal of Business & Economic Statistics* 21, no. 2, 2003. Reinhard Hujer and Dubravko Radić, "Evaluating the Impacts of Subsidies on Innovation Activities in Germany," *Scottish Journal of Political Economy* 52, no. 4, 2005; Dirk Czarnitzki and Andrew A. Toole, "Business R&D and the Interplay of R&D Subsidies and Product Market Uncertainty," *Review of Industrial Organization* 31, no. 3 (2007). Katrin Hussinger, "R&D and Subsidies at the Firm Level: An Application of Parametric and Semiparametric Two-Step Selection Models," *Journal of Applied Econometrics* 23, no. 6 (2008). For Belgium, see Hanna Hottenrott and Cindy Lopes-Bento, "(International) R&D Collaboration and SMEs: The Effectiveness of Targeted Public R&D Support Schemes," *Research Policy* 43, no. 6, 2017. For both Germany and Belgium, see Kris Aerts and Tobias Schmidt, "Two for the Price of One?: Additionality Effects of R&D Subsidies: A Comparison Between Flanders and Germany," *Research Policy* 37, no. 5 (2008). For Finland, see Tuomos Takalo, Tanja Tanayama, and Otto Toivanen, "Estimating the Benefits of Targeted R&D Subsidies," *Review of Economics and Statistics* 95, no. 1 (2013). For Israel, see Saul Lach, "Do R&D Subsidies Stimulate or Displace Private R&D? Evidence from Israel," *Journal of Industrial Economics* 50, no. 4 (2002). For Spain, see Xulia González, Jordi Jaumandreu, and Consuelo Pazó, "Barriers to Innovation and Subsidy Effectiveness," *RAND Journal of Economics* (2005). Xulia González and Consuelo Pazó, "Do Public Subsidies Stimulate Private R&D Spending?," *Research Policy* 37, no. 3 (2008). For South Korea, see Soogwan Doh and Byungkyu Kim, "Government Support for SME Innovations in the Regional Industries: The Case of Government Financial Support Program in South Korea," *Research Policy* 43, no. 9 (2014). For the OECD more generally, see Martin Falk, "What Drives Business Research and Development (R&D) Intensity Across Organisation for Economic Co-operation and Development (OECD) Countries?," *Applied Economics* 38, no.

5 (2006). Guntram Wolff and Volker Reinthaler, "The Effectiveness of Subsidies Revisited: Accounting for Wage and Employment Effects in Business R&D," *Research Policy* 37, no. 8 (2008).

CHAPTER 6: AMERICA

1. "Amazon Announces Candidate Cities for HQ2," Amazon, https://www.amazon.com/b?ie=UTF8&node=17044620011. The announcement was made in January 2018. On the same page, the company also says, "Amazon estimates its investments in Seattle from 2010 through 2016 resulted in an additional $38 billion to the city's economy—every dollar invested by Amazon in Seattle generated an additional $1.40 for the city's economy overall."

2. We exclude Hawaii and Alaska. The cost of living in these areas is exceptionally high, so we focus on the mainland states. Average earnings per worker is computed by dividing total household earnings in the MSA by the number of workers and then dividing by a CPI index to create earnings in 2016 dollars.

3. The top ten in 1980: Bridgeport-Stamford-Norwalk, CT; Flint, MI; Detroit-Warren-Dearborn, MI; Midland, MI; Washington-Arlington Alexandria, DC/VA; Saginaw, MI; Midland, TX; Casper, WY; Monroe, MI; and Bremerton-Silverdale, WA. The top ten in 2016: Bridgeport-Stamford-Norwalk, CT; San Jose–Sunnyvale–Santa Clara, CA; San Francisco-Oakland-Heyward, CA; Washington-Arlington-Alexandria, DC/VA; Seattle-Tacoma-Bellevue, WA; Boston-Cambridge-Newton, MA; Trenton, NJ; New York–Newark–Jersey City, NY/NJ; Boulder, CO; Baltimore-Columbia-Towson, MD. All figures here refer to calculations done by the authors from census data. MSA definitions are held constant at their 2016 boundaries for comparison.

4. Authors' calculations, along the same lines as in previous note.

5. This paragraph and the reasoning about agglomeration draws heavily on Enrico Moretti, *The New Geography of Jobs* (New York: Mariner Books, 2013).

6. Kimberly Amadeo, "Silicon Valley, America's Innovative Advantage," *Balance,* updated March 10, 2018, https://www.thebalance.com/what-is-silicon-valley-3305808.

7. "What a Performance," *Economist,* July 28, 2015, https://www.economist.com/graphic-detail/2015/07/28/what-a-performance?fsrc=scn/tw/te/bl/ed/WhatAPErformance.

8. Asma Khalid, "How Boston Became 'The Best Place in the World' to Launch a Biotech Company," WBUR 90.9, June 19, 2017, http://www.wbur.org/bostonomix/2017/06/19/boston-biotech-success.

9. Moretti reviews a large body of literature (most of it his own work) to show that this is true.

10. Enrico Moretti, "The Local and Aggregate Effect of Agglomeration on Innovation: Evidence from High Tech Clusters" (working paper, Berkeley University, Berkeley, CA, 2018).

11. For a nice review of the economics of local agglomeration, see Gilles Duranton and Diego Puga, "Micro-Foundations of Urban Agglomeration Economies," in *Handbook of Urban and Regional Economics*, vol. 4, ed. J. V. Henderson and J.-F. Thisse (Amsterdam: North-Holland, 2004).

12. These facts from Moretti, *The New Geography of Jobs*, Chapter 5, appropriately titled "The Great Divergence."

13. In 2015, the top ten states for public R&D per capita were Maryland, New Mexico, Alabama, Virginia, Massachusetts, Colorado, Connecticut, Rhode Island, California, and Utah.

14. Emily Badger, "What Happened to the American Boomtown?," *New York Times*, December 6, 2017, https://www.nytimes.com/2017/12/06/upshot/what -happened-to-the-american-boomtown.html.

15. Chang-Tai Hsieh and Enrico Moretti, "Housing Constraints and Spatial Misallocation" (working paper #21154, National Bureau of Economic Research, Cambridge, MA, 2017), http://www.nber.org/papers/w21154.

16. Moretti, *The New Geography of Jobs*, p. 169.

17. Divya Raghavan, "Quarter Pounder Index: The Most and Least Expensive Cities in America," NerdWallet, May 12, 2013, https://www.nerdwallet .com/blog/mortgages/home-search/quarter-pounder-index-most-least-expensive -cities/.

18. Moretti, *The New Geography of Jobs*, p. 168.

19. Data on value per owner occupied house from the census. These are self-reported home values, but they should be good indicators of trends in underlying home prices. The data are incomplete for 2016, so we use 2010.

20. E. Glaeser and J. Gyourko, "The Economic Implications of Housing Supply," *Journal of Economic Perspectives* 32, no. 1 (2018).

21. According to the Fair Housing Center of Greater Boston, most suburbs around Boston have large minimum lot requirements—many larger than one acre—in order to preserve open spaces and prevent overdevelopment of suburban land. Of the 187 municipalities of greater Boston, 95 zone over 50 percent of their land area for lot sizes of one acre per home or greater. Of those 95 municipalities, 14 zone more than 90 percent of their land for two-acre lot sizes, and 27 zone more than 90 percent of the land for at least one-acre lot sizes. "1970s–Present: Minimum Lot Size Requirements," Fair Housing Center of Greater Boston, http://www .bostonfairhousing.org/timeline/1970s-present-Local-Land_use-Regulations -4.html.

22. Ibid.

23. "Palo Alto Home Prices & Values," Zillow, https://www.zillow.com /palo-alto-ca/home-values/.

24. Adam Brinklow, "Exclusive interview: Palo Alto Mayor Patrick Burt Fires Back at Housing Critics," *Curbed*, August 23, 2016, https://sf.curbed .com/2016/8/23/12603188/palo-alto-mayor-housing-interview.

25. Elinor Aspegren and Shawna Chen, "Planning Commission Unanimously Recommends Office-Cap Extension," *Palo Alto Online*, July 27, 2017, https://paloaltoonline .com/news/2017/07/27/planning-commission-unanimously-recommends-officeap -extension.

26. Edward Glaeser, *Triumph of the City* (New York: Penguin, 2012), Kindle edition, location 4015.

27. "1950s–1975: Impact of Rte 128 & Rte 495," Fair Housing Center of Greater Boston, http://www.bostonfairhousing.org/timeline/1950s-1975-Suburbs .html. "1970s–Present: The Impact of Zoning," Fair Housing Center of Greater Boston, http://www.bostonfairhousing.org/timeline/1970s-present-Local-Land _use-Regulations-1.html.

28. State policy makers in places like California and Massachusetts have long been cognizant of the pitfalls of zoning controls and have tried to set up processes to circumvent local control. This has met with only limited success. In one case in 2014, a developer proposed replacing a gym property and building 334 apartments, including 81 affordable units, in the Boston suburb of Newton. The developer sought to go through the state process to avoid local opposition but was unable to do so—and the proposal was rejected Layers of restriction in cases like the Newton project shape a decidedly inertial development climate. Scott Van Voorhis, "Housing Proposed for Newton Office Complex," *Boston Globe*, June 11, 2014, https://www.bostonglobe.com/metro/regionals /west/2014/06/11/apartment-complex-proposed-for-route-office-park /SPxooSILRitazfOkRKDhLJ/story.html. Ellen Ishkanian, "Developer Loses Appeal to Build Housing at Wells Avenue Office Park," *Boston Globe*, December 24, 2015, https://www.bostonglobe.com/metro/regionals/west/2015/12/24 /developer-loses-appeal-build-housing-wells-avenue-office-park/UhtZWD bpzQXMHbae9PDBfO/story.html.

29. Hsieh and Moretti, "Housing Constraints."

30. Moretti, *The New Geography of Jobs*, p. 157.

31. Conor Dougherty and Brad Plumer, "A Bold, Divisive Plan to Wean Californians from Cars," *New York Times*, March 16, 2018, https://www.nytimes .com/2018/03/16/business/energy-environment/climate-density.html.

32. Authors' calculations from 2016 census based on self-reported information by workers on their commuting length.

33. Benjamin Schneider, "YIMBYs Defeated as California's Transit Density Bill Stalls," *CityLab*, April 18, 2018, https://www.citylab.com/equity/2018/04 /californias-transit-density-bill-stalls/558341/.

34. As clear evidence of this phenomenon, one study found that when direct flights are introduced between the home location of venture investors and the location of their potential investments, the VCs are more likely to invest. Shai Bernstein, Xavier Giroud, and Richard R. Townsend, "The Impact of Venture Capital Monitoring," *Journal of Finance* 71, no. 4 (2016): 1591–1622.

35. Richard Florida, "A Closer Look at the Geography of Venture Capital in the U.S.," *CityLab*, February 23, 2016, https://www.citylab.com/life/2016/02/the-spiky-geography-of-venture-capital-in-the-us/470208/.

36. Alexander M. Bell, Raj Chetty, Xavier Jaravel, Neviana Petkova, and John Van Reenen, "Who Becomes an Inventor in America? The Importance of Exposure to Innovation" (working paper #24062 National Bureau of Economic Research, Cambridge, MA, November 2017).

37. "There is no sign that the labor market, which is so buoyant at the national level, is helping to heal this [red-blue state labor market] divide. If anything, the divide is growing." Robin Brooks, Jonathan Fortun, and Greg Basile, *Global Macro Views—The Red-Blue Labor Market Split* (Washington DC: Institute for International Finance, 2018).

38. To be clear, the current high level of political polarization in the United States has multiple causes, including shifts in party alliances since the 1960s and the way in which redistricting has been implemented. The economic and geographic dimensions of polarization discussed in this book reinforce the other more political facets of polarization.

39. Richard Florida, "How America's Metro Areas Voted," *CityLab*, November 29, 2016, https://www.citylab.com/equity/2016/11/how-americas-metro-areas-voted/508355/.

40. Since the samples are small in each year (about 1,500 observations nationally), we pool the two most recent years available (2014 and 2016) to get somewhat reliable estimates. Reported results are those for the coefficient of a superstar region dummy variable in a regression controlling for age, gender, race, and education; results reported are statistically significant.

41. For our first fact, respondents are answering a series of questions that are prefaced by "I'm going to read you some statements like those you might find in a newspaper or magazine article. For each statement, please tell me if you strongly agree, agree, disagree, or strongly disagree." Those in the superstar areas are 5.5 percentage points more likely to agree that scientific research should be supported (compared to a national mean of 40 percent).

For our second fact, respondents are told, "We are faced with many problems in this country, none of which can be solved easily or inexpensively. I'm going to name some of these problems . . . and for each one, I'd like you to tell me whether you think we're spending too much money on it, too little money, or about the right amount." Those in superstar areas are 5.2 percentage points more likely to say that we are spending too little on supporting scientific research (compared to a national mean of 42 percent).

For our last fact, respondents are told, "I am going to name some institutions in this country. As far as the people running these institutions are concerned, would you say that you have a great deal of confidence, only some confidence, or hardly any confidence at all in them?" Those in superstar areas are 4.4 percent more likely to say that they have great confidence in educational institutions (compared to 17 percent nationwide).

42. Nick Wingfield and Patricia Cohen, "Amazon Plans Second Headquarters, Opening a Bidding War Among Cities," *New York Times,* September 7, 2017, https://www.nytimes.com/2017/09/07/technology/amazon-headquarters-north-america.html.

43. The only states where no city applied were Arkansas, Hawaii, Montana, North Dakota, South Dakota, Vermont, and Wyoming. We are basing this analysis on the cities that announced they were bidding. Matt Day, "Amazon Receives 238 Bids for Its Second Headquarters," *Seattle Times,* October 23, 2017, https://www.seattletimes.com/business/amazon/amazon-receives-238-bids-for-its-second-headquarters/.

44. Nick Wingfield, "Amazon Chooses 20 Finalists for Second Headquarters," *New York Times,* January 18, 2018, https://www.nytimes.com/2018/01/18/technology/amazon-finalists-headquarters.html.

45. The full list is: Atlanta, GA; Austin, TX; Boston, MA; Chicago, IL; Columbus, OH; Dallas, TX; Denver, CO; Indianapolis, IN; Los Angeles, CA; Miami, FL; Montgomery County, MD; Nashville, TN; Newark, NJ; New York, NY; Northern Virginia; Philadelphia, PA; Pittsburgh, PA; Raleigh, NC; Toronto, Ontario; Washington, DC. From "Where Amazon May Build Its New Headquarters," *New York Times.*

46. Ibid.

47. David M. Levitt, "Christie Backs Newark's Amazon Bid with $7 Billion in Tax Breaks," *Bloomberg,* October 16, 2017, https://www.bloomberg.com/news/articles/2017-10-16/christie-backs-newark-s-amazon-bid-with-7-billion-in-tax-breaks.

48. Robert McCartney and Ovetta Wiggins, "A $5 billion Carrot: Larry Hogan's Historic Offer to win Amazon HQ2," *Washington Post,* January 21, 2018, https://www.washingtonpost.com/local/md-politics/a-5-billion-carrot-larry-hogans-historic-offer-to-win-amazon-hq2/2018/01/21/4d5631d8-fedd-11e7-bb03-722769454f82_story.html?utm_term=.fb448a7316ee.

49. Emily Badger, "In Superstar Cities, the Rich Get Richer, and They Get Amazon," *New York Times,* November 7, 2018, https://www.nytimes.com/2018/11/07/upshot/in-superstar-cities-the-rich-get-richer-and-they-get-amazon.html.

50. Ibid.

51. Moretti, *The New Geography of Jobs.*

52. Authors' tabulations from "American Community Survey (ACS)," United States Census Bureau, https://www.census.gov/programs-surveys/acs/.

53. Every decade, the NRC ranks programs in a variety of scientific fields across a large number of schools. We consider programs in the physical sciences, engineering, and the social sciences. For the latest survey (2005), there are forty-seven fields for which the NRC ranked the top twenty programs. National Research Council, *A Data-Based Assessment of Research-Doctorate Programs in the*

United States (with CD) (Washington, DC: National Academies Press, 2011), https://doi.org/10.17226/12994.http://sites.nationalacademies.org/PGA/resdoc /index.htm.

54. These data are from the National Science Foundation, which does a survey every year of those graduating from graduate schools in the United States. The numbers reported here cover every student graduating from a US PhD program between 2005 and 2015, inclusive. Data were helpfully compiled for us by the NSF.

55. Slightly longer ago, before the 1950s, what is now called Silicon Valley was mostly fruit orchards. We thank the library of the California Historical Society for allowing us to review early maps, photographs, and regional materials.

56. *Necco* stands for the New England Confectionary Company.

57. Jim Miara, "The Reinvention of Kendall Square," *Urban Land,* February 17, 2012, https://urbanland.uli.org/development-business/the-reinvention-of -kendall-square/.

58. Michael Blanding, "The Past and Future of Kendall Square," *MIT Technology Review,* https://www.technologyreview.com/s/540206/the-past-and-future -of-kendall-square/.

59. Ibid.

60. Garret Fitzpatrick, "Duck Pin, We Have a Problem," *MIT Technology Review,* August 21, 2012, https://www.technologyreview.com/s/428696/duck -pin-we-have-a-problem/. Scott Kirsner, "Making Better Use of Parcel in Kendall Square," *Boston Globe,* February 2, 2014, https://www.bostonglobe.com/metro /2014/02/02/underused-parcel-kendall-square-could-put-better-use-government -would-sell/MIxAawAL7tqYvGssmwpJjN/story.html.

61. One of his cofounders, Charles Weissmann, was Swiss.

62. Damian Garde, "Get to Know Kendall Square, Biotech's Booming Epicenter of Big Risks and Bright Minds," *STAT,* May 5, 2016, https://www.statnews .com/2016/05/05/kendall-beating-heart-biotech/.

63. Blanding, "The Past and Future."

64. Ibid.

65. Miara, "The Reinvention."

66. Cambridge Innovation Center, https://cic.com/.

67. Authors' tabulations from "American Community Survey (ACS)," US Census Bureau.

68. This section draws directly from Moretti, *The New Geography of Jobs.* In his assessment, "Seattle was not an obvious choice for a software company. In fact, it seemed like a terrible place. Far from being the high-flying hub it is today, it was a struggling town. Like many other cities in the Pacific Northwest, it was bleeding jobs every year. It had high unemployment and no clear prospects for future growth. It was closer to today's Detroit than to Silicon Valley."

69. Authors' tabulations from "American Community Survey (ACS)," US Census Bureau.

70. The 1.42 percent figure refers to the profit measure known as *value added,* which is revenues minus input costs. For a detailed overview of the data collection effort and the resulting database, see Timothy J. Bartik, *A New Panel Database on Business Incentives for Economic Development Offered by State and Local Governments in the United States* (Kalamazoo, MI: W. E. Upjohn Institute for Employment Research, 2017), http://research.upjohn.org/cgi/viewcontent.cgi?article =1228&context=reports.

71. Eva Dou, "Foxconn Considers $7 Billion Investment to Build U.S. Factory," *Wall Street Journal,* updated January 23, 2017, http://www.wsj.com/articles/ foxconn-mulls-7-billion-investment-to-build-u-s-factory-1485153535.

72. Danielle Paquette, "Foxconn Deal to Build Massive Factory in Wisconsin Could Cost the State $230,700 Per Worker," *Washington Post,* July 27, 2017, https://www.washingtonpost.com/news/wonk/wp/2017/07/27/foxconn-deal -would-cost-wisconsin-230700-per-worker/.

73. Nelson D. Schwartz, Patricia Cohen, and Julie Hirschfeld Davis, "Wisconsin's Lavish Lure for Foxconn: $3 Billion in Tax Subsidies," *New York Times,* July 27, 2017, https://www.nytimes.com/2017/07/27/business/wisconsin-foxconn -tax-subsidies.html.

74. In addition to the previous article, see Chris Isidore and Julia Horowitz, "Foxconn Got a Really Good Deal from Wisconsin. And It's Getting Better," CNN Money, December 28, 2017, http://money.cnn.com/2017/12/28/news/companies /foxconn-wisconsin-incentive-package/index.html.

75. Wisconsin Legislature Legislative Fiscal Bureau, "2017 Wisconsin Act 58 (Foxconn/Fiserv)," October 4, 2017, http://docs.legis.wisconsin.gov/misc/lfb/bill _summaries/2017_19/0001_2017_wisconsin_act_58_foxconn_fiserv_10_4_17.pdf.

76. Nathan M. Jensen, "Exit Options in Firm-Government Negotiations: An Evaluation of the Texas Chapter 313 Program" (working paper, University of Texas at Austin, 2017), http://www.natemjensen.com/wp-content/uploads/2017 /02/Jensen-Chapter-313-Policy-Brief-1.pdf.

77. Michael Greenstone, Richard Hornbeck, and Enrico Moretti, "Identifying Agglomeration Spillovers: Evidence from Winners and Losers of Large Plant Openings," *Journal of Political Economy* 118, no. 3 (2010).

78. On average currently, the federal government raises around 19 percent of GDP in taxes, while state and local government raise about 12 percent. Important categories of spending, such as education, are almost entirely the responsibility of local government. "World Economic Outlook (April 2018)," International Monetary Fund, https://www.imf.org/en/Publications/WEO/Issues/2018/03/20 /world-economic-outlook-april-2018. "The Budget and Economic Outlook: 2018 to 2028," Congressional Budget Office, https://www.cbo.gov/publication/53651.

79. Most recently popularized by the song "The Room Where It Happens" in the hit musical *Hamilton.*

80. "Transcript of Morrill Act (1862)," Our Documents, https://www .ourdocuments.gov/doc.php?flash=false&doc=33&page=transcript.

81. Arthur A. Hauck, "Maine's University and the Land-Grant Tradition," *General University of Maine Publications* 174 (1954). "Holmes Hall," University of Maine, https://umaine.edu/150/a-chapter-in-history/a-walk-through-history/holmes-hall/.

82. Shimeng Liu, "Spillovers from Universities: Evidence from the Land-Grant Program," *Journal of Urban Economics* 87 (2015), https://lusk.usc.edu/sites/default/files/Spillovers_from_Universities_Land_grant_Program.pdf.

83. Enrico Moretti, "Estimating the Social Return to Higher Education: Evidence from Longitudinal and Repeated Cross-Sectional Data," *Journal of Econometrics* 121 (2004): 175–212.

84. Pat Kline and Enrico Moretti, "Local Economic Development, Agglomeration Economies, and the Big Push: 100 Years of Evidence from the Tennessee Valley Authority," *Quarterly Journal of Economics* 129 (2014).

85. Updating the $20 billion figure from Kline and Moretti, "Local Economic Development," by the 33 percent inflation from 2000 to 2016.

86. Ibid.

87. "UTIA Study Finds $1M-Per-Mile Economic Impact of TVA Reservoirs," Tennessee Valley Authority, May 1, 2017, https://www.tva.gov/Newsroom/Press-Releases/UTIA-Study-Finds-1-Million-Per-Mile-Economic-Impact-of-TVA-Reservoirs.

88. Rick Perlstein, *Before the Storm: Barry Goldwater and the Unmaking of the American Consensus* (New York: Nation Books, 2009).

89. The TVA is currently a government-owned independent corporation. It's now fully self-financed, makes no profit, and receives no tax money. The Obama administration was considering divesting part or all ownership because the TVA's anticipated capital needs looked like they would exceed the agency's statutory cap. Then new private owners would divide up the TVA electric power system. Sue Sturgis, "The Strange Politics of TVA Privatization," *Facing South*, April 16, 2013, https://www.facingsouth.org/2013/04/the-strange-politics-of-tva-privatization.html. Philip Bump, "Goodbye, New Deal: Obama Proposes Selling the TVA," *Atlantic*, April 11, 2013, https://www.theatlantic.com/politics/archive/2013/04/goodbye-new-deal-obama-proposes-selling-tva/316380/. "TVA at a Glance," Tennessee Valley Authority, https://www.tva.gov/About-TVA/TVA-at-a-Glance.

90. Kline and Moretti, "Local Economic Development."

91. Dwight D. Eisenhower, "To Frank Goad Clement," Internet Archive, https://web.archive.org/web/20101122171602/http://www.eisenhowermemorial.org/presidential-papers/first-term/documents/1132.cfm.

92. Kline and Moretti, "Local Economic Development."

93. "Military's Impact on State Economies," National Conference of State Legislatures, April 9, 2018, http://www.ncsl.org/research/military-and-veterans-affairs/military-s-impact-on-state-economies.aspx.

94. "Economic Data," State of California Governor's Military Council, https://militarycouncil.ca.gov/s_economicdata/.

95. "History of Malmstrom Air Force Base," Malmstrom Air Force Base, http://www.malmstrom.af.mil/About-Us/History/Malmstrom-History/.

96. "Airport History," Great Falls International Airport, http://flygtf.com/?p=History.

97. *Malmstrom Air Force Base & Central Montana: Partners in One Community* (Malmstrom AFB, MT: 341st Missile Wing Public Affairs Office, 2016), https://greatfallsmt.net/sites/default/files/fileattachments/community/page/40351/malmstromafbcentralmtpartnerscommunityflyer.pdf.

98. Benjamin A. Austin, Edward L. Glaeser, and Lawrence H. Summers, "Jobs for the Heartland: Place-Based Policies in 21st Century America" (working paper #24548, National Bureau of Economic Research, Cambridge, MA, 2018).

99. Austin, Glaeser, and Summers, "Jobs for the Heartland," refer to the lack of evidence in favor of a European Union policy that tries to reduce income disparities across areas in Europe. On the other hand, the Zonenrandgebeit (ZRG) initiative in Germany in 1971, as discussed in Maximilian von Ehrlich and Tobias Seidel, "The Persistent Effects of Place-Based Policy: Evidence from the West-German Zonenrandgebeit" (working paper series #5373, CESifo, Munich, Germany, 2015), had more positive impacts. This initiative consisted of a large-scale transfer program to stimulate economic development in a well-defined geographical area adjacent to the Iron Curtain, to compensate residents for being cut off from East German markets. Incomes in this area, relative to nearby areas, were 30–50 percent higher by 1986, and this difference persisted until at least 2010.

100. This is also a line of investigation that has been pursued by Fiona Murray and Phil Budden—for example, in "A Systematic MIT Approach for assessing 'Innovation-Driven Entrepreneurship' in Ecosystems (iEcosystems)" (working paper, MIT Lab for Innovation Science and Policy, Cambridge, MA, September 2017), and "An MIT Framework for Innovation Ecosystem Policy: Developing Policies to support Vibrant Innovation Ecosystems (iEcosystems)" (working paper, MIT Lab for Innovation Science and Policy, Cambridge, MA, October 2018).

101. These 378 areas are not an exhaustive list of places that could be considered for new technology hubs; indeed, some of the initial Amazon applicants were not on this list of metropolitan statistical areas (MSAs). But all the Amazon finalists are MSAs, so MSAs provide a natural starting point for thinking about the criteria for technology hub centers.

102. We can see this by comparing the NRC rankings of top graduate programs in 1982 to the rankings in 2005. For example, according to NRC rankings from 1982, Johns Hopkins University had four top twenty programs in sciences and engineering; by 2005, they had eighteen, including newly minted top twenty programs in statistics, astrophysics, and materials science and engineering. Pennsylvania State University had only three top-twenty programs in 1982 and had twenty-eight by 2005, including statistics, biochemistry, and physiology.

103. Research on reported well-being shows that commuting is the activity that contributes most to unhappiness, more than work, housework, and taking care

of children, yet people living in the superstar cities endure longer and longer commutes. Daniel Kahneman, Alan B. Krueger, David A. Schkade, Norbert Schwarz, and Arthur A. Stone, "A Survey Method for Characterizing Daily Life Experience: The Day Reconstruction Method," *Science* 306, no. 5702 (2004).

104. Within each category, we use data on the ranking within the list of potential economic areas, so we are averaging across rankings in all these calculations—getting at the idea that you just need to be more attractive as a location than other places.

105. This list uses the division labels (i.e., within regions) from "Census Regions and Divisions of the United States," US Census Bureau, https://www2 .census.gov/geo/pdfs/maps-data/maps/reference/us_regdiv.pdf.

106. We use the latest available Kauffman Index, which is for 2017: "Metropolitan Areas Rankings: Growth Entrepreneurship—Data Table," Kauffman Index, https://www.kauffman.org/kauffman-index/rankings?report=growth&indicator =growth-rate&type=metro.

107. "Repeat Defenders," *Site Selection*, March 2018, pp. 108–125. There are thirty-two cities on these three lists combined, due to some ties.

108. At the time of its founding (mid-1880s), Stanford University was apparently referred to in some newspapers as an "asylum for decayed sea-captains in Switzerland"—implying presumably that it was not needed in a place such as California. This is according to chancellor emeritus David Starr Jordan, "Early Days of Stanford," *Daily Palo Alto Times Memorial Number*, Stanford edition (no date, but the context in its content suggests it was published just after the end of World War I).

CHAPTER 7: INNOVATION FOR GROWTH

1. Owning and managing patents in this fashion is controversial. However, the sentiments expressed in this quote are exactly on target.

2. Abraham Aboraya, "7 Things You Didn't Know About Research Park Near UCF," *Orlando Business Journal*, updated May 23, 2014, http://www.bizjournals .com/orlando/blog/2014/05/7-things-you-didn-t-know-about-the-ucf-research .html. Updated through conversations with CFRP manager Joe Wallace.

3. The statistical unit is called the Union Park county subdivision, but locals know it as East Orange County (as opposed to the Disney-dominated West Orange County).

4. Charlie Jean, "Orlando Leader Martin Andersen Dies: Former Publisher Helped Set Course for Central Florida," *Orlando Sentinel*, May 7, 1986, http://articles.orlandosentinel.com/1986-05-07/news/0220130227_1_martin -andersen-orlando-central-florida.

5. The focus of NTDC was on combat simulation and had previously been located in Long Island. "The History," RTC Orlando, http://rtcorlando.homestead .com/.

6. Based on conversations with CFRP manager Joe Wallace.

7. In 1983, President Reagan signed a bill for $23.5 million to pay for a new simulation center in CFRP.

8. Susan G. Strother, "2 Move to Research Park Training-simulation Companies Hope to Tap Area's Military Market," *Orlando Sentinel*, March 2, 1987, http://articles.orlandosentinel.com/1987-03-02/business/0110260180_1_florida-research-park-simulation-and-training-training-simulation. Also conversation with CFRP manager Joe Wallace.

9. "Historical Enrollment," Institutional Knowledge Management, https://ikm.ucf.edu/historical-enrollment/.

10. *Resource Square One and Three: Offering Summary* (Miami, FL: HFF, 2018), https://my.hfflp.com/GetDocument?DT=DealDocument&ID=175837.

11. *Impacts of Florida Modeling, Simulation and Training* (Orlando, FL: National Center for Simulation, 2012), https://www.simulationinformation.com/sites/default/files/news/2013-01-10/258-impacts-florida-modeling-simulation-training-research-project-dr.guy-hagen-tuckerhall/uploads/guy-hagen-2012-mst-study-final.pdf.

12. Estimates provided by Joe Wallace.

13. Marco Santana, "Orlando Ranks No. 2 In Florida in Venture Capital Activity, Report Says," *Orlando Sentinel*, January 27, 2016, http://www.orlandosentinel.com/business/os-investment-in-orlando-companies-dropped-8-percent-last-year-report-says-20160127-post.html.

14. Mary Shanklin, "With Defense Cuts, Vacancies Rise at Central Florida Research Park," *Orlando Sentinel*, December 8, 2013, http://articles.orlandosentinel.com/2013-12-08/business/os-cfb-cover-research-park-20131208_1_central-florida-research-park-defense-cuts-cubic-corp. Richard Burnett, "Cubic Corp. Orlando Unit Wins Training Contract," *Orlando Sentinel*, December 4, 2013, http://articles.orlandosentinel.com/2013-12-04/business/os-orlando-team—big-training-deal-20131204_1_cubic-corp-orlando-unit-mission-bay-trainer.

15. "Best States for Pre-K–12," *US News & World Report*, https://www.usnews.com/news/best-states/rankings/education/prek-12.

16. Conversation with CFRP manager Joe Wallace.

17. Maryann Feldman and Lauren Lanahan, "State Science Policy Experiments," in *The Changing Frontier: Rethinking Science and Innovation Policy*, ed. Adam Jaffe and Benjamin Jones (Chicago: University of Chicago Press, 2015). Georgia Research Alliance, http://gra.org.

18. As discussed in Chapter 5, an investment of 0.5 percent of GDP could accelerate economic growth rate by at least 7 percent relative to what would otherwise be its baseline: a growth rate that would otherwise be 2 percent per annum would now become 2.14 percent.

19. As discussed in Chapter 5, we estimated statistical models to ascertain the relationship between university R&D funding and jobs. We are grateful to Trinh Le for her assistance with this calculation for New Zealand.

20. Gabriel Chodorow-Reich, "Geographic Cross-Sectional Fiscal Spending Multipliers: What Have We Learned" (working paper #23577, National Bureau of Economic Research, Cambridge, MA, 2017). Chodorow-Reich estimates that the cost per job of the highway spending part of the 2009 American Recovery and Reinvestment Act was $50,000.

21. Josh Lerner, *Boulevard of Broken Dreams* (Princeton, NJ: Princeton University Press, 2009).

22. "The organization will be led by a four-star general and tasked with overseeing the planning and purchasing of everything from futuristic helicopters to direct-energy weapons that the Pentagon believes can someday be used in missile defense." Dan Lamothe, "Why the Army Decided to Put Its New High-Tech Futures Command in Texas," *Washington Post,* July 14, 2018, https://www.washingtonpost.com/news/checkpoint/wp/2018/07/14/understanding-the-armys-reasons-for-putting-its-new-high-tech-futures-command-in-texas/?utm_term=.89065c6fa6f5.

23. Harry Holzer, "Raising Job Quality and Skills for American Workers: Creating More-Effective Education and Workforce Development Systems in the States," Brookings Institution, November 30, 2011, https://www.brookings.edu/research/raising-job-quality-and-skills-for-american-workers-creating-more-effective-education-and-workforce-development-systems-in-the-states/. Michael Greenstone and Adam Looney, "Building America's Job Skills with Effective Workforce Programs: A Training Strategy to Raise Wages and Increase Work Opportunities," Brookings Institution, November 30, 2011, https://www.brookings.edu/research/building-americas-job-skills-with-effective-workforce-programs-a-training-strategy-to-raise-wages-and-increase-work-opportunities/. Martha Laboissiere and Mona Mourshed, "Closing the Skills Gap: Creating Workforce-Development Programs That Work for Everyone," McKinsey & Company, February 2017, https://www.mckinsey.com/industries/social-sector/our-insights/closing-the-skills-gap-creating-workforce-development-programs-that-work-for-everyone. "CEA Report: Addressing America's Reskilling Challenge," White House, July 17, 2018, https://www.whitehouse.gov/briefings-statements/cea-report-addressing-americas-reskilling-challenge/.

24. These data are for people who received bachelor's degrees in 2015. Given how these data are reported, this number is likely to be an underestimate. See Christine DiGangi, "The Average Student Loan Debt in Every State," *USA Today,* April 28, 2017, https://www.usatoday.com/story/money/personalfinance/2017/04/28/average-student-loan-debt-every-state/100893668/.

25. This headline number is the operating revenue of all higher (postsecondary) education and includes some government support for public colleges and also through Pell Grants: "Postsecondary Revenues by Source," National Center for Education Statistics, https://nces.ed.gov/programs/coe/pdf/Indicator_CUD/coe_cud_2015_06.pdf. The National Center for Education Statistics gives more detail on average tuition by type of institution: "Postsecondary Institution Revenues,"

updated May 2018, National Center for Education Statistics, https://nces.ed.gov
/programs/coe/indicator_cud.asp.

26. These scandals include the failure of two large for-profit educational chains
that defrauded students who borrowed billions in federal student loans. See Erica
L. Green, "DeVos to Eliminate Rules Aimed at Abuses by For-Profit Colleges,"
New York Times, July 26, 2018, https://www.nytimes.com/2018/07/26/us/politics
/betsy-devos-for-profit-colleges.html.

27. For an existing effort along these lines in the state of Montana, see Jon Marcus and Kirk Carapezza, "One State Uses Labor Market Data to Shape What Colleges Teach," WGBH, November 7, 2018, https://www.wgbh.org/news/education
/2018/11/07/one-state-uses-labor-market-data-to-shape-what-colleges-teach.
We are well aware that there was a perceived glut of STEM graduates at various
times, including when public research and development was cut at the end of the
1960s and again after the end of the Cold War. However, most of these talented
people eventually found good jobs, including through starting their own companies or working for start-ups.

28. Paul Lewis, *How to Create Skills for an Emerging Industry: The Case of
Technician Skills and Training in Cell Therapy* (London: Gatsby Charitable Foundation, 2017), http://www.gatsby.org.uk/uploads/education/reports/pdf/paul-lewis
-cell-therapy-jan2017.pdf.

29. "CEA Report," White House.

30. In 1939/40, on the eve of World War II, there were 1,708 American
institutions of higher education (i.e., colleges of all kinds) employing just under
150,000 professional staff and about 111,000 instructional staff. In 1959/60, just
after Sputnik, there were 380,000 professional staff and 281,500 instructors in
2,004 colleges. By 1989/90, there were 1.5 million professional staff and nearly
1 million instructors in 3,535 colleges. Enrollment increased from 1.5 million
students before the war to 3.6 million in 1959/60 and to 13.5 million in 1989/90.
National Center for Education Statistics, *120 Years of American Education: A Statistical Portrait* (Washington, DC: US Department of Education, 1993), https://nces
.ed.gov/pubs93/93442.pdf.

31. For confirmation on the AIP, see p. 9, footnote 2, Amicus Brief filed in 2016 by
Airports Council International—North America in the case of *The City of Santa Monica v. FAA.* Eligible projects include land acquisition, airport safety, capacity, security,
and environmental studies. *Principles of Federal Appropriations Law: Annual Update of
the Third Edition* (Washington, DC: US Government Accountability Office, 2009),
https://www.nasa.gov/pdf/436198main_GAO_Redbook_Vol_I_Ch_5_and
_2009_Update-1-508.pdf. United States Court of Appeals for the Ninth Circuit,
"The City of Santa Monica v. Federal Aviation Administration," City of Santa
Monica, https://www.smgov.net/uploadedFiles/Departments/Airport/Litigation
/2016.12.23%20Brief%20of%20Amicus%20Curiae%20Airports%20Council
%20International%20-%20North%20America.pdf. "Overview: What is AIP?," Federal Aviation Administration, https://www.faa.gov/airports/aip/overview/.

32. For tax rates by sector, see Kevin Carmichael and Andrea Jones-Rooy, "The GOP's Corporate Tax Cut May Not Be as Big as It Looks," *FiveThirtyEight*, December 15, 2017, https://fivethirtyeight.com/features/the-gops-corporate-tax -cut-may-not-be-as-big-as-it-looks/.

33. For a summary of the Trump tax cuts and their impacts, see Jonathan Gruber, *Public Finance and Public Policy*, 6th ed. (New York: Macmillan, 2019).

34. Rebecca Spalding, "Kendall Square: How a Rundown Area Near Boston Birthed a Biotech Boom and Real Estate Empire," *Boston Globe*, October 15, 2018, http://realestate.boston.com/news/2018/10/15/kendall-square-rundown-area -near-boston-birthed-biotech-boom-real-estate-empire/.

35. Ibid.

36. *FY 2011 Federal Real Property Report* (Washington, DC: US General Services Administration, n.d.), https://www.gsa.gov/cdnstatic/FY_2011_FRPP_intro _508.pdf.

37. Rob Matheson, "MIT Signs Agreement to Redevelop Volpe Center," *MIT News*, January 18, 2017, http://news.mit.edu/2017/agreement-redevelop -volpe-center-kendall-square-0118. We were not involved in any way with this transaction.

38. Shayndi Raice and Keiko Morris, "Search for Amazon HQ2 Sparks Real-Estate Speculation," *Wall Street Journal*, updated October 22, 2018, https://www .wsj.com/articles/search-for-amazon-hq2-sparks-real-estate-speculation-1540200601 ?mod=cx_picks&cx_navSource=cx_picks&cx_tag=collabctx&cx_artPos=1 #cxrecs_s.

39. William C. Wheaton, "Percentage Rent in Retail Leasing: The Alignment of Landlord-Tenant Interests," *Real Estate Economics* 28, no. 2 (2000). We thank Bill Wheaton for very helpful discussions on this and other real estate–related points.

40. No doubt politicians will spend some time debating what "everyone" means here. We propose that everyone, irrespective of age, who has a Social Security number should receive an equal dividend.

41. Scott Goldsmith, "The Alaska Permanent Fund Dividend: An Experiment in Wealth Distribution," 2002, http://www.basicincome.org/bien/pdf/2002 Goldsmith.pdf.

42. "Investing for Alaska, Investing for the Long Run," Alaska Permanent Fund Corporation, http://www.apfc.org/home/Content/aboutFund/fundFAQ.cfm.

43. Ibid.

44. Nathaniel Herz, "Gov. Walker's Veto Cuts Alaska Permanent Fund Dividends to $1,022," *Anchorage Daily News*, updated October 19, 2016, https://www.adn.com/politics/2016/09/23/gov-walkers-veto-shaves-alaska -permanent-fund-dividends-to-1022/.

45. Michelle Theriault Boots, "UAA Research Shows Impact of PFD on Poverty Rates in Alaska," *Anchorage Daily News*, updated October 20, 2016, https:// www.adn.com/alaska-news/2016/10/19/new-uaa-research-shows-impact-of-pfd -on-poverty-rates-in-alaska/.

46. Gloria Guzman, "Household Income: 2016," US Census Bureau, September 24, 2017, https://www.census.gov/library/publications/2017/acs/acsbr16 -02.html.

47. "California Climate Credit," California Public Utilities Commission, http://www.cpuc.ca.gov/climatecredit/. California may be taking this lesson further. A recent proposal would revise a cap-and-trade system for emissions regulations so as to distribute most of the revenues from their initiative to a per capita dividend for state residents. David Roberts, "California Is About to Revolutionize Climate Policy . . . Again," *Vox*, Mary 3, 2017, https://www.vox.com /energy-and-environment/2017/5/3/15512258/california-revolutionize-cap -and-trade.

CHAPTER 8: BIG SCIENCE AND THE INDUSTRIES OF THE FUTURE

1. Alvin M. Weinberg, "Impact of Large-Scale Science on the United States," *Science* 134, no. 347 (1961). Weinberg was director of the Oak Ridge National Laboratory.

2. This description of Lawrence's innovation and its funding draws on Michael Hiltzik, *Big Science: Ernest Lawrence and the Invention That Launched the Military-Industrial Complex* (New York: Simon & Schuster, 2015), in particular Chapter 3.

3. This was the Research Corporation, founded in 1912, by Frederick Cottrell. Ibid., pp. 59–60.

4. "Malaria Mortality Among Children Under Five Is Concentrated in Sub-Saharan Africa," Unicef, June 2018, https://data.unicef.org/topic/child-health /malaria/.

5. Roll Back Malaria Partnership Secretariat, *Economic Costs of Malaria* (Geneva, Switzerland: World Health Organization, n.d.), https://www.malaria consortium.org/userfiles/file/Malaria%20resources/RBM%20Economic%20 costs%20of%20malaria.pdf.

6. "Chinese Nobel Prize Winner Tu Youyou's Drug Has Saved Lives of Millions of Malaria Sufferers," *South China Morning Post,* October 6, 2015, http:// www.scmp.com/news/china/society/article/1864597/drug-chinas-nobel-prize -winner-tu-youyou-worked-has-saved.

7. *World Malaria Report 2008* (Geneva, Switzerland: World Health Organization, 2008), http://apps.who.int/iris/bitstream/handle/10665/43939/9789241563697 _eng.pdf?sequence=1.

8. Mark Peplow, "Synthetic Biology's First Malaria Drug Meets Market Resistance," *Nature* 530, no. 7591 (2016), https://www.nature.com/news /synthetic-biology-s-first-malaria-drug-meets-market-resistance-1.19426#/market.

9. Dae-Kyun Ro, Eric M. Paradise, Mario Ouellet, Karl J. Fisher, Karyn L. Newman, John M. Ndungu, Kimberly A. Ho, Rachel A. Eachus, Timothy S. Ham, James Kirby, Michelle C. Y. Chang, Sydnor T. Withers, Yoichiro Shiba,

Richmond Sarpong, and Jay D. Keasling, "Production of the Antimalarial Drug Precursor Artemisinic Acid in Engineered Yeast," *Nature* 440 (2006) describes how they engineered yeast to produce artemisinic acid. In 2008, Sanofi licensed the yeast developed by the team and began industrial-scale production. Mark Peplow, "Malaria Drug Made in Yeast Causes Market Ferment," *Nature* 494, no. 7436 (2013), https://www.nature.com/news/malaria-drug-made-in-yeast-causes-market-ferment-1.12417. The researchers set up the company Amyris to produce artemisinin, and much of the funding for its development came from the Bill & Melinda Gates Foundation; our source is Eric Althoff (founder, Arzeda), in discussion with the authors.

10. The Affordable Medicines Facility-Malaria (AMFm) program was run by the Global Fund to Fight AIDS/TB/Malaria and was the main funding route for the finished treatments. Peplow, "Malaria Drug."

11. Tong Si and Huimin Zhao, "A Brief Overview of Synthetic Biology Research Programs and Roadmap Studies in the United States," *Synthetic and Systems Biology* 1, no. 4 (2016), https://www.sciencedirect.com/science/article/pii/S2405805X1630031X.

12. Tanel Ozdemir, Alex J. H. Fedorec, Tal Danino, Chris P. Barnes, "Synthetic Biology and Engineered Live Biotherapeutics: Toward Increasing System Complexity," *Cell* 7, no. 1 (2018), https://www.cell.com/cell-systems/abstract/S2405-4712(18)30248-5.

13. Projections suggest that the growth in world population to nine billion by 2050 will require 60 percent more calories than we produce today. But food production is getting harder and harder. The Food and Agricultural Organization of the United Nations reported that arable land per person shrank by more than one-third from 1970 to 2000 and is projected to decline by another one-third from 2000 to 2050. Soil has been eroding at a pace of up to one hundred times greater than the rate of soil formation. *Achieving Sustainable Gains in Agriculture* (Rome: Food and Agriculture Organization, n.d.), http://www.fao.org/docrep/014/am859e/am859e01.pdf. Oliver Milman, "Earth Has Lost a Third of Arable Land in Past 40 Years, Scientists Say," *Guardian*, December 2, 2015, https://www.theguardian.com/environment/2015/dec/02/arable-land-soil-food-security-shortage.

14. One company doing so is Perfect Day, a Berkeley-based start-up formerly known as Muufri. Michael Pellman Rowland, "This Futuristic Startup Could Disrupt the Dairy Industry," *Forbes*, February 27, 2018, https://www.forbes.com/sites/michaelpellmanrowland/2018/02/27/perfectday-disrupts-dairy/#70d101e85f61.

15. Cellular agriculture is the application of disciplines like tissue engineering, molecular bio, and synthetic bio to produce products typically associated with traditional agriculture, such as meat and dairy. Christine Gould, "5 Inspiring Ways Synthetic Biology Will Revolutionize Food and Agriculture," *Medium*, October 28, 2016, https://medium.com/age-of-awareness/5-inspiring-ways-synthetic-biology-will-revolutionize-food-and-agriculture-3601c25438b5.

16. *Synthetic Microorganisms for Agricultural Use* (Raleigh: North Carolina State University Genetic Engineering and Society Center, 2017), https://research .ncsu.edu/ges/files/2017/07/Issue-brief-Synbio-in-agriculture-01.2017-v3.pdf.

17. David Freeman, "Artificial Photosynthesis Advance Hailed as Major Breakthrough," *Huffington Post,* April 20, 2015, https://www.huffingtonpost .com/2015/04/20/artificial-photosynthesis-environment-energy_n_7088830.html.

18. "Current Uses of Synthetic Biology," Biotechnology Innovation Organization, https://www.bio.org/articles/current-uses-synthetic-biology.

19. Ibid.

20. A. Rahman and C. D. Miller, "Microalgae as a Source of Bioplastics," in *Algal Green Chemistry: Recent Progress in Biotechnology,* ed. Rajesh Prasad Rastogi, Datta Madamwar, and Ashok Pandey (Amsterdam: Elsevier, 2017), https://www .sciencedirect.com/science/article/pii/B9780444637840000060.

21. Figure on tons added to landfills extrapolated from Norm Schriever, "Plastic Water Bottles Causing Flood of Harm to Our Environment," *Huffington Post,* updated December 6, 2017, https://www.huffingtonpost.com/norm-schriever/post _5218_b_3613577.html.

22. Alex Janin, "Can a Bottle Made from Algae End the World's Plastic Addiction?," *Takepart,* April 6, 2016, http://www.takepart.com/article/2016/04/06 /algae-bottle-end-planets-plastic-addiction.

23. "America's Bioeconomy Grow Opportunities," United States Department of Agriculture, https://www.biopreferred.gov/BPResources/files/BP_InfoGraphic.pdf.

24. D. Ewen Cameron, Caleb J. Bashor, and James J. Collins, "A Brief History of Synthetic Biology," *Nature Reviews Microbiology* 12, no. 5 (2014), http:// collinslab.mit.edu/files/nrm_cameron.pdf.

25. The first international conference for the field, Synthetic Biology 1.0 (SB1.0), was held in the summer of 2004 at MIT and was significant because it provided an identifiable community and helped to consolidate efforts in the field.

26. Todd Kuiken, "U.S. Trends in Synthetic Biology Research Funding," Wilson Center, September 15, 2015, https://www.wilsoncenter.org/publication /us-trends-synthetic-biology-research-funding.

27. Ibid.

28. Si and Zhao, "A Brief Overview."

29. Ibid.

30. *Sustainability Initiative Initial Findings & Recommendations* (New York: Nancy J. Kelley & Associates, 2017), http://nancyjkelley.com/wp-content/uploads /Final-Synberc-Sustainability-Report.pdf.

31. "Award Abstract #1818248," National Science Foundation, https://nsf .gov/awardsearch/showAward?AWD_ID=1818248&HistoricalAwards=false. Perhaps the largest funder of research in synthetic biology in recent years has been DARPA, within the Department of Defense. While DARPA was providing almost no funding to synthetic biology in 2010, the organization had increased its investment to $100 million per year by 2014. The DARPA program Living Foundries:

1000 Molecules will invest $110 million through 2019 to enable facilities to generate organisms capable of producing one thousand molecules of industrial and defense interest. Harriet Taylor, "Why the Pentagon Is Paying Nearly $2 Million for a Custom-Designed Bacteria," CNBC, August 15, 2016, https://www.cnbc.com/2016/08/15/why-the-pentagon-is-paying-nearly-2-million-for-a-custom-designed-bacteria.html.

Despite these successes, DARPA is not an ideal organization to serve as the primary federal funder of synthetic biology research. DARPA continues to view its mission primarily as focused on military purposes. "The Mansfield amendment was repealed the following year, but its impact lingered. The DoD adjusted its own policies to conform to the law, and it left the adjustments in place. Congress had given clear notice that it wanted to see direct military payoff for the research-and-development dollars spent by DoD. The same enthusiasm led Congress in 1972 to change ARPA's name to DARPA . . . a reminder that DARPA was not at liberty to support any technology it might find interesting. Rather it was to support only those projects with clear and present application to the military mission of the armed forces." Alex Roland and Philip Shiman, *Strategic Computing: DARPA and the Quest for Machine Intelligence, 1983–1993* (Cambridge, MA: MIT Press, 2002), p. 29.

32. "SynBio Map," Synthetic Biology Project, 2018, http://www.synbioproject.org/sbmap/.

33. Shaun Moshasha, "The Rapid Growth of Synthetic Biology in China," SynBioBeta, March 24, 2016, https://synbiobeta.com/news/rapid-growth-synthetic-biology-china/.

34. "Schools Participating in iGEM 2006," iGEM, https://2006.igem.org/wiki/index.php/Schools_Participating_in_iGEM_2006. "2018 iGEM Calendar," iGEM, http://2018.igem.org/Calendar.

35. "Convergence: The Future of Health," Convergence Revolution, 2016, http://www.convergencerevolution.net/2016-report/.

36. The NSF established the Engineering Research Center for Cell Manufacturing Technologies in September 2017 with a budget of just $20 million. The center has three stated goals: to advance new tools, to develop regulatory guidelines, and to improve workforce development—but not to increase manufacturing capacity. Charlene Betourney, "UGA Partner in Cell Research Consortium," *UGA Today*, September 13, 2017, https://news.uga.edu/uga-a-major-partner-in-cell-manufacturing-research-consortium/.

37. *The Future Is Unfolding: From Cells to Solutions* (Toronto, ON: Center for Commercialization of Regenerative Medicine, 2017), https://www.ccrm.ca/sites/default/files/CCRM%20ANNUAL%20REPORT%202017%20SML.pdf. CCRM describes itself as a "not-for-profit, public-private consortium supporting the development of foundational technologies that accelerate the commercialization of cell and gene therapies, and regenerative medicine technologies." "Executive Summary," Center for Commercialization of Regenerative Medicine, 2018, https://www.ccrm.ca/regenerative-medicine-executive-summary.

38. Recognizing that research-and-development teams are hit hardest by an inability to access manufacturing, CCRM will use the facility exclusively to produce materials for clinical trials, with the hope of helping "companies, researchers, and non-profit organizations to take the steps necessary toward regulatory approval of their cell therapies." "Partnership to Develop Personalized Therapeutics for B-cell Lymphoma and Leukemia," Center for Commercialization of Regenerative Medicine, September 29, 2017, https://www.ccrm.ca/sites/default/files/media_room /CCRM-Affigen%20Launch%20Press%20Release%20FINAL_0.pdf.

39. K. Thompson and E. P. Foster, "The Cell Therapy Catapult: Growing a U.K. Cell Therapy Industry Generating Health and Wealth," *Stem Cells and Development* 22, suppl. 1 (2013): 35–39, https://www.ncbi.nlm.nih.gov/pubmed/24304073.

40. Indeed, CGT Catapult's 2016 Advanced Therapies Manufacturing Action Plan proposes a series of action items that coordinate industry, government, and academia to "secure [the UK's] position as a global hub for advanced therapies." Proposed action items include an extended tax credit for research and development related to manufacturing, £30 million (US$40 million) annually in government-supported competitive funding for increased manufacturing capacity, establishment of a network of treatment centers with £30 million (US$40 million) in government funding delivered through a competitive process, collaboration between industry and educators to develop a talent plan for industry-funded training at all skill levels, and engagement between industry and academic researchers to identify and address gaps in regulatory standards for manufacturing. "Cell and Gene Therapy Catapult Opens Manufacturing Centre to Accelerate Growth of the Industry in the UK," Catapult Cell and Gene Therapy, April 23, 2018, https://ct.catapult.org.uk/news-media /manufacturing-news/cell-and-gene-therapy-catapult-opens-manufacturing-centre.

41. "Use of Oil," US Energy Information Administration, September 19, 2017, https://www.eia.gov/energyexplained/index.cfm?page=oil_use.

42. "U.S. Imports of Crude Oil," United States Census Bureau, https://www .census.gov/foreign-trade/statistics/historical/petr.pdf. "Gross Domestic Product," Federal Reserve Bank of St. Louis, August 29, 2018, https://fred.stlouisfed.org /series/GDP.

43. "Fast Facts on Transportation Greenhouse Gas Emissions," EPA, August 27, 2018, https://www.epa.gov/greenvehicles/fast-facts-transportation-greenhouse -gas-emissions.

44. Mashael Yazdanie, Fabrizio Noembrini, Steve Heinen, Augusto Espinel, and Konstantinos Boulouchos, "Well-to-Wheel Costs, Primary Energy Demand, and Greenhouse Gas Emissions for the Production and Operation of Conventional and Alternative Vehicles," *Transportation Research Part D: Transport and Environment* 48 (2016): 63–84. Päivi T. Aakko-Saksa, Chris Cook, Jari Kiviaho, and Timo Repo, "Liquid Organic Hydrogen Carriers for Transportation and Storing of Renewable Energy—Review and Discussion," *Journal of Power Sources* 396 (2018): 803–823. Wentao Wang, Jose Herreros, Athanasios Tsolakis, and Andrew York, "Ammonia as Hydrogen Carrier for Transportation; Investigation of the

Ammonia Exhaust Gas Fuel Reforming," *International Journal of Hydrogen Energy* 38 (2013): 9907–9917.

45. *How Clean Are Hydrogen Fuel Cell Electric Vehicles?* (Cambridge, MA: Union of Concerned Scientists, 2014), https://www.ucsusa.org/sites/default/files /attach/2014/10/How-Clean-Are-Hydrogen-Fuel-Cells-Fact-Sheet.pdf.

46. Donald L. Barlett and J. B. Steele, "Hydrogen Is in His Dreams," *Time,* July 14, 2003, http://content.time.com/time/magazine/article/0,9171,464641,00.html. "History," Fuel Cell Today, http://www.fuelcelltoday.com/history#The%201990s.

47. Nicholas Brown, "Insiders and Experts Are Ripping on Hydrogen Cars, but Why?," *Kompulsa,* May 21, 2015, https://www.kompulsa.com/2015/05/21 /insiders-and-experts-are-ripping-on-hydrogen-cars-but-why/.

48. Ian Bickis, "Hydrogen Fuel Cells Making an Automotive Comeback," *Canadian Manufacturing,* March 31, 2016, https://www.canadianmanufacturing .com/environment-and-safety/hydrogen-fuel-cells-making-automotive-comeback -164989/.

49. "Are Hydrogen Cars Making a Comeback?," CBS News, November 22, 2013, https://www.cbsnews.com/news/are-hydrogen-cars-making-a-comeback/.

50. "5 Fast Facts About Hydrogen and Fuel Cells," Office of Energy Efficiency and Renewable Energy, October 4, 2017, https://www.energy.gov/eere/articles/5 -fast-facts-about-hydrogen-and-fuel-cells. Tests run by the Union of Concerned Scientists on a Hyundai Tucson show emissions reductions of 34 percent using natural gas and 60 percent using 46 percent renewable energy. *How Clean are Hydrogen Fuel Cell Electric Vehicles?,* Union of Concerned Scientists.

51. *Effects of a Transition to a Hydrogen Economy on Employment in the United States Report to Congress* (Washington, DC: US Department of Energy, 2008), https://www.hydrogen.energy.gov/pdfs/epact1820_employment_study.pdf. This study may be overly optimistic given the development of electric vehicles and trends in energy prices since the study was done. A more recent projection from the Department of Energy based on current trends suggests a rise in employment of "only" 267,000. But this is a projection based on current trends, not if there is more aggressive investment in the hydrogen economy as in the 2008 report.

52. *State of the States: Fuel Cells in America 2016,* 7th ed. (Washington, DC: US Department of Energy, 2016), https://www.energy.gov/sites/prod/files/2016/11 /f34/fcto_state_of_states_2016_0.pdf.

53. DOE FY05 budget justification tables suggest that FY04 had appropriations of $81.9 million for hydrogen research and $65.1 million for fuel cells; "FY 2005 Budget Justification," US Department of Energy, https://www.energy.gov/cfo /downloads/fy-2005-budget-justification.

DOE FY09 budget justification tables suggest that FY08 had appropriations of $211 million for hydrogen research and $55 million for fuel cells; "FY 2009 Budget Justification," US Department of Energy, https://www.energy.gov/cfo /downloads/fy-2009-budget-justification.

DOE FY18 budget justification tables suggest that FY17 had appropriations of $101 million for hydrogen and fuel cell research combined; "FY 2018 Budget Justification," US Department of Energy https://www.energy.gov/cfo/downloads /fy-2018-budget-justification

54. *Fuel Cell Technologies Market Report 2016* (Washington, DC: US Department of Energy, 2016), https://www.energy.gov/sites/prod/files/2017/10/f37/fcto _2016_market_report.pdf.

55. *Fuel Cell Technologies Market Report 2014* (Washington, DC: US Department of Energy), 2014 https://www.energy.gov/sites/prod/files/2015/10/f27/fcto _2014_market_report.pdf.

56. "Hydrogen Basics," Alternative Fuels Data Center, July 2, 2018, https:// www.afdc.energy.gov/fuels/hydrogen_basics.html.

57. Daniel Fraile, Jean-Christophe Lanoix, Patrick Maio, Azalea Rangel, and Angelica Torres, *Overview of the Market Segmentation for Hydrogen Across Potential Customer Groups, Based on Key Application Areas* (Brussels: CertifHy, 2015), https://www.fch.europa.eu/sites/default/files/project_results_and_deliverables/D %201.2.%20Overview%20of%20the%20market%20segmenatation%20for%20 hydrogen%20across%20potential%20customer%20groups%20based%20on%20 key%20application%20areas.pdf.

58. "Japan Builds 'Hydrogen Society of the Future,'" Invest with Values, August 30, 2017, https://investwithvalues.com/news/japan-builds-hydrogen-society -future/.

59. Lun Jingguang, "Hydrogen-Fuel Cell Vehicle Development in China," United Nations,http://www.un.org/esa/sustdev/csd/csd14/lc/presentation/hydrogen 4.pdf.

60. Fangzhu Zhang and Philip Cooke, "Hydrogen and Fuel Cell Development in China: A Review," *European Planning Studies* 18, no. 7 (2010). Many of these organizations appear to be small.

61. Yang Yi, "World's First Hydrogen Tram Runs in China,"XinhuaNet, October 27, 2017, http://www.xinhuanet.com/english/2017-10/27/c_136709647.htm. "China Develops World's First Hydrogen-Powered Train," IFL Science, https:// www.iflscience.com/technology/china-develops-worlds-first-hydrogen-powered -tram/.

62. Yamei, "Wuhan to House China's First Industry Park for Developing Hydrogen Fuel Cells," XinhuaNet, December 24, 2017, http://www.xinhuanet .com/english/2017-12/24/c_136849031.htm.

63. Andrew Kadak, "The Status of the US High-Temperature Gas Reactors," *Engineering* 2 (2016): 119–123.

64. Idaho National Laboratory, "An Analysis of the Effect of Reactor Outlet Temperature of a High Temperature Reactor on Electric Power Generation, Hydrogen Production, and Process Heat" (technical evaluation study project no. 23843, September 14, 2010).

65. A. Abdulla, "A Retrospective Analysis of Funding and Focus in US Advanced Fission Innovation," *Environmental Research Letters* 12 (2017): 084016.

66. Mark Hibbs, *The Future of Nuclear Power in China* (Washington, DC: Carnegie Endowment for International Peace, 2018). Abby Harvey, "China Advances HTGR Technology," *Power*, November 2017, https://www.powermag.com/china-advances-htgr-technology/. "HTR-PM steam generator passes pressure tests," World Nuclear News, October 2018, http://www.world-nuclear-news.org/Articles/HTR-PM-steam-generator-passes-pressure-tests.

67. "TerraPower, CNNC Team Up on Travelling Wave Reactor," World Nuclear News, September 25, 2015, http://www.world-nuclear-news.org/NN-TerraPower-CNNC-team-up-on-travelling-wave-reactor-25091501.html.

68. NASA has a space exploration budget of $3.8 billion, while NOAA has an exploration budget of only $23.7 million. Michael Conathan, "Rockets Top Submarines: Space Exploration Dollars Dwarf Ocean Spending," Center for American Progress, June 18, 2018, https://www.americanprogress.org/issues/green/news/2013/06/18/66956/rockets-top-submarines-space-exploration-dollars-dwarf-ocean-spending/e.

69. Ibid.

70. "Deepwater Technology," National Energy Technology Laboratory, https://www.netl.doe.gov/research/oil-and-gas/deepwater-technologies.

71. "Cobalt Demand Worldwide from 2010 to 2015 (in 1,000 Tons)," Statista, 2018, https://www.statista.com/statistics/875808/cobalt-demand-worldwide/. Robert Ferris, "Technology Is Fueling the Growing Demand for the Once-Obscure Element Cobalt," CNBC, April 16, 2018, https://www.cnbc.com/2018/04/16/technology-is-fueling-the-growing-demand-for-the-once-obscure-element-cobalt.html. Frank Holmes, "The World's Cobalt Supply Is in Jeopardy," *Forbes*, February 27, 2018, https://www.forbes.com/sites/greatspeculations/2018/02/27/the-worlds-cobalt-supply-is-in-jeopardy/#703d71fd1be5.

72. "Deep Sea Mining: The Basics," Pew Charitable Trusts, February 3, 2017, https://www.pewtrusts.org/en/research-and-analysis/fact-sheets/2017/02/deep-sea-mining-the-basics. Thomas Peacock and Matthew H. Alford, "Is Deep-Sea Mining Worth It?," *Scientific American*, April 17, 2018.

73. Peacock and Alford, "Is Deep-Sea Mining Worth It?"

74. Yutaro Takaya, Kazutaka Yasukawa, Takehiro Kawasaki, Koichiro Fujinaga, Junichiro Ohta, Yoichi Usui, Kentaro Nakamura, Jun-Ichi Kimura, Qing Chang, Morihisa Hamada, Gjergj Dodbiba, Tatsuo Nozaki, Koichi Iijima, Tomohiro Morisawa, Takuma Kuwahara, Yasuyuki Ishida, Takao Ichimura, Masaki Kitazume, Toyohisa Fujita, and Yasuhiro Kato, "The Tremendous Potential of Deep-Sea Mud as a Source of Rare-Earth Elements," *Scientific Reports* 8 (2018).

75. "Rare Earth Elements," MIT: The Future of Strategic Natural Resources, 2016, http://web.mit.edu/12.000/www/m2016/finalwebsite/elements/ree.html.

76. The top producers are China, Australia, and Russia. *Rare Earths* (Reston, VA: United States Geological Survey, 2017), https://minerals.usgs.gov/minerals /pubs/commodity/rare_earths/mcs-2017-raree.pdf.

77. Clifford Coonan, "Rare-Earth Metal Prices Spike as China Stockpiles Supplies," *Independent,* June 21, 2011, https://www.independent.co.uk /environment/rare-earth-metal-prices-spike-as-china-stockpiles-supplies-2300303 .html.

78. Christine Parthemore, "Rare Earth Woes Could Mean Trouble for U.S. Stealth Fleet," *Wired,* May 11, 2011, https://www.wired.com/2011/05/rare -earth-woes-could-mean-trouble-for-u-s-stealth-fleet/.

79. "Deep Sea Mining," MIT: The Future of Strategic Natural Resources, 2016, http://web.mit.edu/12.000/www/m2016/finalwebsite/solutions/oceans.html.

80. "Why Are Hadal Zones Important?," University of South Denmark, August 31, 2018, https://www.sdu.dk/en/om_sdu/institutter_centre/i_biologi/forskning /forskningsprojekter/benthic+diagenesis+and+microbiology+of+hadal+trenches /environment/why.

81. "Deep-Sea Corals," Smithsonian Institute, https://ocean.si.edu/ecosystems /coral-reefs/deep-sea-corals.

82. *Earth's Final Frontier: A U.S. Strategy for Ocean Exploration* (Silver Spring, MD: National Oceanic and Atmospheric Administration, 2000), https:// oceanexplorer.noaa.gov/about/what-we-do/program-review/presidents-panel -on-ocean-exploration-report.pdf.

83. There are also autonomous underwater vehicles (AUV, like ROV but not connected to the ship).

84. As of 2015, about 50 percent of WHOI funding is from government sources. Bryan Bender, "Woods Hole Allies with Energy Firms," *Boston Globe,* May 25, 2014, https://www.bostonglobe.com/news/nation/2014/05/24/woods -hole-feeling-budget-squeeze-looks-partner-with-energy-industry/sScPY15 XErNsnU5PdtANzI/story.html. "History and Legacy," Woods Hole Oceanographic Institution, http://www.whoi.edu/main/history-legacy.

85. "Hybrid Remotely Operated Vehicle *Nereus* Reaches Deepest Part of the Ocean," Woods Hole Oceanographic Institution, June 2, 2009, http://www.whoi .edu/page.do?pid=7545&tid=7342&cid=57586.

86. Daniel Cressey, "Ocean-Diving Robot Nereus Will Not Be Replaced," *Nature* 528, no. 7581 (2015), http://www.nature.com/news/ocean-diving-robot -nereus-will-not-be-replaced-1.18972. Instead, the United States is leaning on private organizations such as the Schmidt Ocean Institute (the foundation of Google former chairman Eric Schmidt) to lead the development of new deepwater vehicles, but there has been little progress to date.

87. Feng Liu, Wei Cheng Cui, and Xiang Yang Li. "China's First Deep Manned Submersible, JIAOLONG," *Science China Earth Sciences* 53, no. 10 (2010).

88. Xie Chuanjiao and Zhao Lei, "China's Deep-Sea Submersible Goes on Global Mission," *Telegraph,* July 28, 2017, http://www.telegraph.co.uk/news/world /china-watch/technology/chinas-deep-sea-submersible/.

89. "China Finds Sulfide Deposits in Indian Ocean," *People's Daily Online,* August 14, 2018, http://en.people.cn/n3/2018/0814/c90000-9490361.html (page discontinued).

90. Damian Carrington, "Is Deep Sea Mining Vital for a Greener Future— Even If It Destroys Ecosystems?," *Guardian,* June 4, 2017, https://www.theguardian .com/environment/2017/jun/04/is-deep-sea-mining-vital-for-greener-future -even-if-it-means-destroying-precious-ecosystems.

91. Data from OECD R&D statistics. All comparisons are restricted to the twenty other nations that have information on total R&D and government R&D relative to GDP: Austria, Belgium, Canada, Denmark, Finland, France, Germany, Greece, Ireland, Israel, Italy, Japan, Netherlands, New Zealand, Norway, Portugal, Spain, Sweden, Switzerland, and Great Britain. For fifteen of the nations, we use data for 1981 and 2015. For Belgium and Portugal, data aren't available for 1981, so we use 1982 (Belgium) and 1983 (Portugal) instead. For Sweden, data aren't available for 2015, so we use 2013 instead. "Gross Domestic Spending on R&D," OECD, 2018, https://data.oecd.org/rd/gross-domestic-spending-on-r-d.htm.

92. For government R&D, only the UK spent more than 1 percent of GDP, while only France, Germany, and Sweden spent more than 0.8 percent of GDP. For total R&D, Japan and the UK were slightly behind the United States at 2.2 percent of GDP, with Germany at 2.1 percent and Switzerland at 2 percent.

93. All facts in this paragraph and next are from Richard B. Freeman and Wei Huang, "China's 'Great Leap Forward' in Science and Engineering" (working paper #21081, National Bureau of Economic Research, Cambridge, MA, 2015).

94. Mikhail A. Prokofiev, M. G. Chilikin, and S. I. Tulpanov, "Higher Education in the USSR," UNESCO Educational studies and documents, vol. 39, 1961.

95. Freeman and Huang, "China's 'Great Leap Forward.'"

96. "The Recruitment Program for Innovative Talents (Long Term)," Recruitment Plan of Global Experts, http://www.1000plan.org/en/.

97. Anthony Capaccio, "U.S. Faces 'Unprecedented Threat' from China on Tech Takeover," *Bloomberg,* June 22, 2018, https://www.bloomberg.com/news /articles/2018-06-22/china-s-thousand-talents-called-key-in-seizing-u-s-expertise.

98. It is notoriously difficult to obtain reliable data on Chinese R&D and in particular the distribution between the public and private sectors.

99. Jeff Tollefson, "China Declared World's Largest Producer of Scientific Articles," *Nature,* January 18, 2018, https://www.nature.com/articles/d41586-018 -00927-4. China does have a low rate of international coauthorship, raising issues about the quality of the research by international standards; indeed, China's share of international citations has been declining over time, although this may just reflect the even rapider growth in domestic citations.

100. This goal was stated in China's 13th Five-Year Plan in Chapter 3, Box 2. "The 13th Five-Year Plan for Economic and Social Development of the People's Republic of China (2016–2020)," Central Committee of the Communist Party of China, Compilation, and Translation Bureau, http://en.ndrc.gov.cn/newsrelease/201612/P020161207645765233498.pdf.

101. Tarmo Lemola, "Finland: Building the Base for Telecom Breakthrough" (presented at Industrial Policy for New Growth Areas and Entrepreneurial Ecosystem conference, Helsinki, Finland, November 28–29, 2016), https://tem.fi/documents/1410877/4430406/Tarmo_Lemola.pdf/8893ba55-c46c-4e53-8346-186dbc5dd147/Tarmo_Lemola.pdf.

102. Edwin Lane, "Nokia: Life After the Fall of a Mobile Phone Giant," BBC News, March 18, 2016, https://www.bbc.com/news/business-35807556.

103. Naomi Powell, "How Finland's Economy Became Hooked on Nokia," *Globe and Mail*, October 26, 2011, https://www.theglobeandmail.com/report-on-business/economy/economy-lab/how-finlands-economy-became-hooked-on-nokia/article618622/.

104. *How America's 4G Leadership Propelled the U.S. Economy* (Dedham, MA: Recon Analytics, 2018), https://api.ctia.org/wp-content/uploads/2018/04/Recon-Analytics_How-Americas-4G-Leadership-Propelled-US-Economy_2018.pdf.

105. Steve Pociask, "The Global Race for 5G Technology Is On, and It's Not Looking Good," *Forbes*, April 17, 2018, https://www.forbes.com/sites/stevepociask/2018/04/17/the-global-race-for-5g-technology-is-on-and-its-not-looking-good/#667007b7555b.

106. *The Global Race to 5G* (Washington, DC: CTIA, 2018), https://api.ctia.org/wp-content/uploads/2018/04/Race-to-5G-Report.pdf.

107. *How America's 4G Leadership Propelled the U.S. Economy*.

108. Roma Eisenstark, "Why China and the US Are Fighting Over 5G," *TechNode*, March 30, 2018, https://technode.com/2018/03/30/5g/. "The U.S., China, and Others Race to Develop 5G Mobile Networks," Stratfor, April 3, 2018, https://worldview.stratfor.com/article/us-china-and-others-race-develop-5g-mobile-networks.

109. Edison Lee, *Telecom Services: The Geopolitics of 5G and IoT* (New York: Jeffries Financial Group, 2017), http://www.jefferies.com/CMSFiles/Jefferies.com/files/Insights/TelecomServ.pdf.

110. "Many economists have said, yeah, there's some legitimate issues here," said Laura D. Tyson, an economist at the Haas School of Business of the University of California–Berkeley, who headed the Council of Economic Advisers under President Bill Clinton. "I haven't seen any who have said the appropriate response is a series of tariffs on a bunch of goods, most of which don't have any real link to the underlying issue." Because tariffs would raise prices for American businesses and consumers that buy imported goods, "you're hurting yourself if you follow through with it," Mr. Mankiw said. "It just seems to me to be a not very smart

threat to be making, given that it would not be rational to follow through with it." Jim Tankersley, "Economists Say U.S. Tariffs Are Wrong Move on a Valid Issue," *New York Times,* April 11, 2018, https://www.nytimes.com/2018/04/11/business/economy/trump-economists.html.

111. Rebecca Trager, "Countries Poised to Roll Out Deep Sea Mining in New 'Gold Rush,'" *Chemistry World,* March 7, 2017, https://www.chemistryworld.com/news/countries-poised-to-roll-out-deep-sea-mining-in-new-gold-rush/2500509.article.

112. A. R. Thurber, A. K. Sweetman, B. E. Narayanaswamy, D. O. B. Jones, J. Ingels, and R. L. Hansman, "Ecosystem Function and Services Provided by the Deep Sea," *Biogeosciences* 11, no. 14 (2014), https://www.biogeosciences.net/11/3941/2014/bg-11-3941-2014.pdf.

113. Technically, the ISA controls DSM outside of exclusive economic zones (EEZs) of individual countries (i.e., water that is more than two hundred kilometers from a country's coast). Countries control regulations within their EEZ.

114. Mike Ives, "Drive to Mine the Deep Sea Raises Concerns Over Impacts," October 20, 2014, *Yale Environment 360,* https://e360.yale.edu/features/drive_to_mine_the_deep_sea_raises_concerns_over_impacts.

115. Cary Funk and Brian Kennedy, "3. Public Opinion About Genetically Modified Foods and Trust in Scientists Connected with These Foods," Pew Research Center, December 1, 2016, http://www.pewinternet.org/2016/12/01/public-opinion-about-genetically-modified-foods-and-trust-in-scientists-connected-with-these-foods/.

116. Anne Q. Hoy, "Agricultural Advances Draw Opposition That Blunts Innovation," *Science* 360, no. 6396 (2018), http://science.sciencemag.org/content/360/6396/1413.

117. Kelly Servick, "How Will We Keep Controversial Gene Drive Technology in Check?," *Science,* July 19, 2017, http://www.sciencemag.org/news/2017/07/how-will-we-keep-controversial-gene-drive-technology-check.

118. Gigi Kwik Gronvall, "US Competitiveness in Synthetic Biology," *Health Security* 13, no. 6 (2015), https://www.ncbi.nlm.nih.gov/pmc/articles/PMC4685481/.

119. A more modern version would likely include residential and commercial space, for the reasons we discussed in earlier chapters.

120. "How Important Is the Semiconductor Industry to Taiwan?," *Financial Times,* November 22, 2015, https://www.ft.com/content/f49958fc-8f32-11e5-8be4-3506bf20cc2b.

121. Ralph Jennings, "China Looks to Chip Away at Taiwan's Semiconductor Dominance," *Forbes,* November 9, 2017, https://www.forbes.com/sites/ralphjennings/2017/11/09/an-upstart-upstream-high-tech-sector-in-china-threatens-now-dominant-taiwan/#3768d66f5930.

122. Tain-ly Chen, "The Emergence of Hsinchu Science Park as an IT Cluster," in *Growing Industrial Clusters in Asia: Serendipity and Science,* ed. Shahid Yusuf, Kaoru Nabeshima, and Shoichi Yamashita (Washington, DC: World Bank, 2008).

123. Yu Zheng, *Governance and Foreign Investment in China, India, and Taiwan: Credibility, Flexibility, and International Business* (Ann Arbor: University of Michigan Press, 2014). Info on Chang can be found in this IEEE profile: Tekla S. Perry, "Morris Chang: Foundry Father," IEEE Spectrum, April 19, 2011, https://spectrum.ieee.org/at-work/tech-careers/morris-chang-foundry-father.

124. George Clancy, "Intelligent Island to Biopolis: Smart Minds, Sick Bodies and Millennial Turns in Singapore," *Science, Technology & Society* 17, no. 1 (2012).

125. Information derived from the SARS genome helped the Genome Institute of Singapore (GIS)'s scientists "design new molecular probes that will aid in the confirmation of diagnosis," "assist in the early diagnosis," and identify possible viral gene targets for vaccines and drugs. "Singapore Scientists Determine Complete Genetic Code of SARS Virus," Agency of Science, Technology, and Research, April 17, 2003, https://www.a-star.edu.sg/News-and-Events/News/Press-Releases/ID/490.

126. Clancy, "Intelligent Island to Biopolis."

127. "Singapore's Biopolis: A Success Story," Agency for Science Technology and Research, October 16, 2013, http://www.nas.gov.sg/archivesonline/speeches/record-details/530a0796-63db-11e3-bb37-0050568939ad.

128. V. V. Krishna and Sohan Prasad Sha, "Building Science Community by Attracting Global Talents: The Case of Singapore Biopolis," *Science, Technology & Society* 20, no. 3 (2015).

129. "Scientific American Worldview Scorecard Methodology," Scientific American Worldview, 2018, http://www.saworldview.com/scorecard/scientific-american-worldview-scorecard-methodology/.

130. "Singapore Rising," Scientific American Worldview, 2018, http://www.saworldview.com/scorecard/singapore-rising/.

131. "Biopolis: Ten Years On," A-Star Research, November 20, 2013, https://www.research.a-star.edu.sg/feature-and-innovation/6861/biopolis-058-ten-years-on.

132. "Global Innovation Powerhouse Benefits from Network in Biopolis @ One-North," JTC Corporation, June 29, 2017, https://www.jtc.gov.sg/news-and-publications/featured-stories/Pages/Global-innovation-powerhouse-benefits-from-network-in-Biopolis-@-one-north.aspx.

133. "worldVIEWguide," Scientific American Worldview, http://www.saworldview.com/scorecard/worldviewguide/.

134. Steve Blank, "China Startup Report: Torch, the World's Most Successful Startup Program (Part 2 of 5)," Startup Grind, 2015, https://www.startupgrind.com/blog/china-startup-report-torch-the-worlds-most-successful-startup-program-part-2-of-5/.

135. The Torch program is the largest and most successful government R&D program, and it was this program that spurred creation of national science/technology industrial parks. "Torch Program in the Past 15 Years," China Internet Information Center, September 17, 2003, http://www.china.org.cn/english/2003/Sep/75302.htm.

136. Cheng-Hua Tzeng, "The State, the Social Sector, and the Market in the Making of China's First Entrepreneurial Venture," *Business and Economic History* 6 (2008), https://www.thebhc.org/sites/default/files/tzeng.pdf.

137. The company was originally named New Technology Development Company of the Computing Technology Institute of Chinese Academy of Science.

138. "Lenovo Overview," Glassdoor, https://www.glassdoor.com/Overview /Working-at-Lenovo-EI_IE8034.11,17.htm.

139. Annual reports for the park are available at "Zhongguancun (Annual Reports)," May 17, 2018, https://docs.google.com/spreadsheets/d/1JNx7aq _YgNw1L_BG6dO1f5iN5IPW7AtZbJmN0uW1Zr0/edit?usp=sharing.

140. Researchers used ten data points to determine the rankings, including software engineer salaries, how long it takes to get a business up and running, cost of living and monthly rent prices, growth index, startup output, and other factors. Casey Hynes, "Beijing—Not Silicon Valley—Is the World's Top Tech Hub, Report Says," *Forbes,* November 2, 2017, https://www.forbes.com/sites/chynes/2017/11 /02/has-beijing-unseated-silicon-valley-as-the-worlds-top-tech-hub-one-report -says-yes/#417f49a7acf2.

141. The Chinese Academy of Science has always been an integral part of the park, since many of the early start-ups originated from CAS talent. The CAS also contributed to ZGC's growth by creating a policy framework called One Academy, Two Systems. The first of the Two Systems involved keeping a small number of scientists and engineers in basic research, while the second system was designed to encourage most researchers to seek outside funding for applied research that directly benefits the economy and that serves market needs.

142. Highest percentage of alumni in CAS: "USTC Introduction," University of Science and Technology of China, October 14, 2016, http://en.ustc.edu.cn /about/201101/t20110113_87798.html.

Student populations for each college:

PKU: "Peking University 2017 Basic Data," Peking University, December 2017, http://xxgk.pku.edu.cn/docs/20180410192941232836.pdf.

Tsinghua: "General Information," Tsinghua University, 2018, https://www .tsinghua.edu.cn/publish/thu2018en/newthuen_cnt/01-about-1.html.

USTC: "USTC Introduction," University of Science and Technology of China, October 14, 2016, http://en.ustc.edu.cn/about/201101/t20110113_87798.html.

Uniqueness of having two national labs: Ibid.

143. "Anhui Statistical Yearbook—1999," China Statistics Publishing House, http://www.ahtjj.gov.cn/tjjweb/web/tjnj_view.jsp?strColId=13787135717978521 &_index=1. "Anhui Statistical Yearbook—2017," China Statistics Publishing House, http://www.ahtjj.gov.cn/tjjweb/web/tjnj_view.jsp?strColId=13787135717978521 &_index=1.

144. Of course, none of these impressive facts *prove* that the research park strategy has worked in China—all this growth in companies and population movement may have happened even without the Chinese research park strategy.

145. "Our Results," Mars Discovery District, 2018, https://www.marsdd.com /about/results/.

146. Information in this section from the Auditor General's 2014 Annual Ontario report on the MaRS Phase 2 development (Chapter 3, Section 3.06 Appendix) and the update in 2016 (Chapter 1, Section 1.06). Office of the Auditor General of Ontario, "Infrastructure Ontario's Loans Program" in *Annual Report 2014* (Toronto: Queen's Printer for Ontario, 2014), http://www.auditor.on.ca/en /content/annualreports/arreports/en14/306en14.pdf. Office of the Auditor General of Ontario, "Infrastructure Ontario's Loans Program" in *Annual Report 2016*, vol. 2 (Toronto: Queen's Printer for Ontario, 2016). *MaRS Discovery District* (Toronto: PricewaterhouseCoopers, 2016), https://www.marsdd.com/wp-content /uploads/2017/05/MaRS-DISCOVERY-DISTRICT-FS-2016.pdf.

147. Robert Benzie, "Booming MaRS Repays 290m Government Loan Three Years Early," *Star*, February 7, 2017, https://www.thestar.com/news/queenspark /2017/02/09/booming-mars-repays-290m-government-loan-three-years-early.html.

148. *The Economic Impact of MaRS Discovery District Activities on the Ontario Economy* (Milton, ON: Centre for Spatial Economics, 2014), http://www.c4se .com/documents/MarsReport.pdf.

Index

Jonathan Gruber is the Ford Professor of Economics at MIT. An architect of both Romneycare and Obamacare, he appears regularly on news outlets ranging from Fox News to MSNBC. *Slate* has named him one of the top twenty-five "Most Innovative and Practical Thinkers of Our Time." In addition to over 175 academic articles, he is the author of *Health Care Reform* (Hill & Wang), a graphic novel about the Affordable Care Act, *Public Finance and Public Policy* (Worth), the leading textbook in public finance, and six other books.

Simon Johnson is the Ronald A. Kurtz (1954) Professor of Entrepreneurship at MIT and former chief economist at the International Monetary Fund. His much-viewed opinion pieces have appeared in the *New York Times,* the *Wall Street Journal,* the *Financial Times,* the *Atlantic,* and elsewhere. With law professor James Kwak, Simon is the coauthor of the best sellers *13 Bankers* and *White House Burning* and a founder of the widely cited economics blog *The Baseline Scenario.* He is also coauthor, with Daron Acemoglu, of *Power and Progress: Our Thousand-Year Struggle Over Technology and Prosperity.*

102 PLACES FOR JUMP-STARTING AMERICA

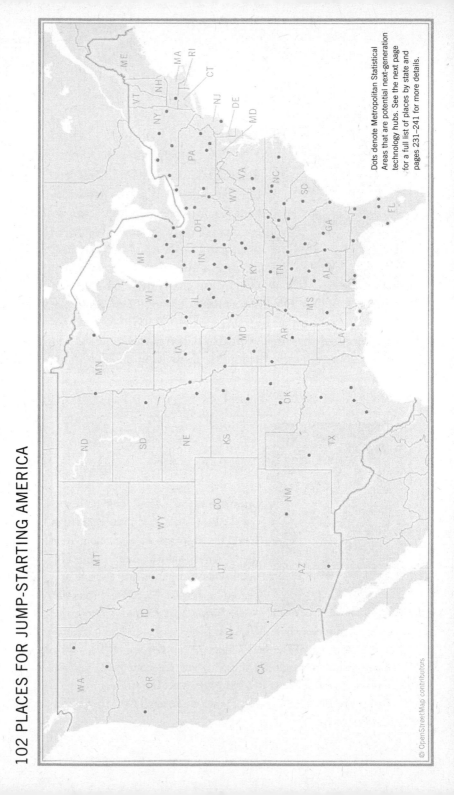

Dots denote Metropolitan Statistical Areas that are potential next-generation technology hubs. See the next page for a full list of places by state and pages 231–241 for more details.

© OpenStreetMap contributors

102 PLACES FOR JUMP-STARTING AMERICA

Metropolitan Statistical Areas (MSAs) Shown on Map

Birmingham-Hoover, AL
Daphne-Fairhope-Foley/Mobile, AL
Huntsville, AL
Montgomery, AL
Tuscaloosa, AL
Little Rock-North Little Rock-Conway, AR
Fayetteville-Springdale-Rogers, AR-MO
Tucson, AZ
Gainesville, FL
Jacksonville, FL
Orlando-Kissimmee-Sanford, FL
Palm Bay-Melbourne-Titusville, FL
Pensacola-Ferry Pass-Brent, FL
Tallahassee, FL
Tampa-St. Petersburg-Clearwater, FL
Atlanta-Sandy Springs-Roswell, GA
Savannah, GA
Warner Robins, GA
Auburn-Opelika/Columbus, GA-AL
Ames/Des Moines-West Des Moines, IA
Cedar Rapids/Iowa City, IA
Davenport-Moline-Rock Island, IA-IL
Boise City, ID
Idaho Falls/Pocatello, ID
Bloomington/Champaign-Urbana, IL
Decatur/Springfield, IL
Peoria, IL

Bloomington/Columbus, IN
Fort Wayne, IN
Indianapolis-Carmel-Anderson/Lafayette-West Lafayette, IN
Niles-Benton Harbor/South Bend-Mishawaka, IN-MI
Lawrence/Manhattan/Topeka, KS
Wichita, KS
Lexington-Fayette, KY
Louisville/Jefferson County, KY-IN
Baton Rouge, LA
New Orleans-Metairie, LA
Springfield, MA
Ann Arbor/Jackson, MI
Battle Creek/Kalamazoo-Portage, MI
Detroit-Warren-Dearborn, MI
Grand Rapids-Wyoming, MI
Lansing-East Lansing, MI
Midland/Saginaw, MI
Rochester, MN
Duluth, MN-WI
Columbia/Jefferson City, MO
Springfield, MO
St. Louis, MO-IL
Kansas City, MO-KS
Jackson, MS
Asheville, NC
Greensboro-High Point, NC

Greenville/New Bern, NC
Winston-Salem, NC
Charlotte-Concord-Gastonia, NC-SC
Fargo, ND-MN
Lincoln, NE
Omaha-Council Bluffs, NE-IA
Atlantic City-Hammonton, NJ
Albuquerque, NM
Albany-Schenectady-Troy, NY
Binghamton/Ithaca, NY
Buffalo-Cheektowaga-Niagara Falls, NY
Rochester, NY
Syracuse/Utica-Rome, NY
Akron/Canton-Massillon, OH
Cleveland-Elyria, OH
Columbus, OH
Dayton, OH
Toledo, OH
Cincinnati, OH-KY-IN
Oklahoma City, OK
Tulsa, OK
Eugene, OR
Erie, PA
Harrisburg-Carlisle, PA
Lancaster, PA
Pittsburgh, PA

Allentown-Bethlehem-Easton, PA-NJ
Columbia, SC
Greenville-Anderson-Mauldin, SC
Sioux Falls, SD
Johnson City, TN
Knoxville, TN
Chattanooga, TN-GA
Clarksville/Nashville-Davidson-Murfreesboro-Franklin, TN-KY
Memphis, TN-MS-AR
College Station-Bryan, TX
Dallas-Fort Worth-Arlington, TX
Houston-The Woodlands-Sugar Land, TX
Lubbock, TX
San Antonio-New Braunfels, TX
Logan/Ogden-Clearfield, UT-ID
Blacksburg-Christiansburg-Radford/Roanoke, VA
Lynchburg, VA
Kennewick-Richland, WA
Spokane-Spokane Valley, WA
Appleton/Green Bay/Oshkosh-Neenah, WI
Janesville-Beloit/Madison, WI
Milwaukee-Waukesha-West Allis/Racine, WI
Morgantown/Wheeling, WV-OH

These Metropolitan Statistical Areas (MSAs) meet the criteria for inclusion in the Technology Hub Index System ranking, as explained on pages 231–241. Some MSAs include more than one state.

PublicAffairs is a publishing house founded in 1997. It is a tribute to the standards, values, and flair of three persons who have served as mentors to countless reporters, writers, editors, and book people of all kinds, including me.

I. F. STONE, proprietor of *I. F. Stone's Weekly*, combined a commitment to the First Amendment with entrepreneurial zeal and reporting skill and became one of the great independent journalists in American history. At the age of eighty, Izzy published *The Trial of Socrates*, which was a national bestseller. He wrote the book after he taught himself ancient Greek.

BENJAMIN C. BRADLEE was for nearly thirty years the charismatic editorial leader of *The Washington Post*. It was Ben who gave the *Post* the range and courage to pursue such historic issues as Watergate. He supported his reporters with a tenacity that made them fearless and it is no accident that so many became authors of influential, best-selling books.

ROBERT L. BERNSTEIN, the chief executive of Random House for more than a quarter century, guided one of the nation's premier publishing houses. Bob was personally responsible for many books of political dissent and argument that challenged tyranny around the globe. He is also the founder and longtime chair of Human Rights Watch, one of the most respected human rights organizations in the world.

•   •   •

For fifty years, the banner of Public Affairs Press was carried by its owner Morris B. Schnapper, who published Gandhi, Nasser, Toynbee, Truman, and about 1,500 other authors. In 1983, Schnapper was described by *The Washington Post* as "a redoubtable gadfly." His legacy will endure in the books to come.

Peter Osnos, *Founder*